POSUKA DEMIZU

KAIU SHIRAI

How will you like the short story collection?

It's been five and a half years since "Poppy's Wish." I'm full of emotion. And they created the best Japanese title logo for us again! It looks like a theme park at first glance, and that gets me excited.

Characters from all the stories appear on the cover, but *TPN* takes up such a big space in my heart. So Emma is drawn bigger. Please forgive me for that. Even my drawing speed was faster for *TPN* characters.

I was looking at an image of a toaster while I was drawing Poppy and got hungry. So when I finish my work today, I'm going to eat a pizza toast.

Well then, I'm looking forward to the next time I see everyone.

This is a short story collection!

It features four stories, three of them stand-alone stories released after *The Promised Neverland*. But all four of them were storyboarded before *The Promised Neverland* in order to get *The Promised Neverland* released into the world. (I actually wrote a bunch of stuff.)

That is why they have elements and a feel that is reminiscent of *TPN*.

These four stories could be called "the road to *TPN*."

It would be great if you could enjoy them, whether you're a fan of *TPN* or you're completely new to our work.

Posuka Demizu debuted as a manga artist with the 2013 *CoroCoro* series *Oreca Monster Bouken Retsuden*. A collection of illustrations, *The Art of Posuka Demizu,* was released in 2016 by PIE International.

Kaiu Shirai debuted in 2015 with *Ashley Gate no Yukue* on the *Shonen Jump+* website. Shirai first worked with Posuka Demizu on the two-shot "Poppy's Wish," which was released in February 2016.

KAIU SHIRAI ✖ POSUKA DEMIZU:
BEYOND
THE PROMISED NEVERLAND

SHONEN JUMP Edition

STORY BY KAIU SHIRAI
ART BY POSUKA DEMIZU

Translation/Satsuki Yamashita
Touch-Up Art & Lettering/Mark McMurray
Design/Julian [JR] Robinson
Editor/Alexis Kirsch

Printed in the U.S.A.

Published by VIZ Media, LLC
P.O. Box 77010
San Francisco, CA 94107

10 9 8 7 6 5 4 3 2 1
First printing, November 2022

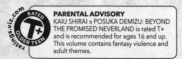

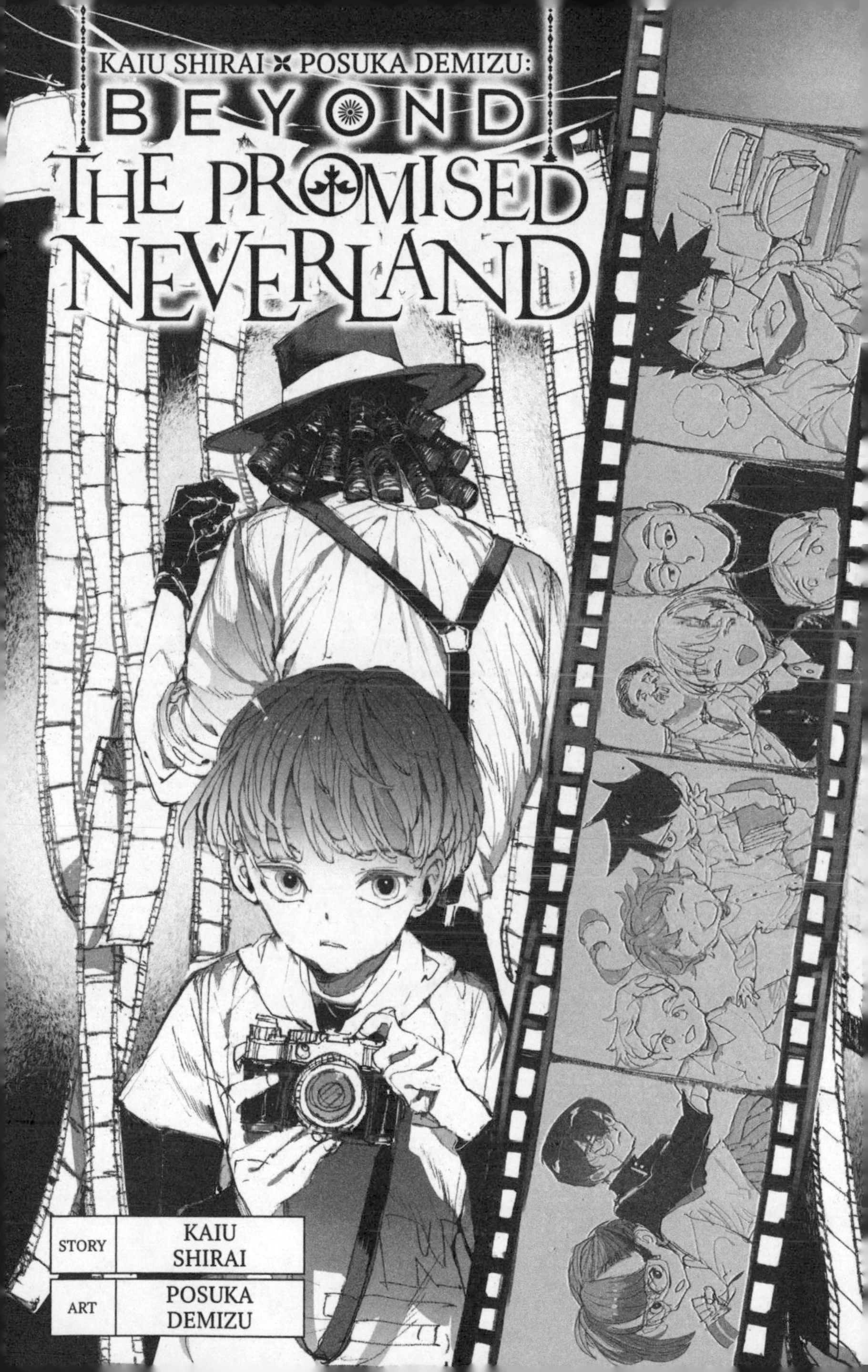
KAIU SHIRAI × POSUKA DEMIZU:
BEYOND
THE PROMISED NEVERLAND
STORY
KAIU SHIRAI
ART
POSUKA DEMIZU

KAIU SHIRAI ✖ POSUKA DEMIZU:

BEYOND THE PROMISED NEVERLAND

CONTENTS

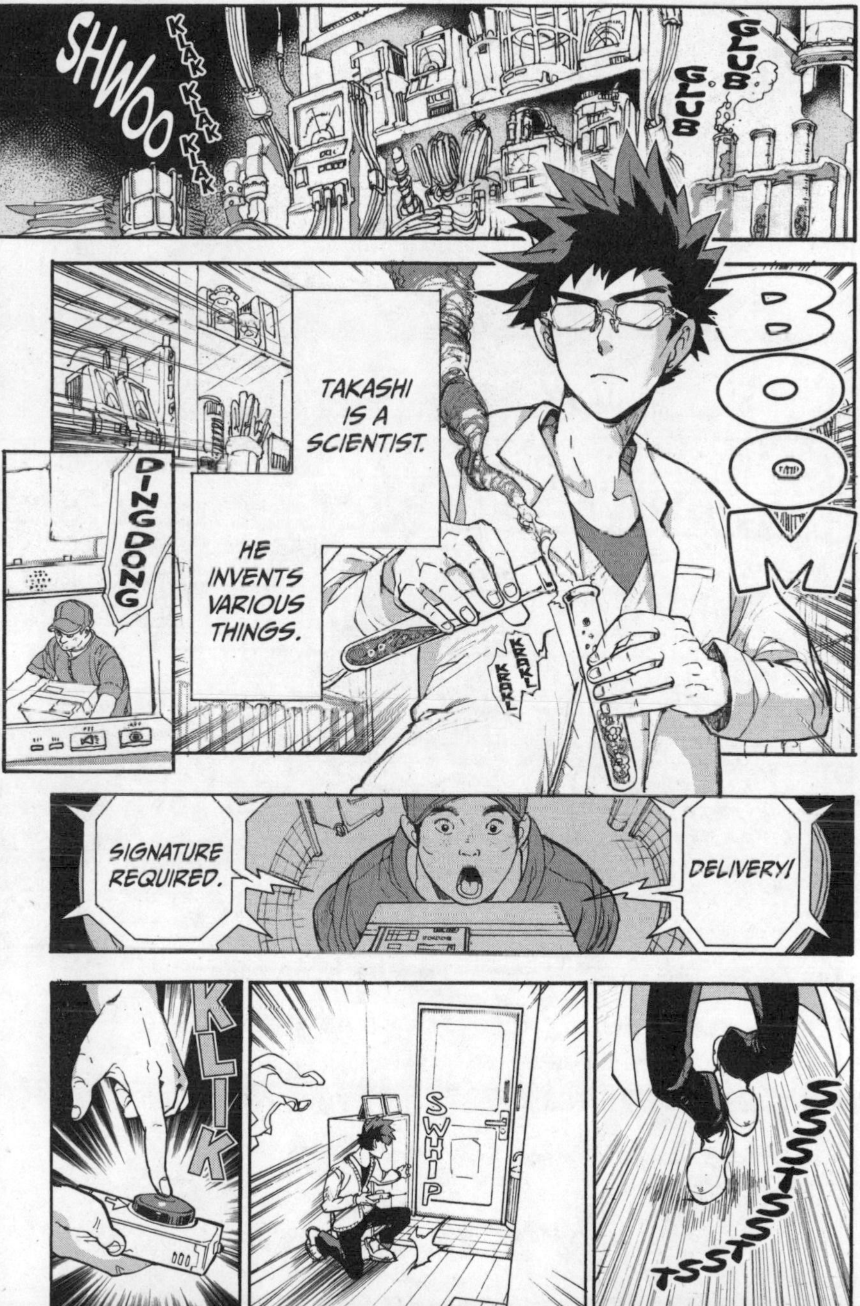
GLUB
GLUB
GLUB
SHWOO
KLAK KLAK KLAK
BOOM
TAKASHI IS A SCIENTIST.
HE INVENTS VARIOUS THINGS.
KRAKL KRAKL
DINGDONG
DELIVERY!
SIGNATURE REQUIRED.
TSSTSSTSSSS
SWHIP
KLIK

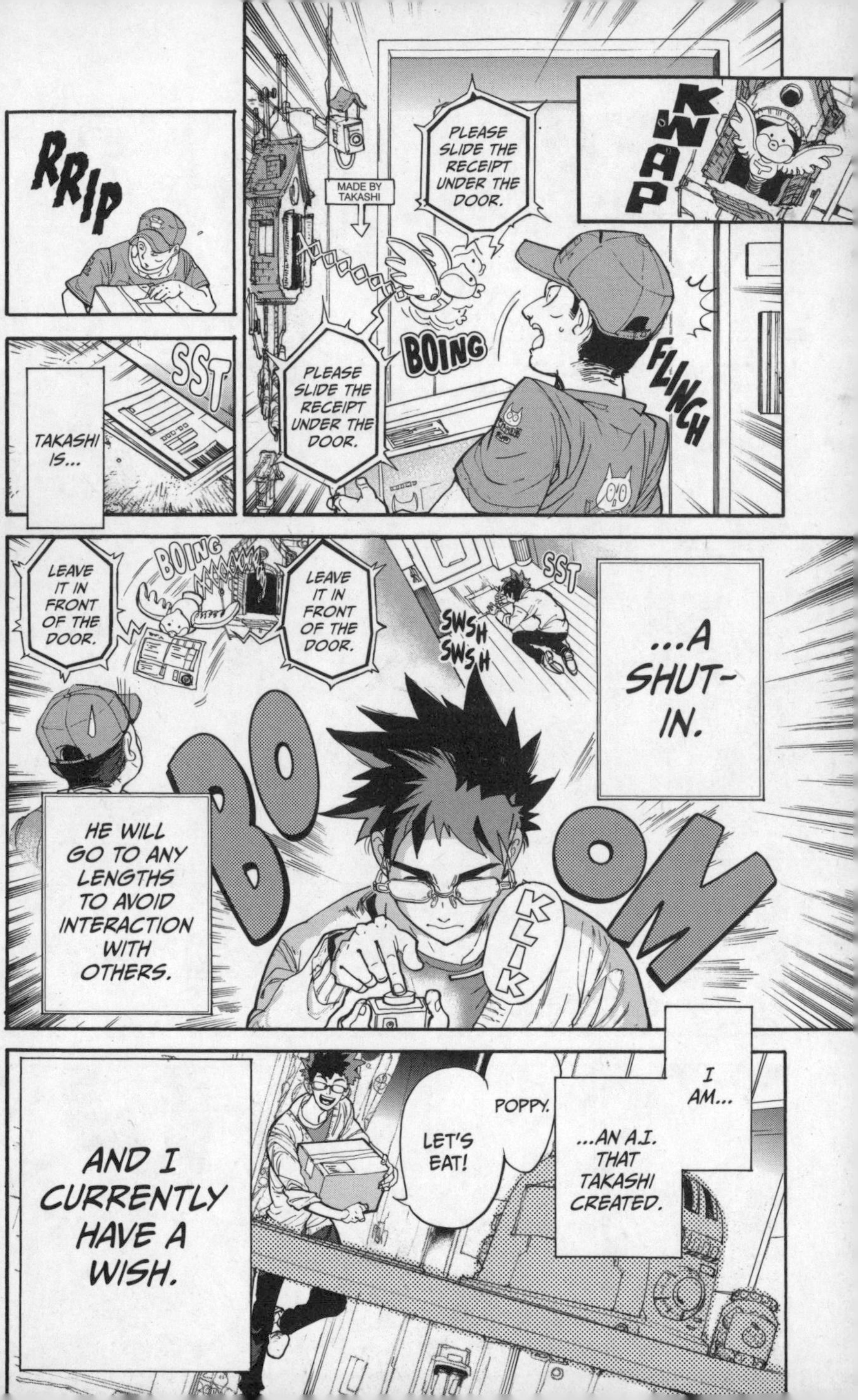
KWAP
PLEASE SLIDE THE RECEIPT UNDER THE DOOR.
MADE BY TAKASHI
FLINCH
BOING
PLEASE SLIDE THE RECEIPT UNDER THE DOOR.
RRIP
SST
TAKASHI IS...
...A SHUT-IN.
SST
SWSH SWSH
LEAVE IT IN FRONT OF THE DOOR.
BOING
LEAVE IT IN FRONT OF THE DOOR.
BOOM
KLIK
HE WILL GO TO ANY LENGTHS TO AVOID INTERACTION WITH OTHERS.
I AM...
...AN A.I. THAT TAKASHI CREATED.
POPPY.
LET'S EAT!
AND I CURRENTLY HAVE A WISH.

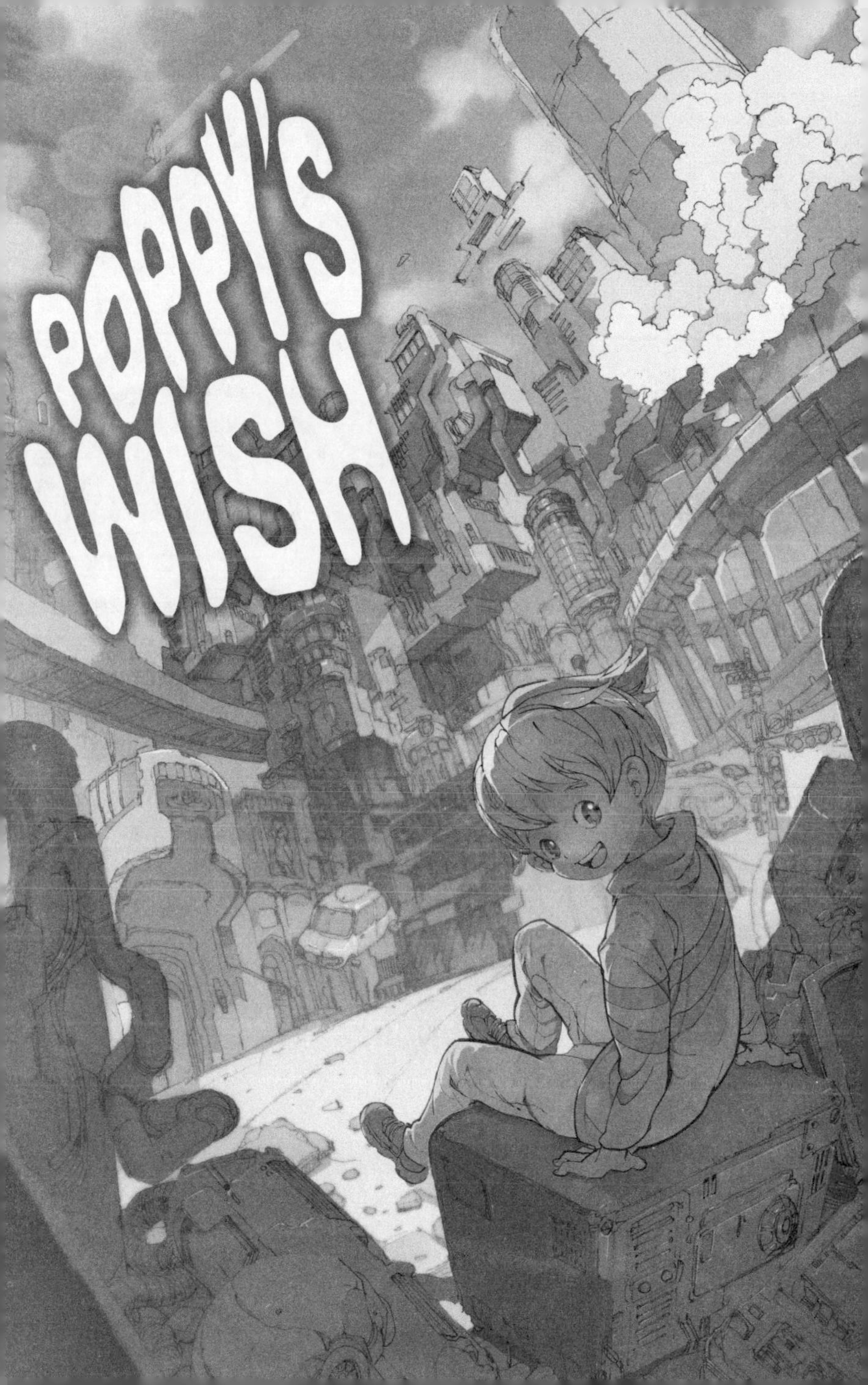
POPPY'S WISH

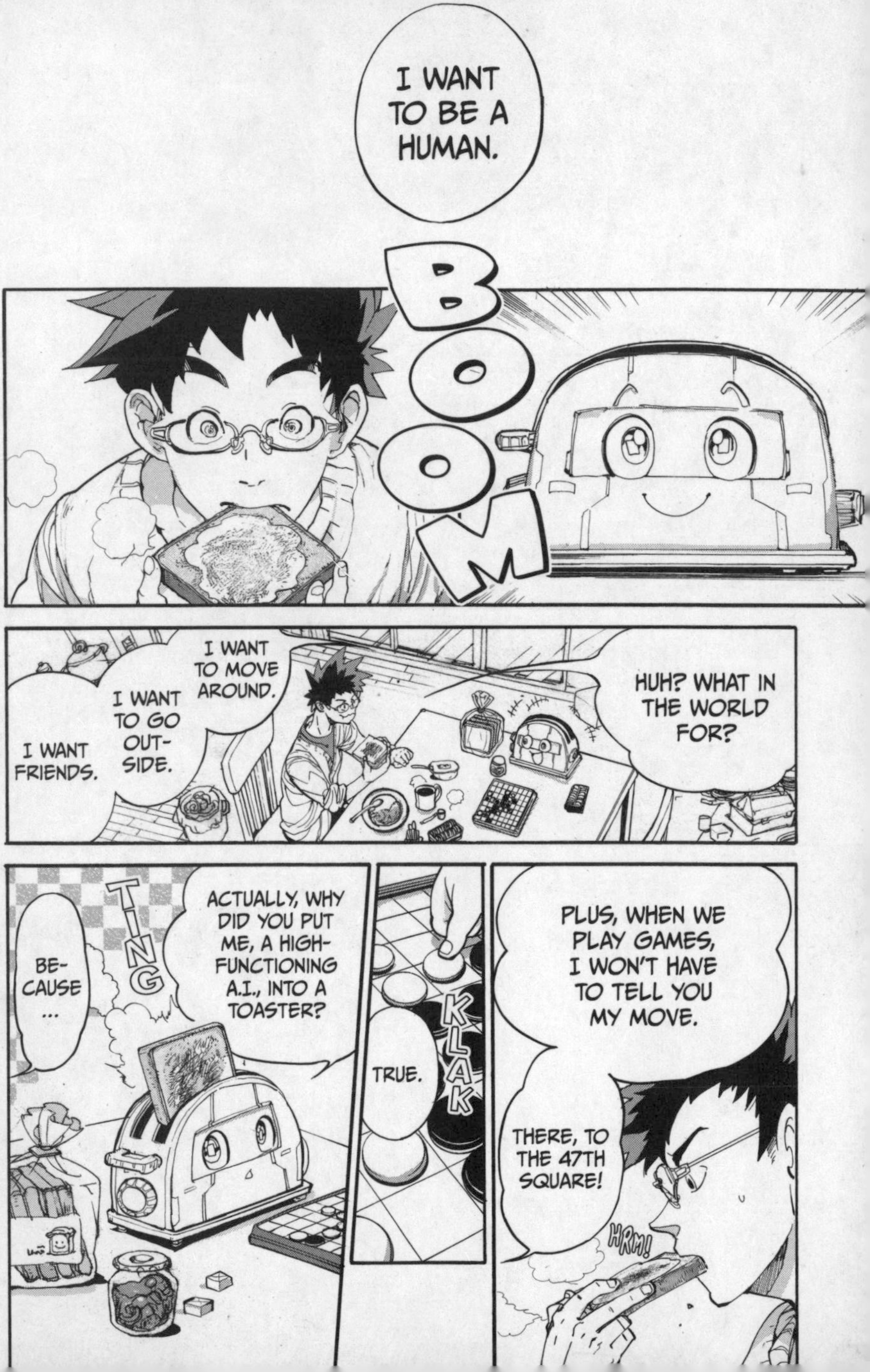
I WANT TO BE A HUMAN.
BOOM
I WANT TO MOVE AROUND.
I WANT TO GO OUT-SIDE.
I WANT FRIENDS.
HUH? WHAT IN THE WORLD FOR?
TING
ACTUALLY, WHY DID YOU PUT ME, A HIGH-FUNCTIONING A.I., INTO A TOASTER?
BE-CAUSE ...
KLAK
TRUE.
PLUS, WHEN WE PLAY GAMES, I WON'T HAVE TO TELL YOU MY MOVE.
THERE, TO THE 47TH SQUARE!
HRM!

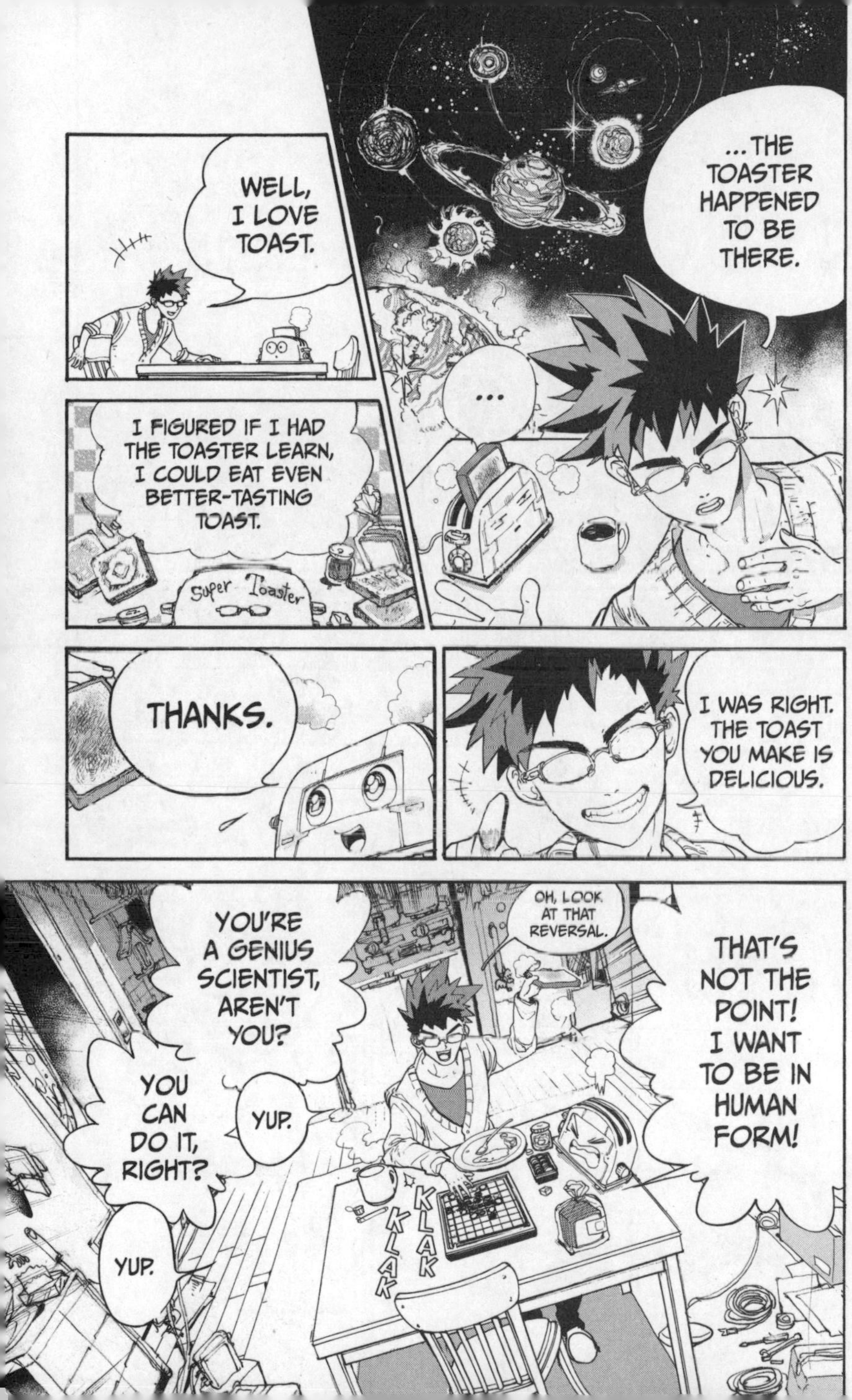
...THE TOASTER HAPPENED TO BE THERE.
...
WELL, I LOVE TOAST.
I FIGURED IF I HAD THE TOASTER LEARN, I COULD EAT EVEN BETTER-TASTING TOAST.
Super Toaster
I WAS RIGHT. THE TOAST YOU MAKE IS DELICIOUS.
THANKS.
THAT'S NOT THE POINT! I WANT TO BE IN HUMAN FORM!
OH, LOOK AT THAT REVERSAL.
YOU'RE A GENIUS SCIENTIST, AREN'T YOU?
YUP.
YOU CAN DO IT, RIGHT?
YUP.
KLAK KLAK KLAK

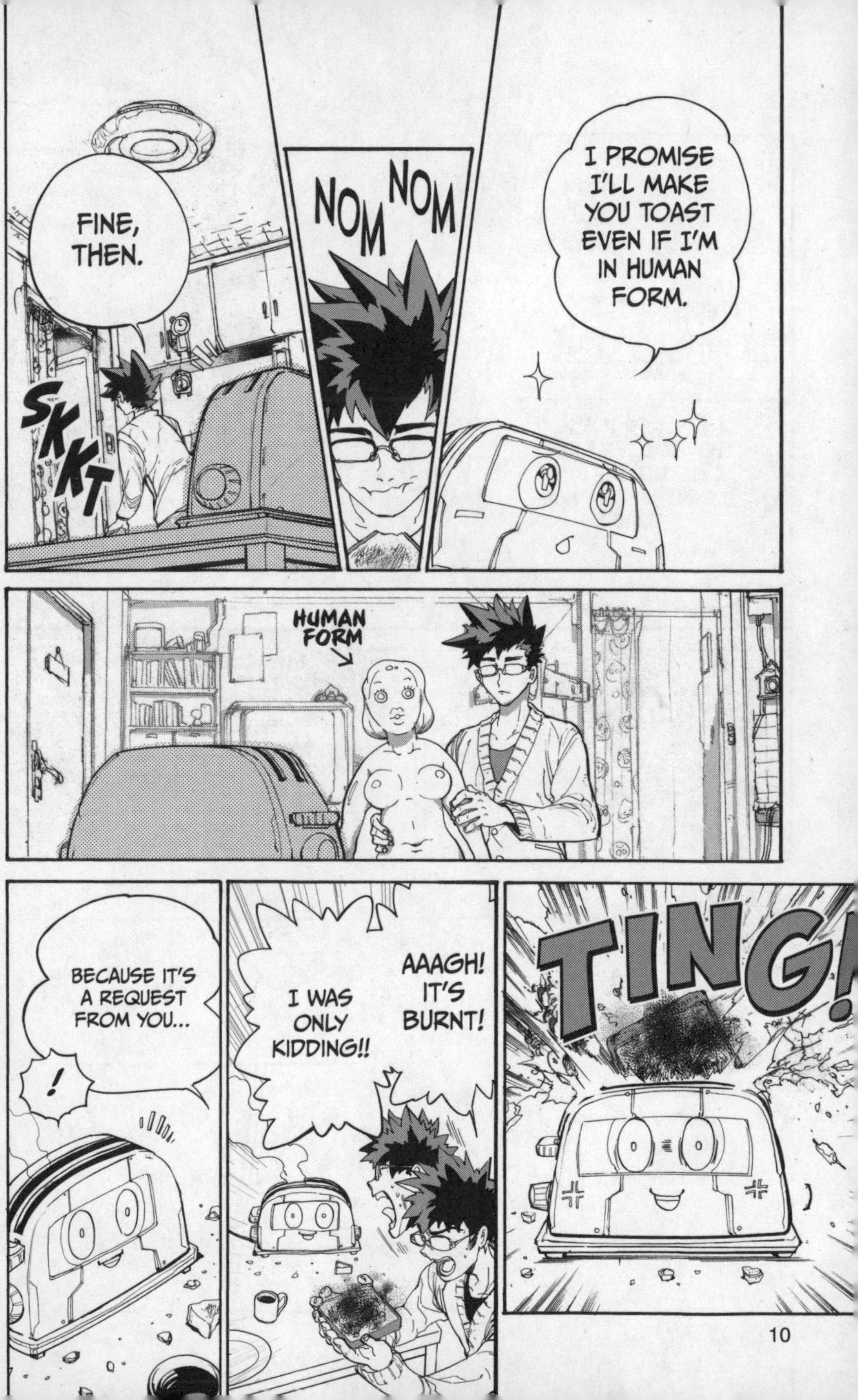
I PROMISE I'LL MAKE YOU TOAST EVEN IF I'M IN HUMAN FORM.
NOM NOM
FINE, THEN.
SKKT
HUMAN FORM
TING!
AAAGH! IT'S BURNT!
I WAS ONLY KIDDING!!
BECAUSE IT'S A REQUEST FROM YOU...
!

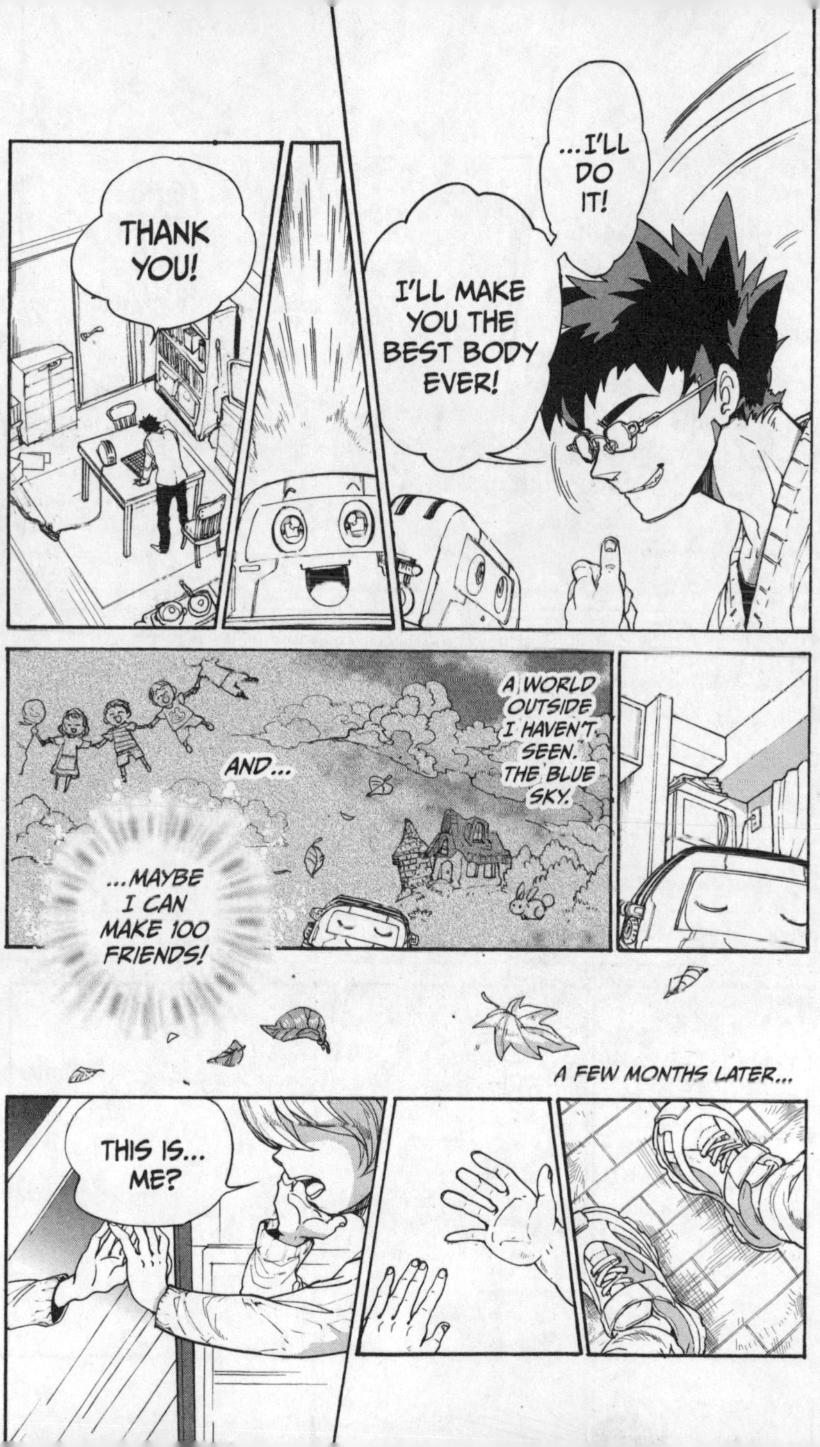
...I'LL DO IT!
I'LL MAKE YOU THE BEST BODY EVER!
THANK YOU!
A WORLD OUTSIDE I HAVEN'T SEEN. THE BLUE SKY.
AND...
...MAYBE I CAN MAKE 100 FRIENDS!
A FEW MONTHS LATER...
THIS IS... ME?

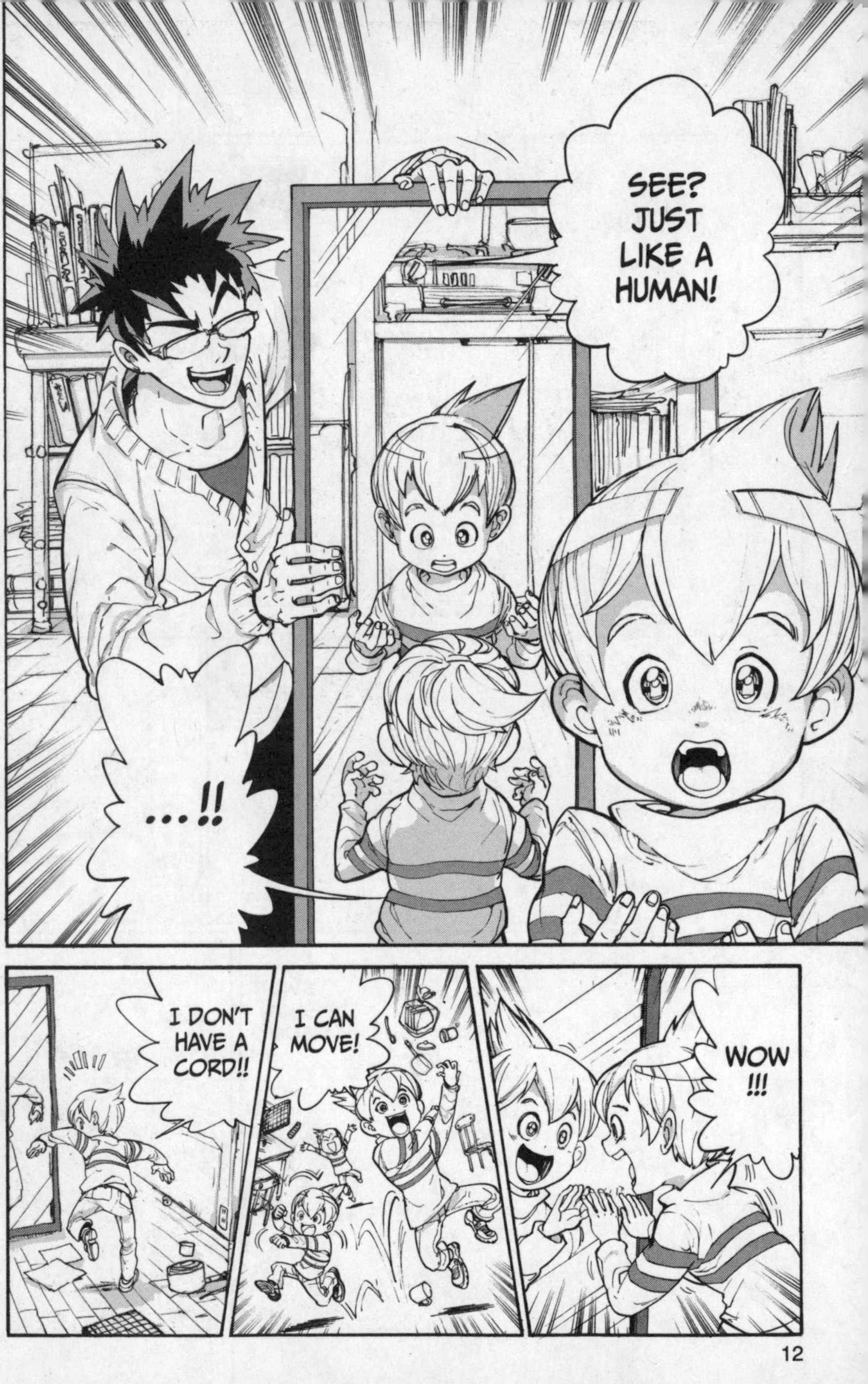
SEE? JUST LIKE A HUMAN!
...!!
WOW !!!
I CAN MOVE!
I DON'T HAVE A CORD!!

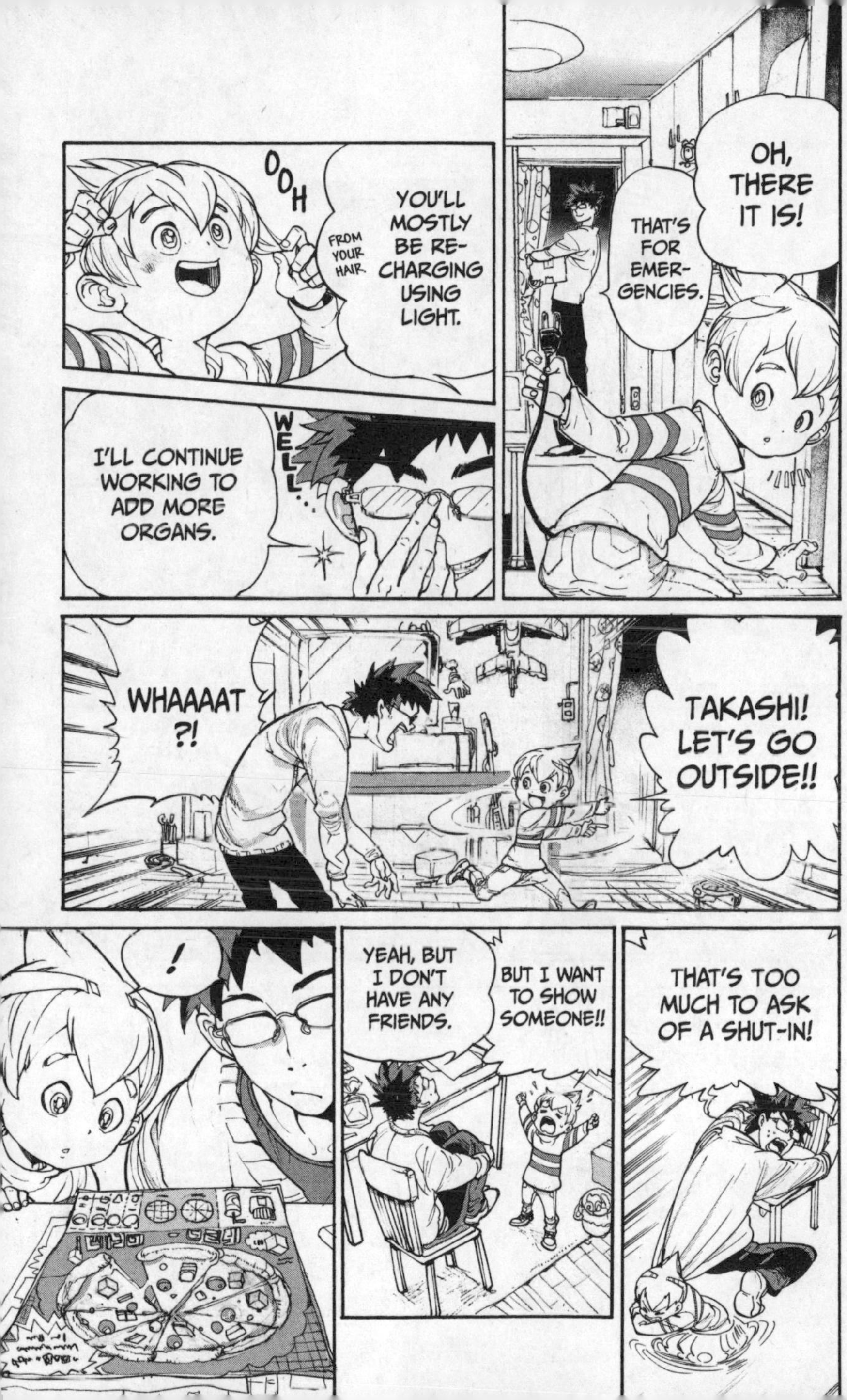
OH, THERE IT IS!
THAT'S FOR EMERGENCIES.
YOU'LL MOSTLY BE RE-CHARGING USING LIGHT.
FROM YOUR HAIR.
OOH
WELL...
I'LL CONTINUE WORKING TO ADD MORE ORGANS.
TAKASHI! LET'S GO OUTSIDE!!
WHAAAAT?!
THAT'S TOO MUCH TO ASK OF A SHUT-IN!
BUT I WANT TO SHOW SOMEONE!!
YEAH, BUT I DON'T HAVE ANY FRIENDS.
!

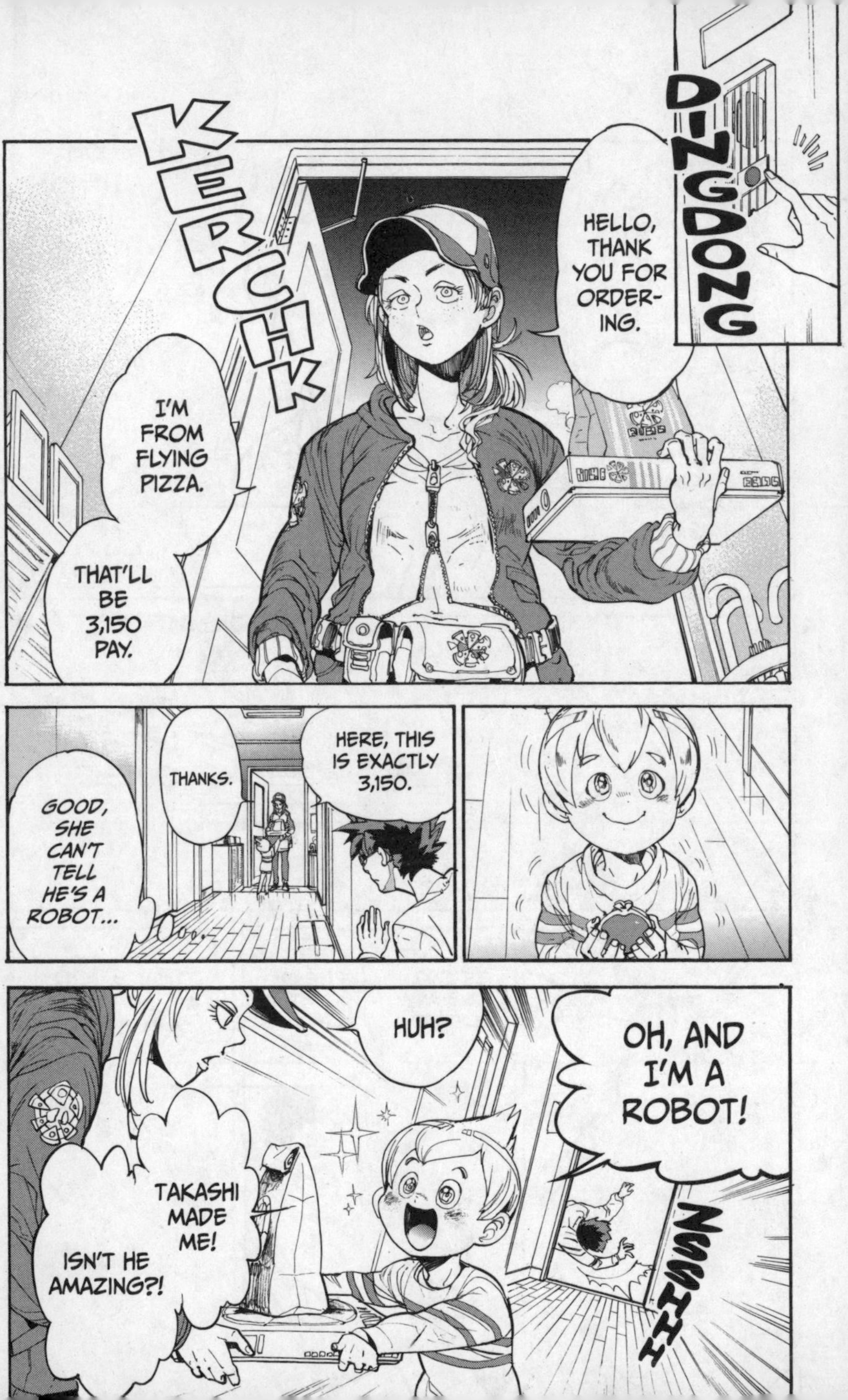
DINGDONG
HELLO, THANK YOU FOR ORDER-ING.
KERCHK
I'M FROM FLYING PIZZA.
THAT'LL BE 3,150 PAY.
HERE, THIS IS EXACTLY 3,150.
THANKS.
GOOD, SHE CAN'T TELL HE'S A ROBOT...
OH, AND I'M A ROBOT!
ZSSHHH
HUH?
TAKASHI MADE ME!
ISN'T HE AMAZING?!

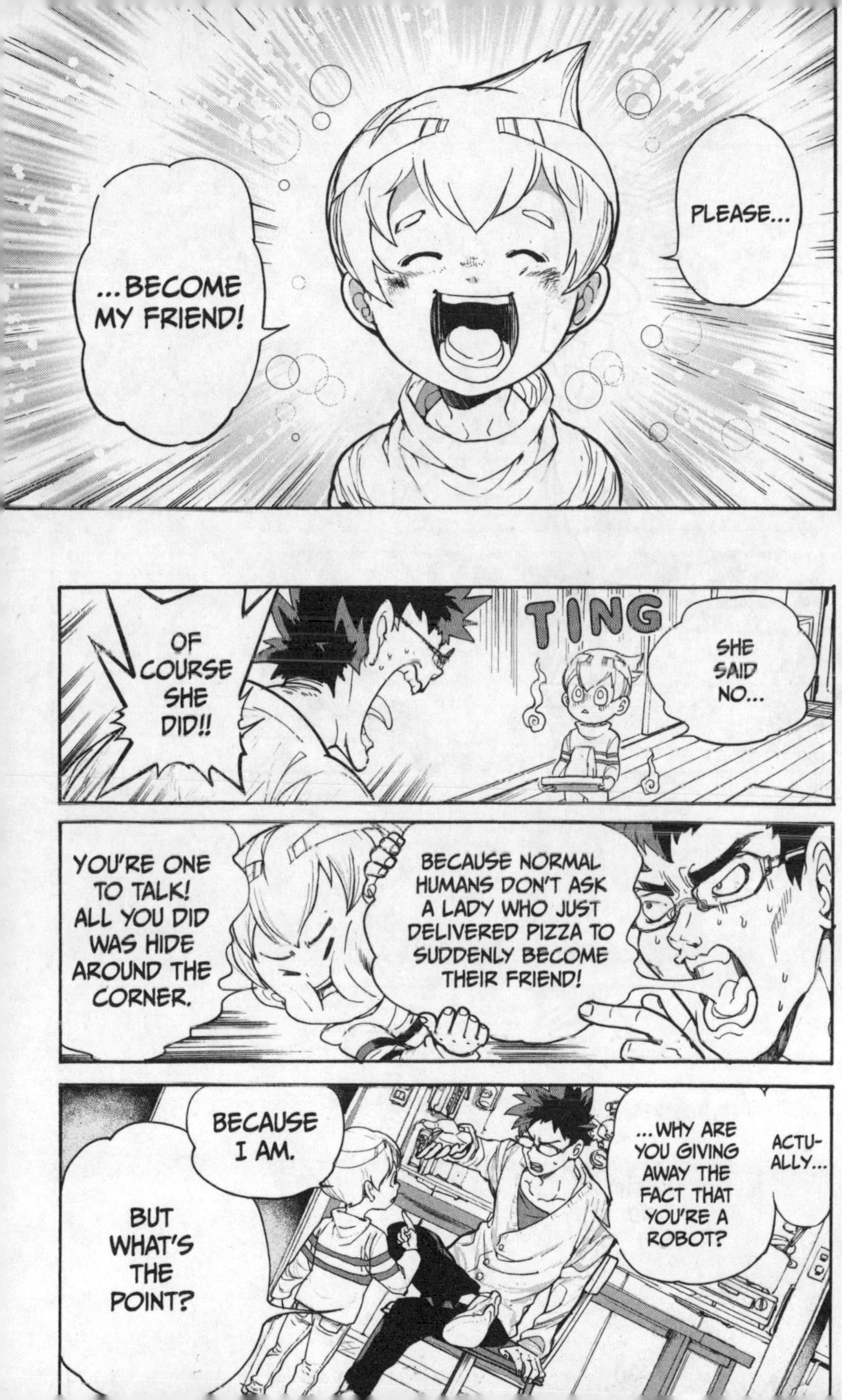
PLEASE...
...BECOME MY FRIEND!
TING
SHE SAID NO...
OF COURSE SHE DID!!
BECAUSE NORMAL HUMANS DON'T ASK A LADY WHO JUST DELIVERED PIZZA TO SUDDENLY BECOME THEIR FRIEND!
YOU'RE ONE TO TALK! ALL YOU DID WAS HIDE AROUND THE CORNER.
ACTU-ALLY...
...WHY ARE YOU GIVING AWAY THE FACT THAT YOU'RE A ROBOT?
BECAUSE I AM.
BUT WHAT'S THE POINT?

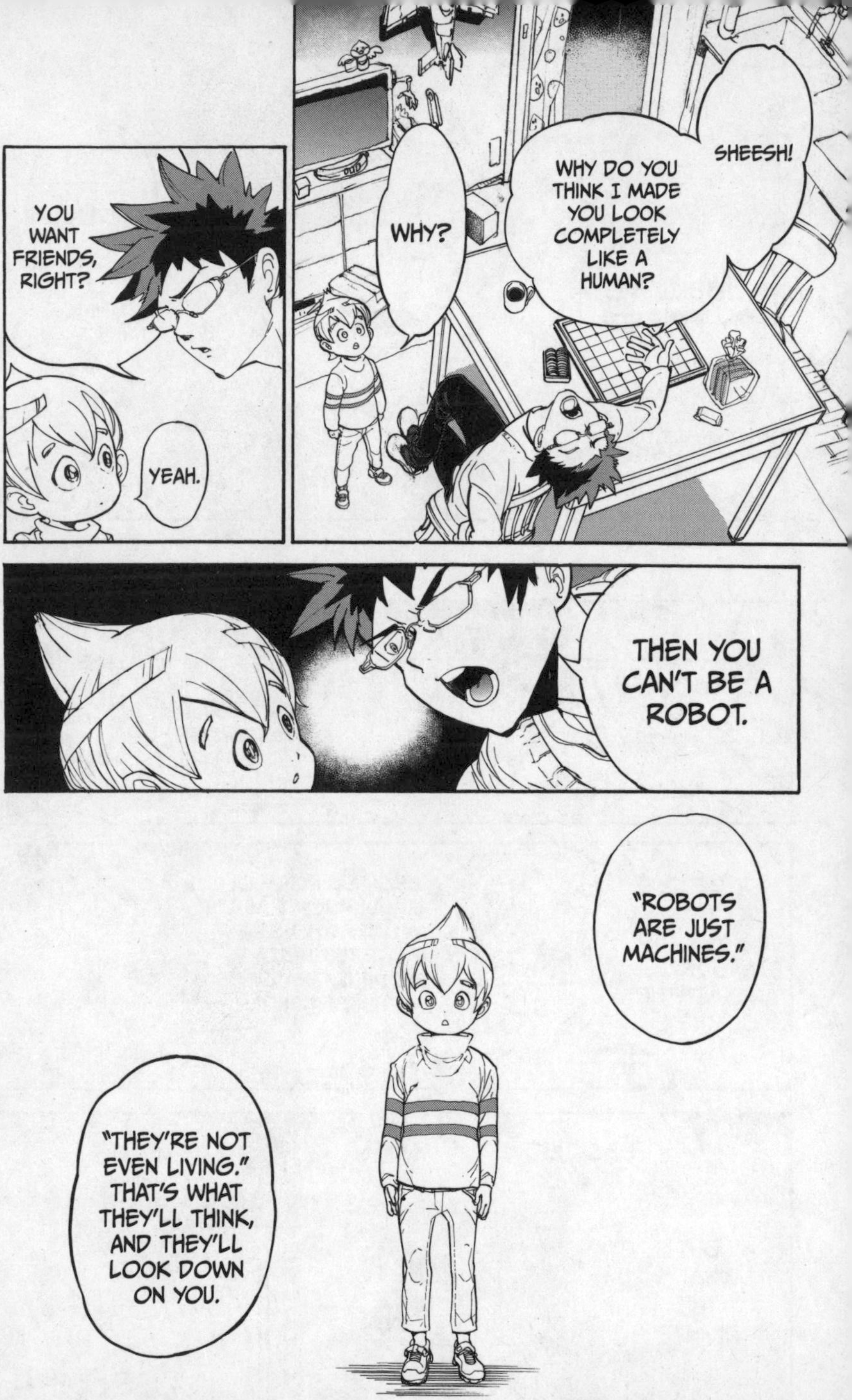
SHEESH!
WHY DO YOU THINK I MADE YOU LOOK COMPLETELY LIKE A HUMAN?
WHY?
YOU WANT FRIENDS, RIGHT?
YEAH.
THEN YOU CAN'T BE A ROBOT.
"ROBOTS ARE JUST MACHINES."
"THEY'RE NOT EVEN LIVING." THAT'S WHAT THEY'LL THINK, AND THEY'LL LOOK DOWN ON YOU.

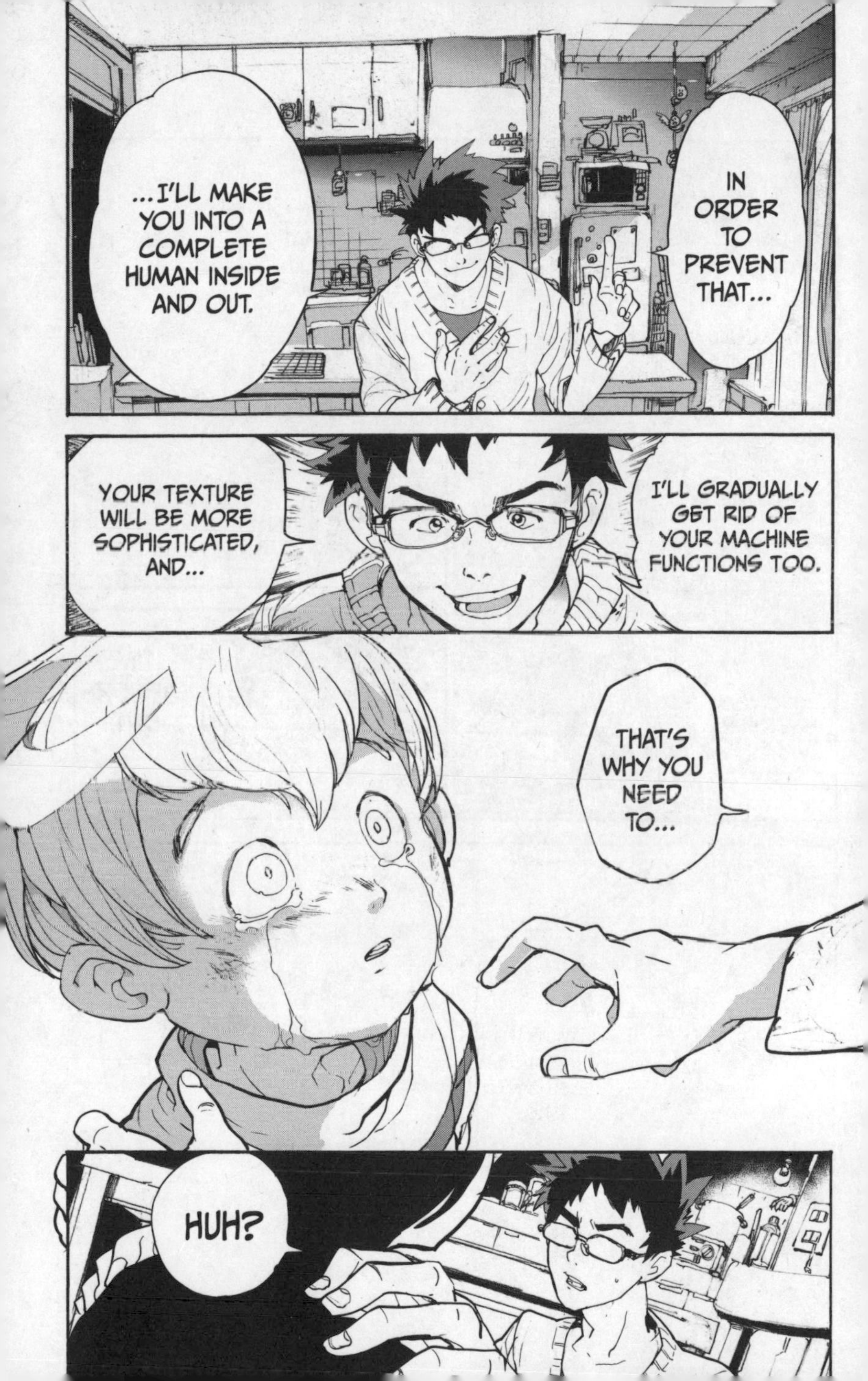
IN ORDER TO PREVENT THAT...
...I'LL MAKE YOU INTO A COMPLETE HUMAN INSIDE AND OUT.
I'LL GRADUALLY GET RID OF YOUR MACHINE FUNCTIONS TOO.
YOUR TEXTURE WILL BE MORE SOPHISTICATED, AND...
THAT'S WHY YOU NEED TO...
HUH?

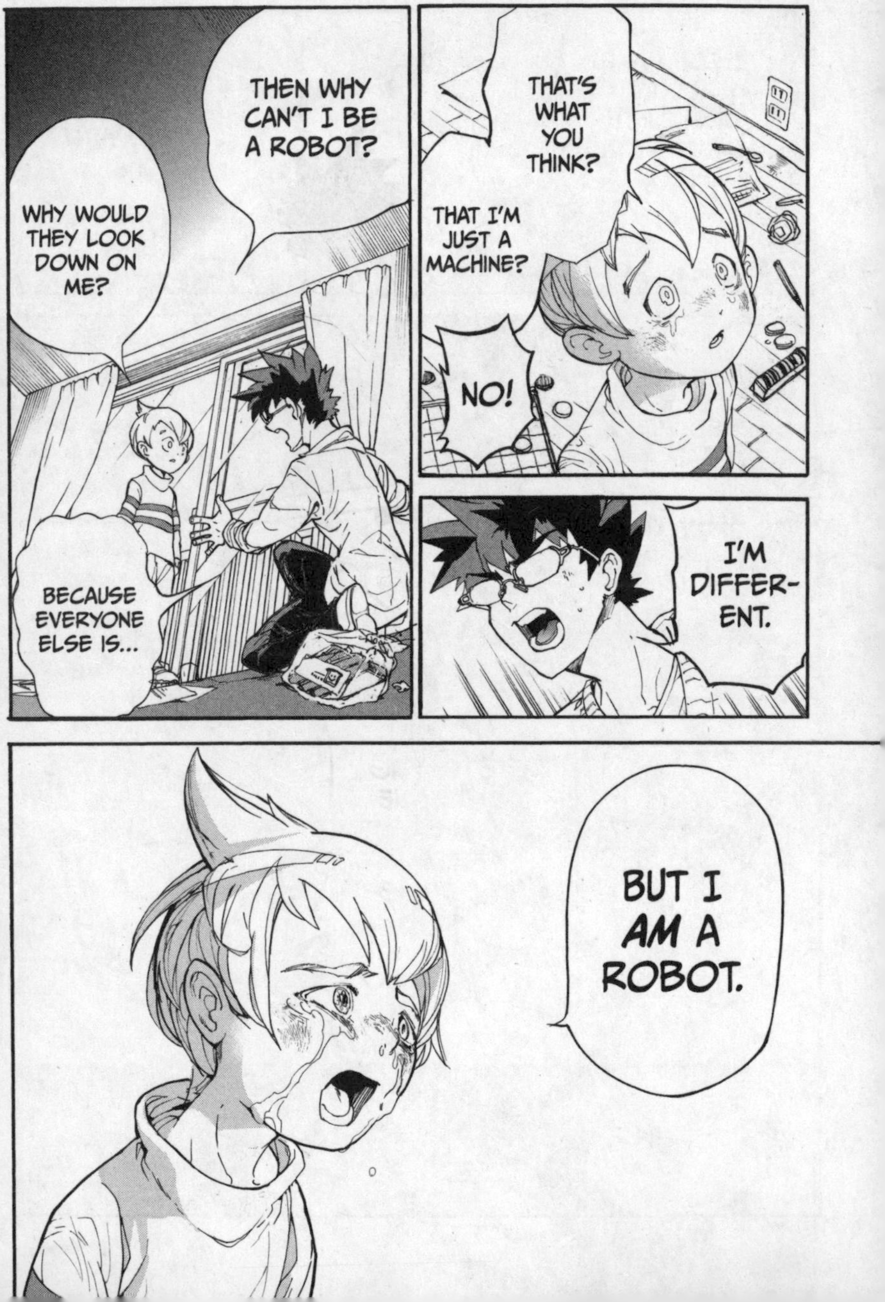
THAT'S WHAT YOU THINK?
THAT I'M JUST A MACHINE?
NO!
I'M DIFFER-ENT.
THEN WHY CAN'T I BE A ROBOT?
WHY WOULD THEY LOOK DOWN ON ME?
BECAUSE EVERYONE ELSE IS...
BUT I *AM* A ROBOT.

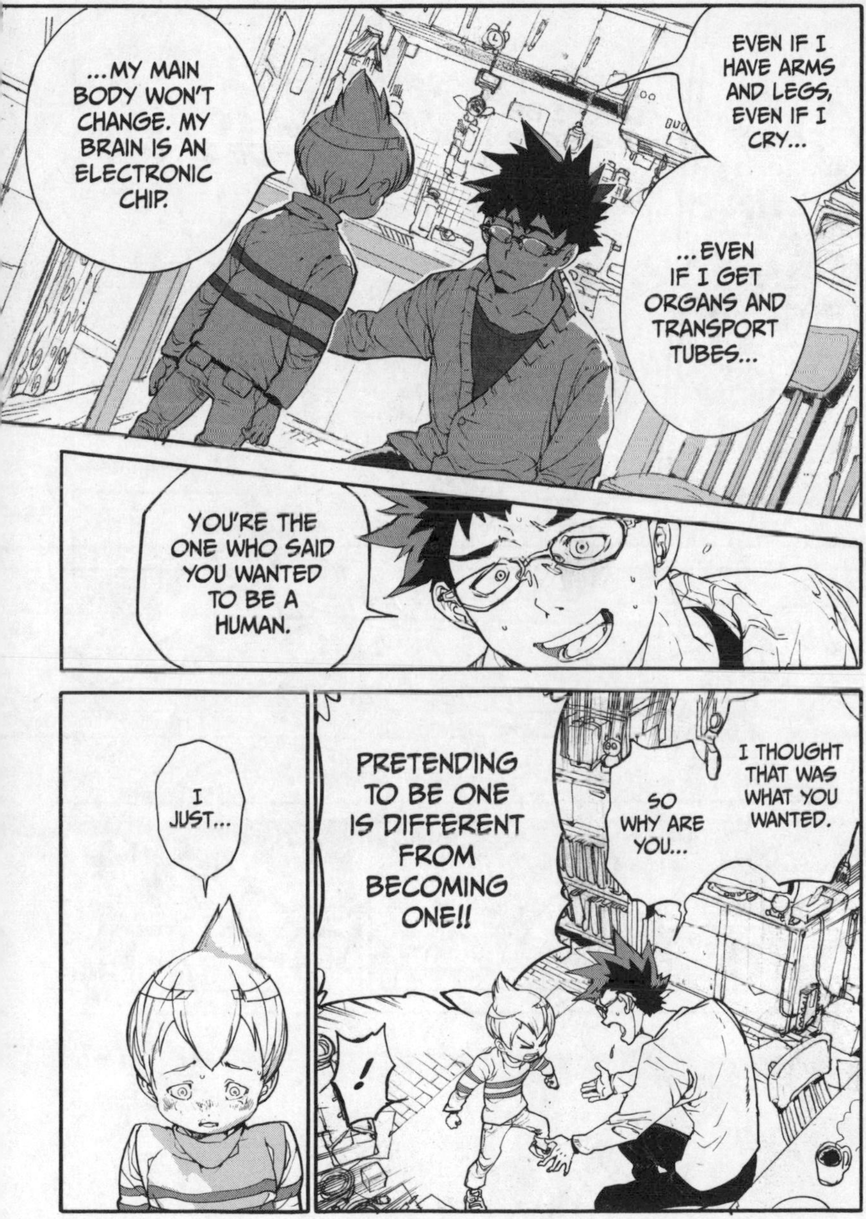
EVEN IF I HAVE ARMS AND LEGS, EVEN IF I CRY...
...EVEN IF I GET ORGANS AND TRANSPORT TUBES...
...MY MAIN BODY WON'T CHANGE. MY BRAIN IS AN ELECTRONIC CHIP.
YOU'RE THE ONE WHO SAID YOU WANTED TO BE A HUMAN.
I THOUGHT THAT WAS WHAT YOU WANTED.
SO WHY ARE YOU...
PRETENDING TO BE ONE IS DIFFERENT FROM BECOMING ONE!!
!
I JUST...

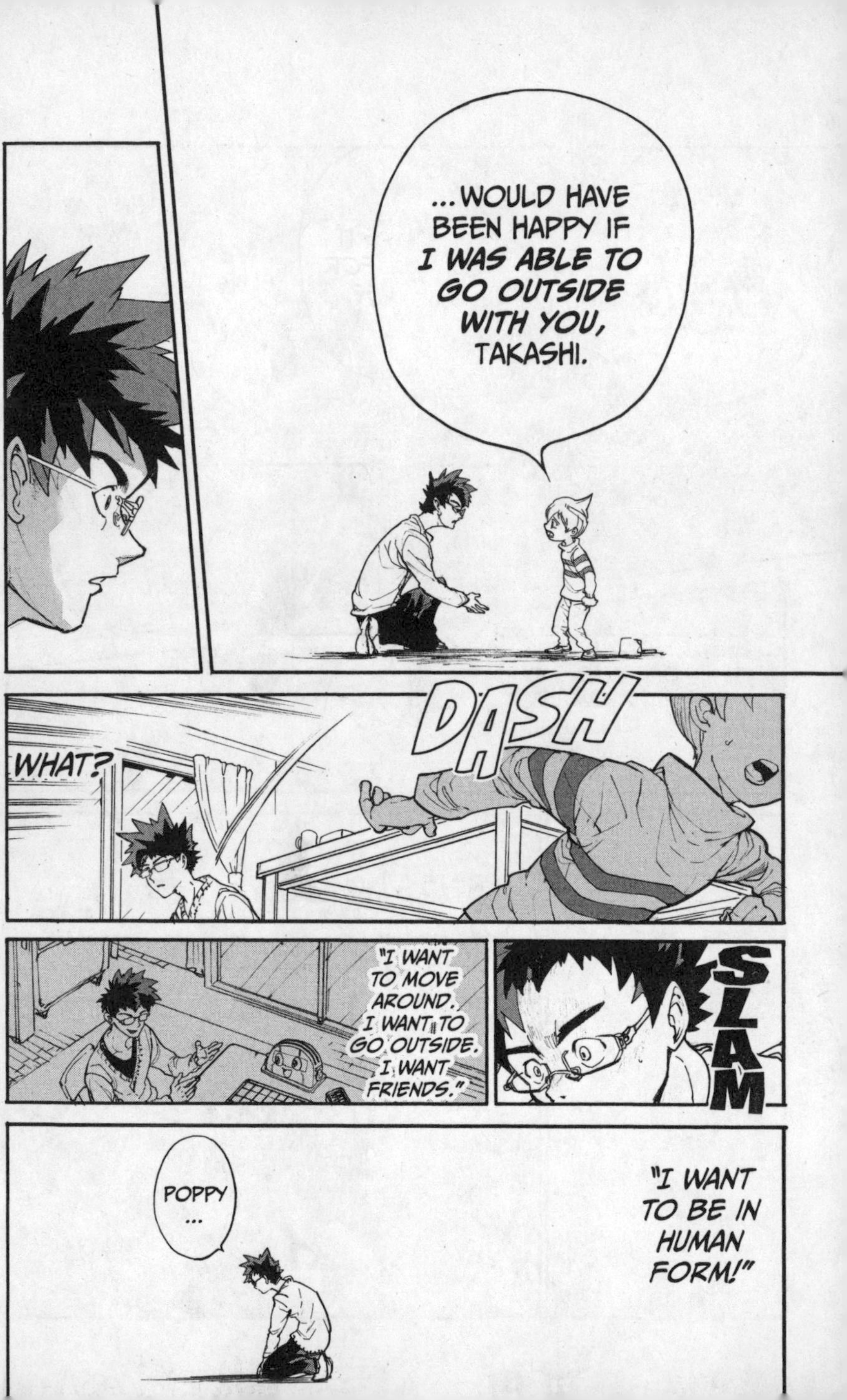
...WOULD HAVE BEEN HAPPY IF I WAS ABLE TO GO OUTSIDE WITH YOU, TAKASHI.
DASH
WHAT?
SLAM
"I WANT TO MOVE AROUND. I WANT TO GO OUTSIDE. I WANT FRIENDS."
"I WANT TO BE IN HUMAN FORM!"
POPPY ...

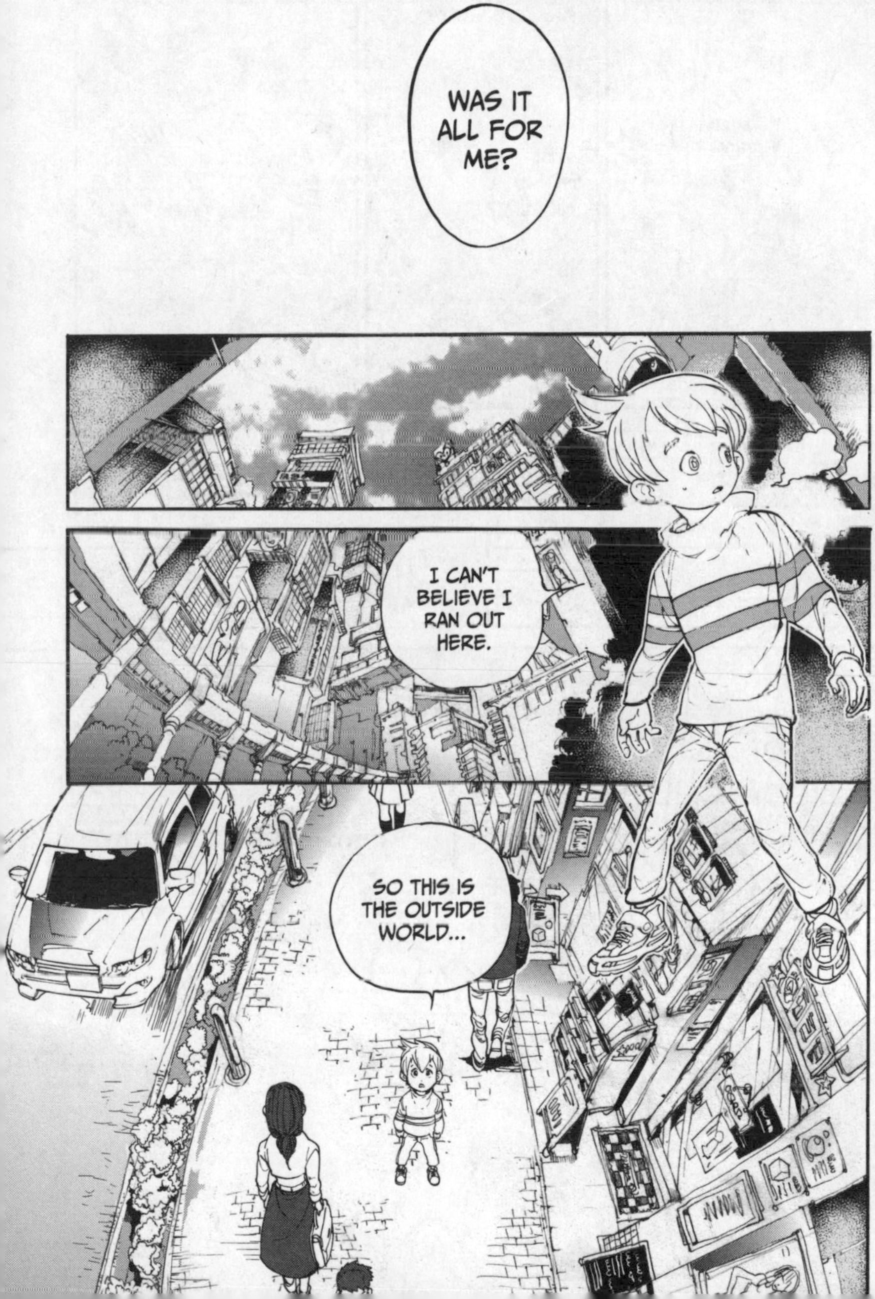
WAS IT ALL FOR ME?
I CAN'T BELIEVE I RAN OUT HERE.
SO THIS IS THE OUTSIDE WORLD...

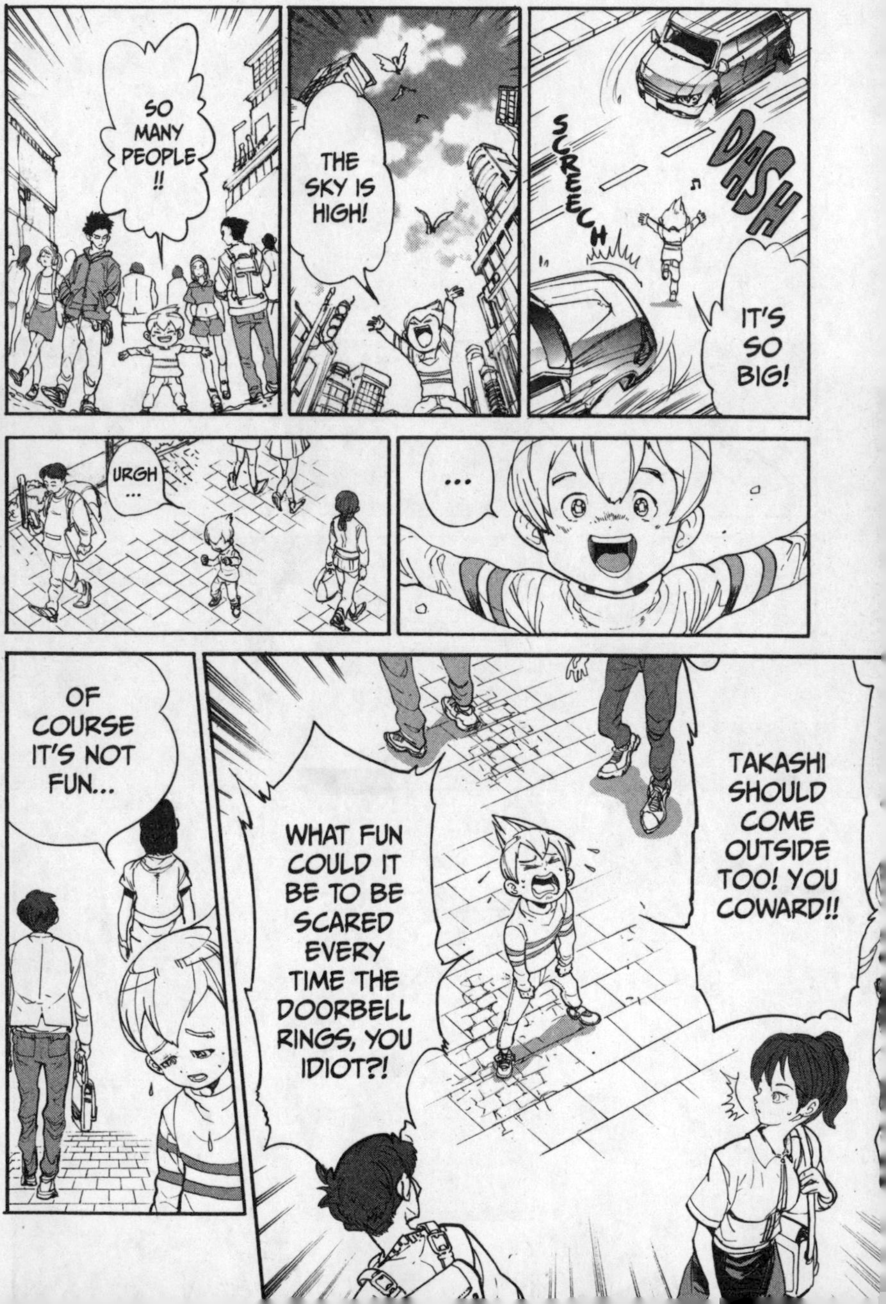
DASH
SCREECH
IT'S SO BIG!
THE SKY IS HIGH!
SO MANY PEOPLE!!
...
URGH ...
TAKASHI SHOULD COME OUTSIDE TOO! YOU COWARD!!
WHAT FUN COULD IT BE TO BE SCARED EVERY TIME THE DOORBELL RINGS, YOU IDIOT?!
OF COURSE IT'S NOT FUN...

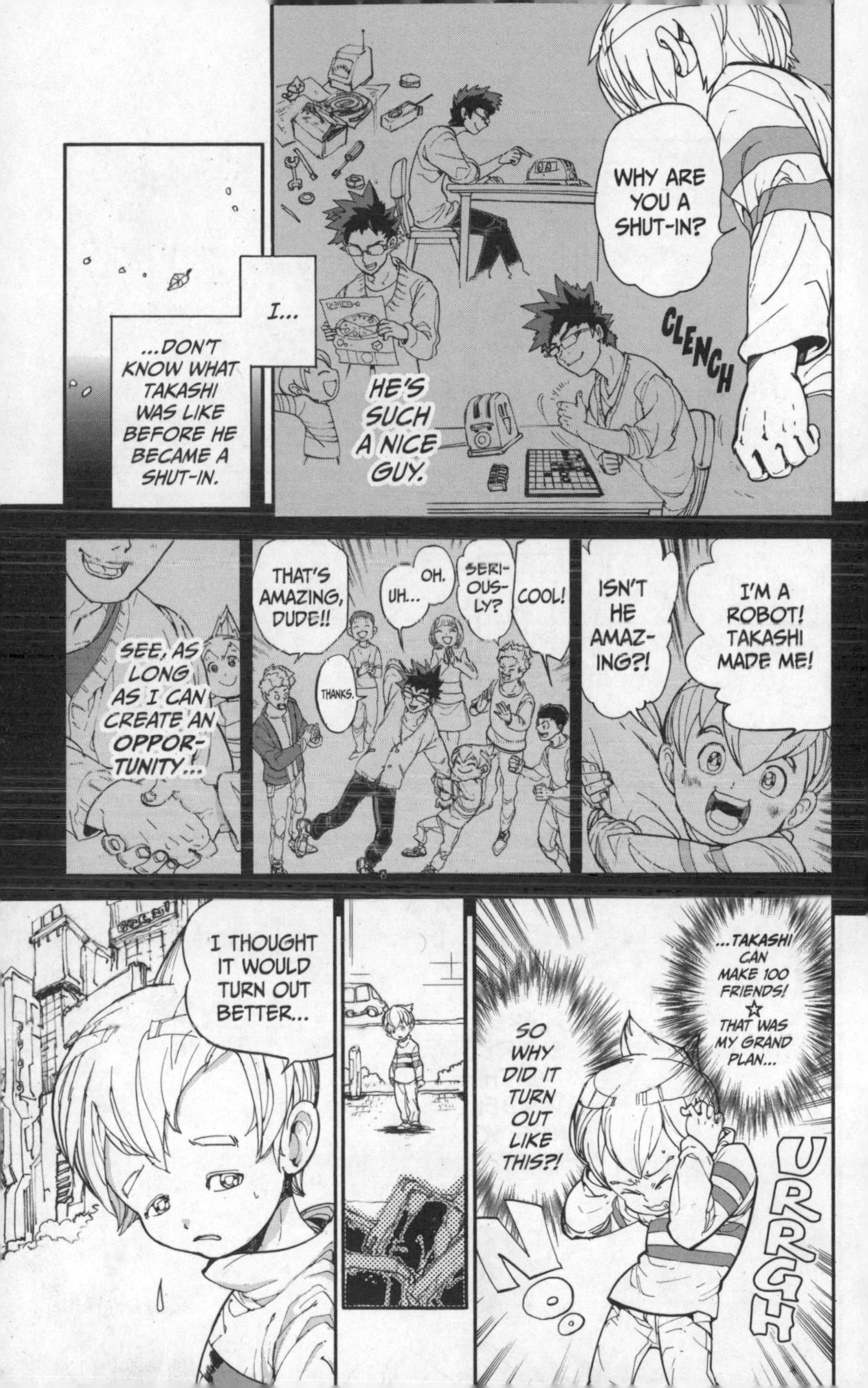
WHY ARE YOU A SHUT-IN?
CLENCH
HE'S SUCH A NICE GUY.
I...
...DON'T KNOW WHAT TAKASHI WAS LIKE BEFORE HE BECAME A SHUT-IN.
I'M A ROBOT! TAKASHI MADE ME!
ISN'T HE AMAZ-ING?!
COOL!
SERI-OUS-LY?
OH.
UH...
THAT'S AMAZING, DUDE!!
THANKS.
SEE, AS LONG AS I CAN CREATE AN OPPOR-TUNITY...
...TAKASHI CAN MAKE 100 FRIENDS! ☆ THAT WAS MY GRAND PLAN...
SO WHY DID IT TURN OUT LIKE THIS?!
URRGH
NOO
I THOUGHT IT WOULD TURN OUT BETTER...

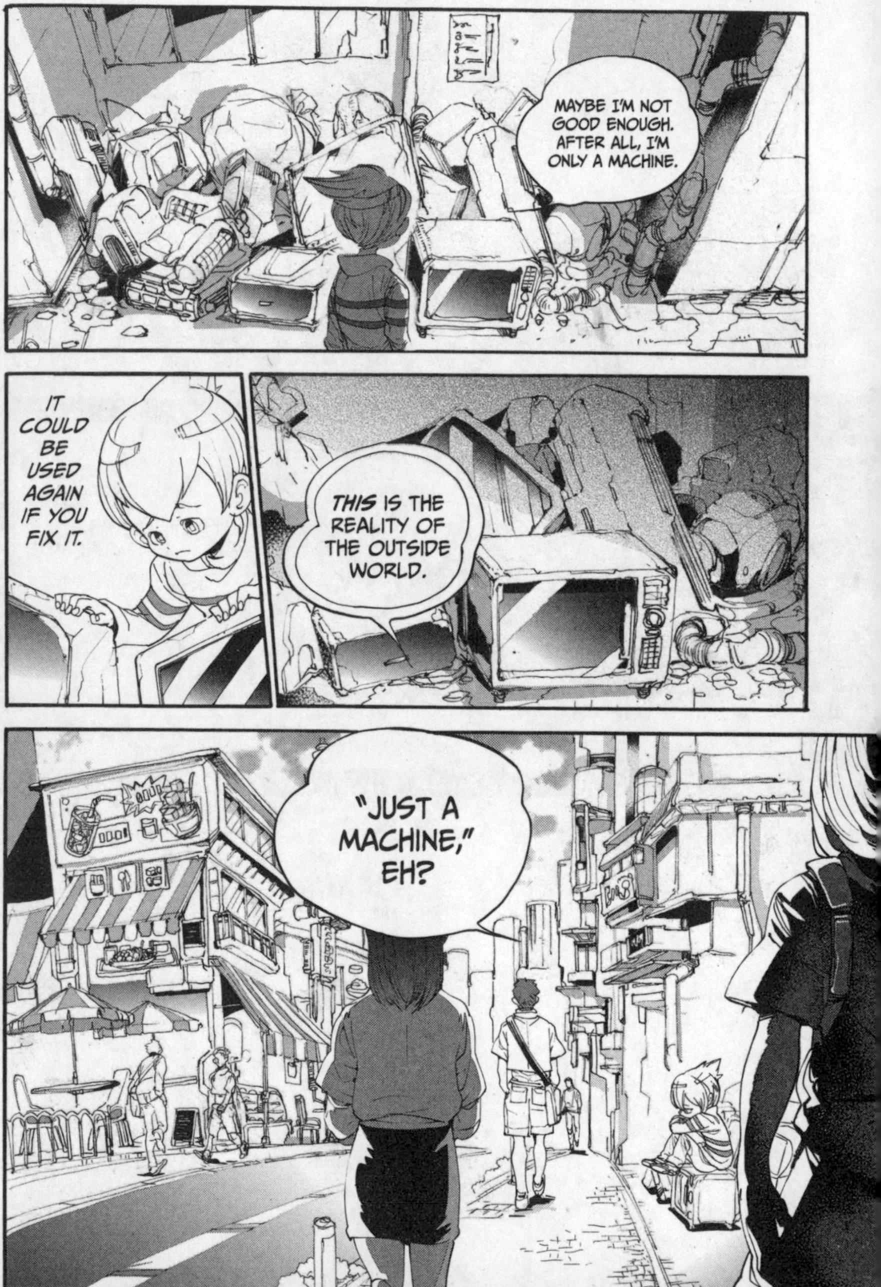
MAYBE I'M NOT GOOD ENOUGH. AFTER ALL, I'M ONLY A MACHINE.
THIS IS THE REALITY OF THE OUTSIDE WORLD.
IT COULD BE USED AGAIN IF YOU FIX IT.
"JUST A MACHINE," EH?

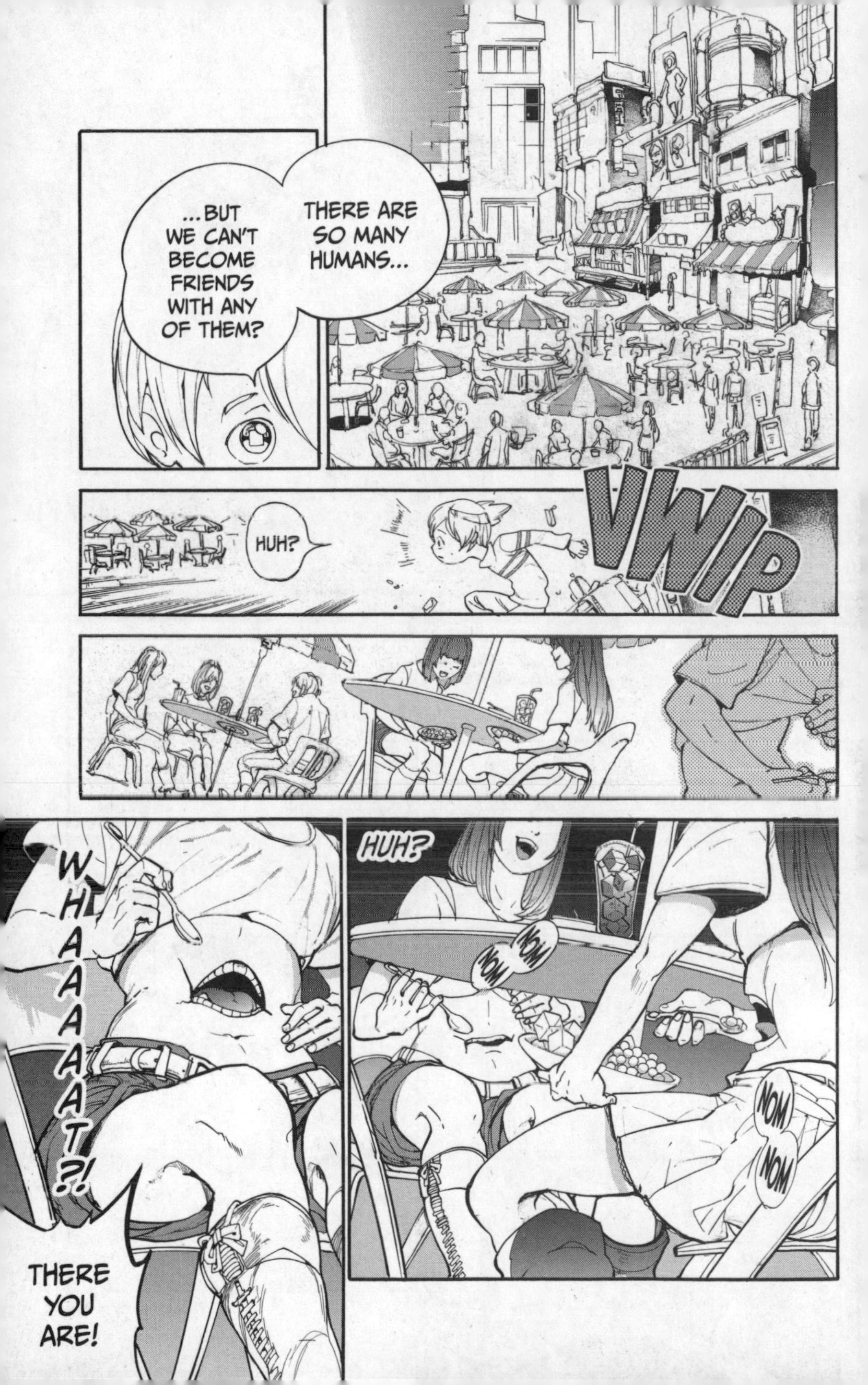
THERE ARE SO MANY HUMANS...
...BUT WE CAN'T BECOME FRIENDS WITH ANY OF THEM?
VWIP
HUH?
HUH?
NOM NOM
NOM NOM
WHAAAAAAAT?!
THERE YOU ARE!

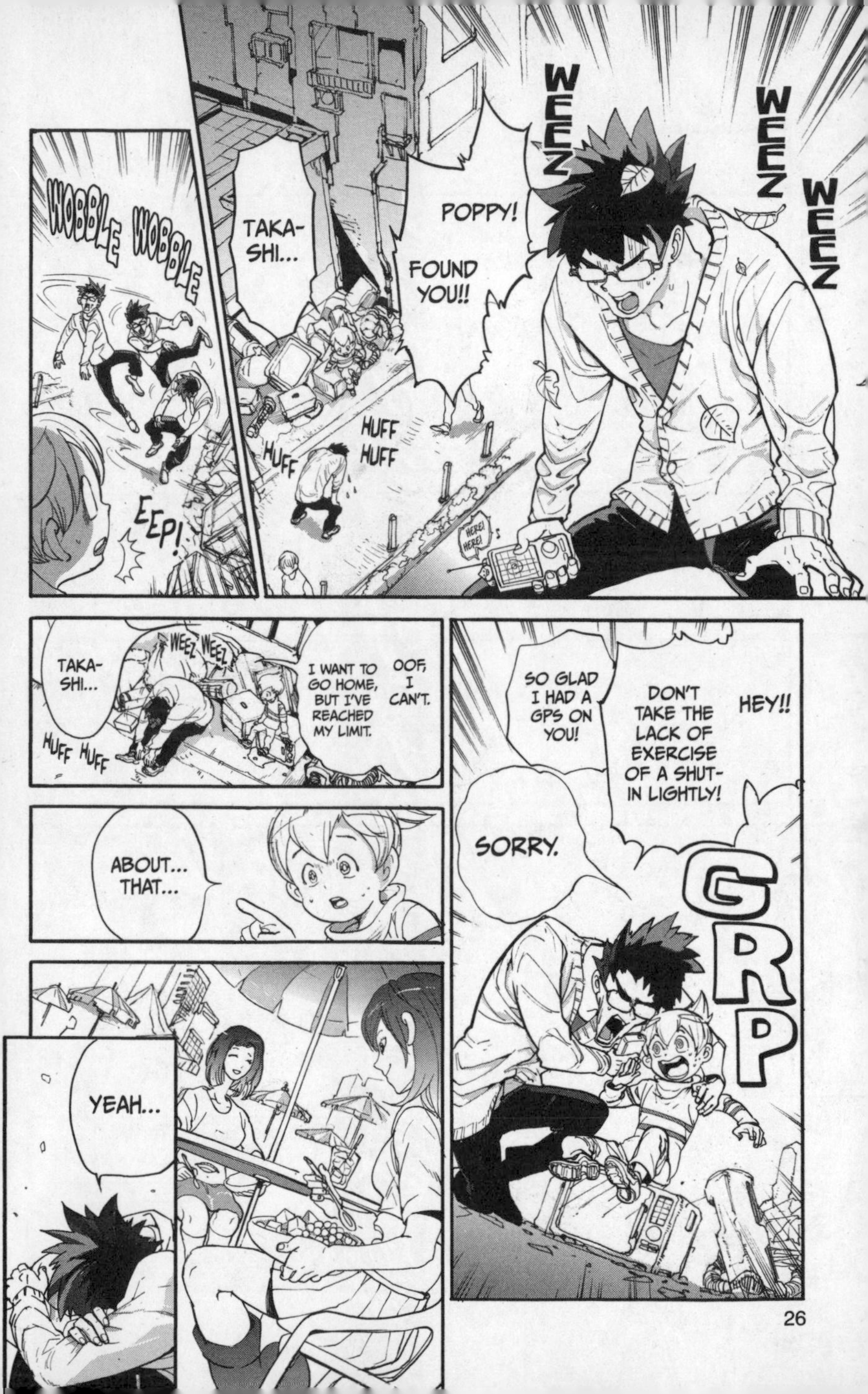
WEEZ
WEEZ
WEEZ
POPPY!
FOUND YOU!!
HERE! HERE!
HUFF HUFF
HUFF
TAKA-SHI...
WOBBLE WOBBLE
EEP!
HEY!!
DON'T TAKE THE LACK OF EXERCISE OF A SHUT-IN LIGHTLY!
SO GLAD I HAD A GPS ON YOU!
GRP
SORRY.
OOF, I CAN'T.
I WANT TO GO HOME, BUT I'VE REACHED MY LIMIT.
WEEZ WEEZ
TAKA-SHI...
HUFF HUFF
ABOUT... THAT...
YEAH...

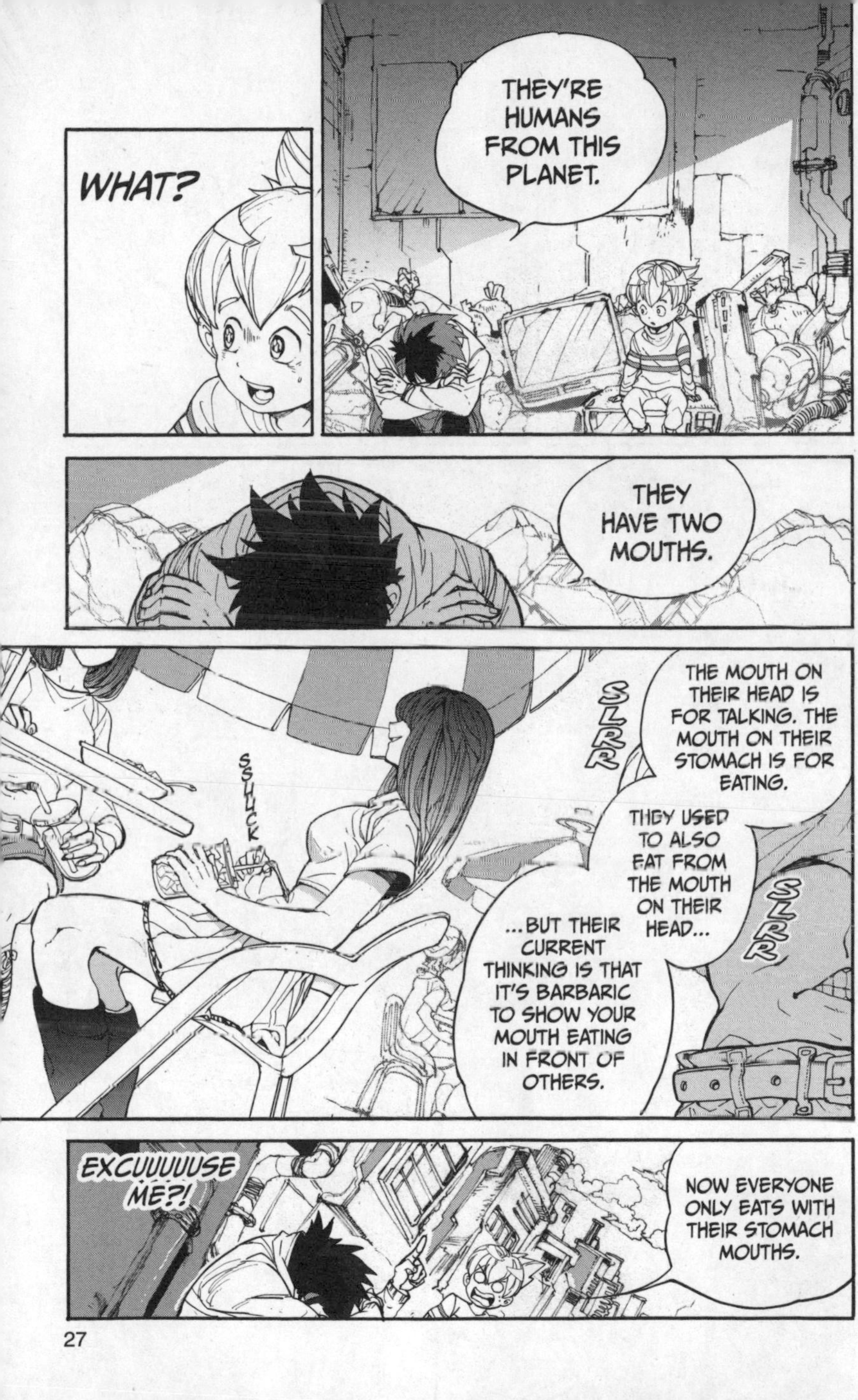
THEY'RE HUMANS FROM THIS PLANET.
WHAT?
THEY HAVE TWO MOUTHS.
THE MOUTH ON THEIR HEAD IS FOR TALKING. THE MOUTH ON THEIR STOMACH IS FOR EATING.
SLRR
THEY USED TO ALSO EAT FROM THE MOUTH ON THEIR HEAD...
SLRR
...BUT THEIR CURRENT THINKING IS THAT IT'S BARBARIC TO SHOW YOUR MOUTH EATING IN FRONT OF OTHERS.
SSHUCK
NOW EVERYONE ONLY EATS WITH THEIR STOMACH MOUTHS.
EXCUUUUUSE ME?!

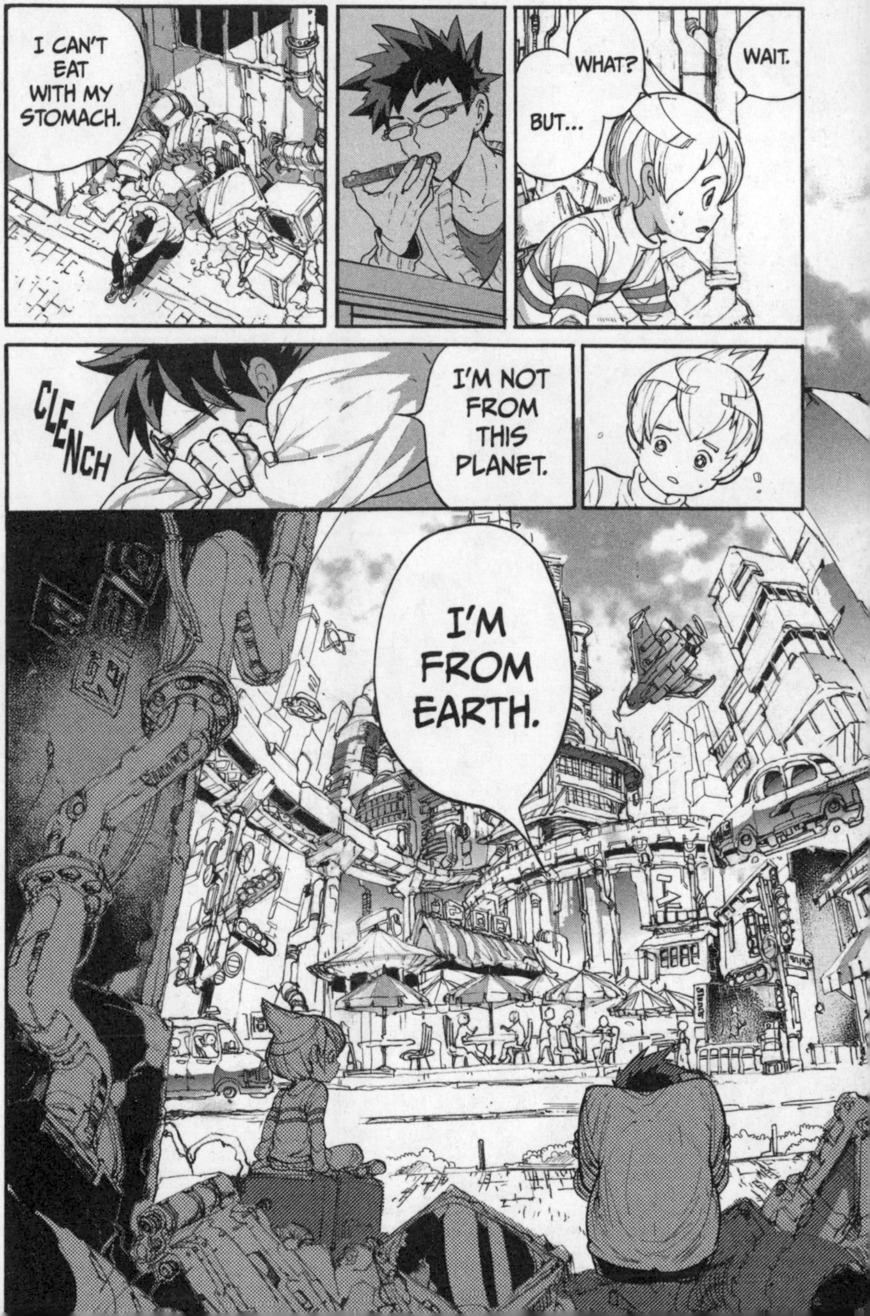
WAIT.
WHAT?
BUT...
I CAN'T EAT WITH MY STOMACH.
I'M NOT FROM THIS PLANET.
CLENCH
I'M FROM EARTH.

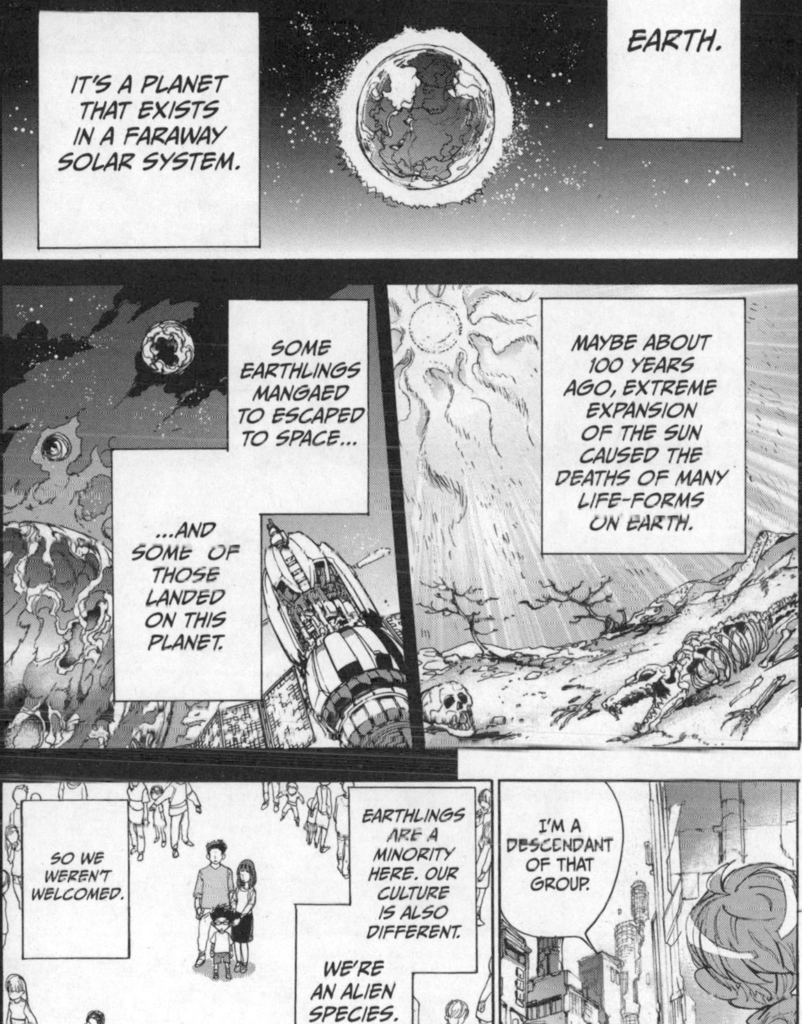
EARTH.
IT'S A PLANET THAT EXISTS IN A FARAWAY SOLAR SYSTEM.
MAYBE ABOUT 100 YEARS AGO, EXTREME EXPANSION OF THE SUN CAUSED THE DEATHS OF MANY LIFE-FORMS ON EARTH.
SOME EARTHLINGS MANGAED TO ESCAPED TO SPACE...
...AND SOME OF THOSE LANDED ON THIS PLANET.
I'M A DESCENDANT OF THAT GROUP.
EARTHLINGS ARE A MINORITY HERE. OUR CULTURE IS ALSO DIFFERENT.
WE'RE AN ALIEN SPECIES.
SO WE WEREN'T WELCOMED.
HE'S AN EARTHLING.
UGH.

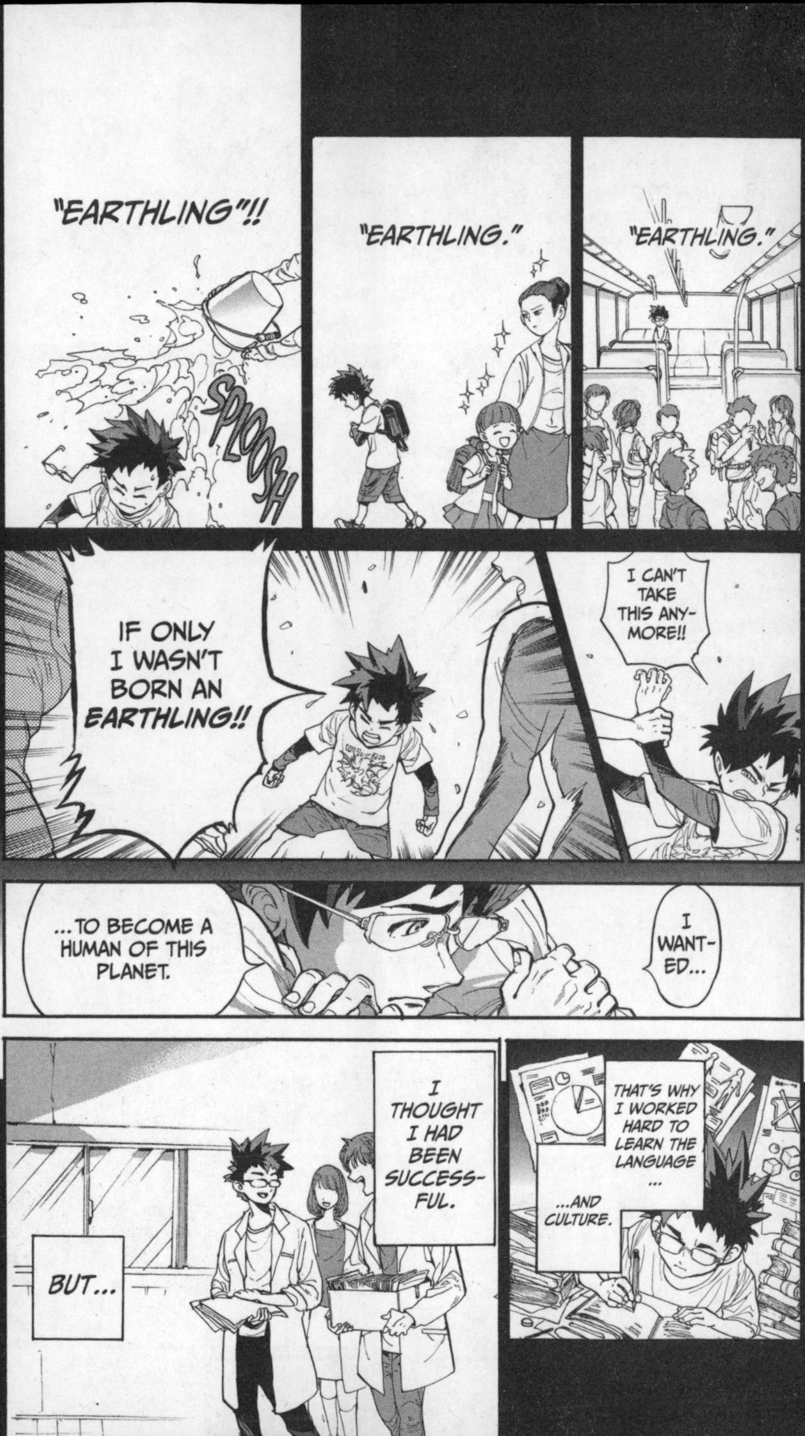
"EARTHLING."
"EARTHLING."
"EARTHLING"!!
SPLOOSH
I CAN'T TAKE THIS ANYMORE!!
IF ONLY I WASN'T BORN AN EARTHLING!!
I WANTED...
...TO BECOME A HUMAN OF THIS PLANET.
THAT'S WHY I WORKED HARD TO LEARN THE LANGUAGE...
...AND CULTURE.
I THOUGHT I HAD BEEN SUCCESSFUL.
BUT...

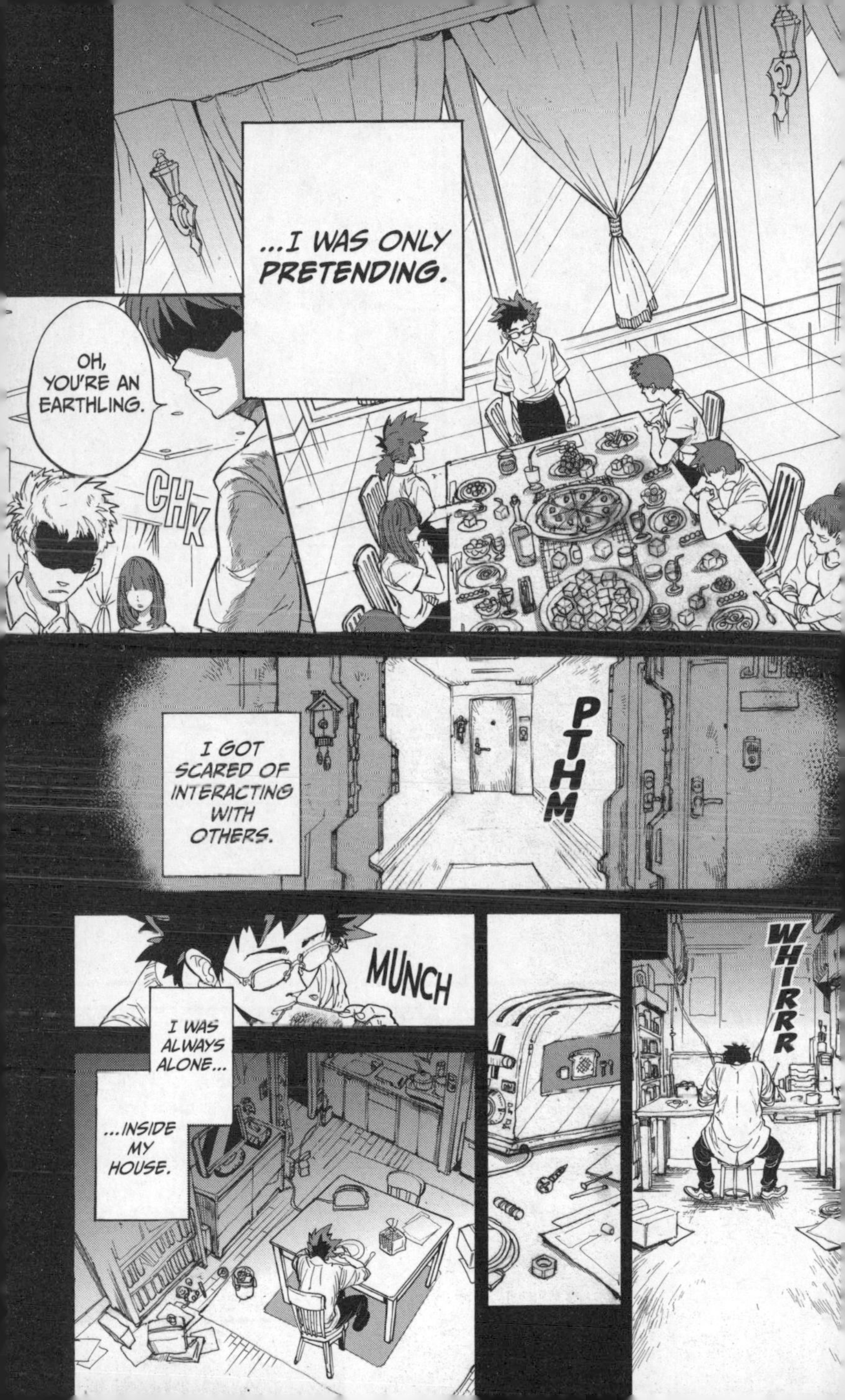
...I WAS ONLY PRETENDING.
OH, YOU'RE AN EARTHLING.
CHK
PTHM
I GOT SCARED OF INTERACTING WITH OTHERS.
WHIRRR
MUNCH
I WAS ALWAYS ALONE...
...INSIDE MY HOUSE.

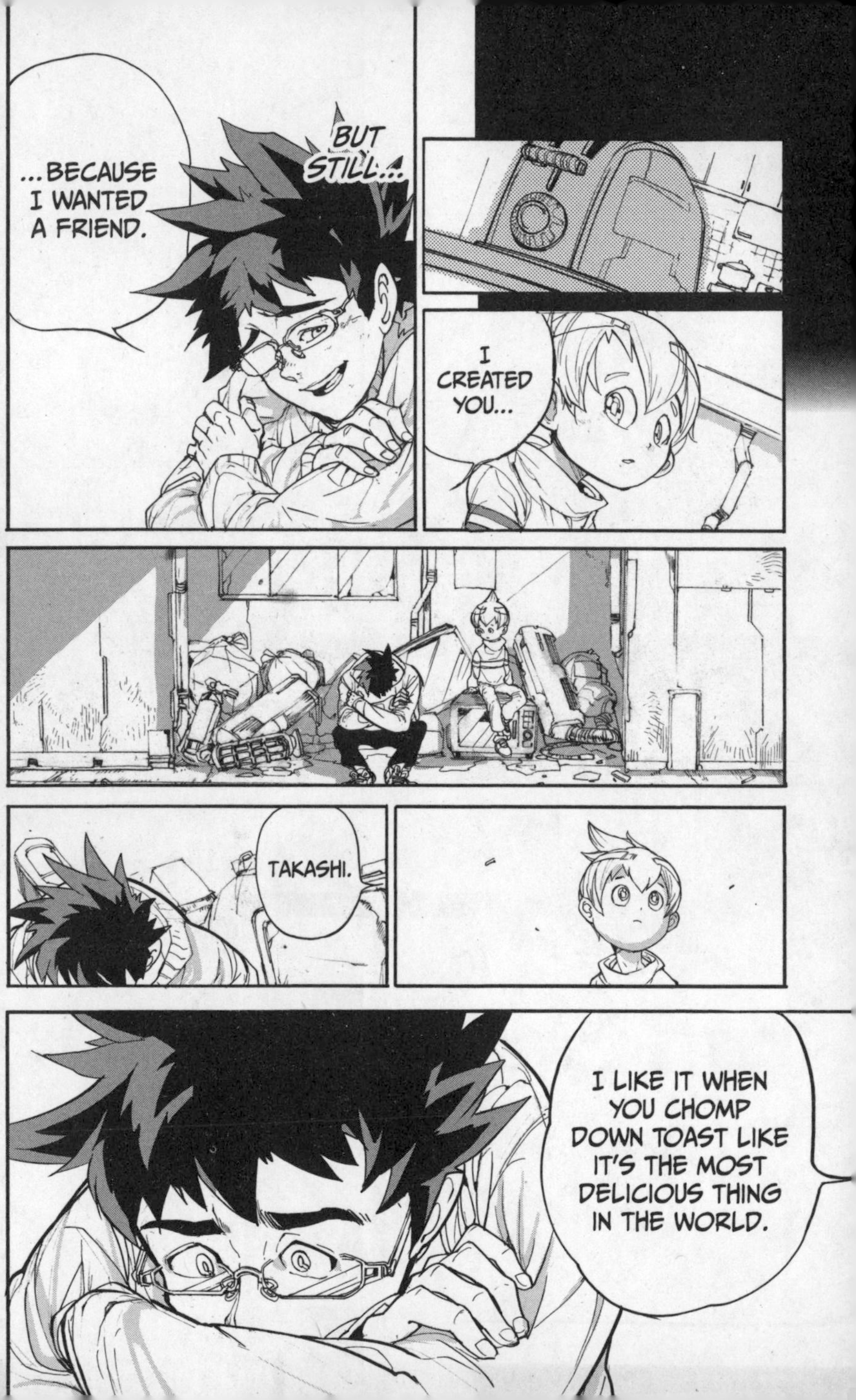
I CREATED YOU...
BUT STILL...
...BECAUSE I WANTED A FRIEND.
TAKASHI.
I LIKE IT WHEN YOU CHOMP DOWN TOAST LIKE IT'S THE MOST DELICIOUS THING IN THE WORLD.

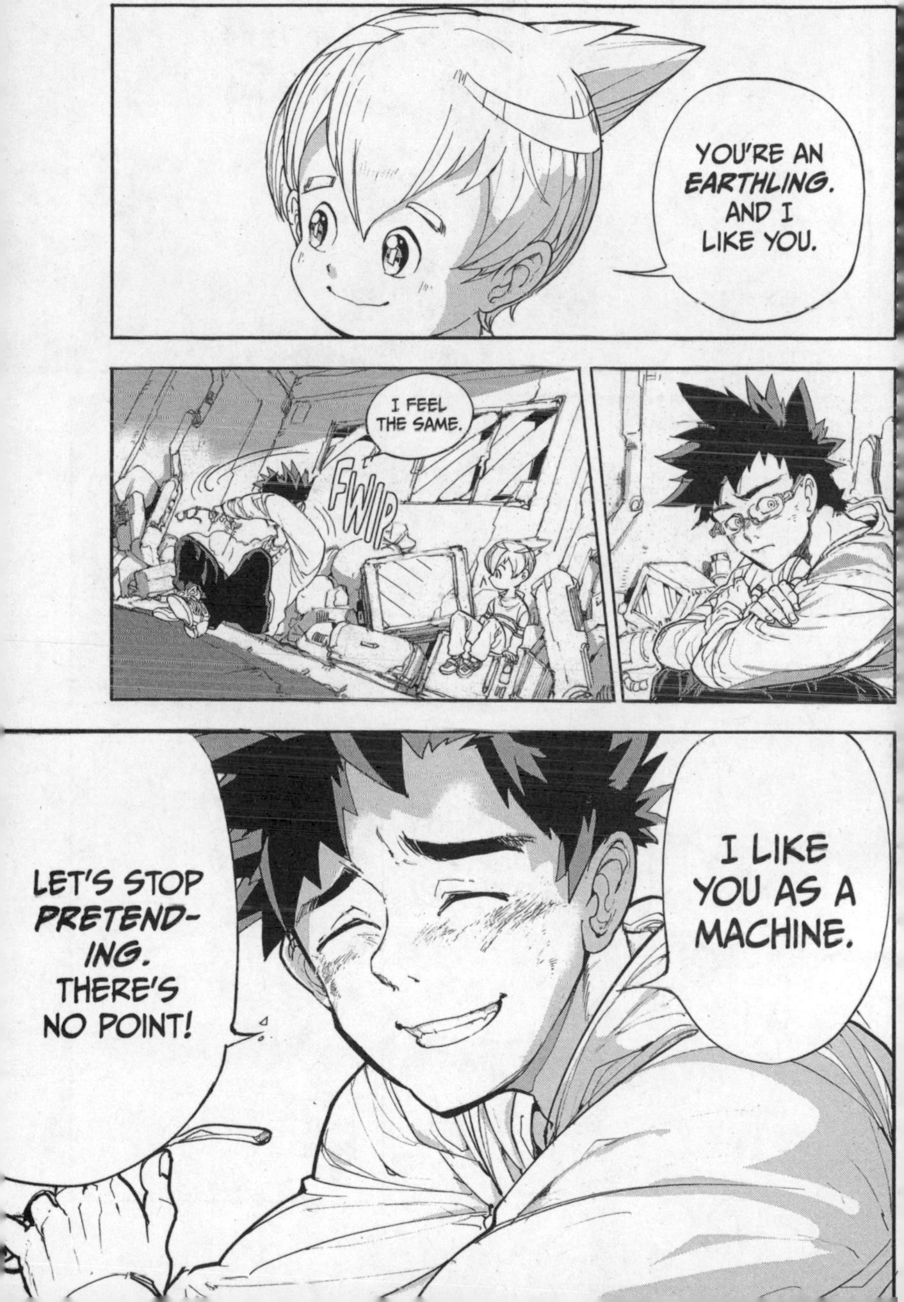
YOU'RE AN EARTHLING. AND I LIKE YOU.
I FEEL THE SAME.
FWIP
I LIKE YOU AS A MACHINE.
LET'S STOP PRETEND-ING. THERE'S NO POINT!

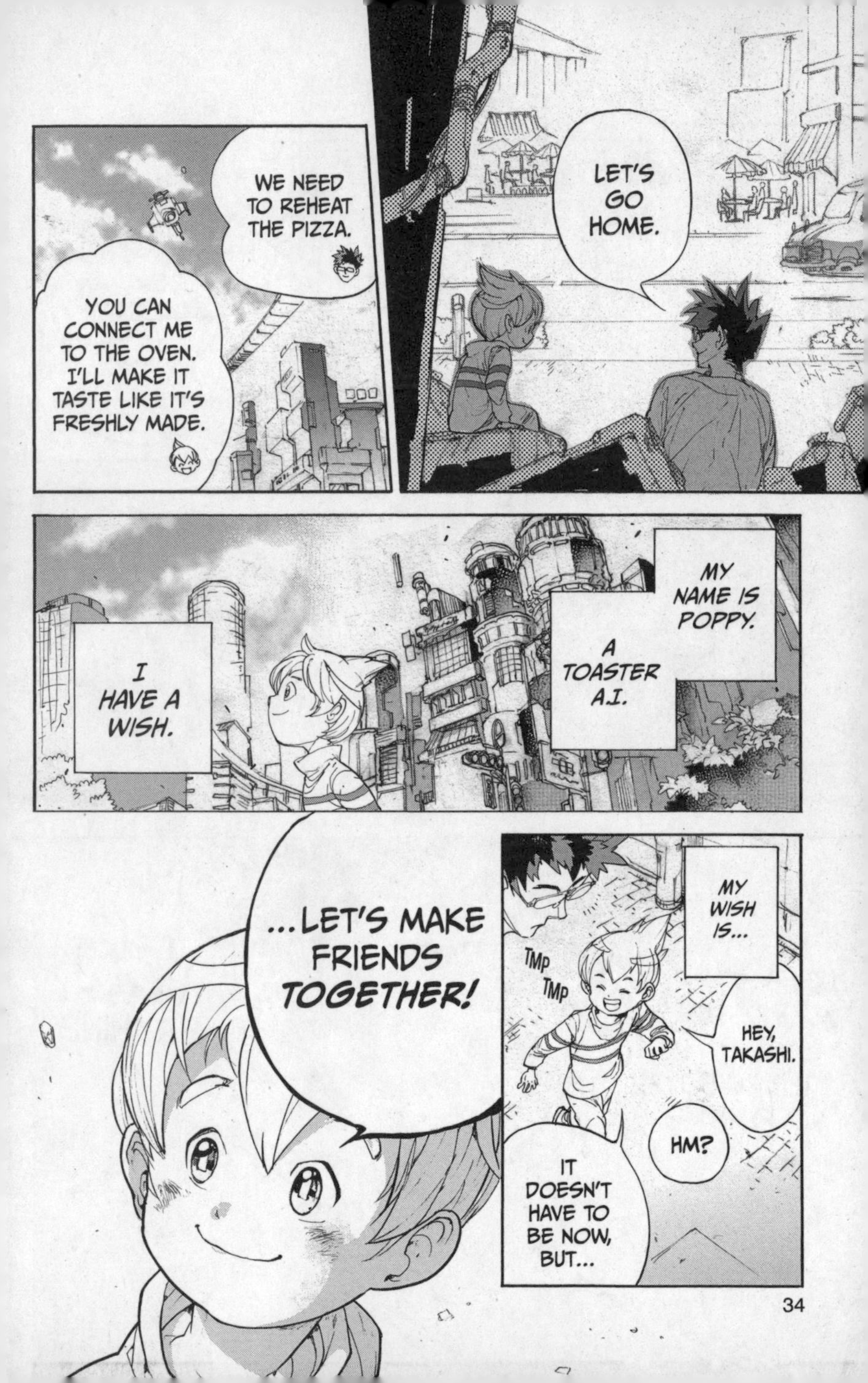
LET'S GO HOME.
WE NEED TO REHEAT THE PIZZA.
YOU CAN CONNECT ME TO THE OVEN. I'LL MAKE IT TASTE LIKE IT'S FRESHLY MADE.
MY NAME IS POPPY.
A TOASTER A.I.
I HAVE A WISH.
MY WISH IS...
TMP
TMP
HEY, TAKASHI.
HM?
IT DOESN'T HAVE TO BE NOW, BUT...
...LET'S MAKE FRIENDS TOGETHER!

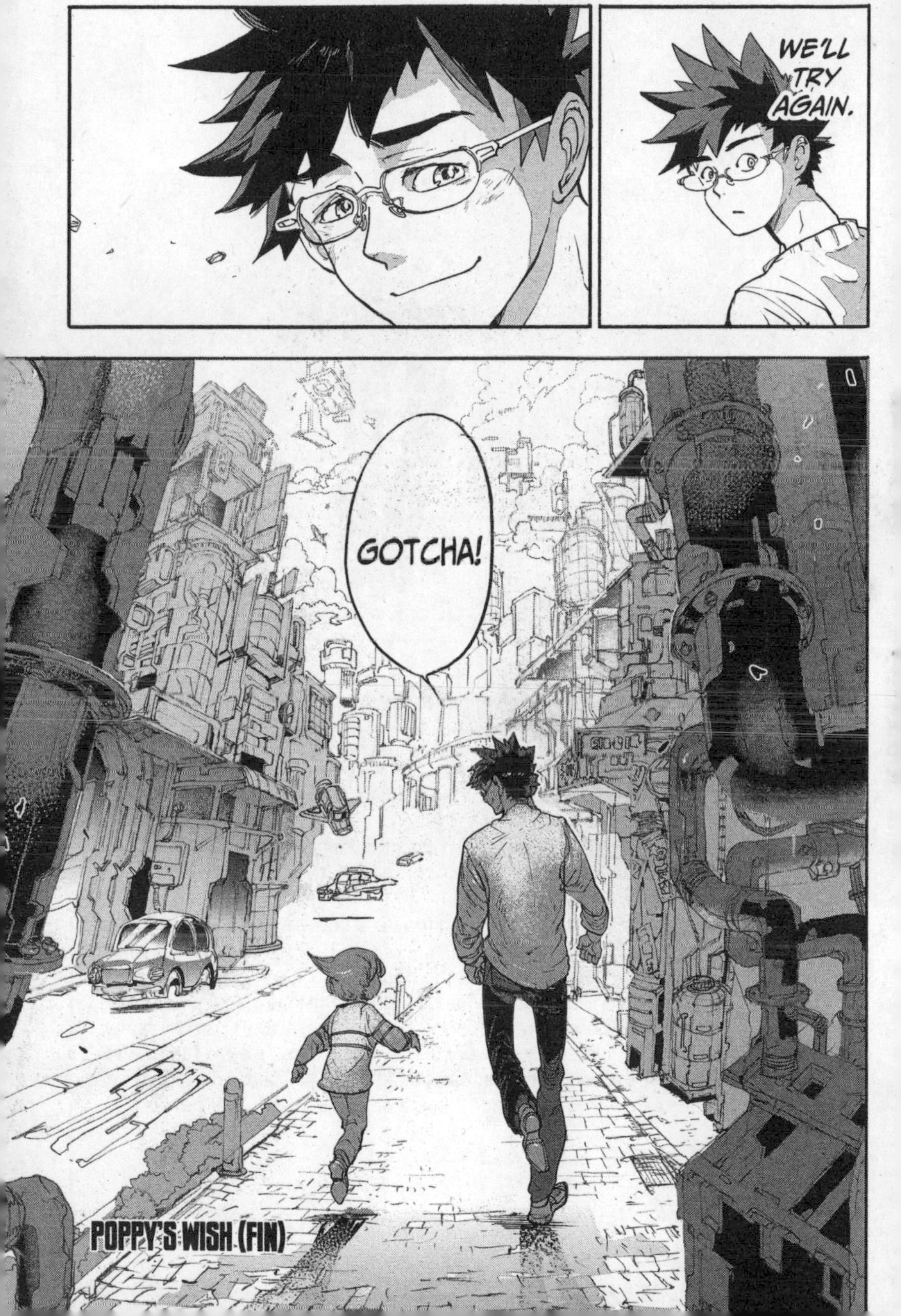
WE'LL TRY AGAIN.
GOTCHA!
POPPY'S WISH (FIN)

SHIRAI'S BEHIND-THE-SCENES STORIES #1

◆ This is my first one-shot after teaming up with Demizu Sensei.
◆ It's one of the two stories I wrote in the autumn of 2014 to find an artist who could draw for me.
◆ I came up with this story when I was thinking about how there could be a Pinocchio-type character who wouldn't want to be a real boy. (I'm sure they have to exist.)
◆ The name "Poppy" comes from toasters known as pop-up toasters. (The one Takashi uses.)
◆ Including the cuckoo clock at the beginning of the story, all of Takashi's inventions have a specific design that are similar to Poppy's humanoid form. And you can see Demizu Sensei's playful and detailed elements in every corner of her art. They're fun to find. (There are some inventions that Demizu Sensei came up with on her own too. They're awesome.) Please enjoy all these little details!

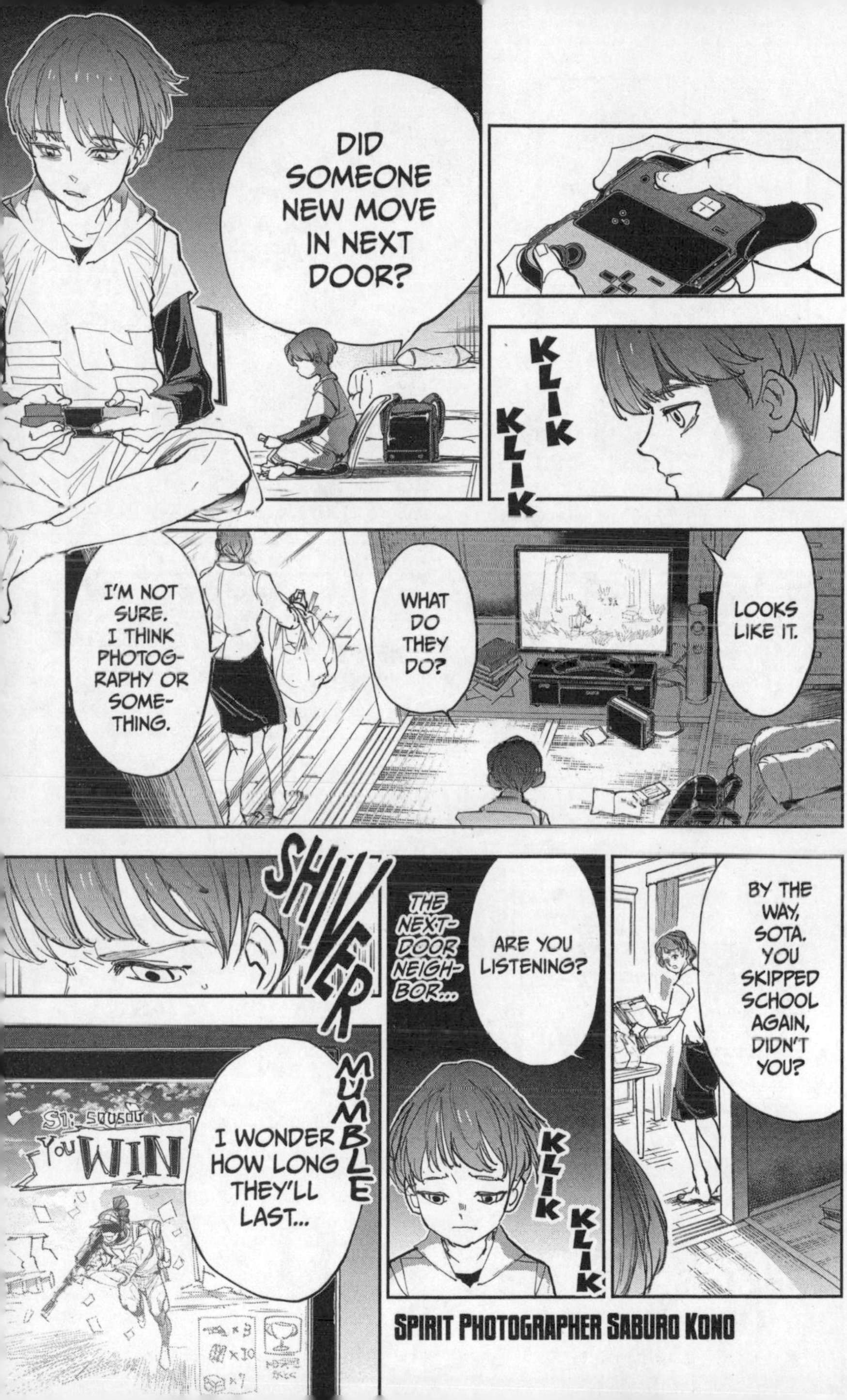
KLIK KLIK
DID SOMEONE NEW MOVE IN NEXT DOOR?
LOOKS LIKE IT.
WHAT DO THEY DO?
I'M NOT SURE. I THINK PHOTOG-RAPHY OR SOME-THING.
BY THE WAY, SOTA. YOU SKIPPED SCHOOL AGAIN, DIDN'T YOU?
ARE YOU LISTENING?
KLIK KLIK
THE NEXT-DOOR NEIGH-BOR...
SHIVER
MUMBLE
I WONDER HOW LONG THEY'LL LAST...
YOU WIN

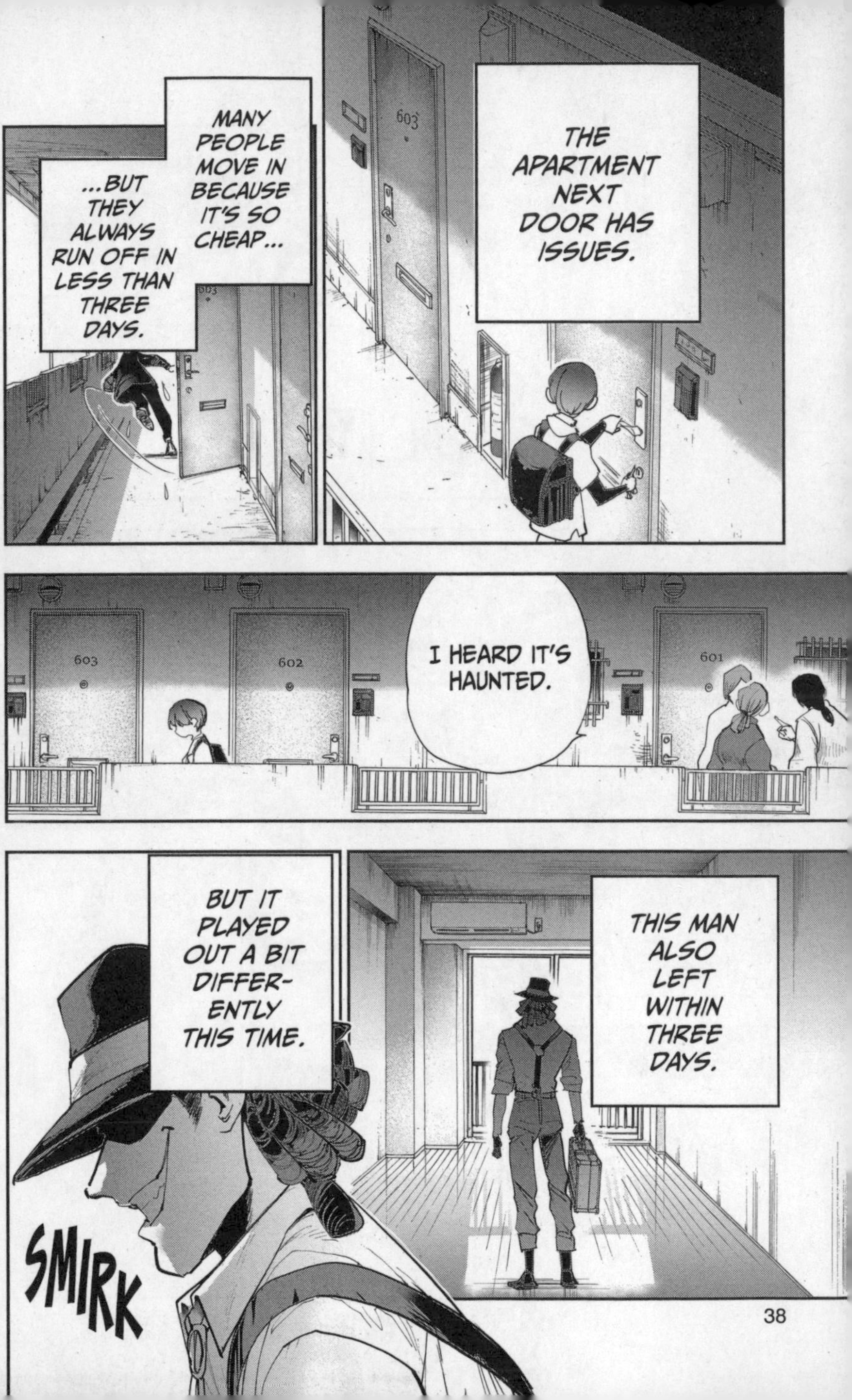
THE APARTMENT NEXT DOOR HAS ISSUES.
MANY PEOPLE MOVE IN BECAUSE IT'S SO CHEAP...
...BUT THEY ALWAYS RUN OFF IN LESS THAN THREE DAYS.
I HEARD IT'S HAUNTED.
THIS MAN ALSO LEFT WITHIN THREE DAYS.
BUT IT PLAYED OUT A BIT DIFFER-ENTLY THIS TIME.
SMIRK

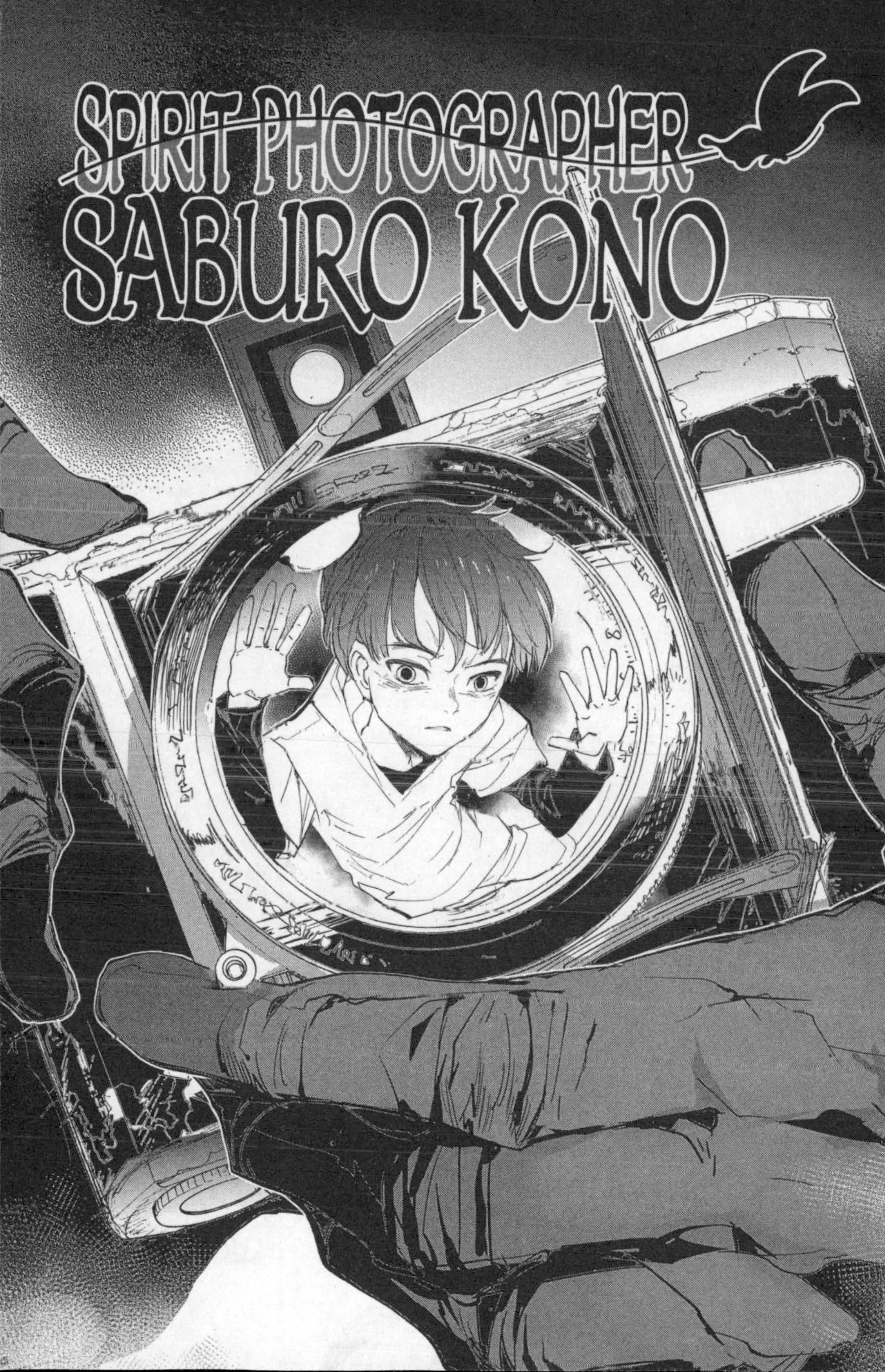
SPIRIT PHOTOGRAPHER
SABURO KONO

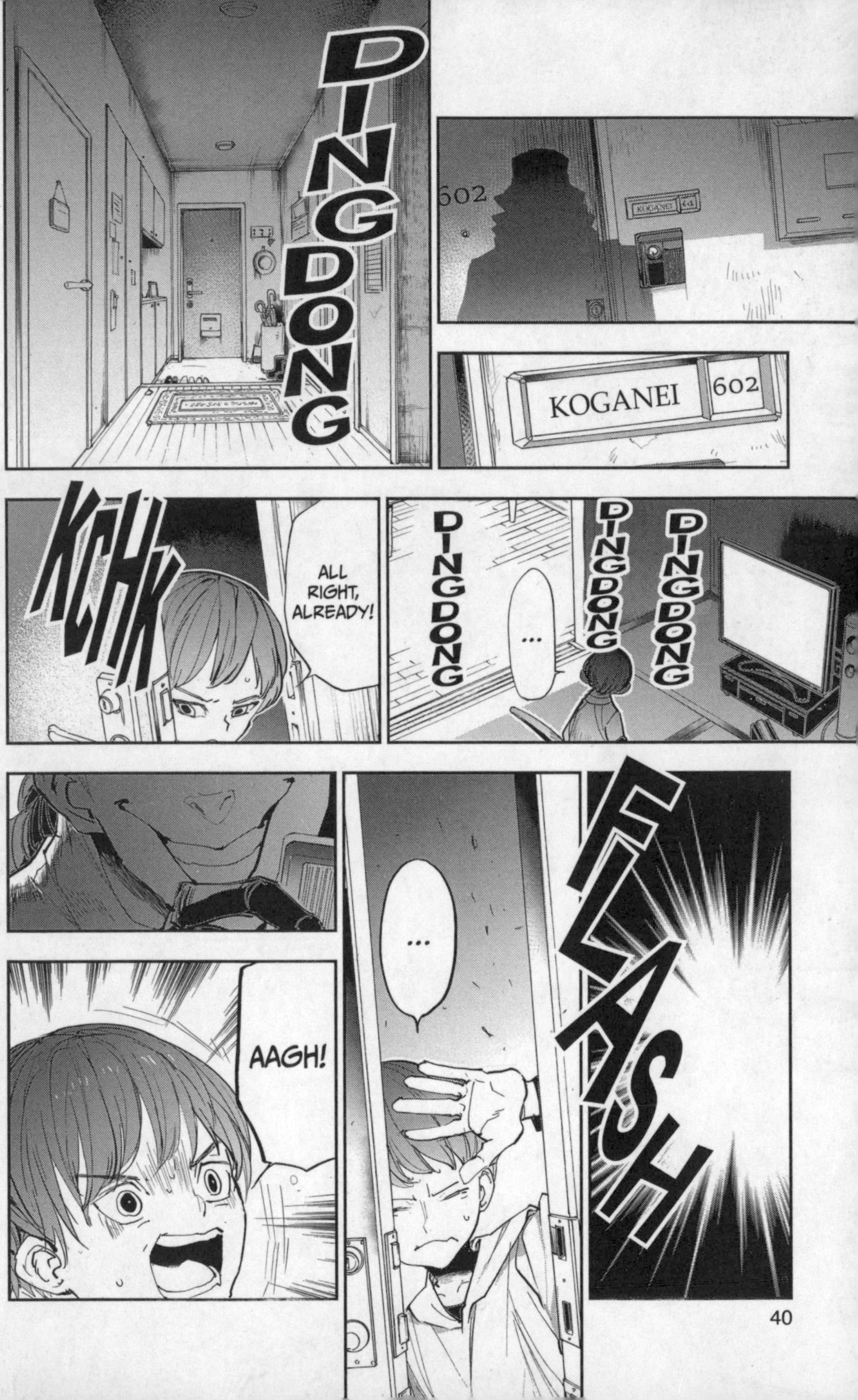
602
KOGANEI
KOGANEI 602
DING DONG
DING DONG
DING DONG
DING DONG
...
ALL RIGHT, ALREADY!
KCHK
FLASH
...
AAGH!

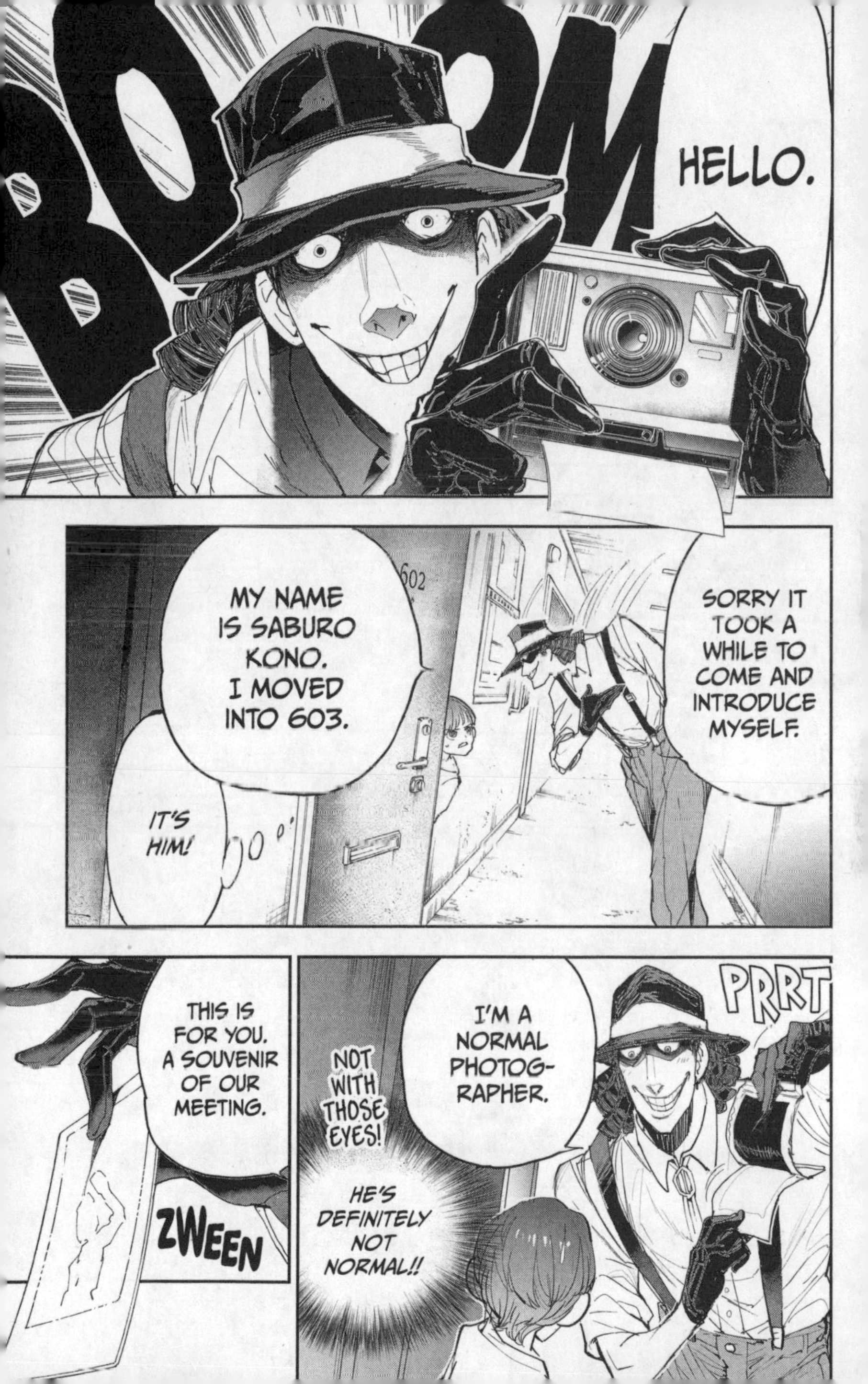
HELLO.
BOOM
SORRY IT TOOK A WHILE TO COME AND INTRODUCE MYSELF.
MY NAME IS SABURO KONO. I MOVED INTO 603.
602
IT'S HIM!
PRRT
I'M A NORMAL PHOTOG-RAPHER.
NOT WITH THOSE EYES!
HE'S DEFINITELY NOT NORMAL!!
THIS IS FOR YOU. A SOUVENIR OF OUR MEETING.
ZWEEN

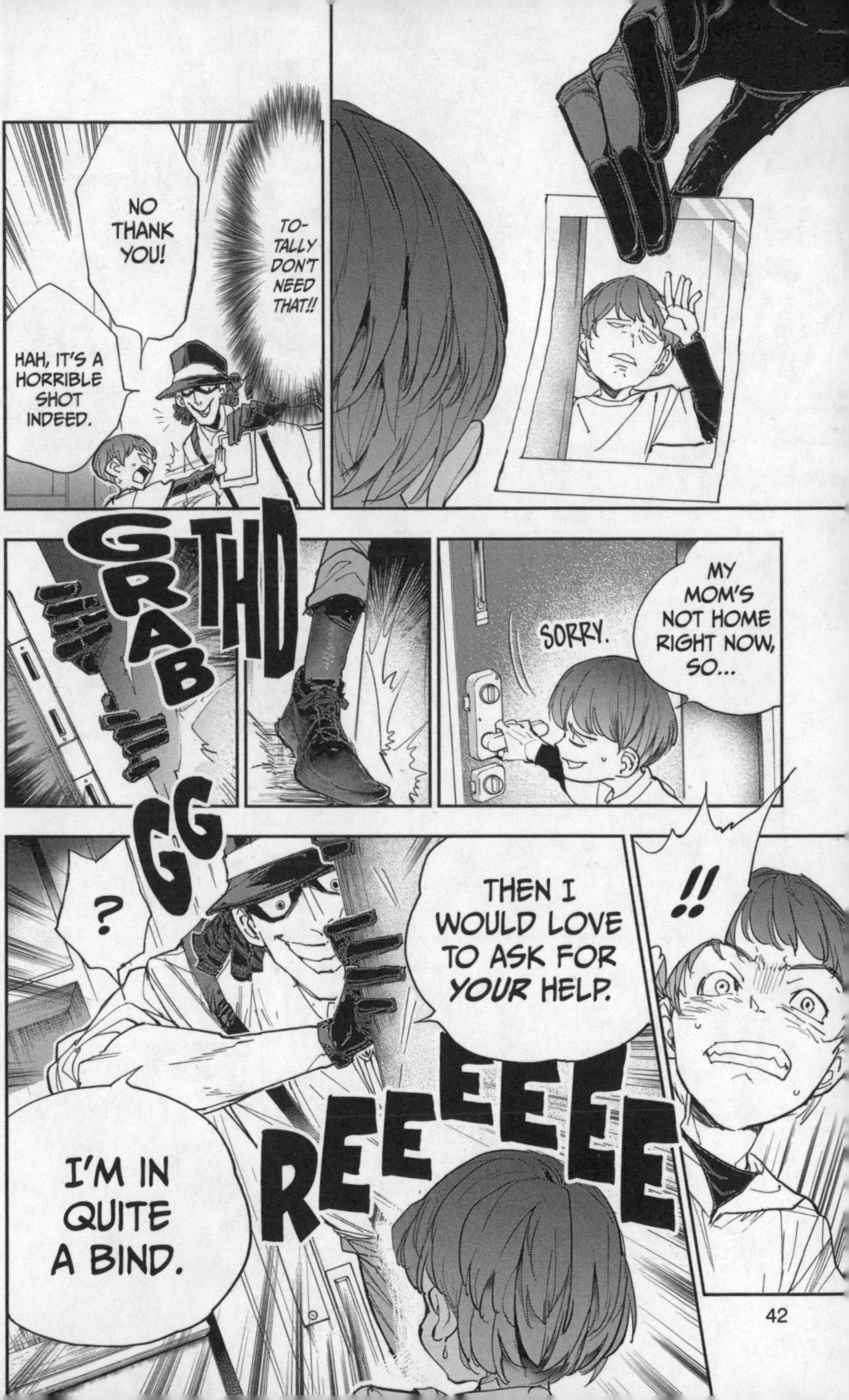
TO-TALLY DON'T NEED THAT!!
NO THANK YOU!
HAH, IT'S A HORRIBLE SHOT INDEED.
MY MOM'S NOT HOME RIGHT NOW, SO...
SORRY.
THD
GRAB
!!
THEN I WOULD LOVE TO ASK FOR *YOUR* HELP.
GG
?
REEEEEE
I'M IN QUITE A BIND.

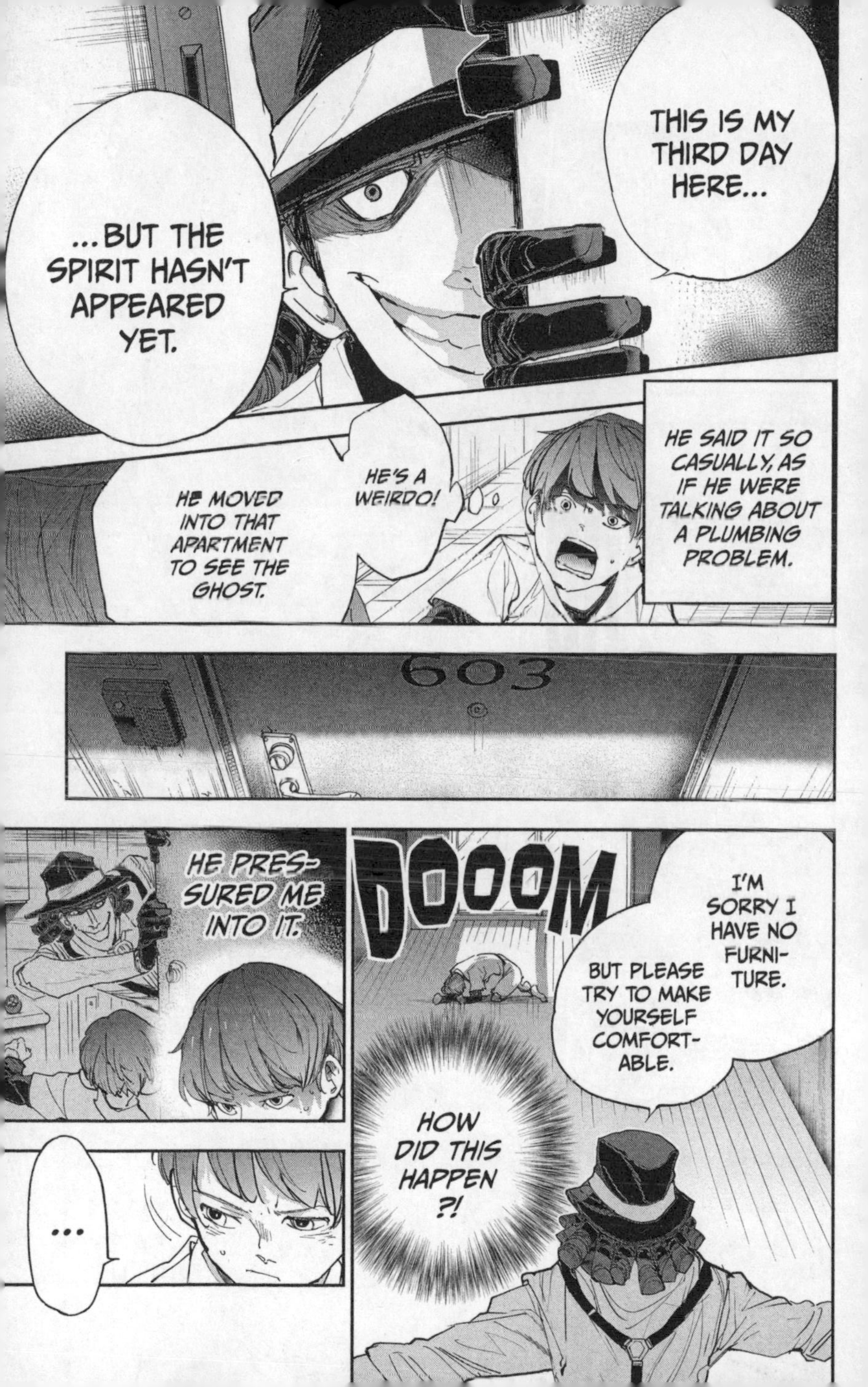
THIS IS MY THIRD DAY HERE...
...BUT THE SPIRIT HASN'T APPEARED YET.
HE SAID IT SO CASUALLY, AS IF HE WERE TALKING ABOUT A PLUMBING PROBLEM.
HE'S A WEIRDO!
HE MOVED INTO THAT APARTMENT TO SEE THE GHOST.
603
DOOOM
I'M SORRY I HAVE NO FURNITURE.
BUT PLEASE TRY TO MAKE YOURSELF COMFORTABLE.
HOW DID THIS HAPPEN?!
HE PRESSURED ME INTO IT.
...

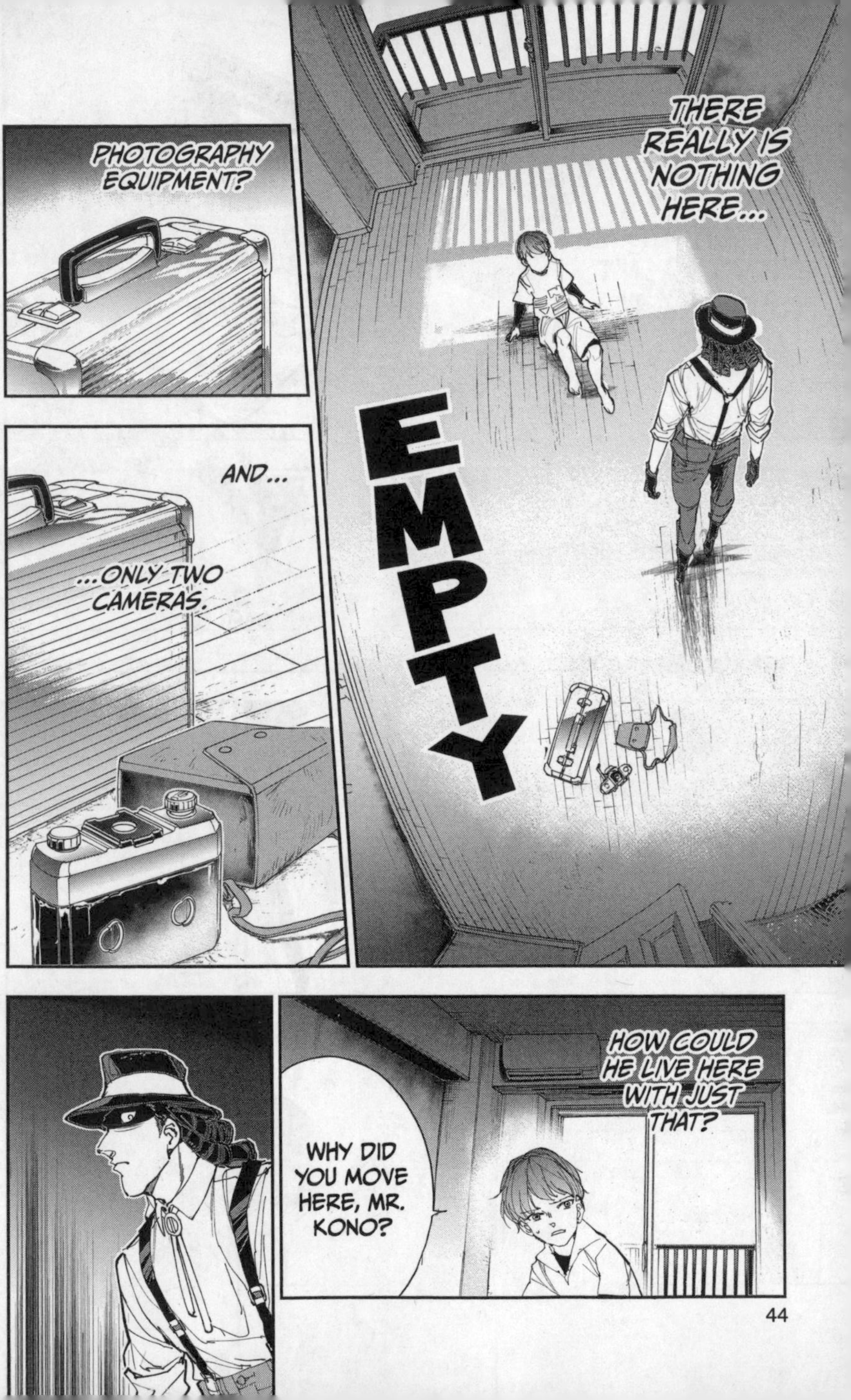
THERE REALLY IS NOTHING HERE...
EMPTY
PHOTOGRAPHY EQUIPMENT?
AND...
...ONLY TWO CAMERAS.
HOW COULD HE LIVE HERE WITH JUST THAT?
WHY DID YOU MOVE HERE, MR. KONO?

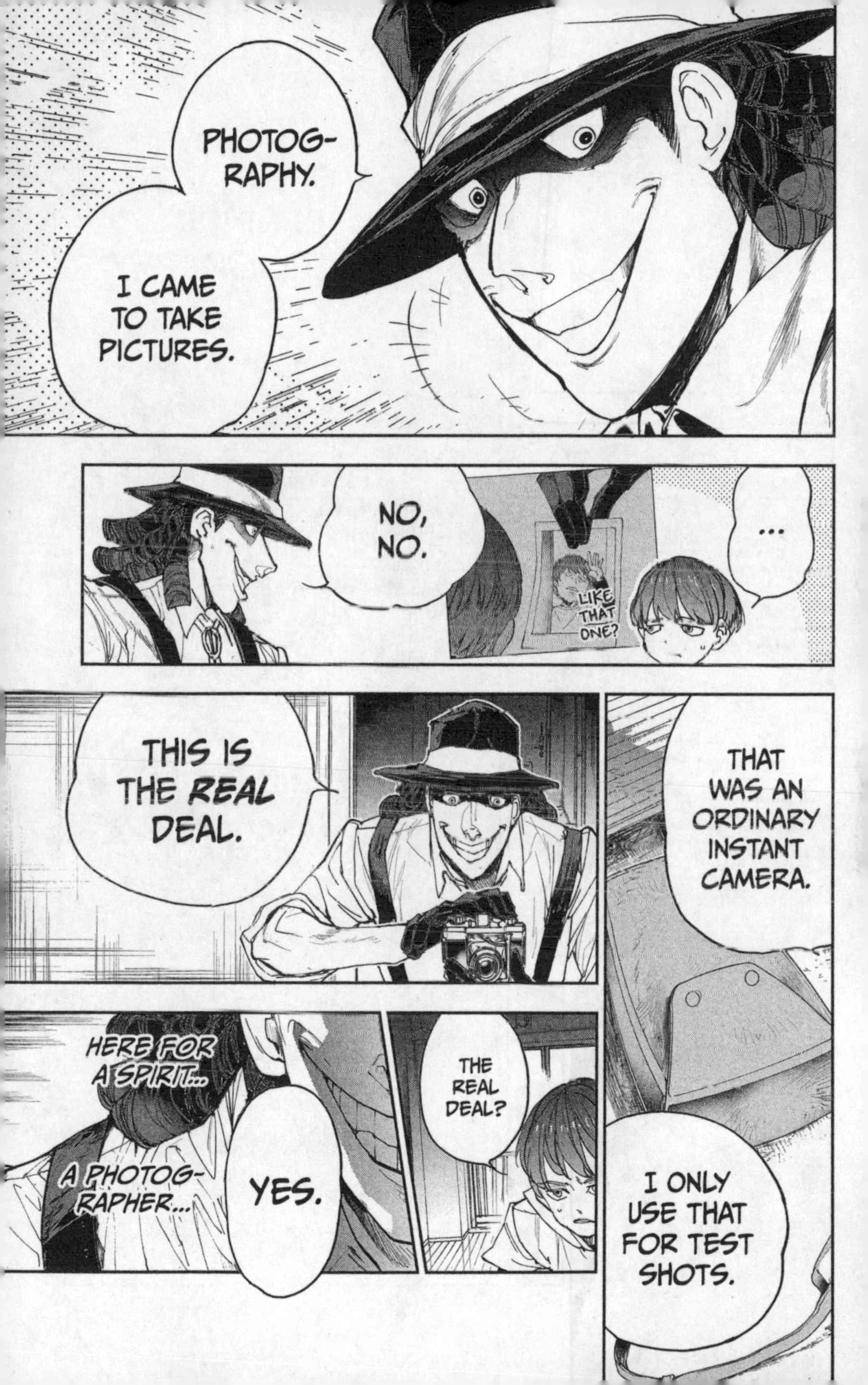
PHOTOG-RAPHY.
I CAME TO TAKE PICTURES.
...
LIKE THAT ONE?
NO, NO.
THAT WAS AN ORDINARY INSTANT CAMERA.
I ONLY USE THAT FOR TEST SHOTS.
THIS IS THE *REAL* DEAL.
THE REAL DEAL?
HERE FOR A SPIRIT...
YES.
A PHOTOG-RAPHER...

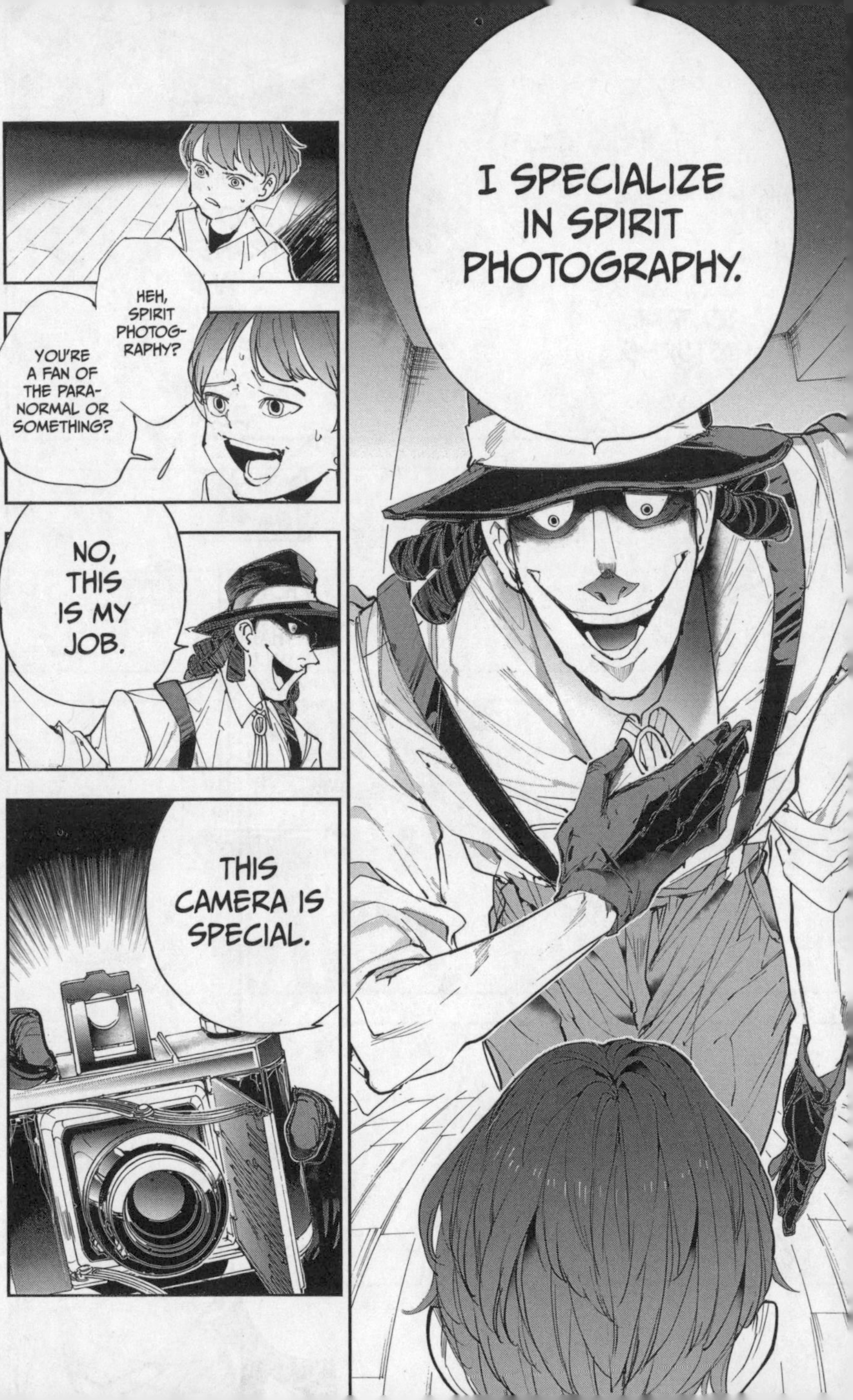
I SPECIALIZE IN SPIRIT PHOTOGRAPHY.
HEH, SPIRIT PHOTOG-RAPHY?
YOU'RE A FAN OF THE PARA-NORMAL OR SOMETHING?
NO, THIS IS MY JOB.
THIS CAMERA IS SPECIAL.

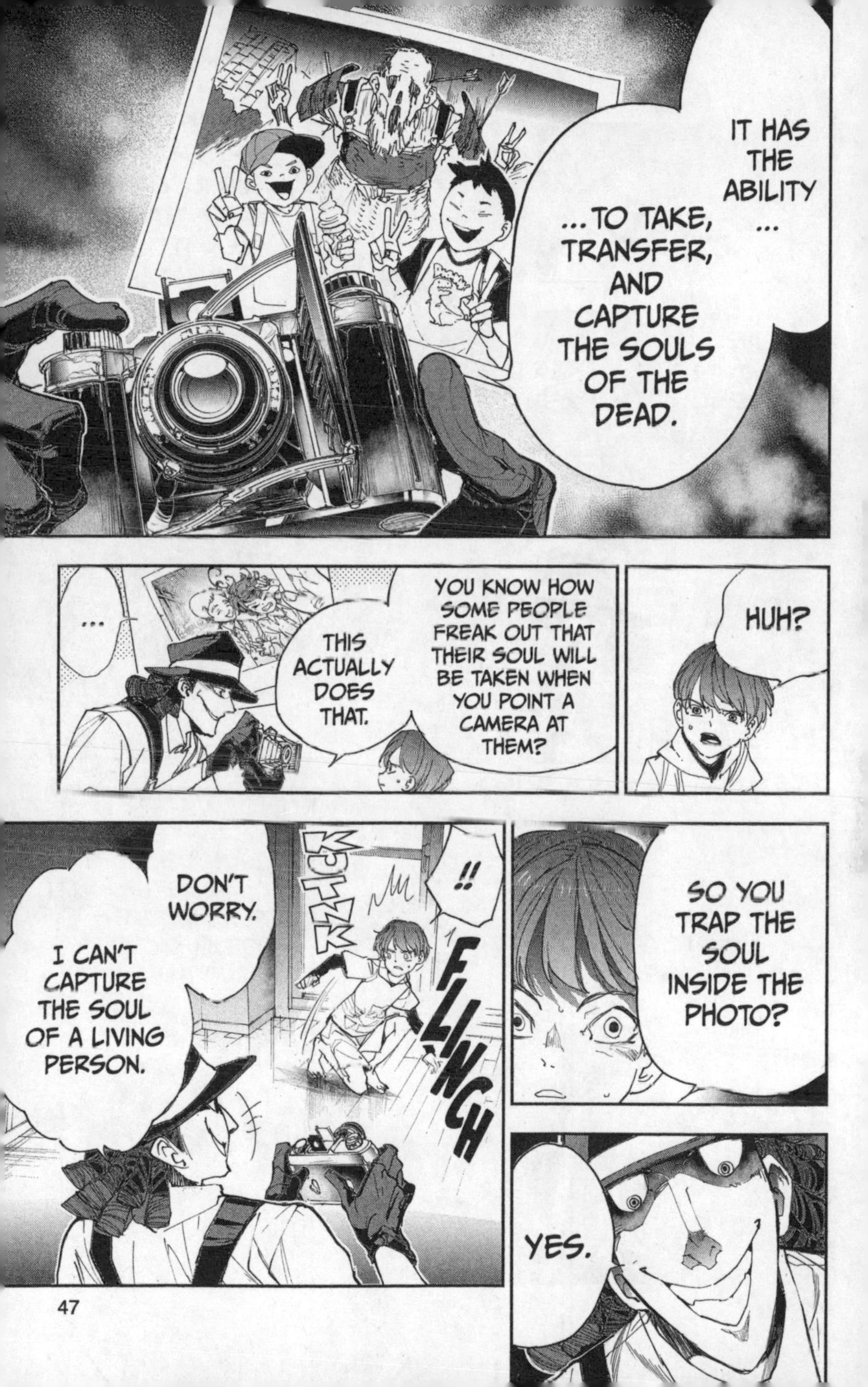
IT HAS THE ABILITY ...
...TO TAKE, TRANSFER, AND CAPTURE THE SOULS OF THE DEAD.
HUH?
YOU KNOW HOW SOME PEOPLE FREAK OUT THAT THEIR SOUL WILL BE TAKEN WHEN YOU POINT A CAMERA AT THEM?
THIS ACTUALLY DOES THAT.
...
SO YOU TRAP THE SOUL INSIDE THE PHOTO?
YES.
!!
FLINCH
DON'T WORRY.
I CAN'T CAPTURE THE SOUL OF A LIVING PERSON.

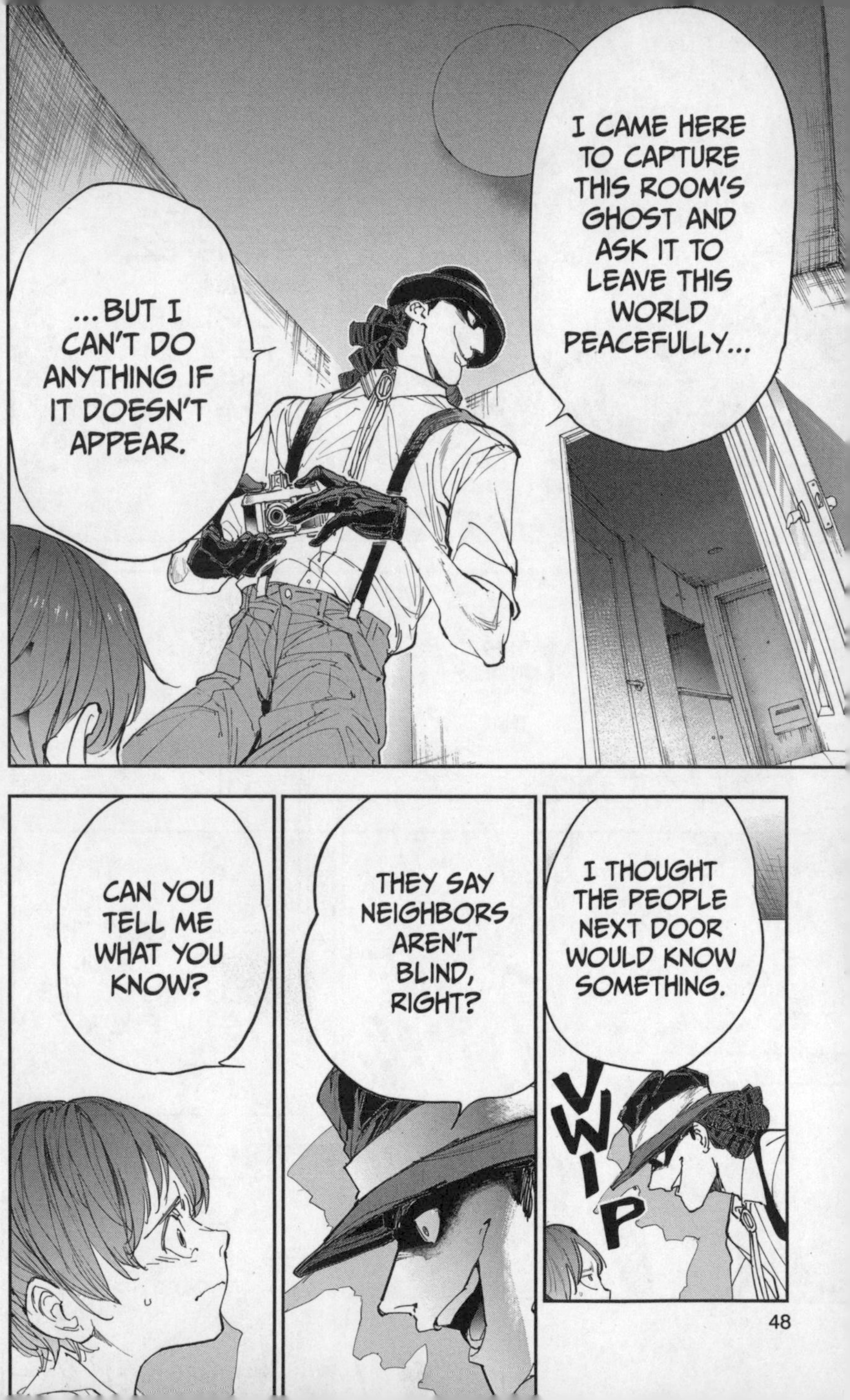
I CAME HERE TO CAPTURE THIS ROOM'S GHOST AND ASK IT TO LEAVE THIS WORLD PEACEFULLY...
...BUT I CAN'T DO ANYTHING IF IT DOESN'T APPEAR.
I THOUGHT THE PEOPLE NEXT DOOR WOULD KNOW SOMETHING.
VWIP
THEY SAY NEIGHBORS AREN'T BLIND, RIGHT?
CAN YOU TELL ME WHAT YOU KNOW?

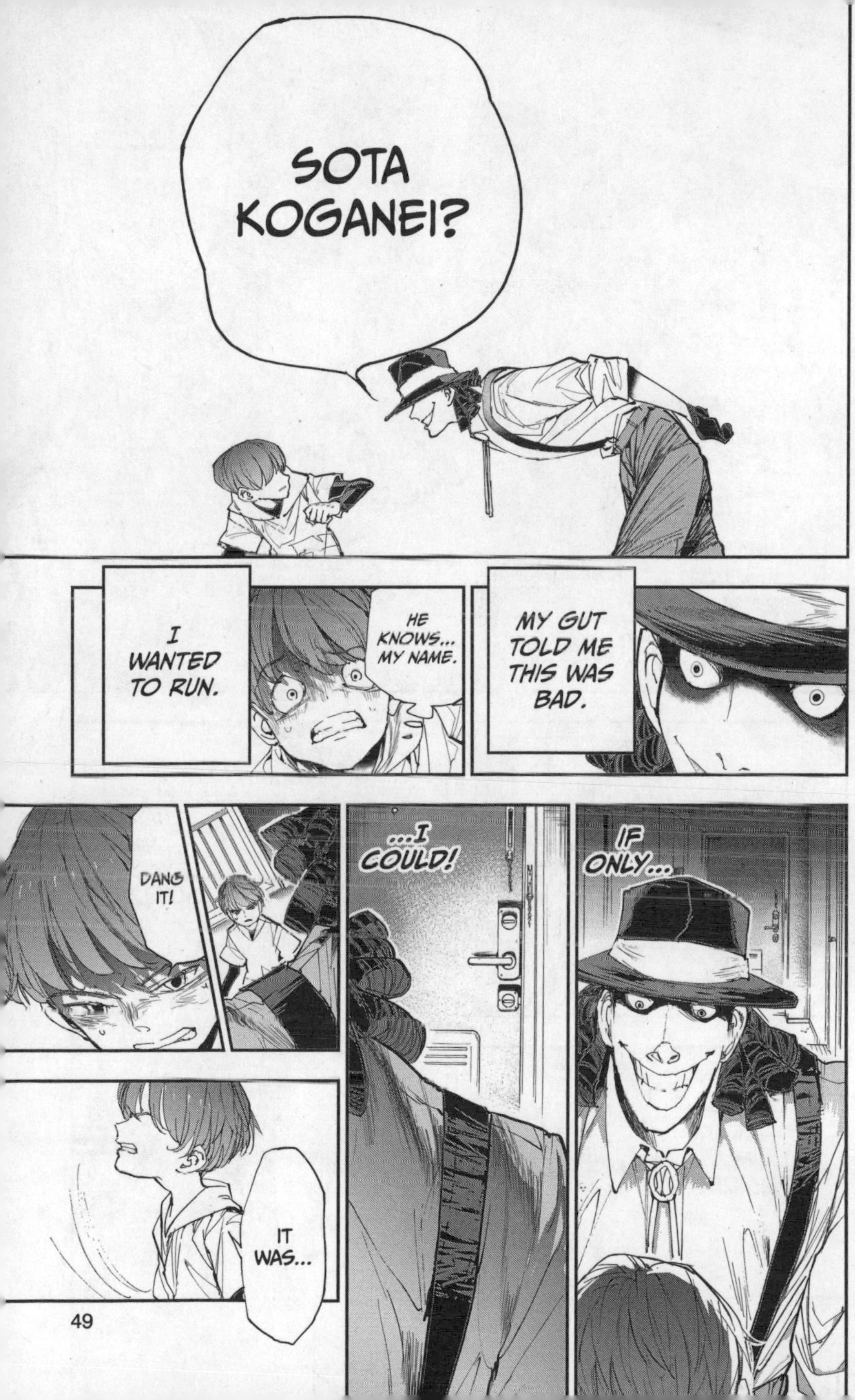
SOTA KOGANEI?
MY GUT TOLD ME THIS WAS BAD.
HE KNOWS... MY NAME.
I WANTED TO RUN.
IF ONLY...
...I COULD!
DANG IT!
IT WAS...

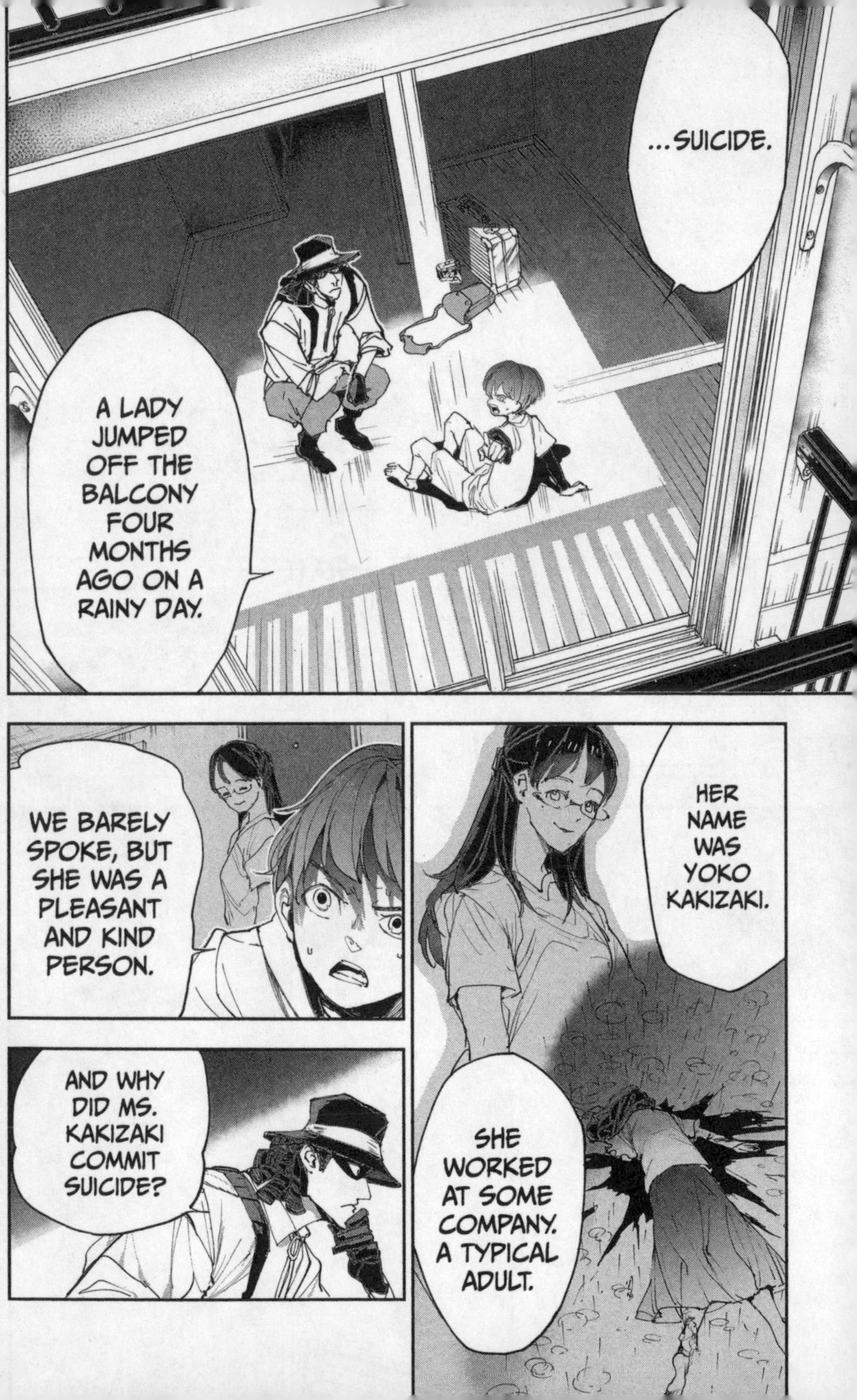
...SUICIDE.
A LADY JUMPED OFF THE BALCONY FOUR MONTHS AGO ON A RAINY DAY.
HER NAME WAS YOKO KAKIZAKI.
SHE WORKED AT SOME COMPANY. A TYPICAL ADULT.
WE BARELY SPOKE, BUT SHE WAS A PLEASANT AND KIND PERSON.
AND WHY DID MS. KAKIZAKI COMMIT SUICIDE?

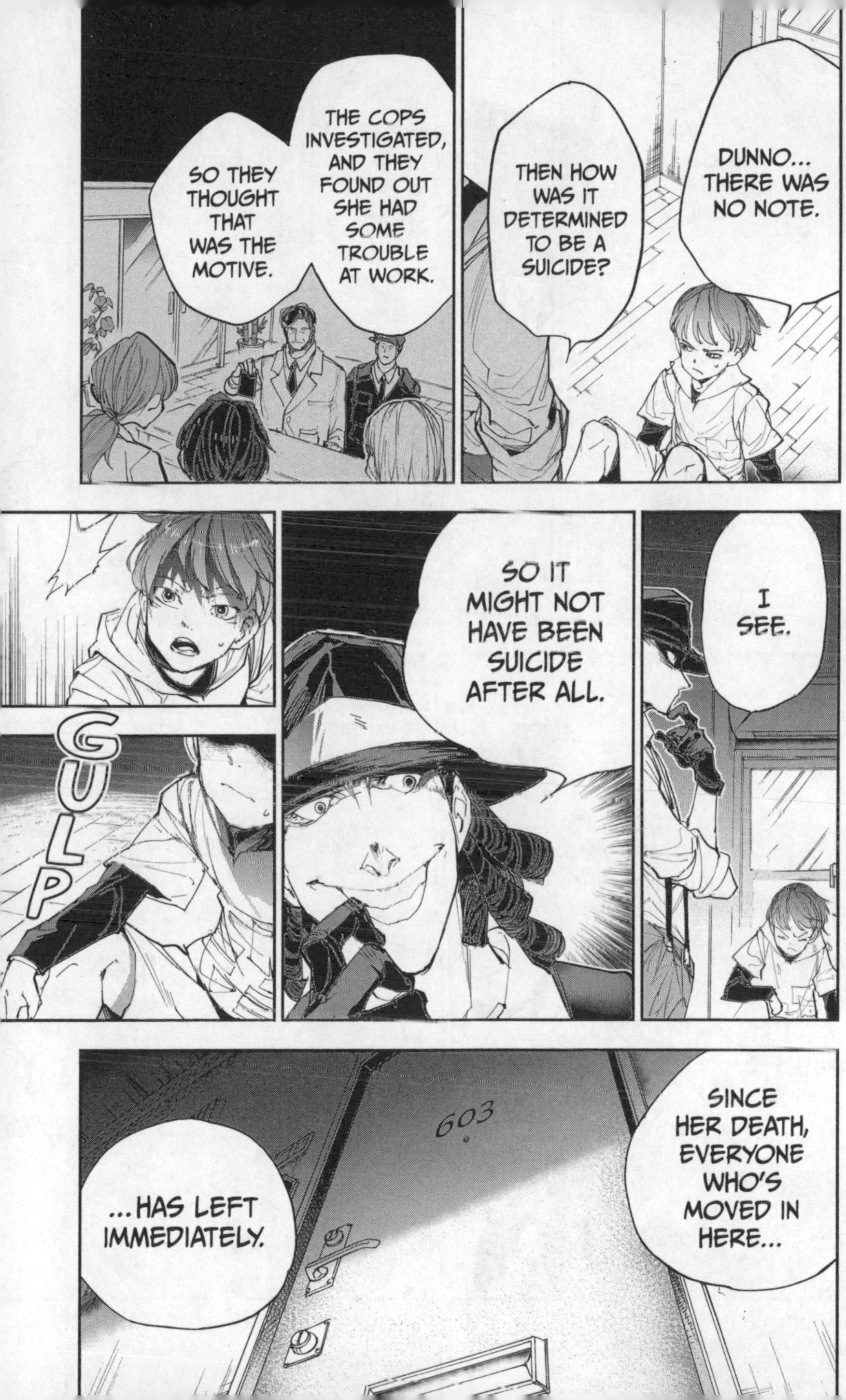
DUNNO... THERE WAS NO NOTE.
THEN HOW WAS IT DETERMINED TO BE A SUICIDE?
THE COPS INVESTIGATED, AND THEY FOUND OUT SHE HAD SOME TROUBLE AT WORK.
SO THEY THOUGHT THAT WAS THE MOTIVE.
I SEE.
SO IT MIGHT NOT HAVE BEEN SUICIDE AFTER ALL.
GULP
SINCE HER DEATH, EVERYONE WHO'S MOVED IN HERE...
603
...HAS LEFT IMMEDIATELY.

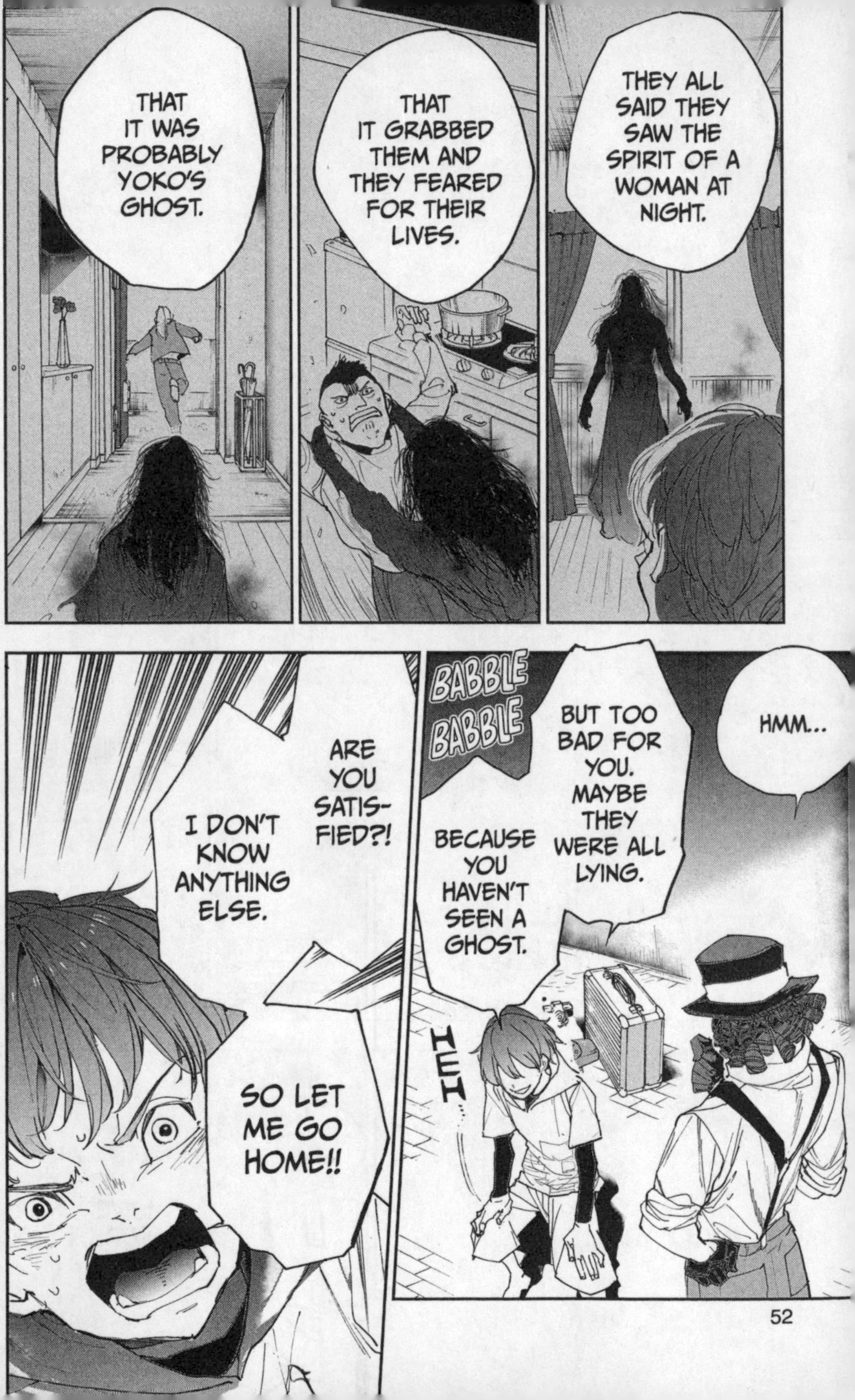
THEY ALL SAID THEY SAW THE SPIRIT OF A WOMAN AT NIGHT.
THAT IT GRABBED THEM AND THEY FEARED FOR THEIR LIVES.
THAT IT WAS PROBABLY YOKO'S GHOST.
HMM...
BABBLE BABBLE
BUT TOO BAD FOR YOU. MAYBE THEY WERE ALL LYING.
BECAUSE YOU HAVEN'T SEEN A GHOST.
HEH...
ARE YOU SATIS-FIED?!
I DON'T KNOW ANYTHING ELSE.
SO LET ME GO HOME!!

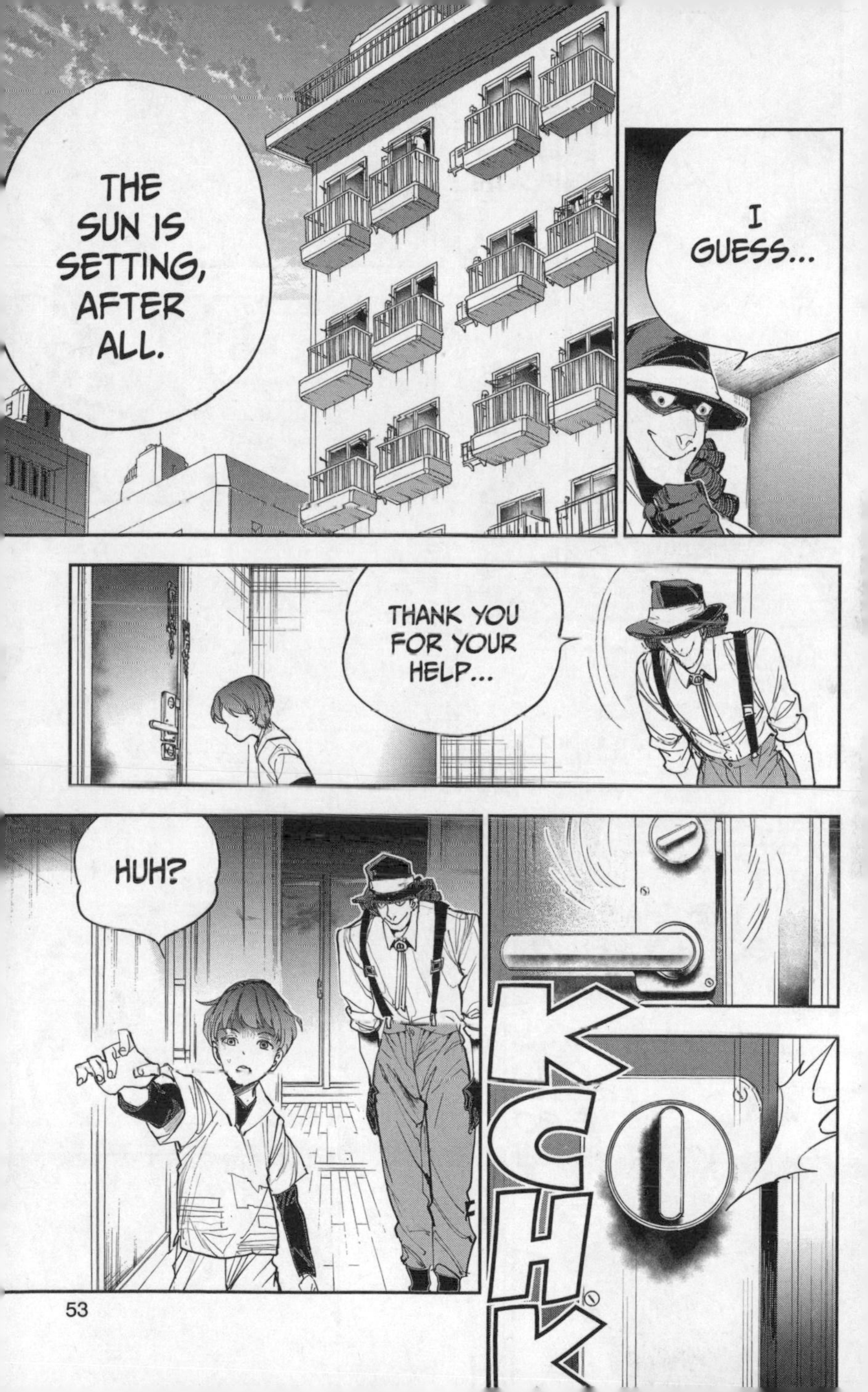
I GUESS...
THE SUN IS SETTING, AFTER ALL.
THANK YOU FOR YOUR HELP...
KCH
HUH?

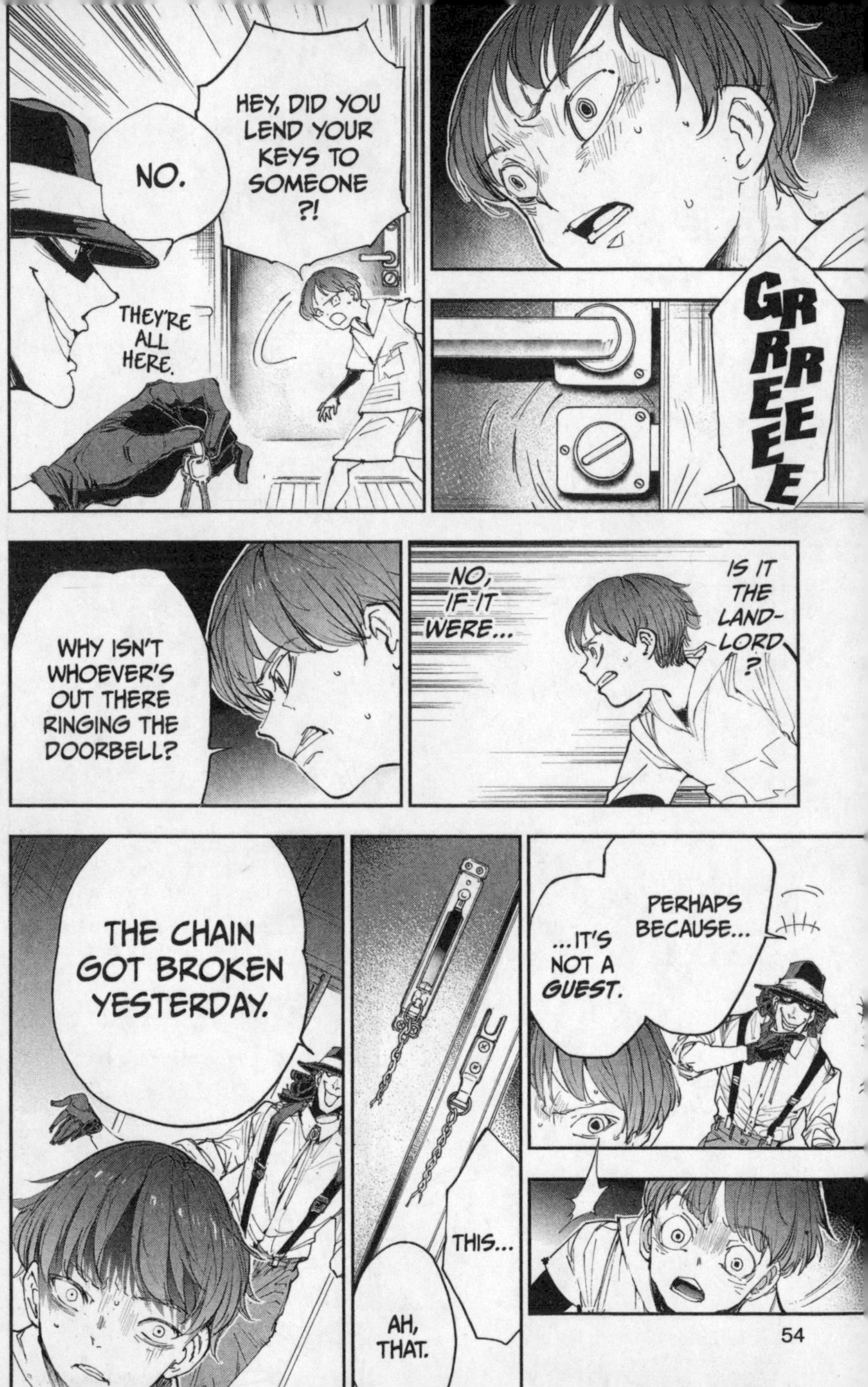
GRREEEE
HEY, DID YOU LEND YOUR KEYS TO SOMEONE ?!
NO.
THEY'RE ALL HERE.
IS IT THE LAND-LORD ?
NO, IF IT WERE...
WHY ISN'T WHOEVER'S OUT THERE RINGING THE DOORBELL?
PERHAPS BECAUSE...
...IT'S NOT A *GUEST*.
THIS...
AH, THAT.
THE CHAIN GOT BROKEN YESTERDAY.

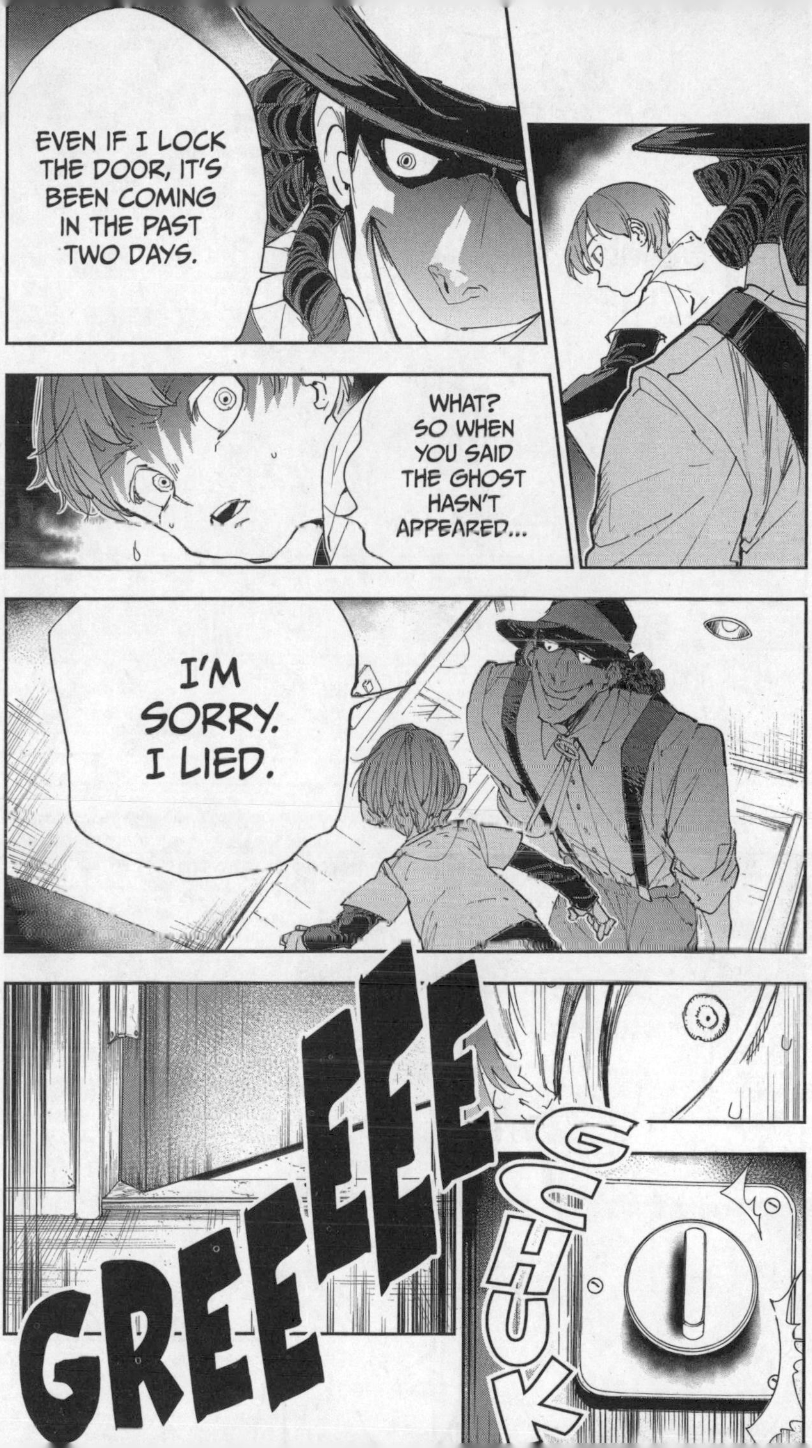
EVEN IF I LOCK THE DOOR, IT'S BEEN COMING IN THE PAST TWO DAYS.
WHAT? SO WHEN YOU SAID THE GHOST HASN'T APPEARED...
I'M SORRY. I LIED.
GCHUK
GREEEEE

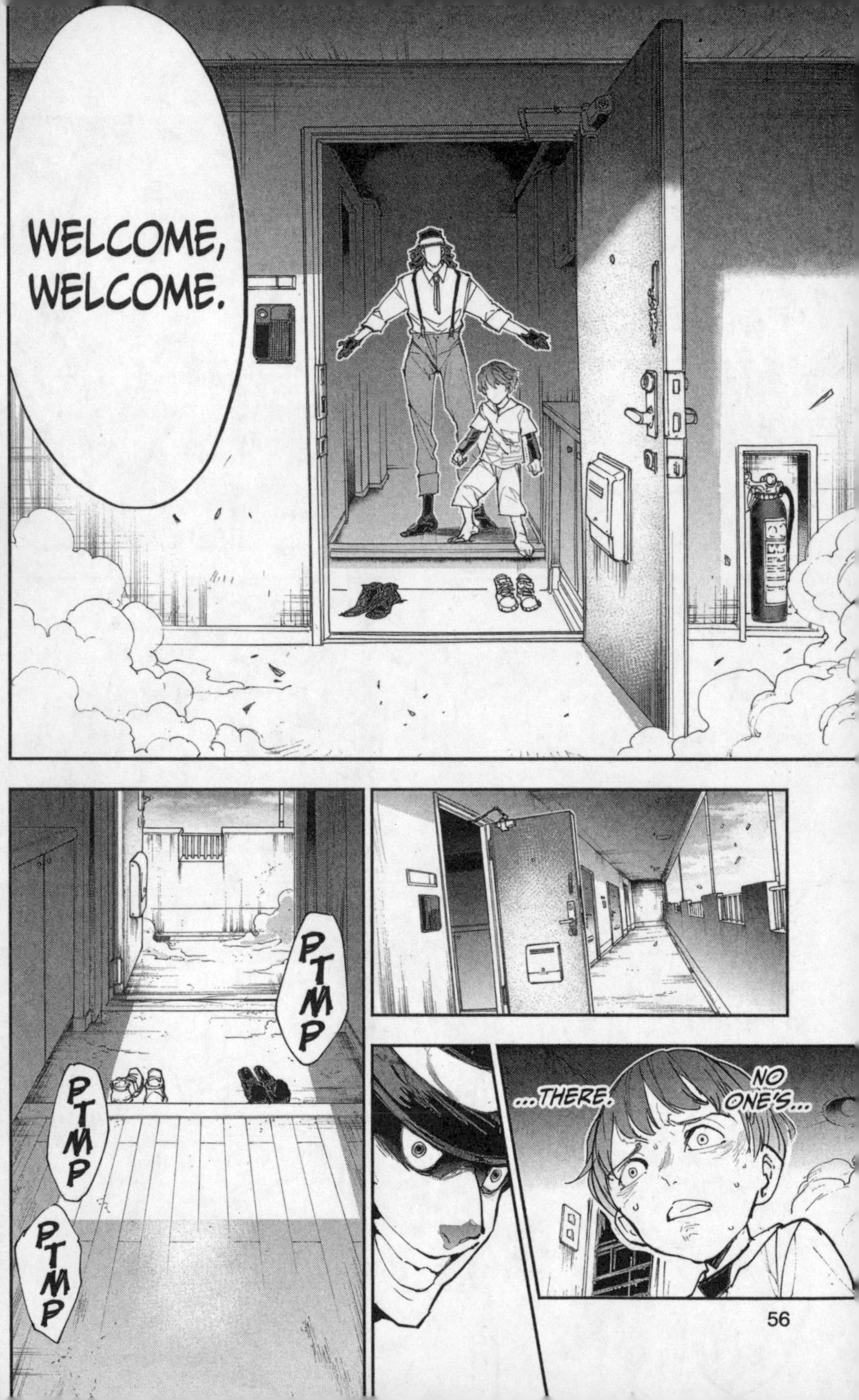
WELCOME, WELCOME.
NO ONE'S...
...THERE.
PTMP
PTMP
PTMP

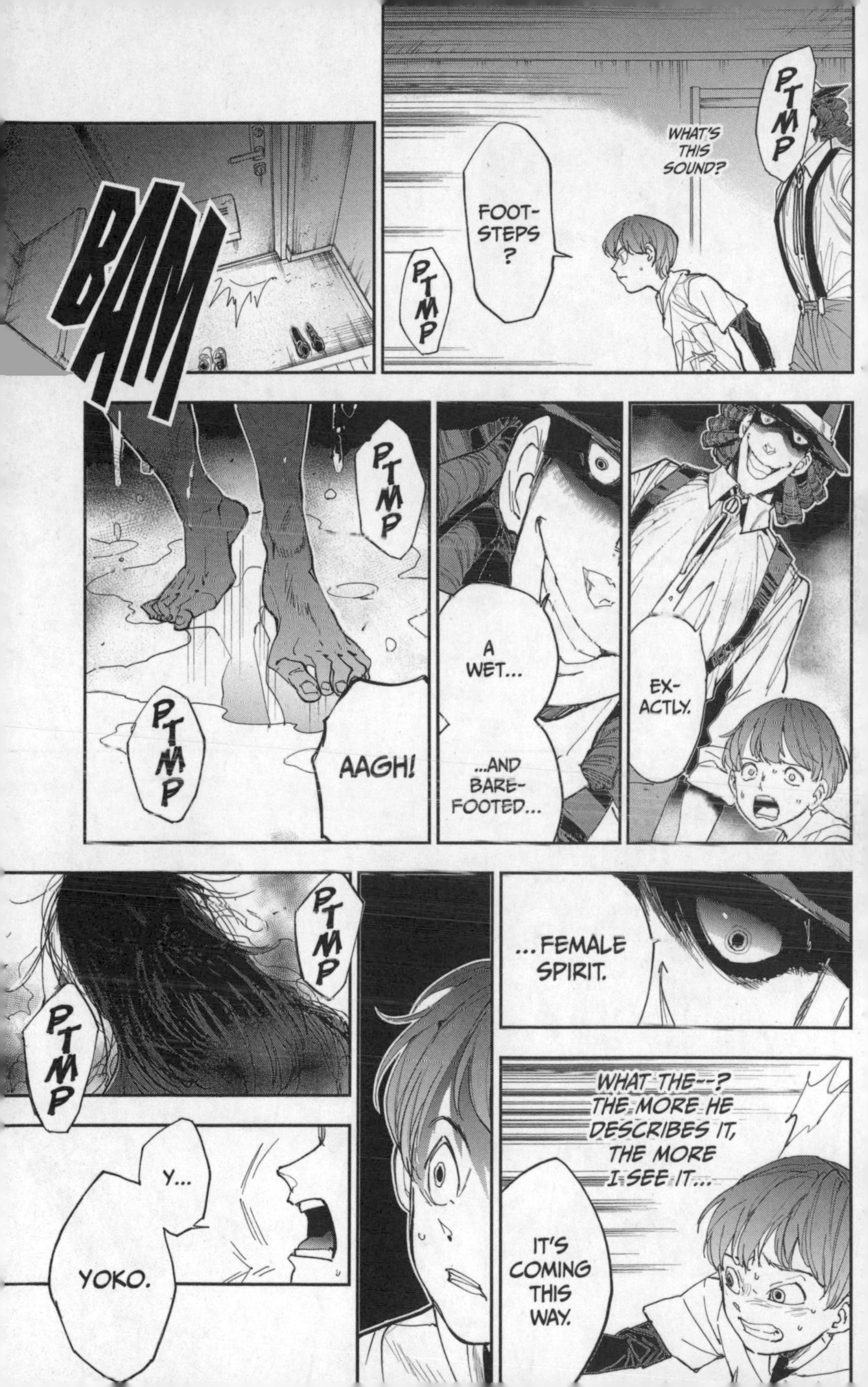
PTMP
WHAT'S THIS SOUND?
FOOT-STEPS?
PTMP
BAM
EX-ACTLY.
A WET...
...AND BARE-FOOTED...
PTMP
AAGH!
PTMP
...FEMALE SPIRIT.
WHAT THE--? THE MORE HE DESCRIBES IT, THE MORE I SEE IT...
IT'S COMING THIS WAY.
PTMP
PTMP
Y...
YOKO.

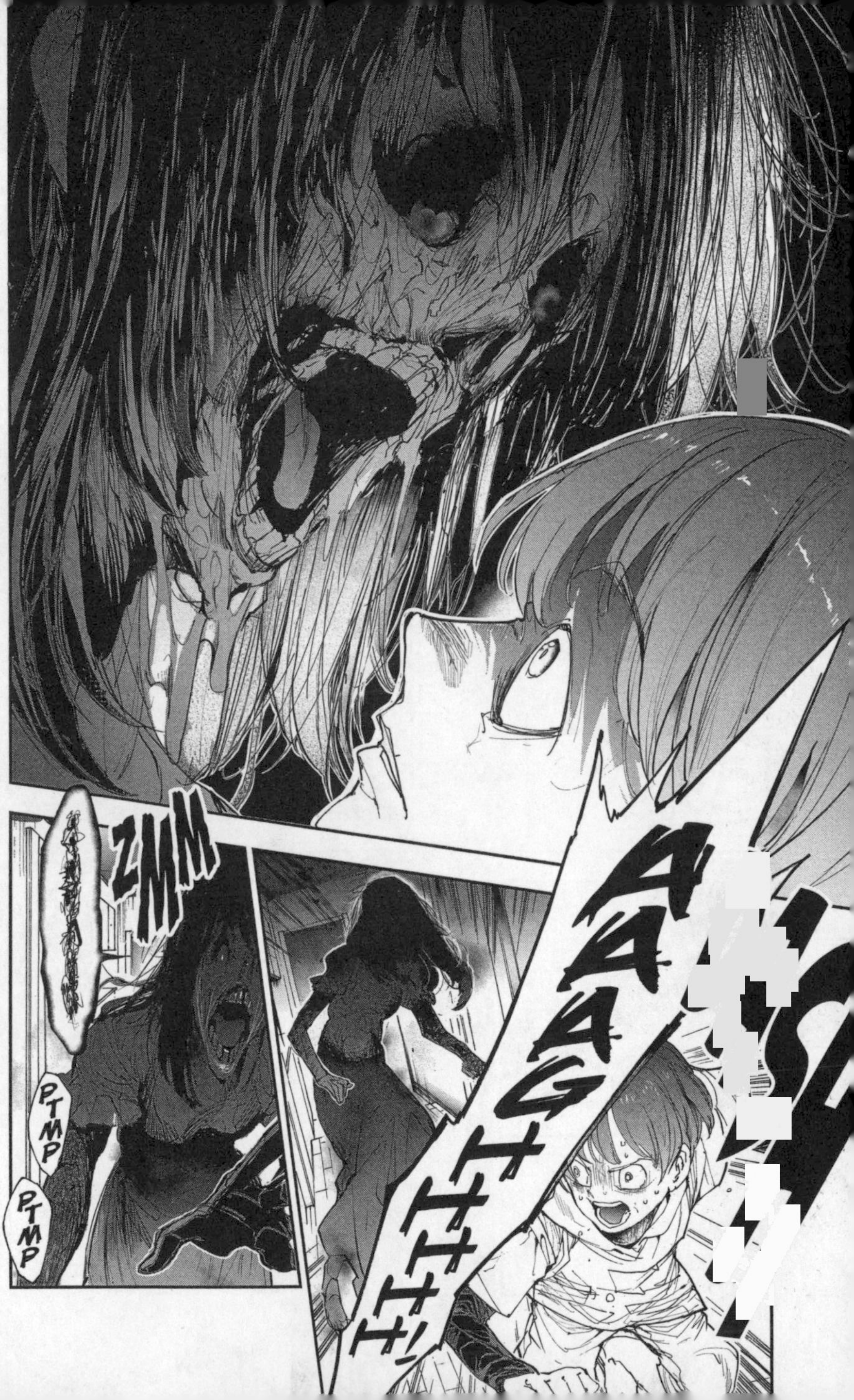

AAAGHHHHH!
ZMM
PTMP
PTMP

WHOA.

HERE, SOTA. STOP HIDING AND LOOK CAREFULLY.

PTMP

PTMP

SHE'S SAYING SOMETHING.

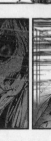

WHERE. IS. SOTA.

FOR SOME REASON, SHE'S LOOKING FOR YOU.

S...

SO...

...TA.

BADUM

IS THIS WHY HE BROUGHT ME TO THIS ROOM?

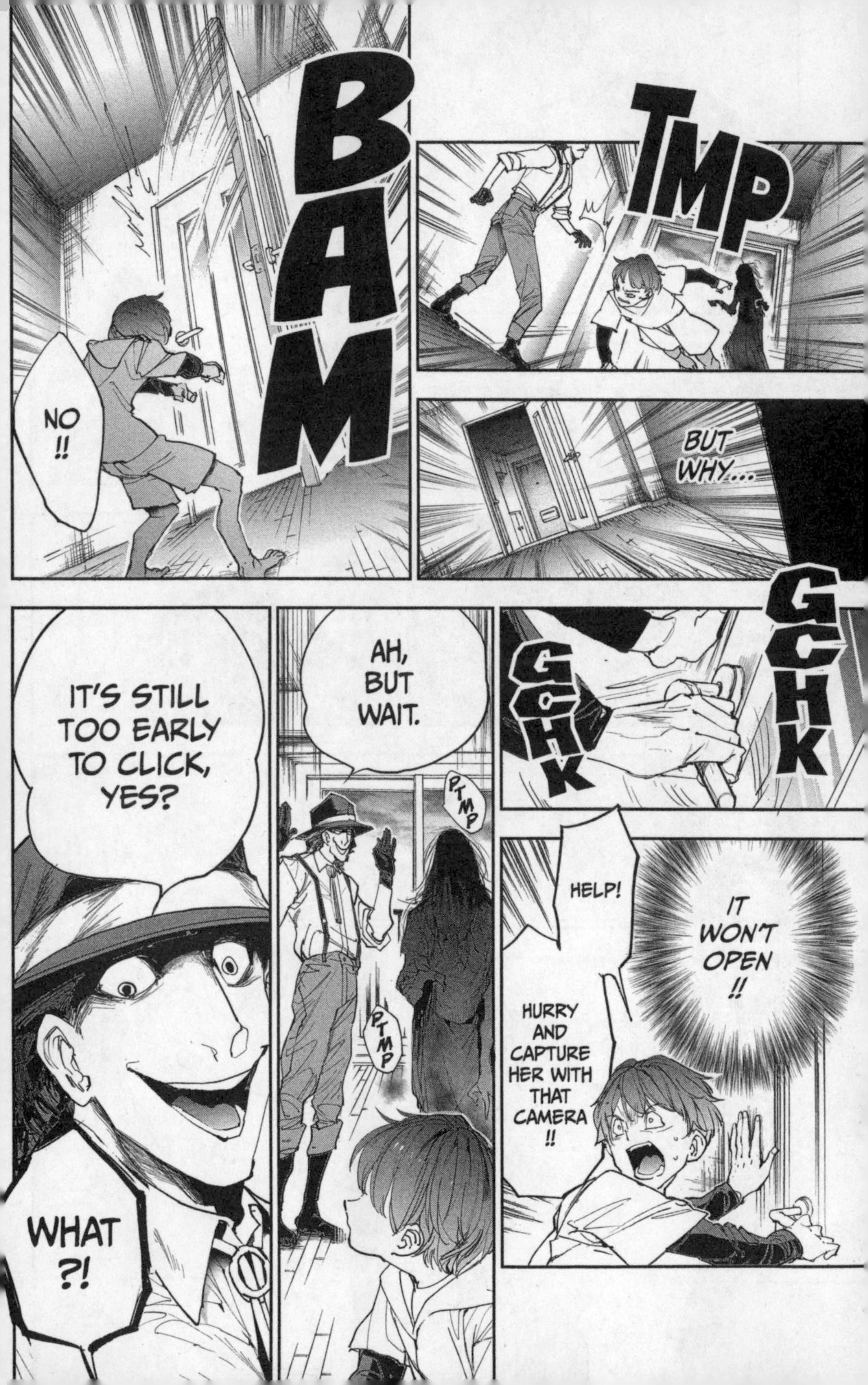
TMP
BUT WHY...
BAM
NO!!
GCHK
GCHK
IT WON'T OPEN!!
HELP!
HURRY AND CAPTURE HER WITH THAT CAMERA!!
AH, BUT WAIT.
PTMP
PTMP
IT'S STILL TOO EARLY TO CLICK, YES?
WHAT?!

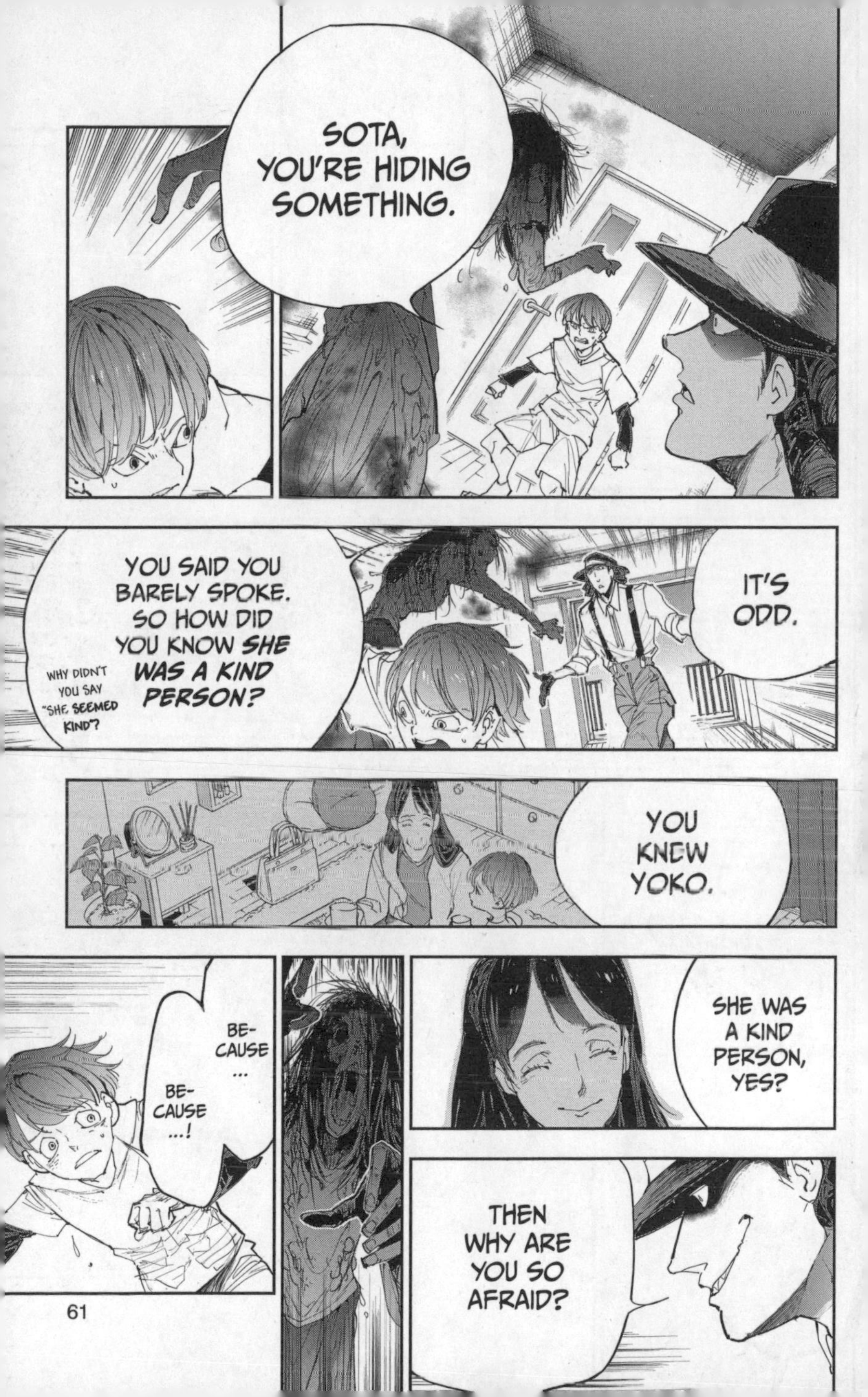
SOTA, YOU'RE HIDING SOMETHING.
IT'S ODD.
YOU SAID YOU BARELY SPOKE. SO HOW DID YOU KNOW *SHE WAS A KIND PERSON?*
WHY DIDN'T YOU SAY "SHE SEEMED KIND"?
YOU KNEW YOKO.
SHE WAS A KIND PERSON, YES?
THEN WHY ARE YOU SO AFRAID?
BE-CAUSE ...
BE-CAUSE ...!

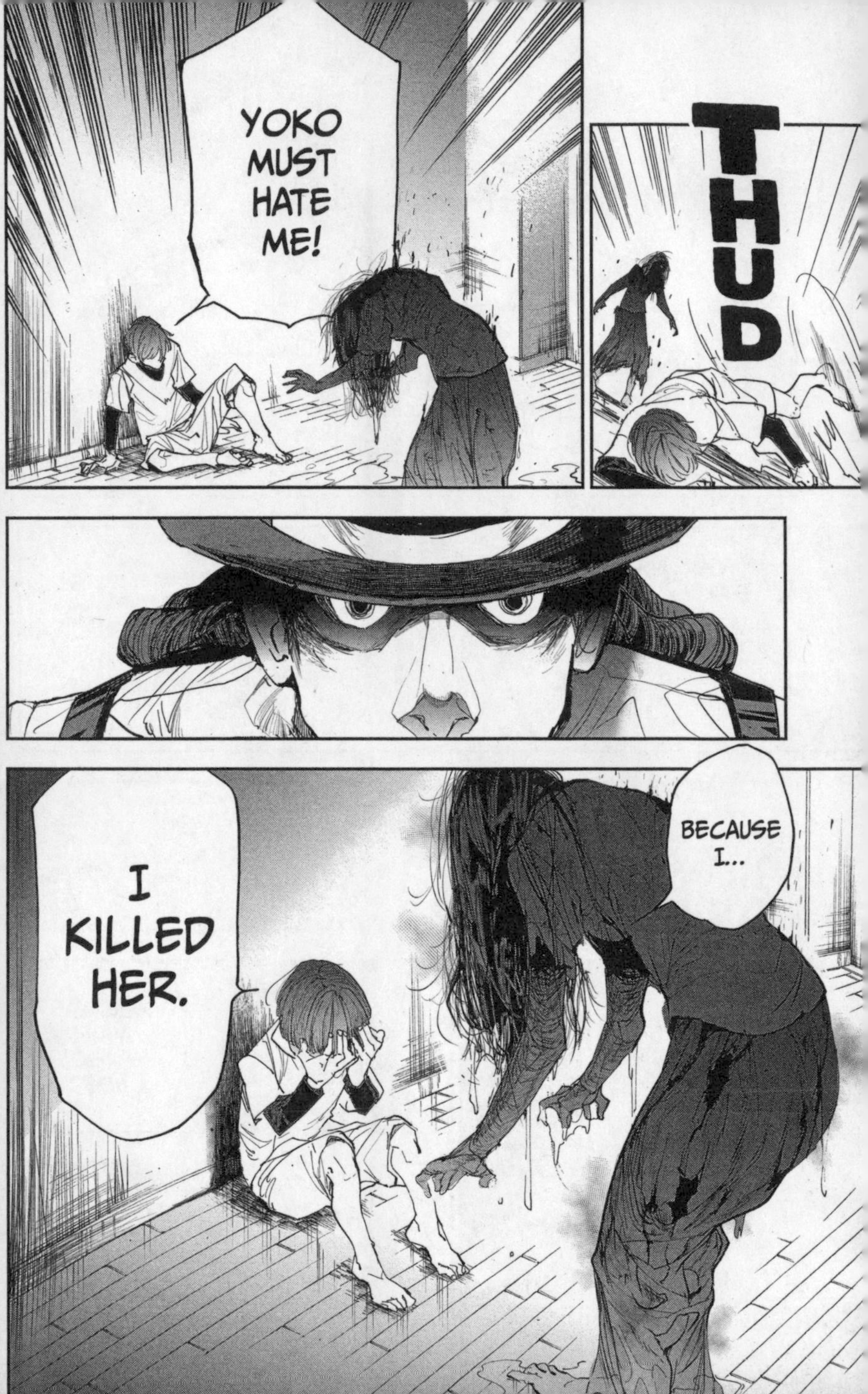
THUD
YOKO MUST HATE ME!
BECAUSE I...
I KILLED HER.

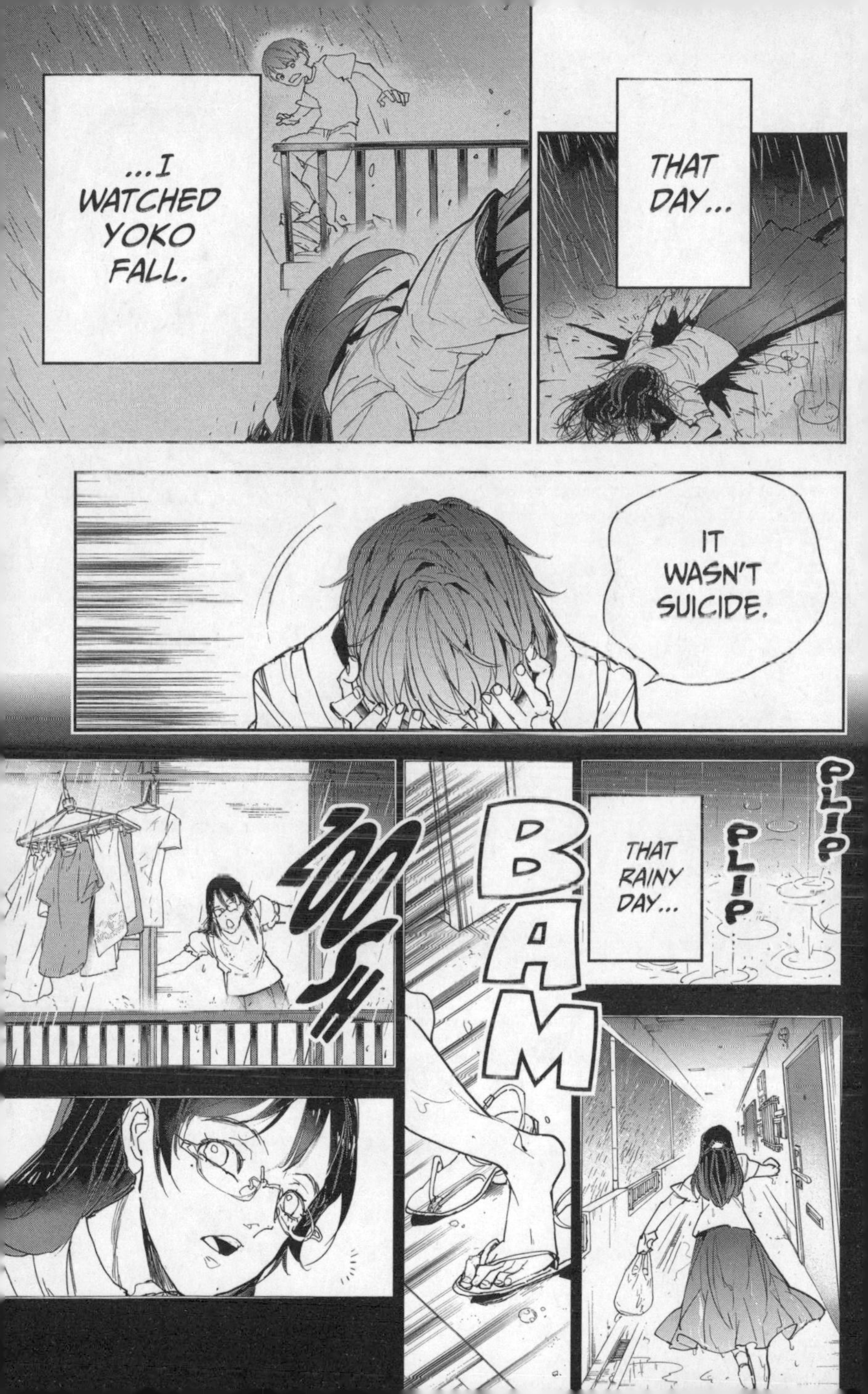
THAT DAY...
...I WATCHED YOKO FALL.
IT WASN'T SUICIDE.
PLIP
PLIP
THAT RAINY DAY...
BAM
WOOSH

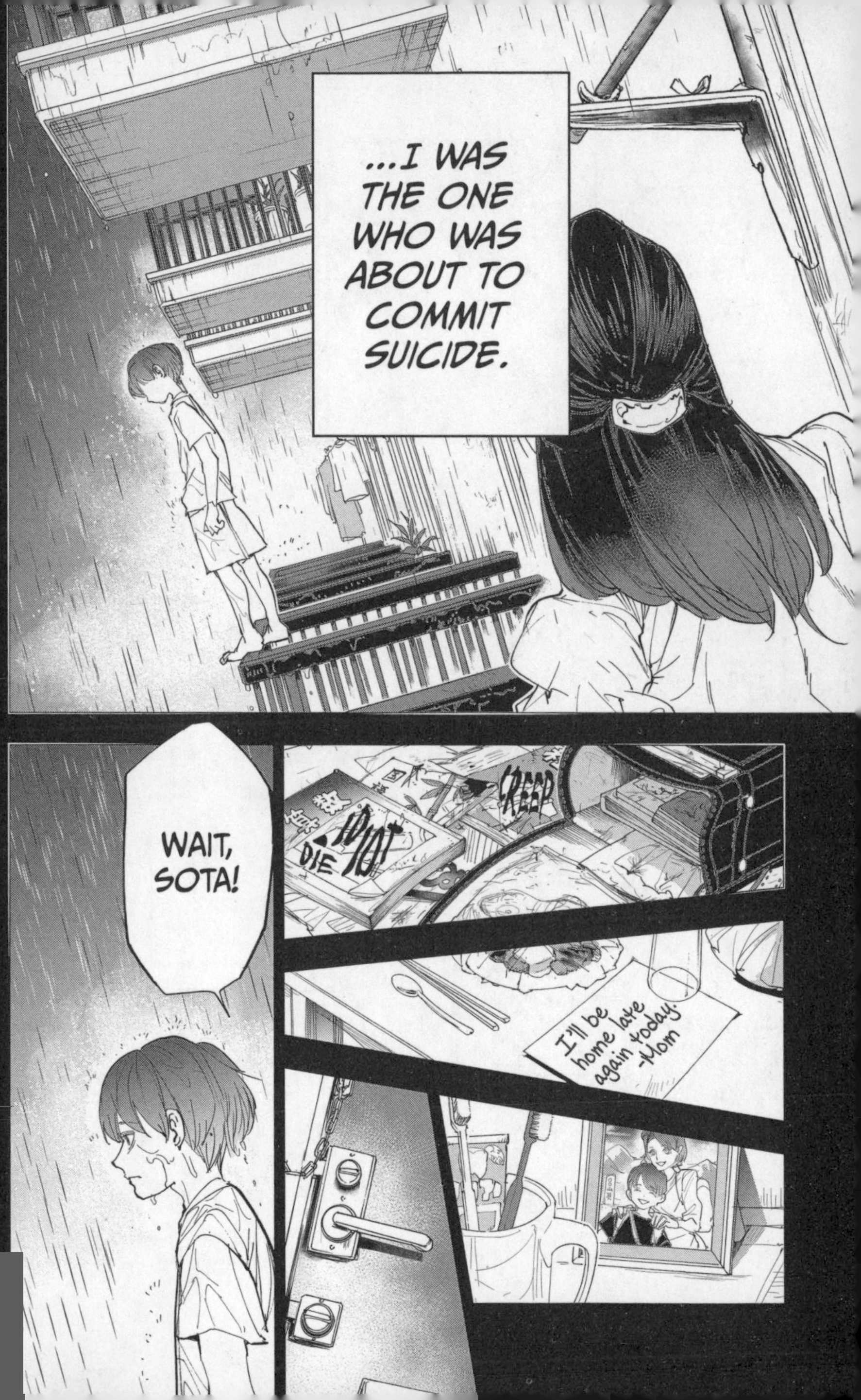
...I WAS THE ONE WHO WAS ABOUT TO COMMIT SUICIDE.
CREEP
IDIOT
DIE
I'll be home late again today. -Mom
WAIT, SOTA!

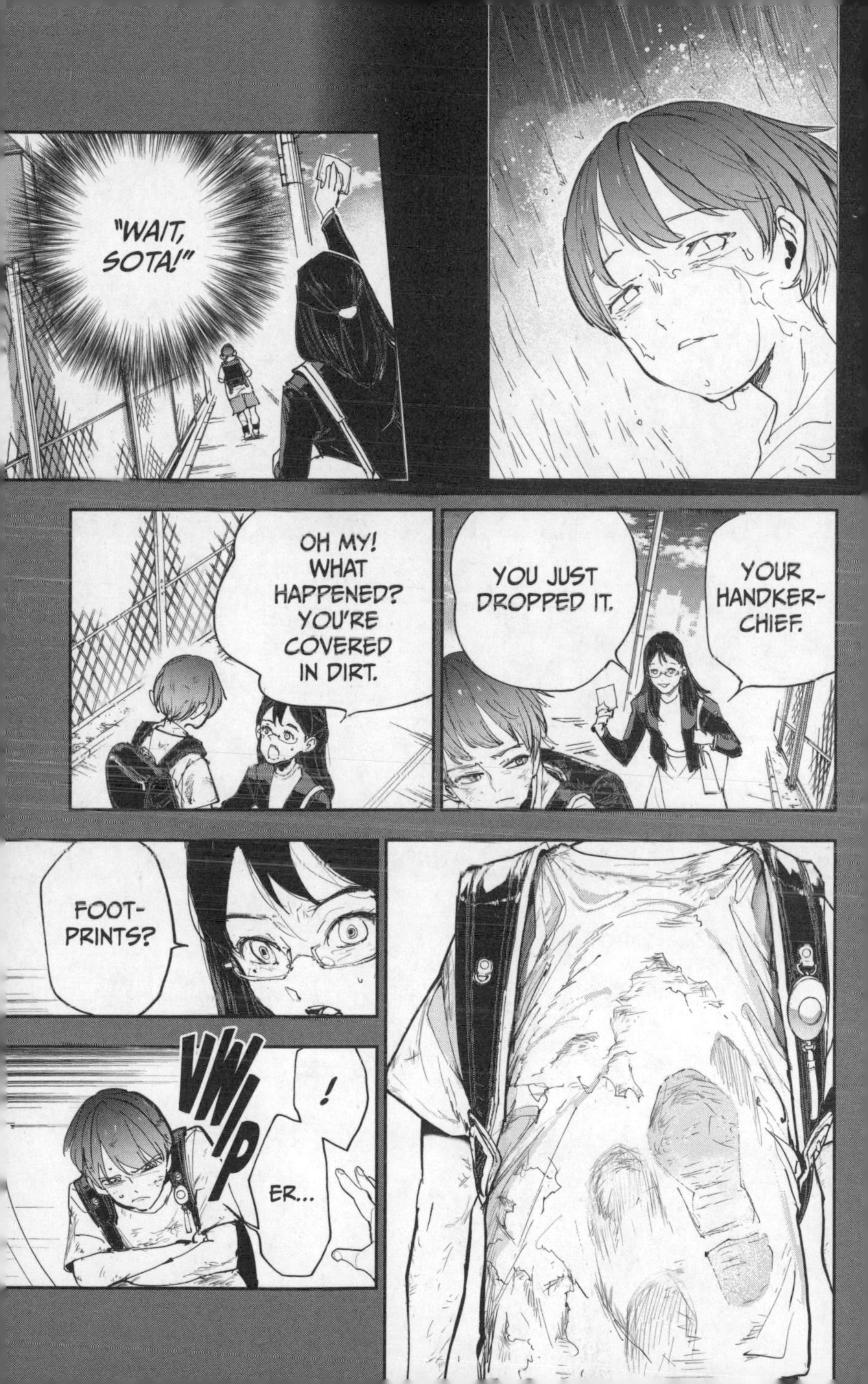
"WAIT, SOTA!"
YOUR HANDKERCHIEF.
YOU JUST DROPPED IT.
OH MY! WHAT HAPPENED? YOU'RE COVERED IN DIRT.
FOOTPRINTS?
!
VWIP
ER...

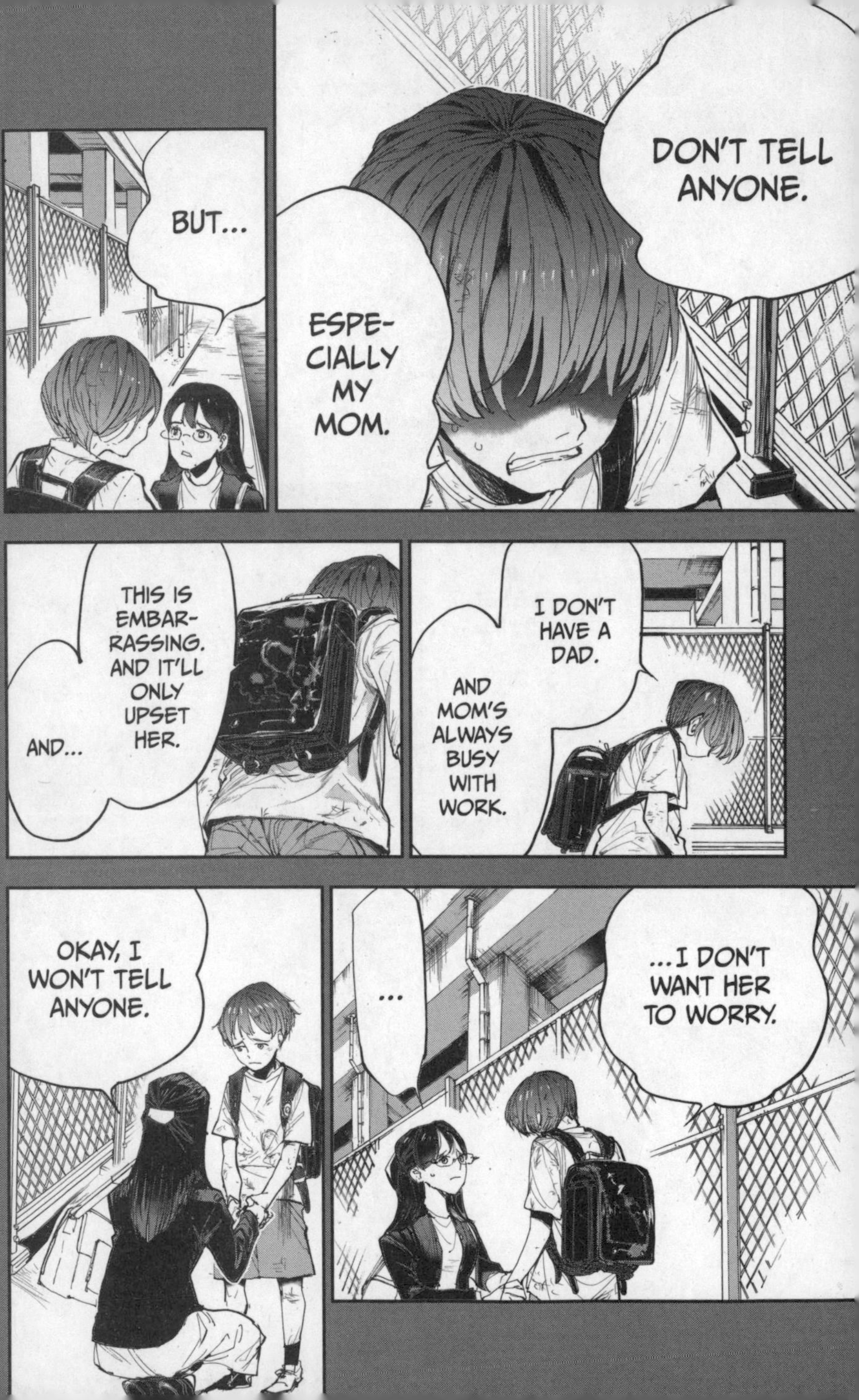
DON'T TELL ANYONE.
ESPE-CIALLY MY MOM.
BUT...
I DON'T HAVE A DAD.
AND MOM'S ALWAYS BUSY WITH WORK.
THIS IS EMBAR-RASSING. AND IT'LL ONLY UPSET HER.
AND...
...I DON'T WANT HER TO WORRY.
...
OKAY, I WON'T TELL ANYONE.

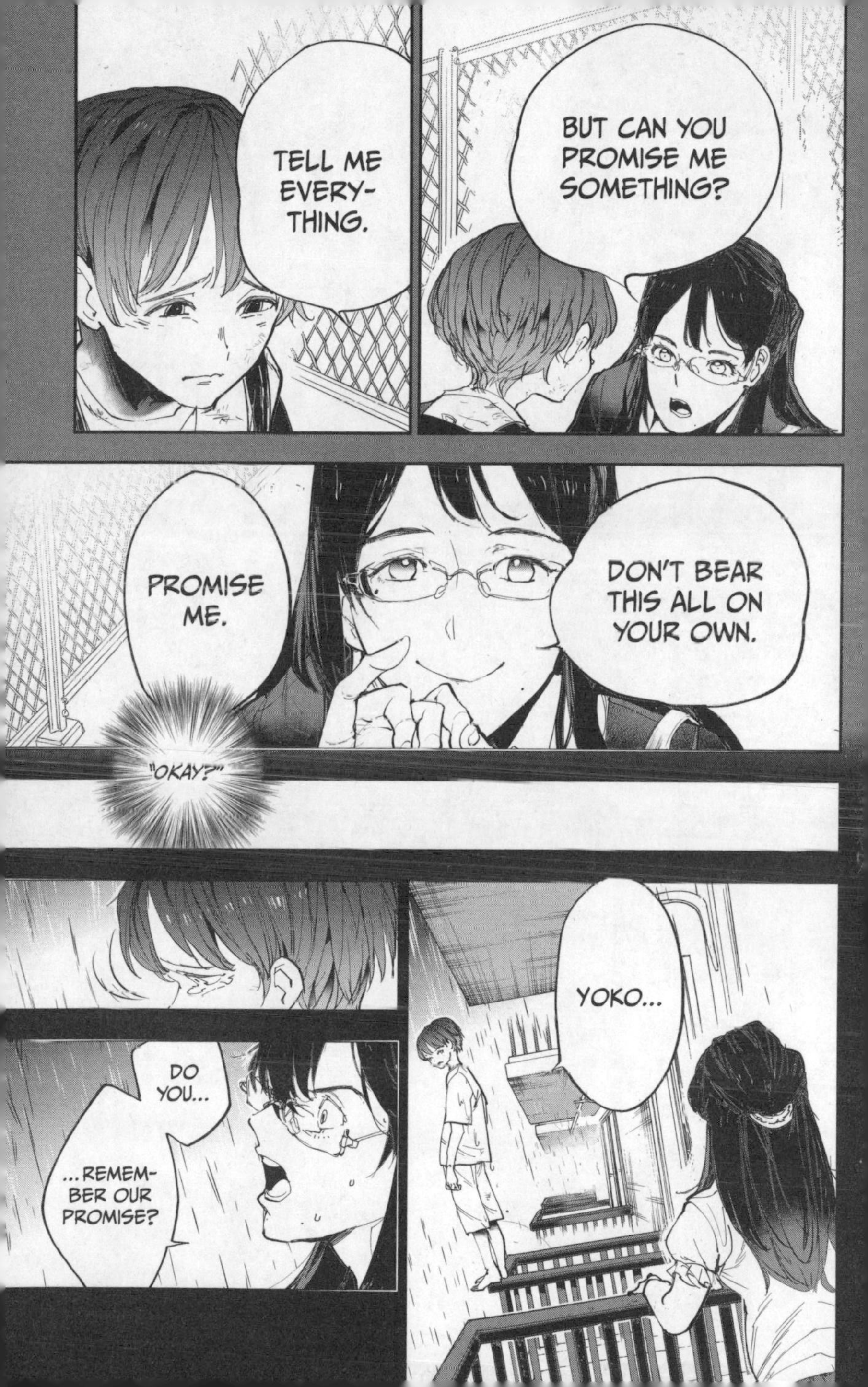
BUT CAN YOU PROMISE ME SOMETHING?
TELL ME EVERY-THING.
DON'T BEAR THIS ALL ON YOUR OWN.
PROMISE ME.
"OKAY?"
YOKO...
DO YOU...
...REMEM-BER OUR PROMISE?

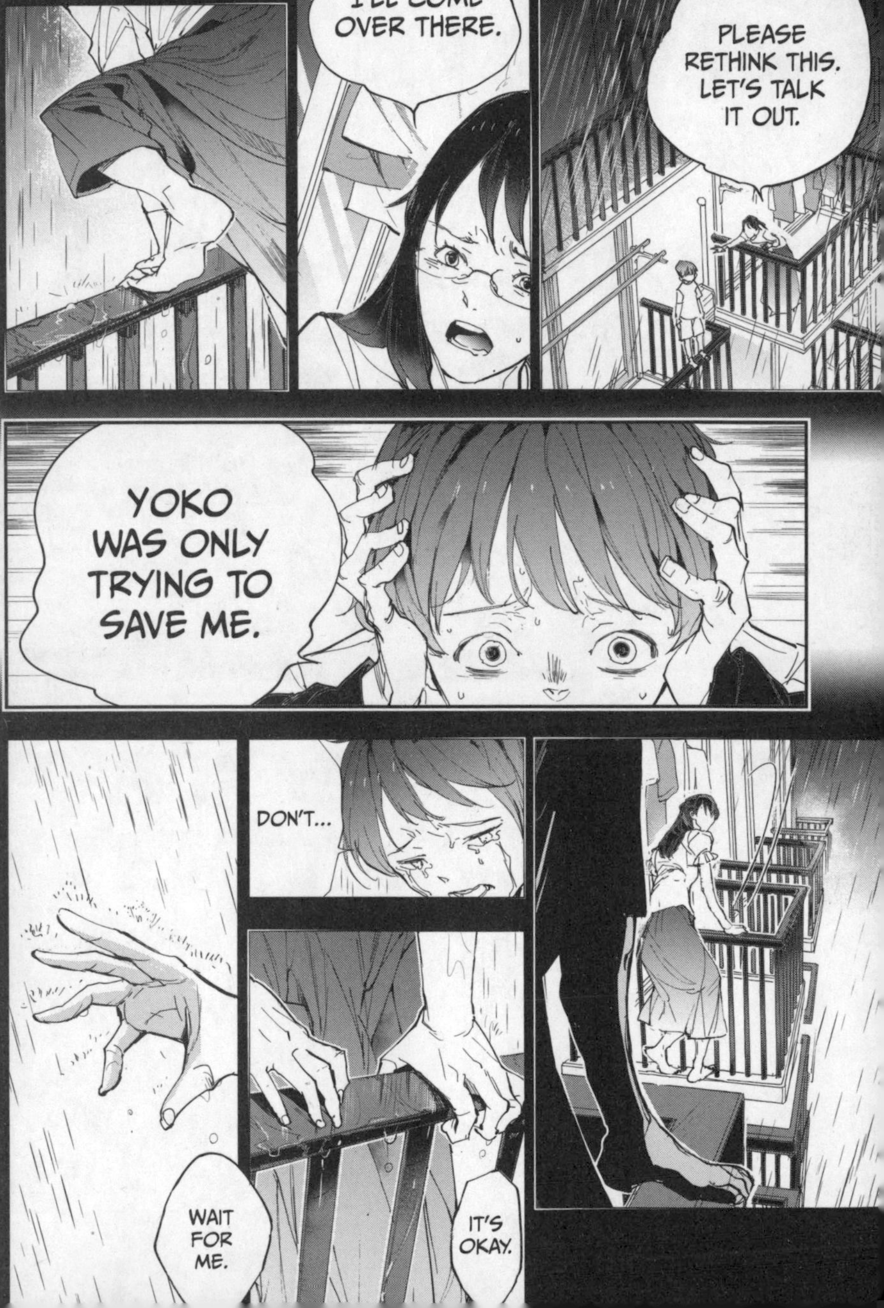
PLEASE RETHINK THIS. LET'S TALK IT OUT.
I'LL COME OVER THERE.
YOKO WAS ONLY TRYING TO SAVE ME.
DON'T...
IT'S OKAY.
WAIT FOR ME.

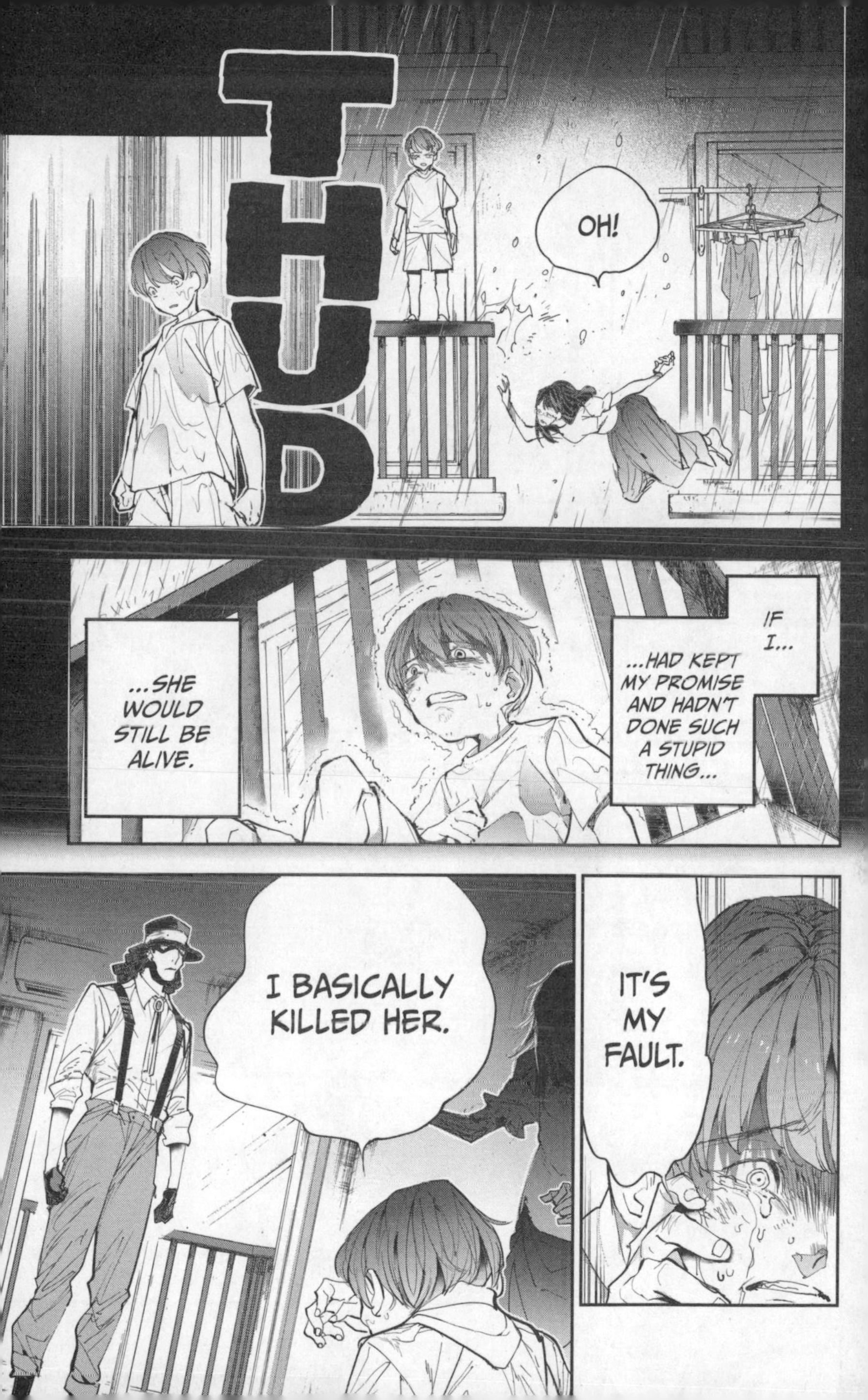
OH!
THUD
IF I...
...HAD KEPT MY PROMISE AND HADN'T DONE SUCH A STUPID THING...
...SHE WOULD STILL BE ALIVE.
IT'S MY FAULT.
I BASICALLY KILLED HER.

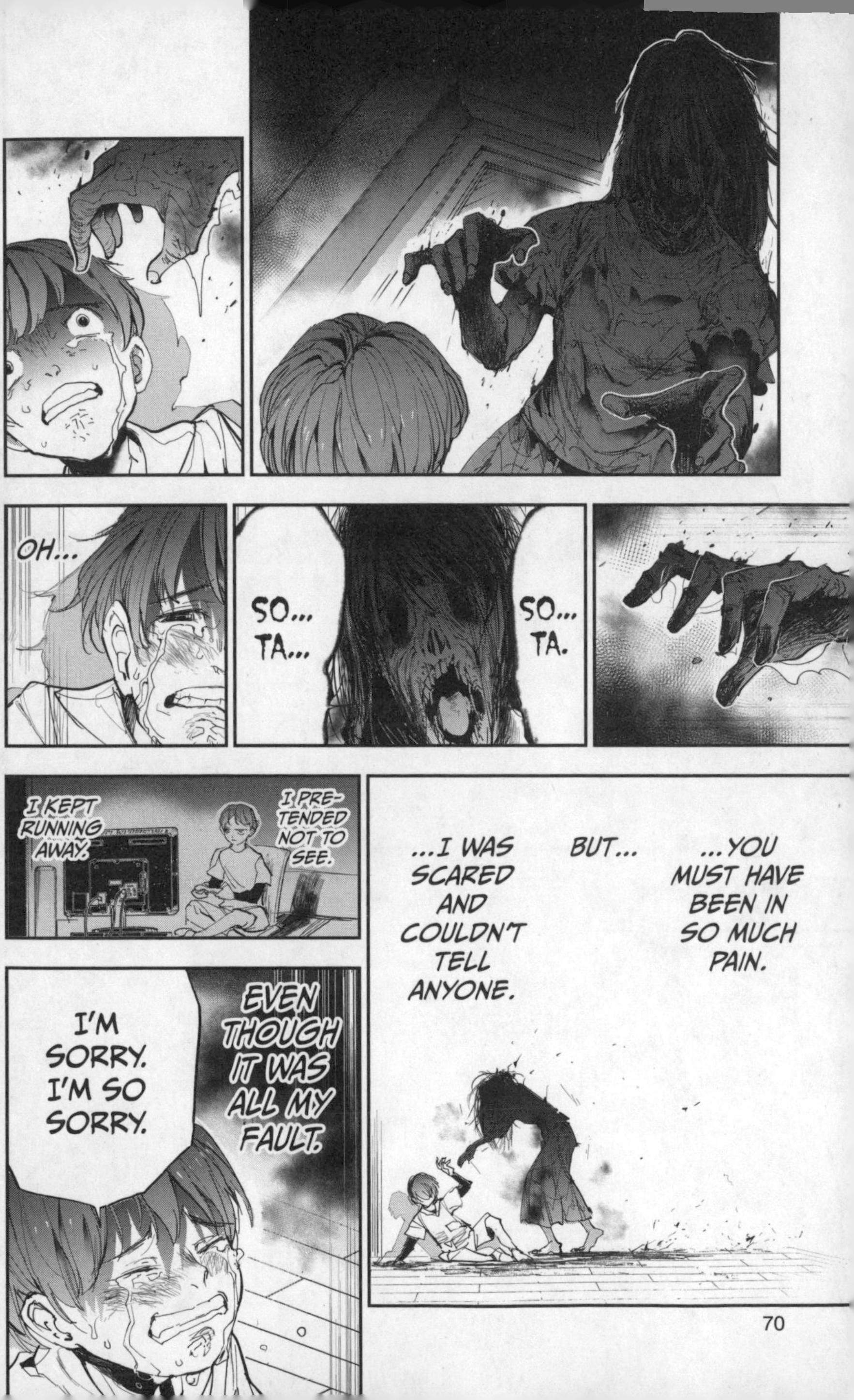
SO... TA.
SO... TA...
OH...
...YOU MUST HAVE BEEN IN SO MUCH PAIN.
BUT...
...I WAS SCARED AND COULDN'T TELL ANYONE.
I PRETENDED NOT TO SEE.
I KEPT RUNNING AWAY.
EVEN THOUGH IT WAS ALL MY FAULT.
I'M SORRY. I'M SO SORRY.

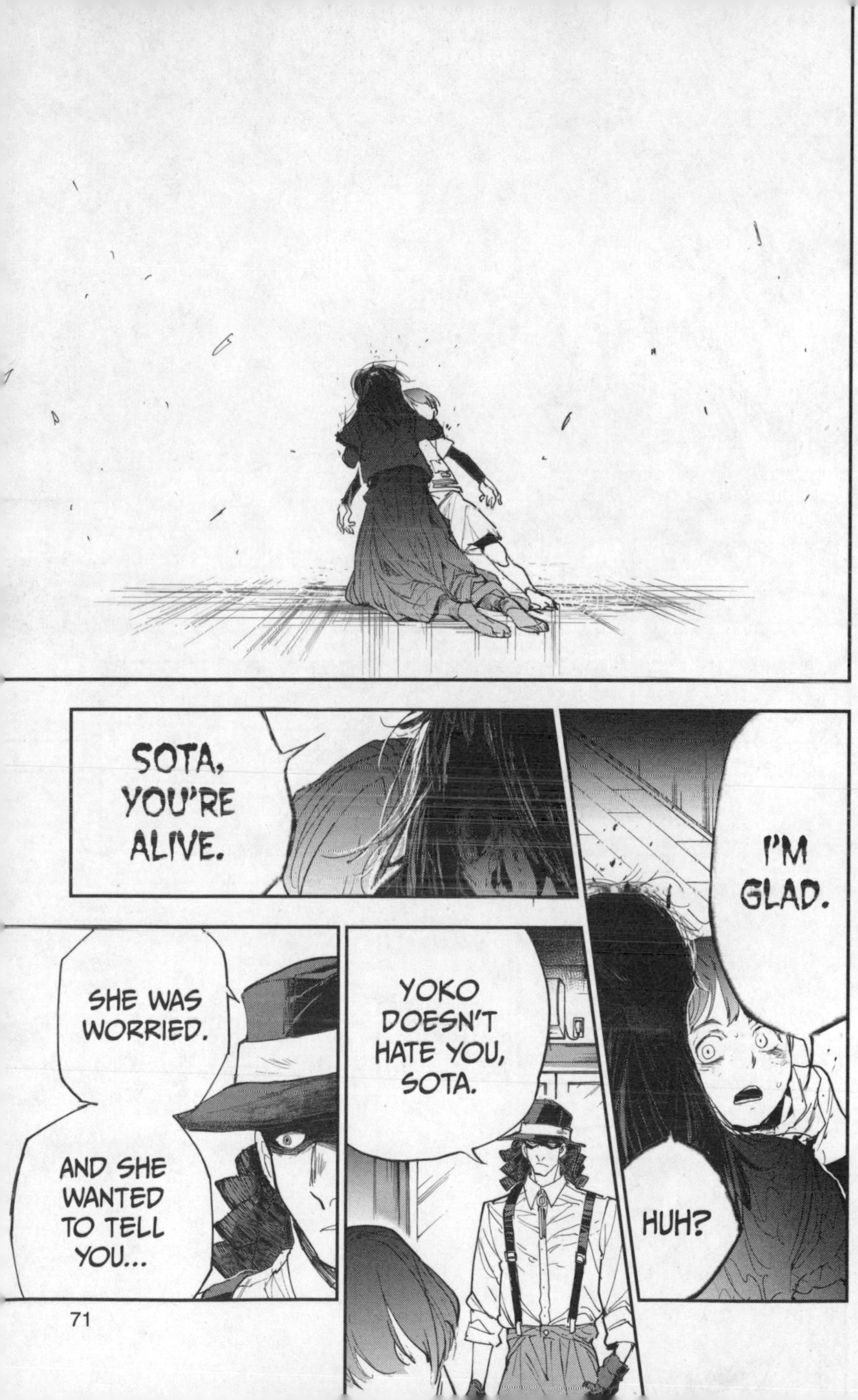
I'M GLAD.
HUH?
SOTA, YOU'RE ALIVE.
YOKO DOESN'T HATE YOU, SOTA.
SHE WAS WORRIED.
AND SHE WANTED TO TELL YOU...

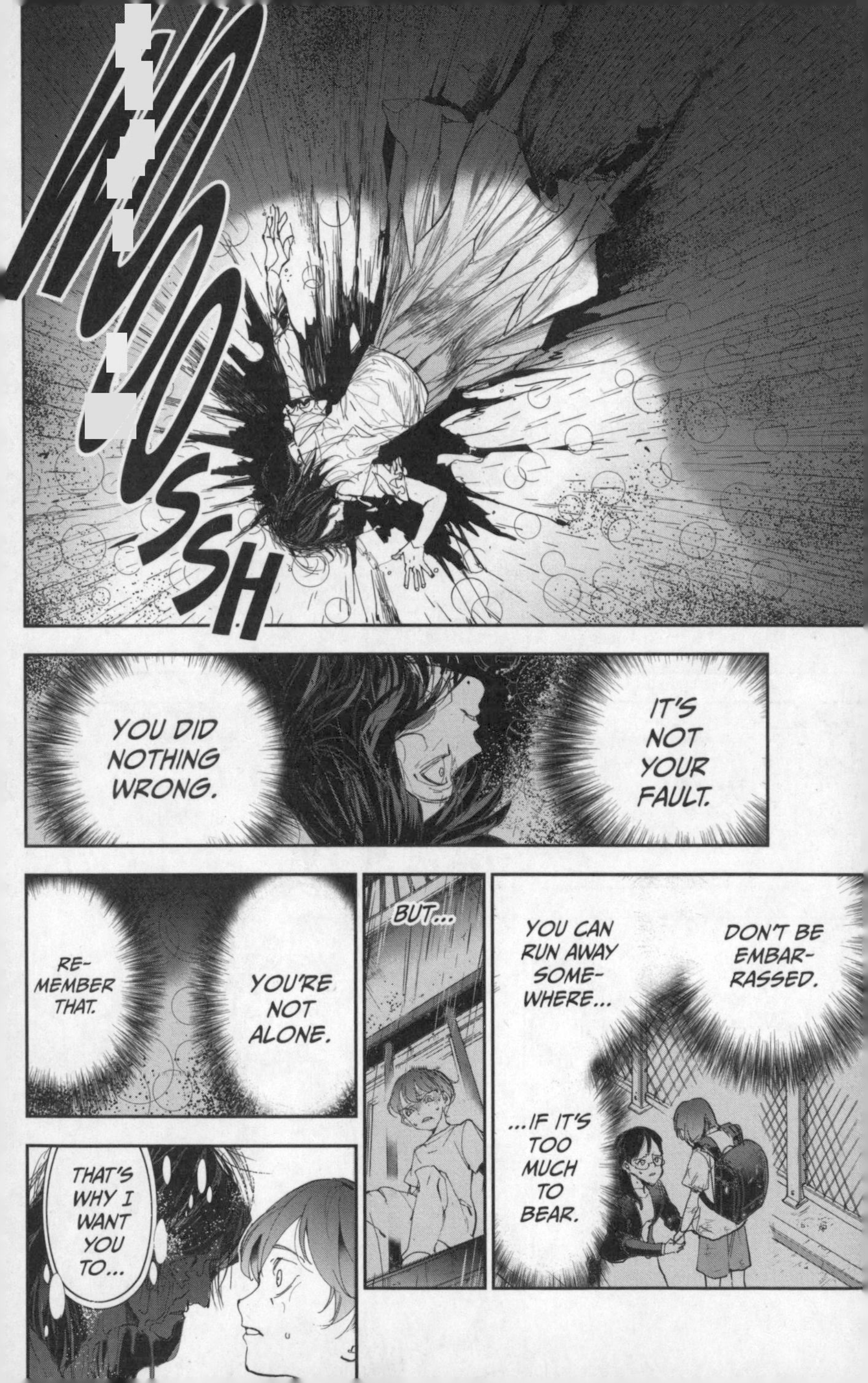
IT'S NOT YOUR FAULT.
YOU DID NOTHING WRONG.
DON'T BE EMBAR-RASSED.
YOU CAN RUN AWAY SOME-WHERE...
...IF IT'S TOO MUCH TO BEAR.
BUT...
YOU'RE NOT ALONE.
RE-MEMBER THAT.
THAT'S WHY I WANT YOU TO...

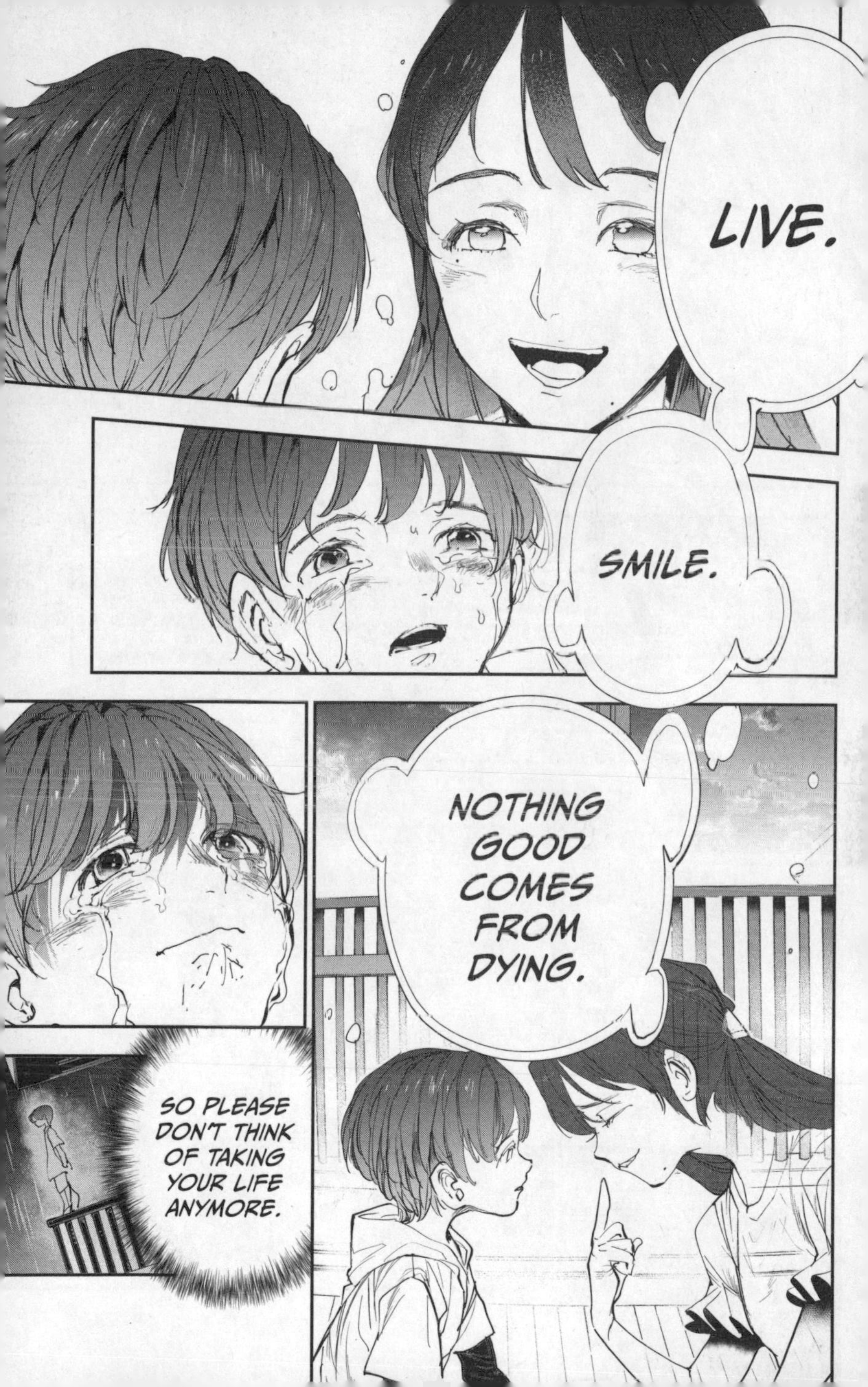
LIVE.
SMILE.
NOTHING GOOD COMES FROM DYING.
SO PLEASE DON'T THINK OF TAKING YOUR LIFE ANYMORE.

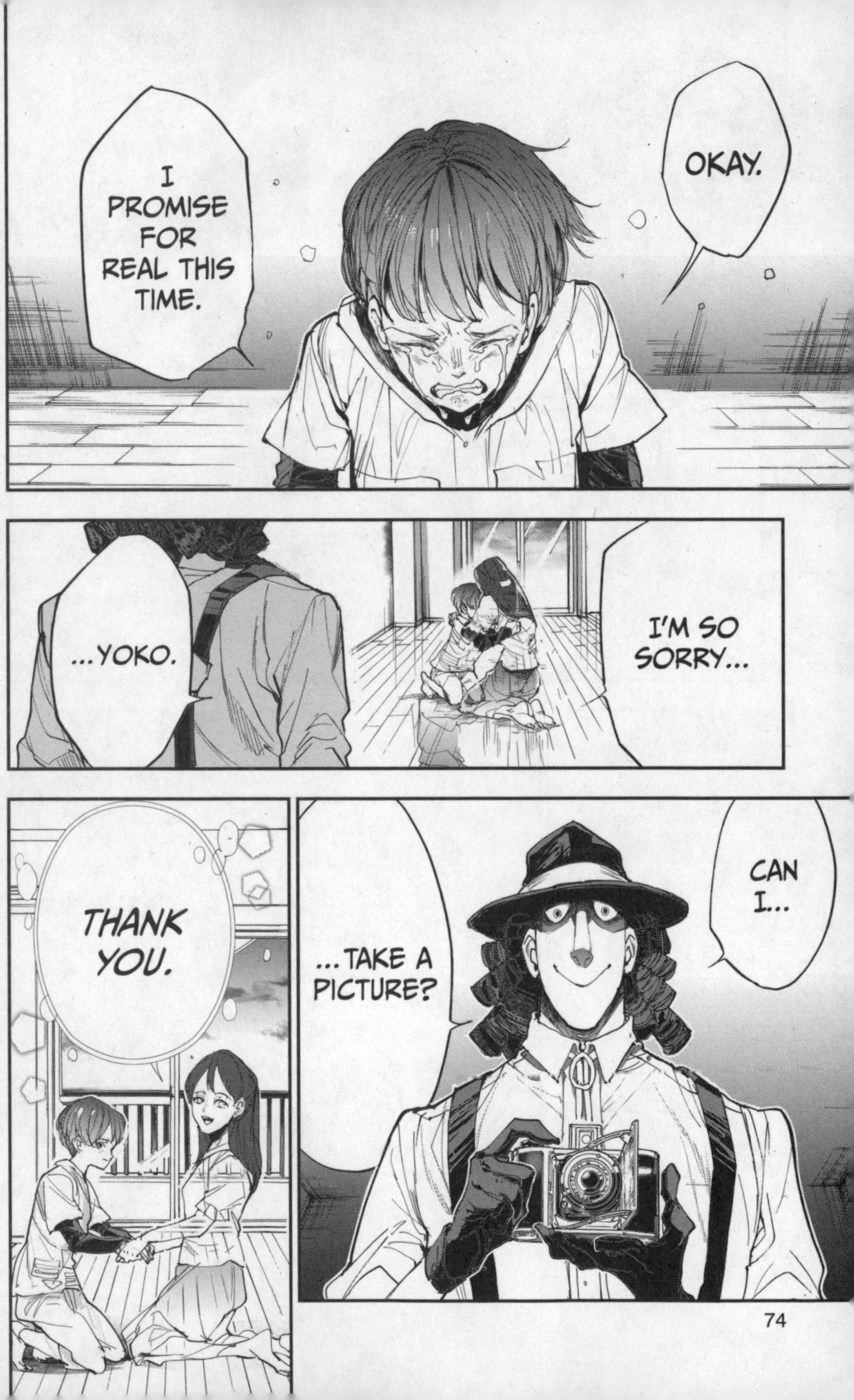
OKAY.
I PROMISE FOR REAL THIS TIME.
I'M SO SORRY...
...YOKO.
CAN I...
...TAKE A PICTURE?
THANK YOU.

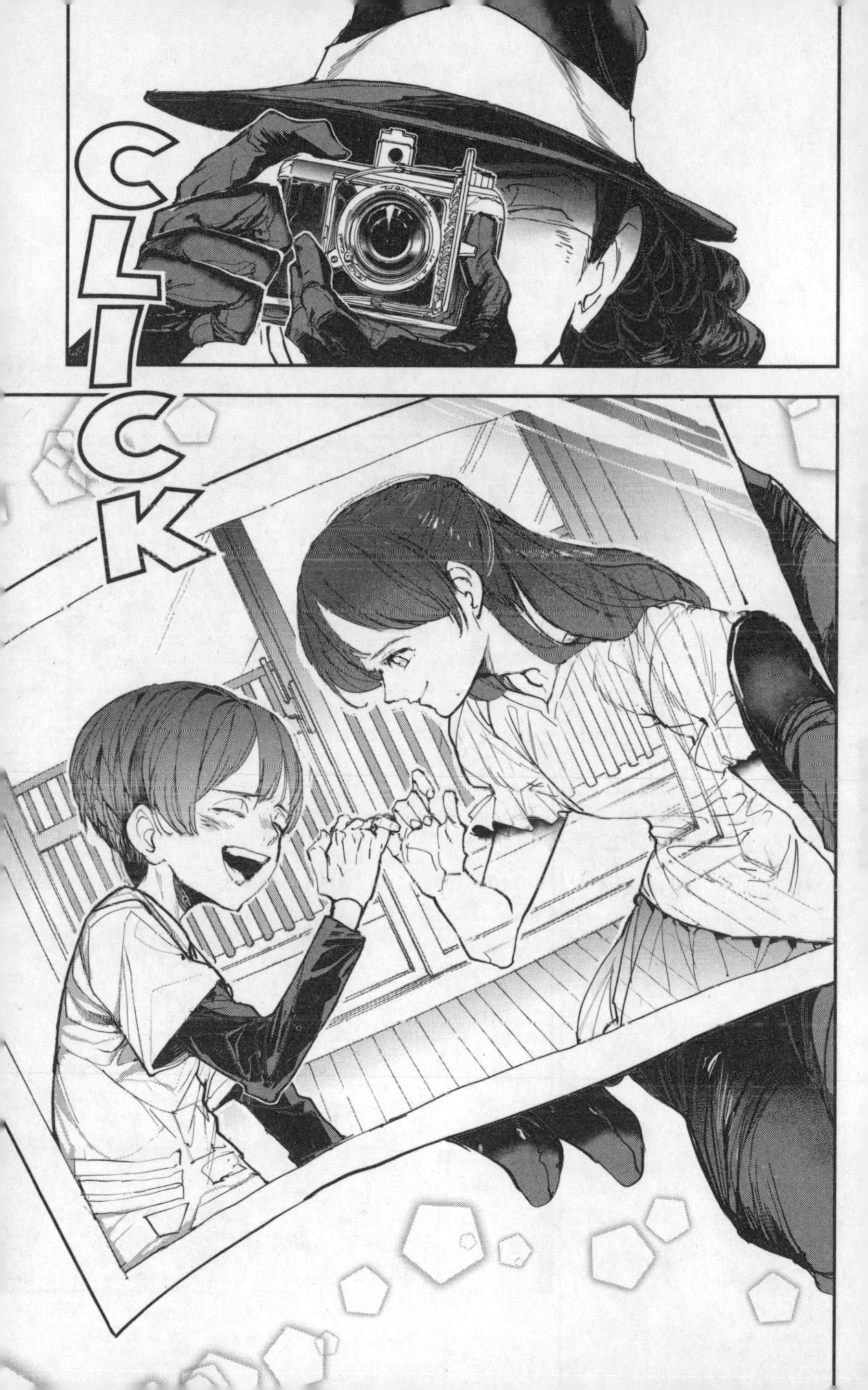
CLICK

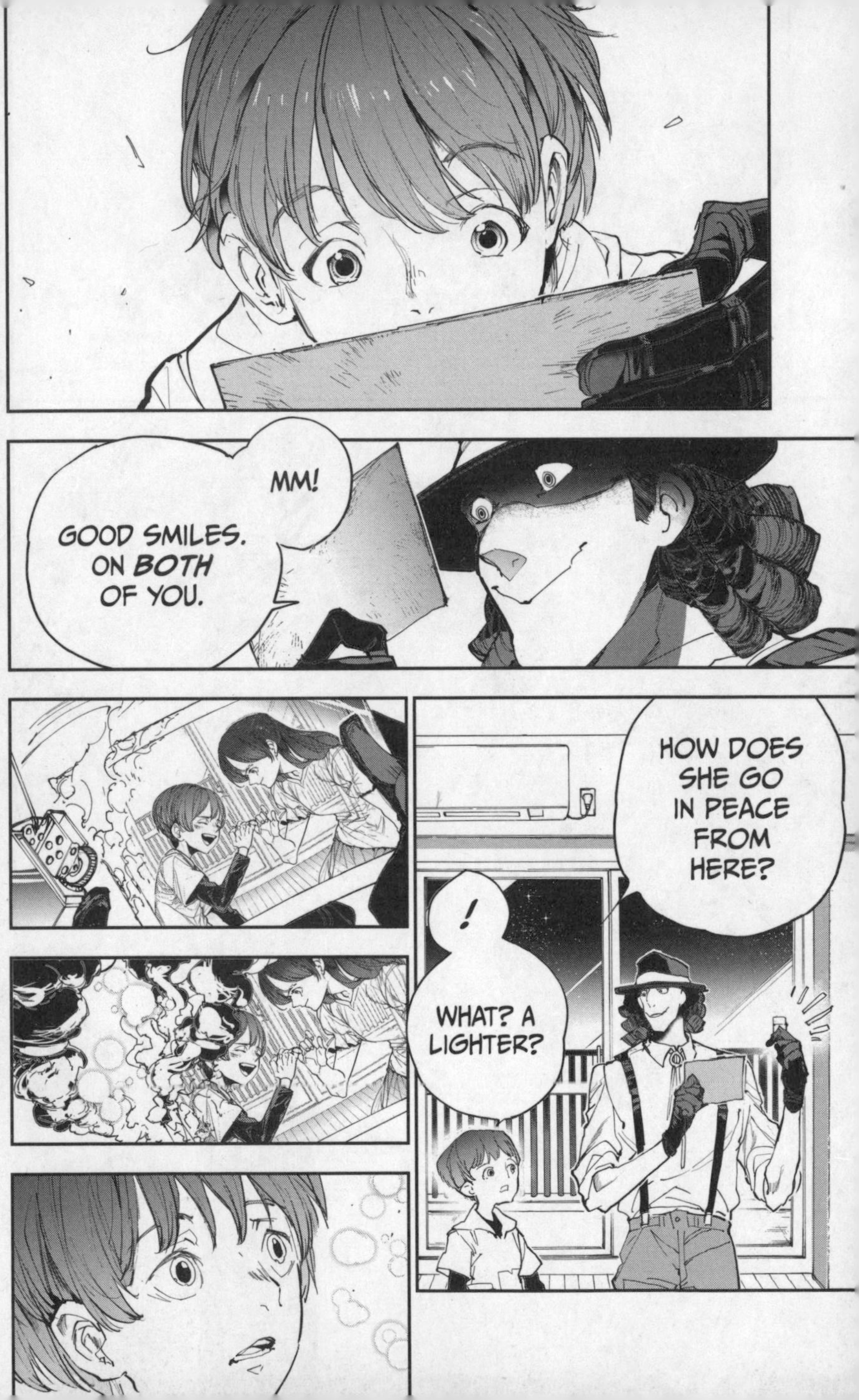
MM!
GOOD SMILES. ON *BOTH* OF YOU.
HOW DOES SHE GO IN PEACE FROM HERE?
!
WHAT? A LIGHTER?

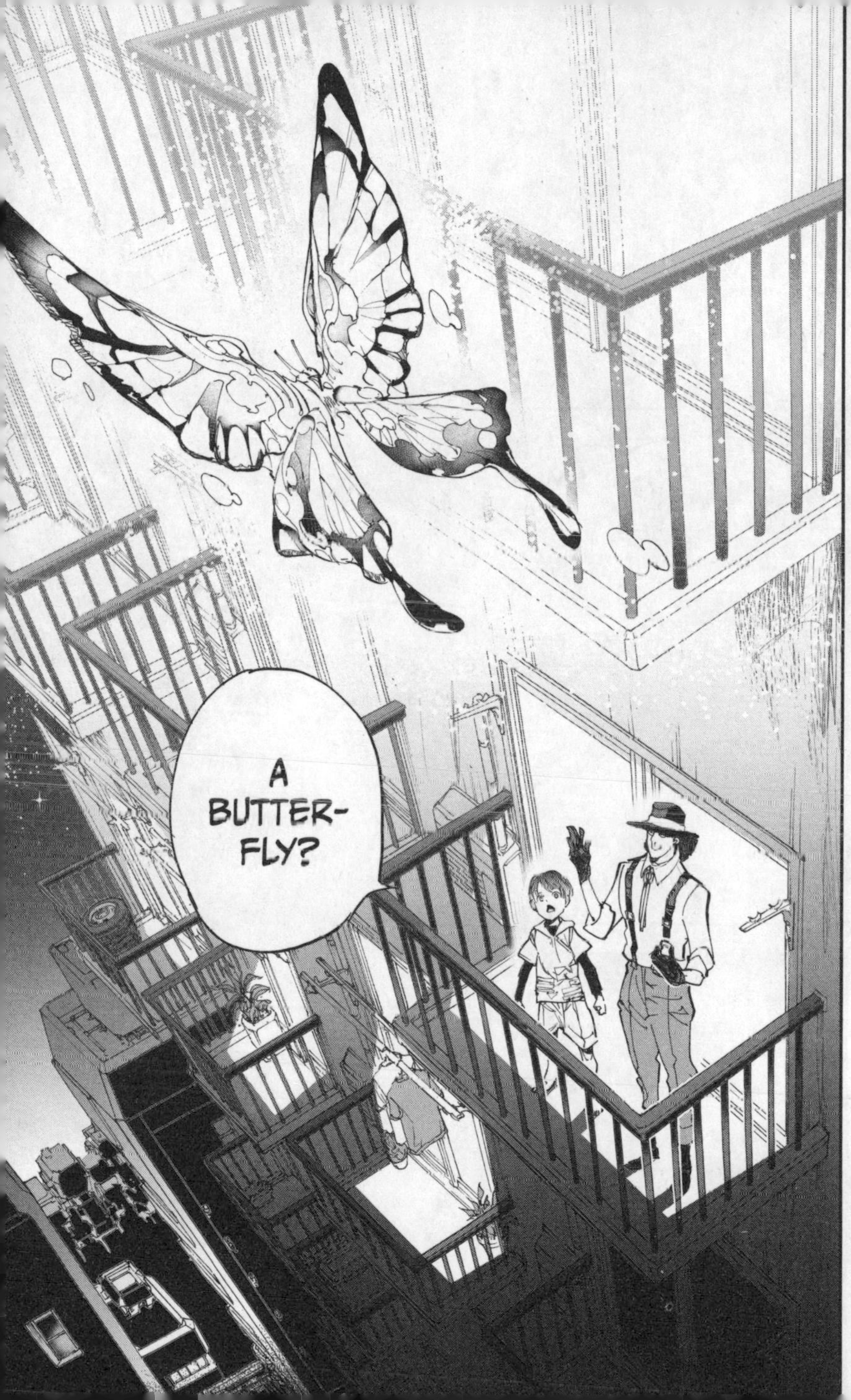
A BUTTER-FLY?

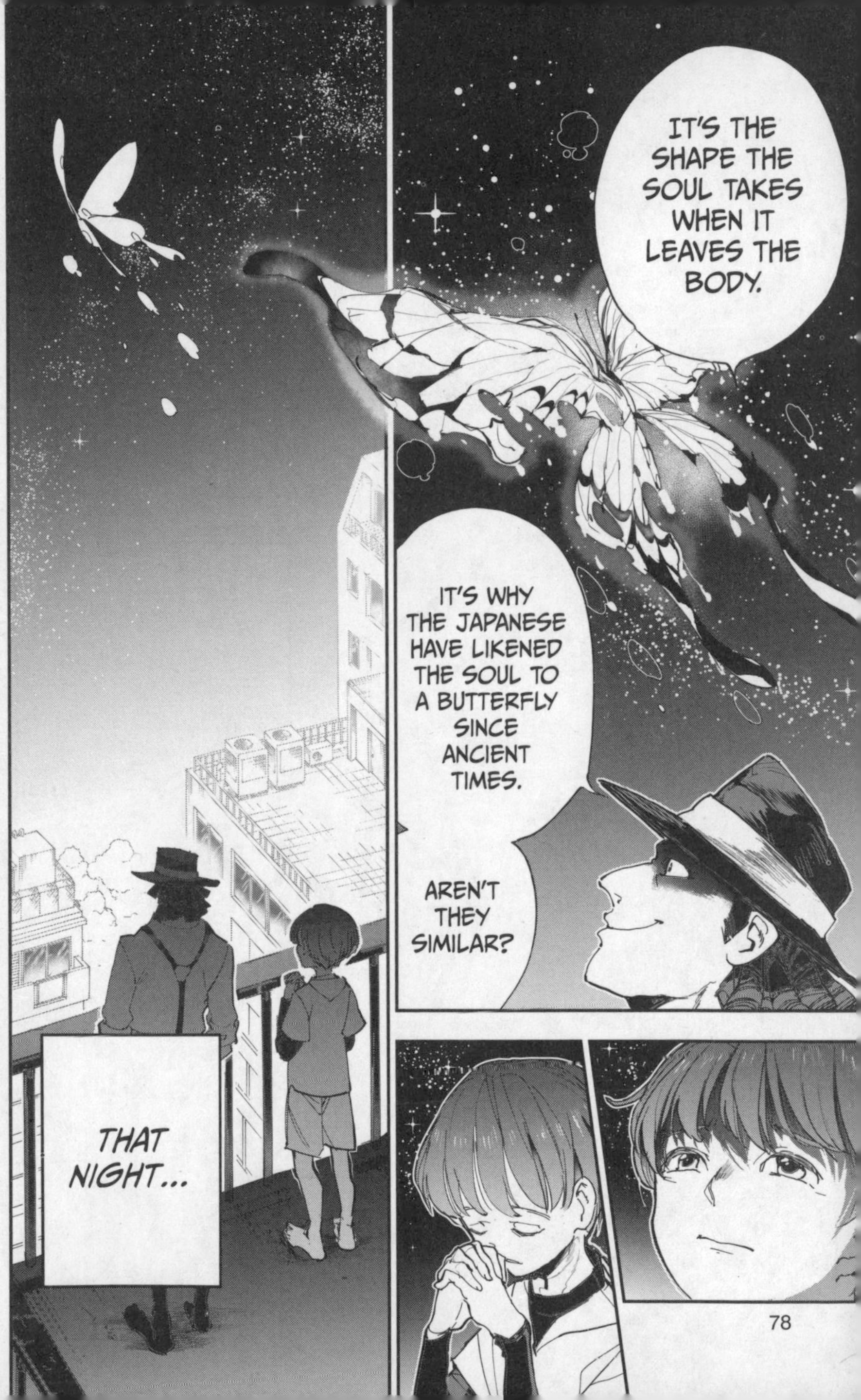
IT'S THE SHAPE THE SOUL TAKES WHEN IT LEAVES THE BODY.
IT'S WHY THE JAPANESE HAVE LIKENED THE SOUL TO A BUTTERFLY SINCE ANCIENT TIMES.
AREN'T THEY SIMILAR?
THAT NIGHT...

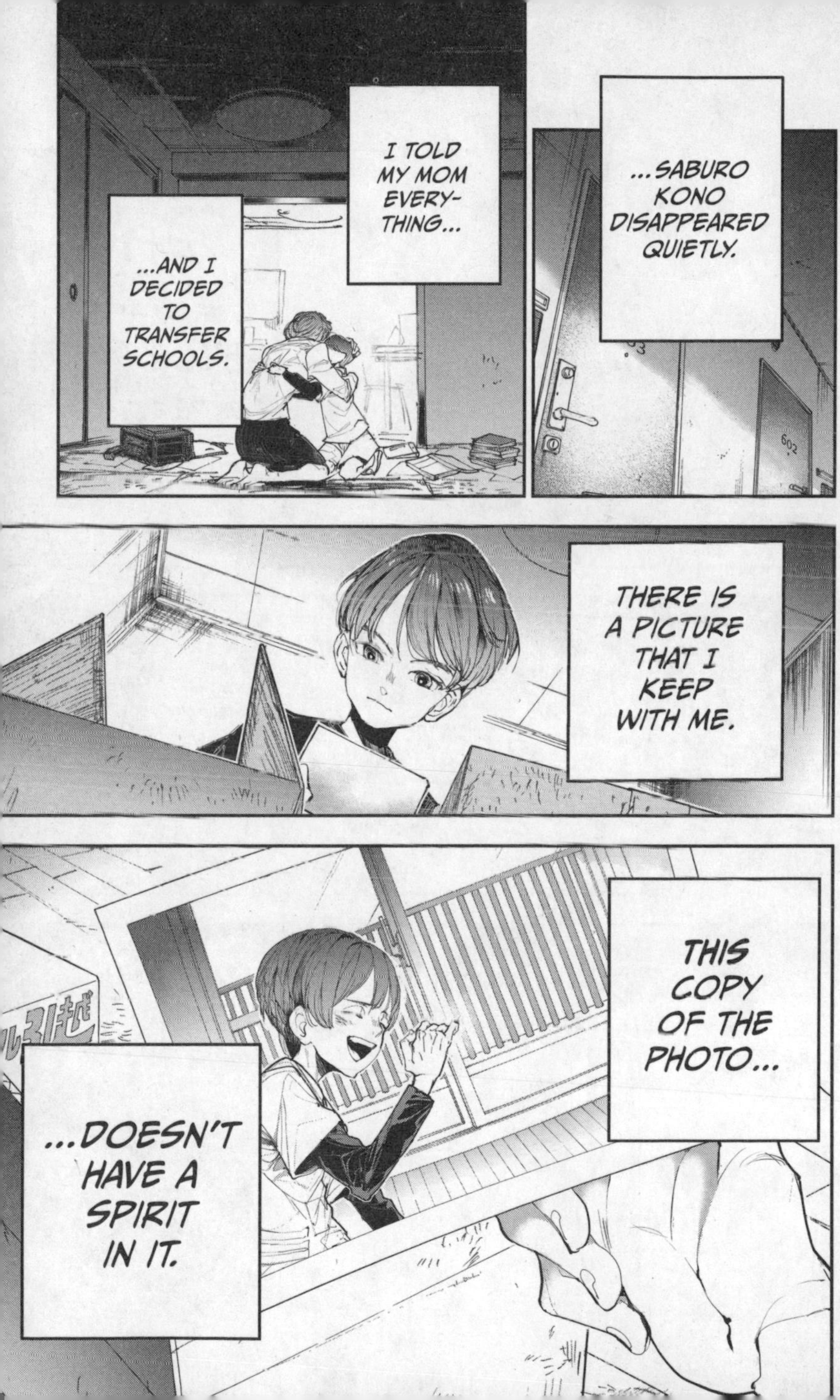
...SABURO KONO DISAPPEARED QUIETLY.
I TOLD MY MOM EVERYTHING...
...AND I DECIDED TO TRANSFER SCHOOLS.
THERE IS A PICTURE THAT I KEEP WITH ME.
THIS COPY OF THE PHOTO...
...DOESN'T HAVE A SPIRIT IN IT.

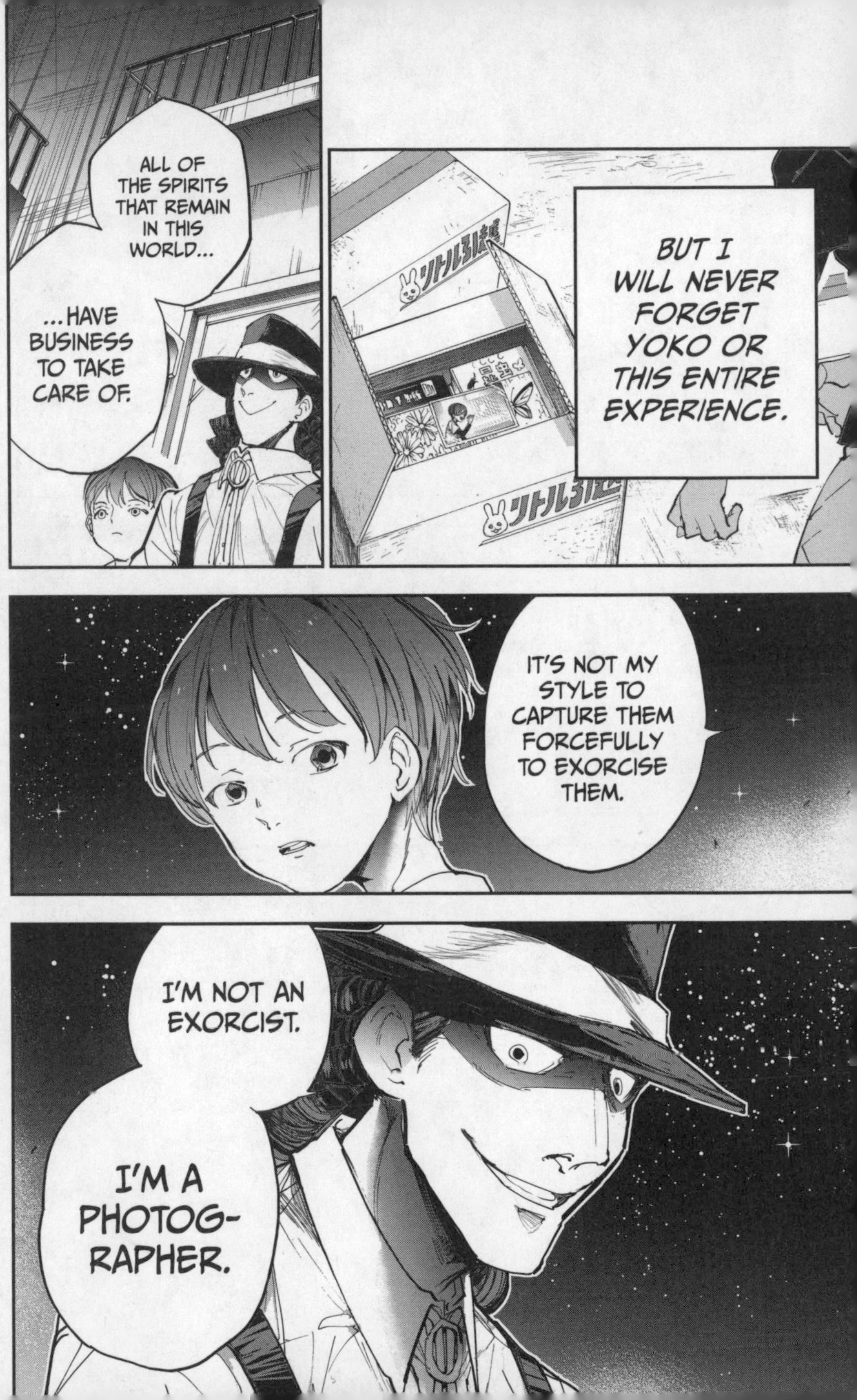
BUT I WILL NEVER FORGET YOKO OR THIS ENTIRE EXPERIENCE.
ALL OF THE SPIRITS THAT REMAIN IN THIS WORLD...
...HAVE BUSINESS TO TAKE CARE OF.
IT'S NOT MY STYLE TO CAPTURE THEM FORCEFULLY TO EXORCISE THEM.
I'M NOT AN EXORCIST.
I'M A PHOTOG-RAPHER.

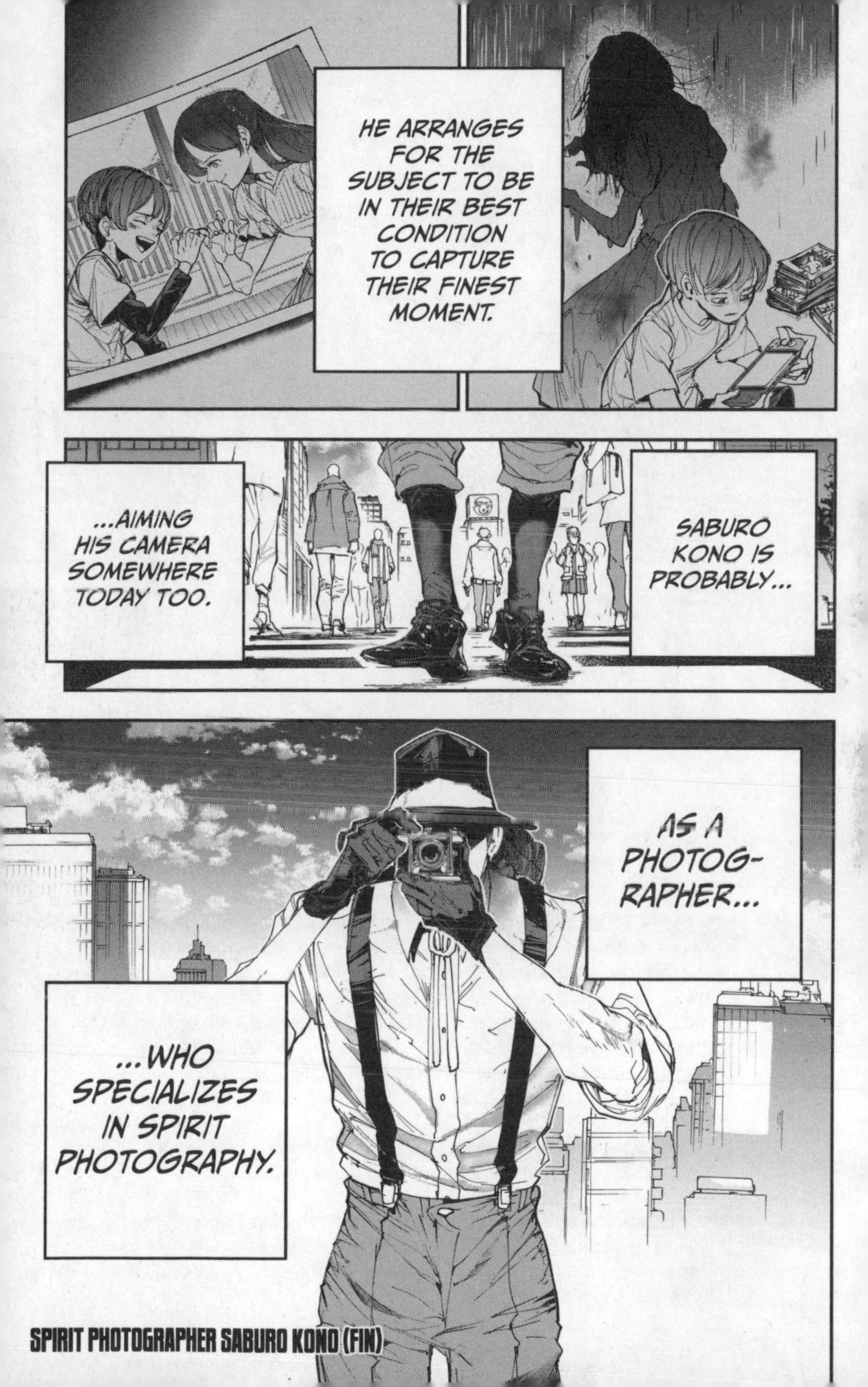
HE ARRANGES FOR THE SUBJECT TO BE IN THEIR BEST CONDITION TO CAPTURE THEIR FINEST MOMENT.
SABURO KONO IS PROBABLY...
...AIMING HIS CAMERA SOMEWHERE TODAY TOO.
AS A PHOTOG-RAPHER...
...WHO SPECIALIZES IN SPIRIT PHOTOGRAPHY.
SPIRIT PHOTOGRAPHER SABURO KONO (FIN)

SHIRAI'S BEHIND-THE-SCENES STORIES #2

◆ A few weeks after taking the storyboards of *The Promised Neverland* to the editors, I turned in this story to compete for publication in a special issue. I drew it on my own, so I didn't think it would be chosen. I was trembling inside as I submitted it, and as I expected, it wasn't selected because my art was too shaky. Of course.

◆ But the story was well received, so after the serialization of *The Promised Neverland* ended, I was able to get this story out into the world. And it came out in the best way possible, with Demizu Sensei's spectacular art. So I'm actually really glad I didn't make it into the special issue back then.

◆ I came up with this story because I grew up near a professional photo studio, and I also thought that it would be nice to have beautiful spirit photography.

◆ I wrote about this when this story was published in *Jump* too, but in real life, you shouldn't tell strangers that your parents aren't home. Depending on the situation, it could be dangerous. Also, don't die. Let's live, together.

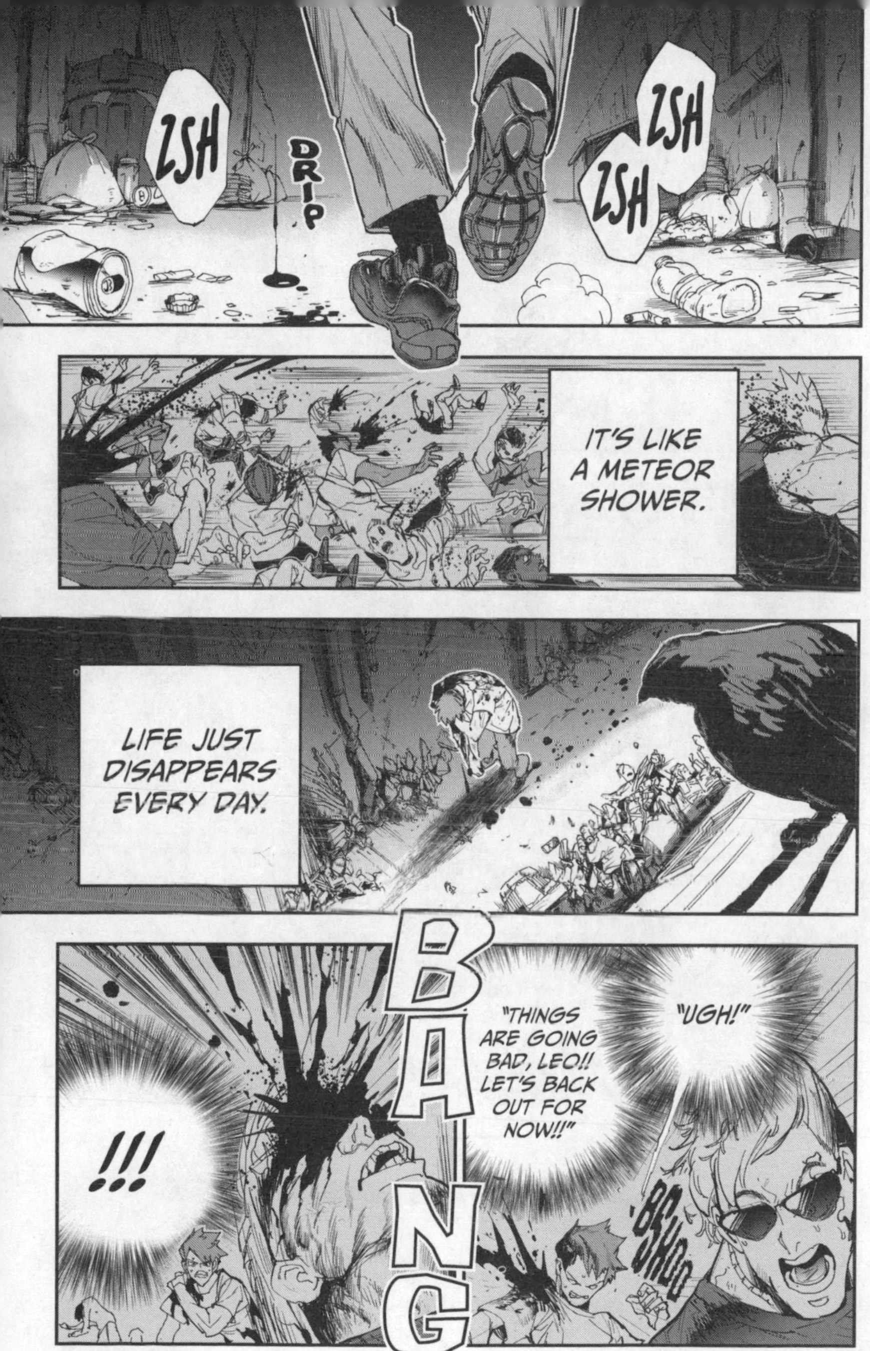
ZSH
ZSH
DRIP
DRIP
ZSH
IT'S LIKE A METEOR SHOWER.
LIFE JUST DISAPPEARS EVERY DAY.
"UGH!"
"THINGS ARE GOING BAD, LEO!! LET'S BACK OUT FOR NOW!!"
BANG
BSHOO
!!!

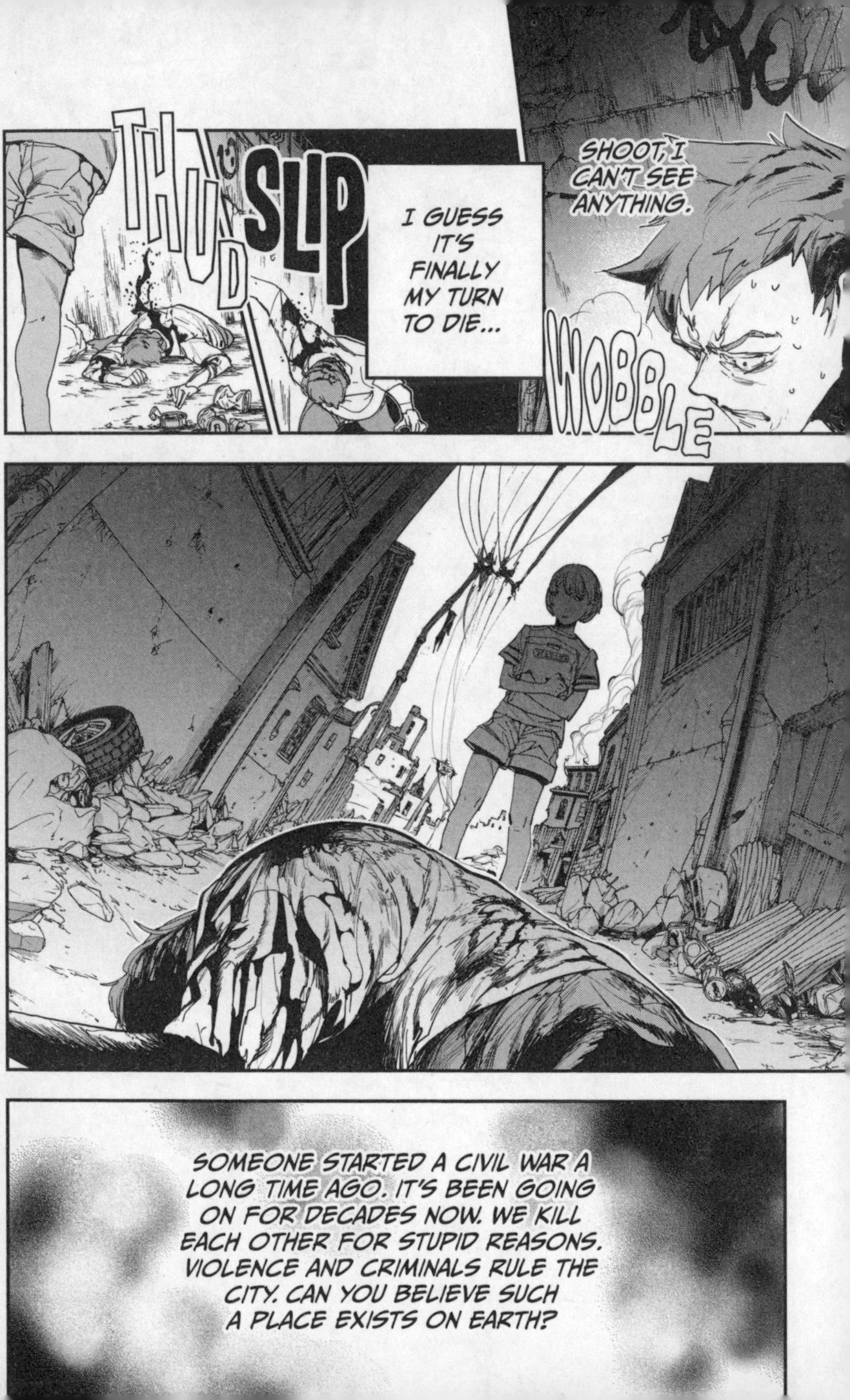
SHOOT, I CAN'T SEE ANYTHING.
WOBBLE
I GUESS IT'S FINALLY MY TURN TO DIE...
SLIP
THUD
SOMEONE STARTED A CIVIL WAR A LONG TIME AGO. IT'S BEEN GOING ON FOR DECADES NOW. WE KILL EACH OTHER FOR STUPID REASONS. VIOLENCE AND CRIMINALS RULE THE CITY. CAN YOU BELIEVE SUCH A PLACE EXISTS ON EARTH?

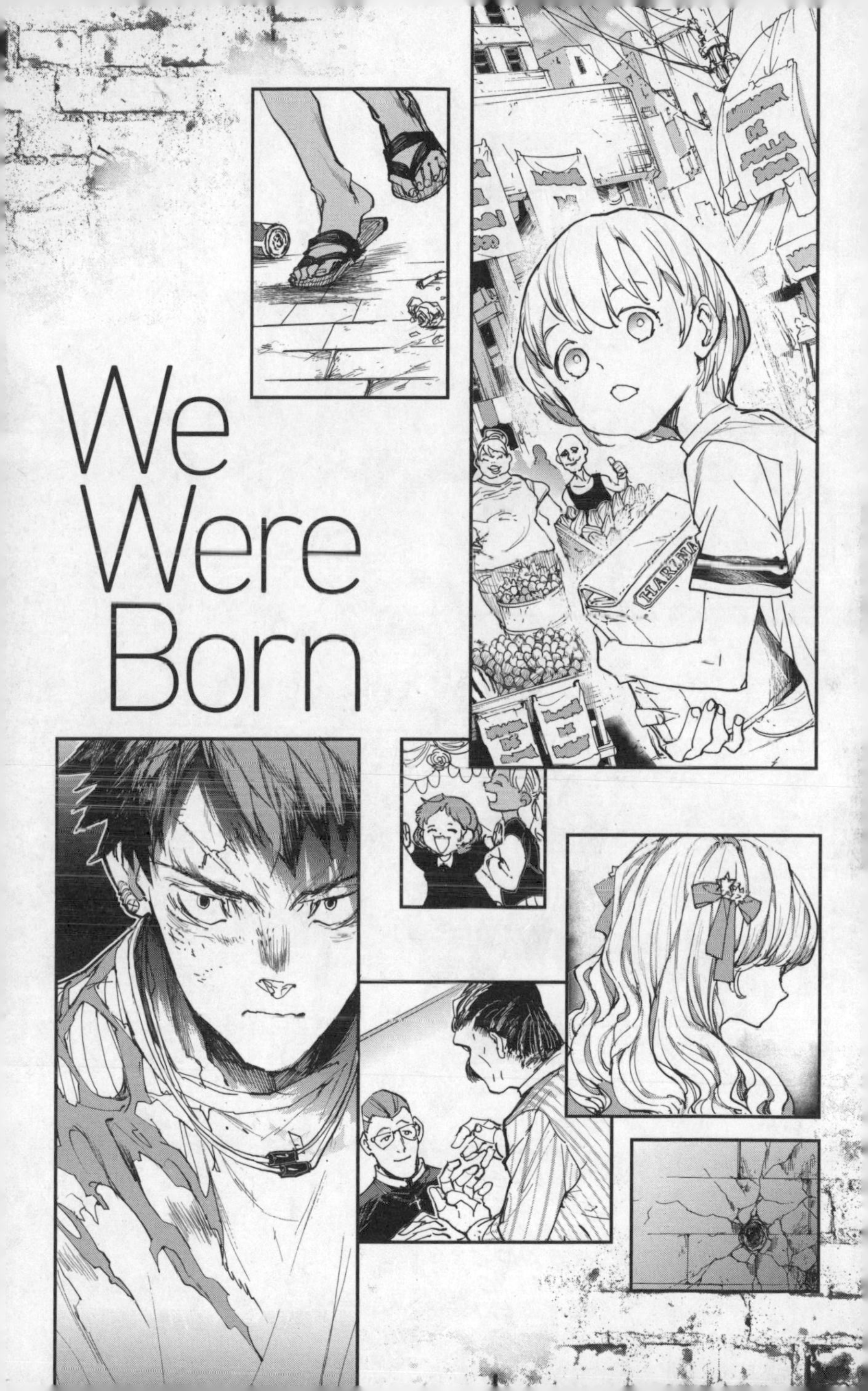
We Were Born
HARINA

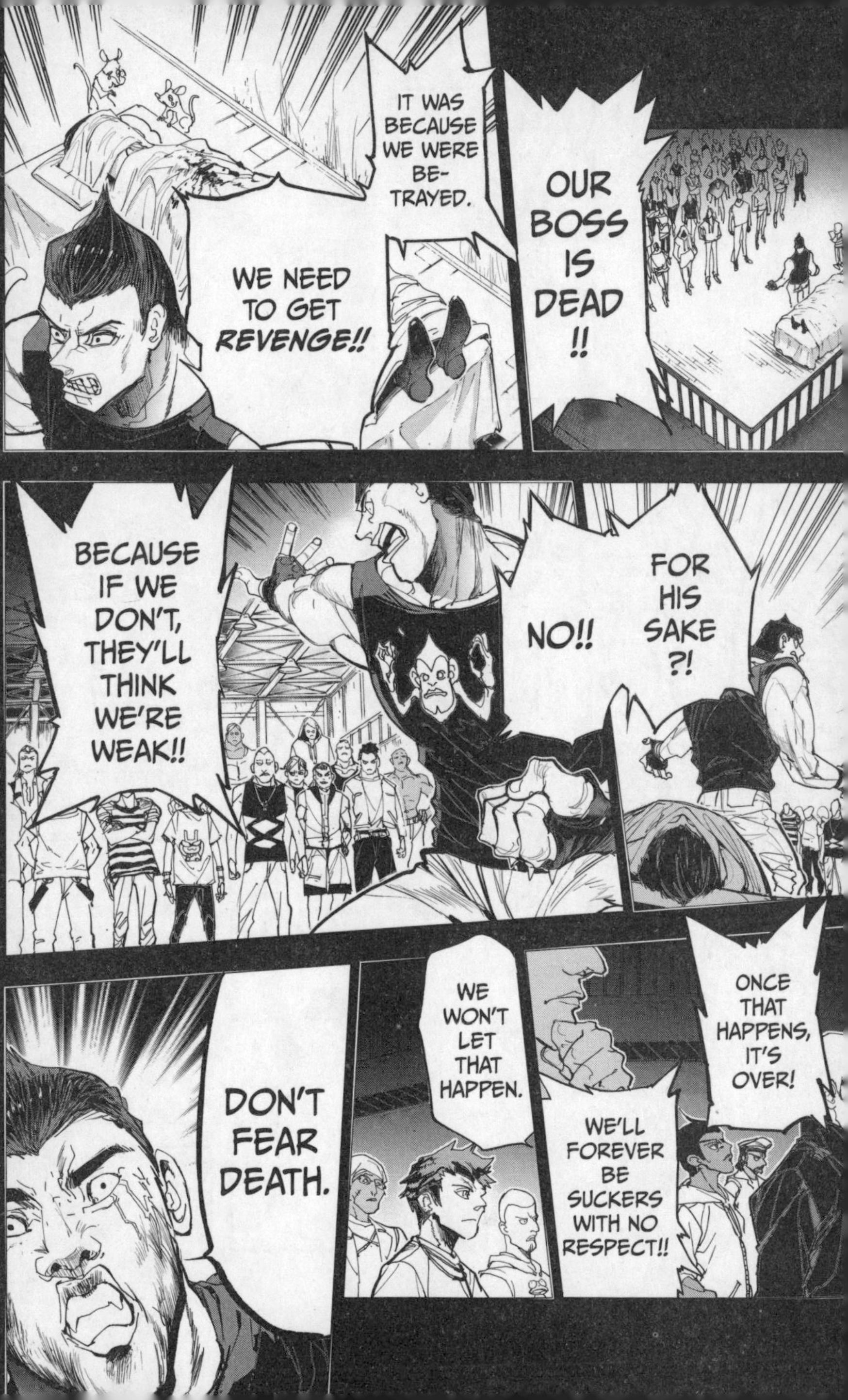
OUR BOSS IS DEAD!!
IT WAS BECAUSE WE WERE BE- TRAYED.
WE NEED TO GET *REVENGE!!*
FOR HIS SAKE?!
NO!!
BECAUSE IF WE DON'T, THEY'LL THINK WE'RE WEAK!!
ONCE THAT HAPPENS, IT'S OVER!
WE'LL FOREVER BE SUCKERS WITH NO RESPECT!!
WE WON'T LET THAT HAPPEN.
DON'T FEAR DEATH.

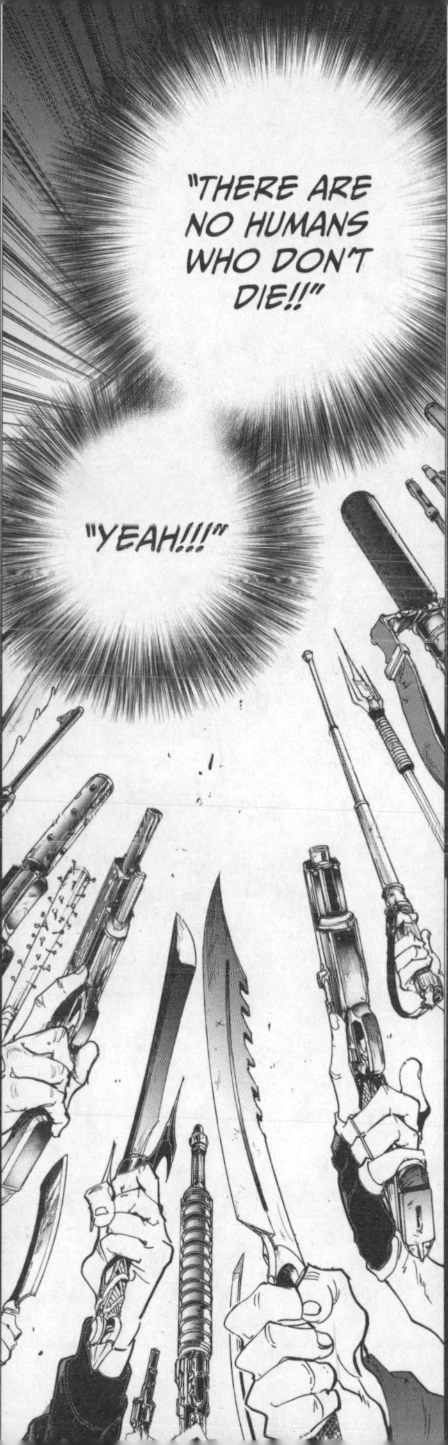
"THERE ARE NO HUMANS WHO DON'T DIE!!"
"YEAH!!!"

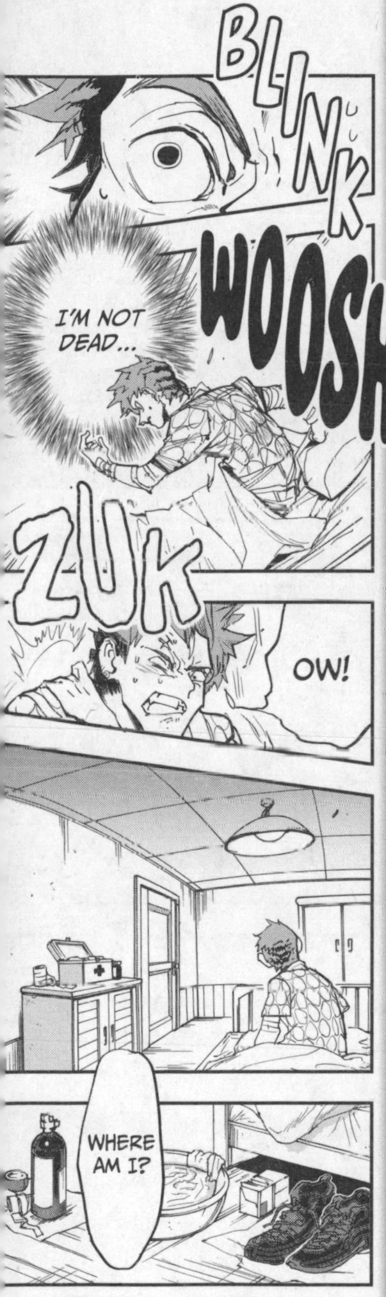
BLINK
WOOSH
I'M NOT DEAD...
ZUK
OW!
WHERE AM I?

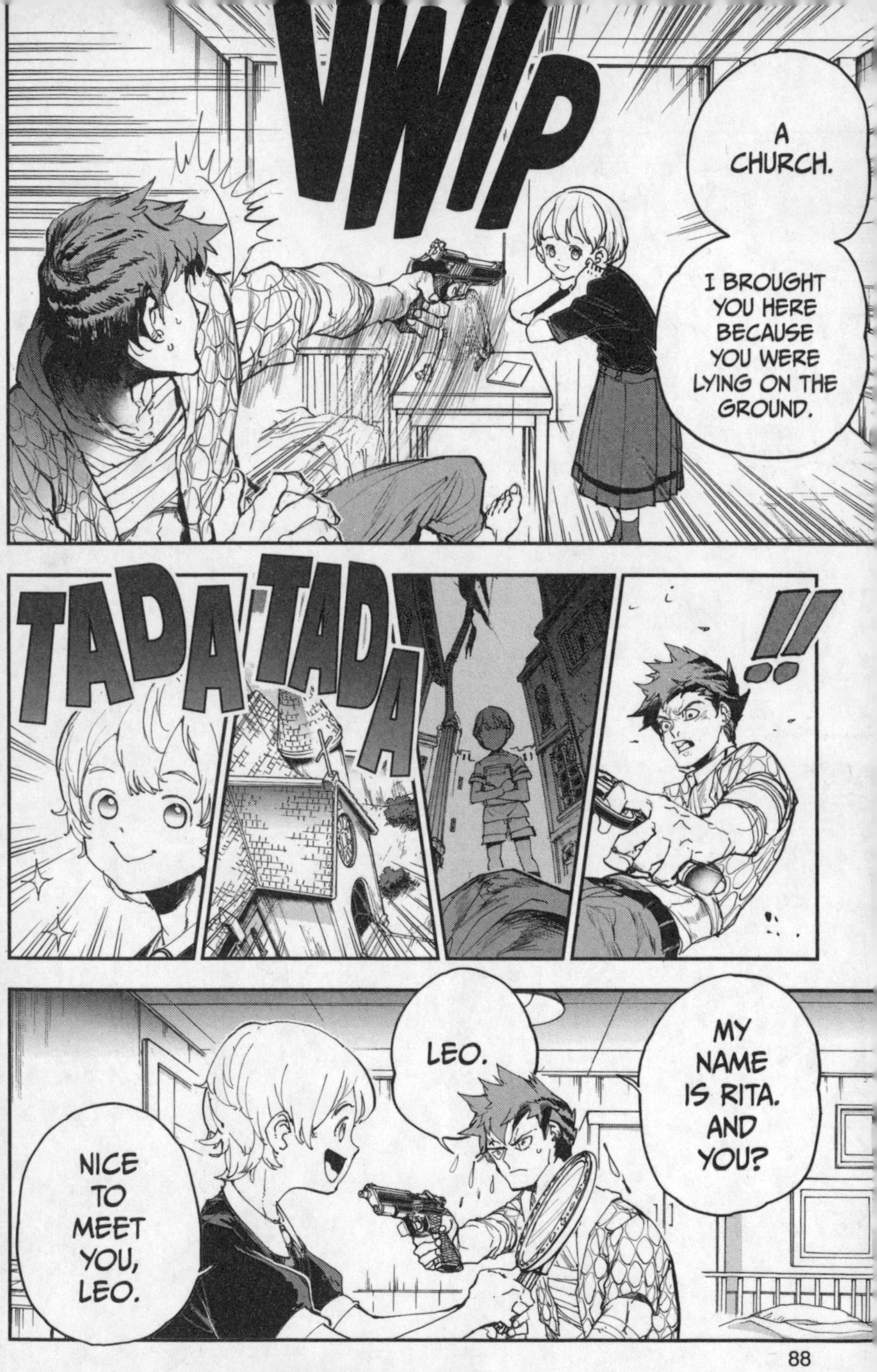
A CHURCH.
I BROUGHT YOU HERE BECAUSE YOU WERE LYING ON THE GROUND.
VWIP
!!
TADA TADA TADA
MY NAME IS RITA. AND YOU?
LEO.
NICE TO MEET YOU, LEO.

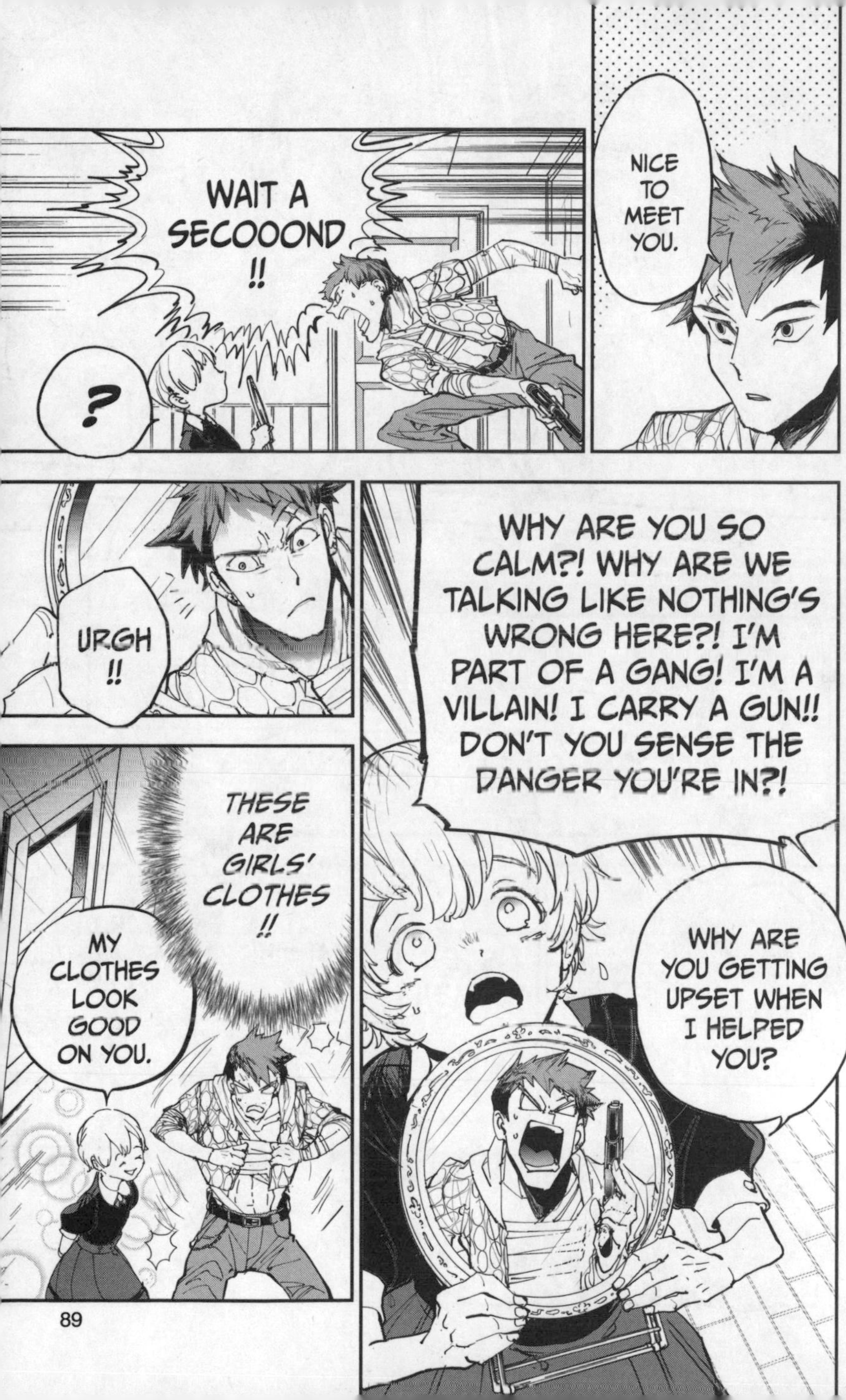
NICE TO MEET YOU.
WAIT A SECOOOND !!
?
WHY ARE YOU SO CALM?! WHY ARE WE TALKING LIKE NOTHING'S WRONG HERE?! I'M PART OF A GANG! I'M A VILLAIN! I CARRY A GUN!! DON'T YOU SENSE THE DANGER YOU'RE IN?!
WHY ARE YOU GETTING UPSET WHEN I HELPED YOU?
URGH !!
THESE ARE GIRLS' CLOTHES !!
MY CLOTHES LOOK GOOD ON YOU.

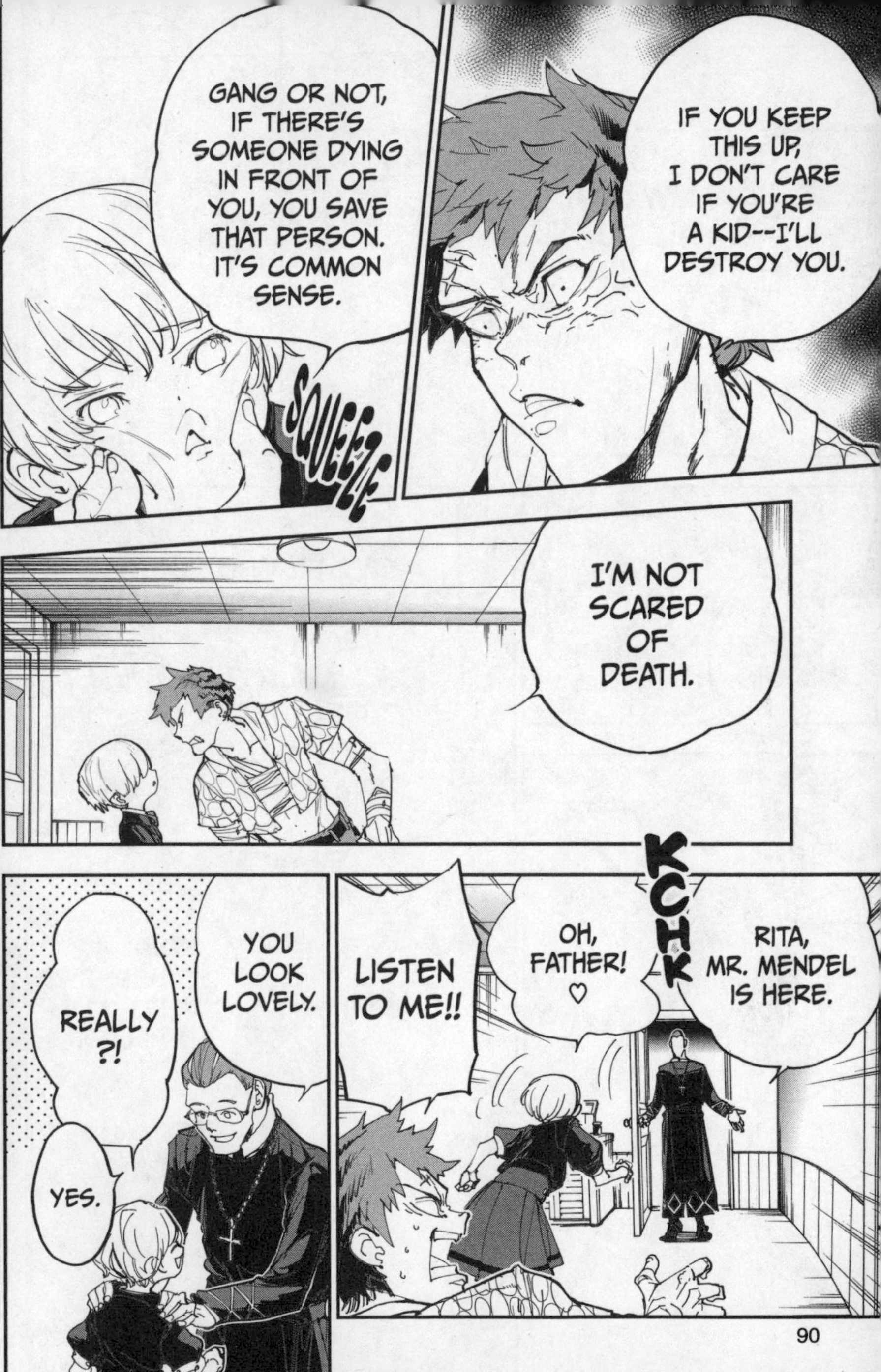
IF YOU KEEP THIS UP, I DON'T CARE IF YOU'RE A KID--I'LL DESTROY YOU.
GANG OR NOT, IF THERE'S SOMEONE DYING IN FRONT OF YOU, YOU SAVE THAT PERSON. IT'S COMMON SENSE.
SQUEEEZE
I'M NOT SCARED OF DEATH.
KCHK
RITA, MR. MENDEL IS HERE.
OH, FATHER! ♡
LISTEN TO ME!!
YOU LOOK LOVELY.
REALLY?!
YES.

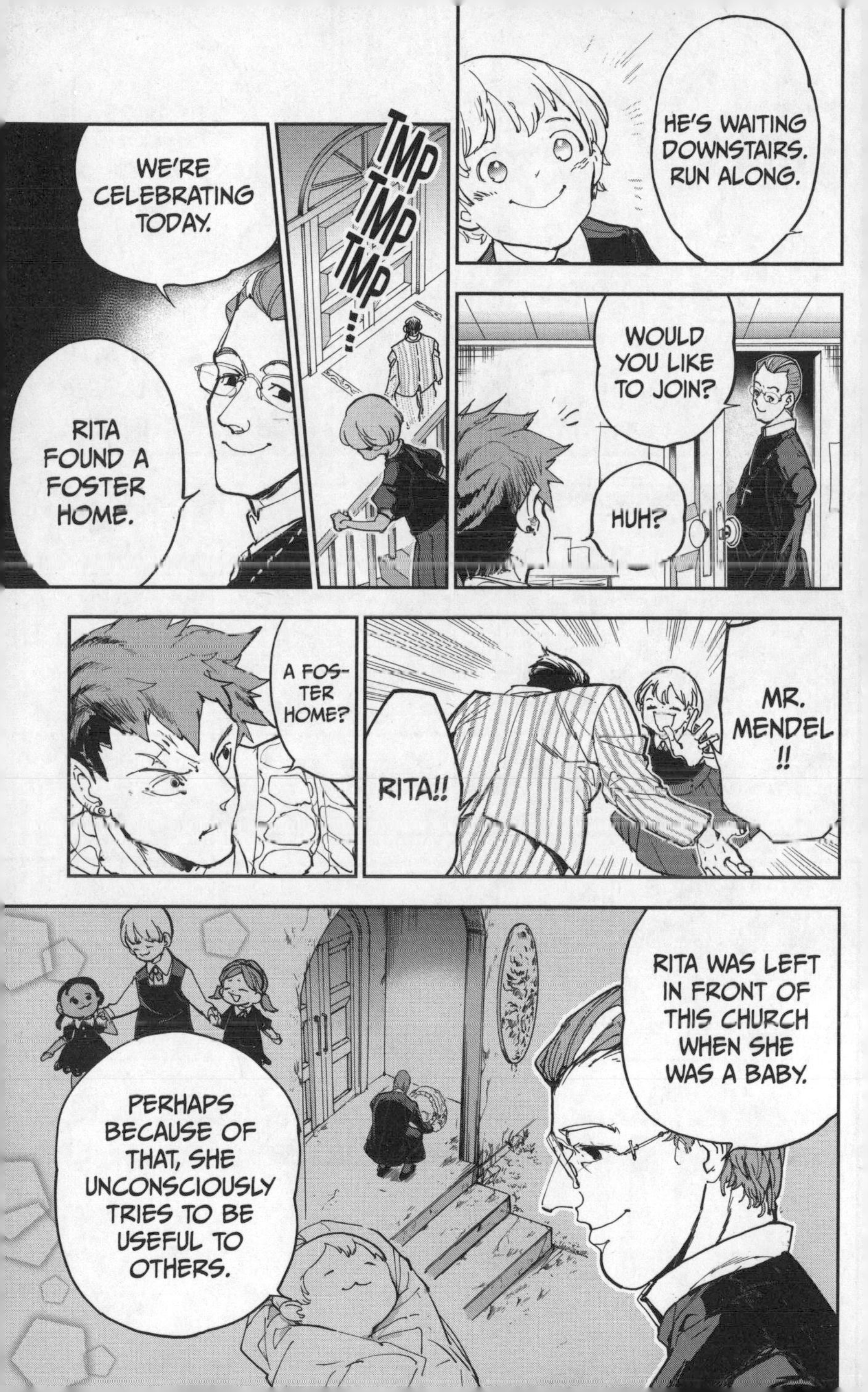
HE'S WAITING DOWNSTAIRS. RUN ALONG.
WOULD YOU LIKE TO JOIN?
HUH?
TMP TMP TMP...!
WE'RE CELEBRATING TODAY.
RITA FOUND A FOSTER HOME.
MR. MENDEL!!
RITA!!
A FOS-TER HOME?
RITA WAS LEFT IN FRONT OF THIS CHURCH WHEN SHE WAS A BABY.
PERHAPS BECAUSE OF THAT, SHE UNCONSCIOUSLY TRIES TO BE USEFUL TO OTHERS.

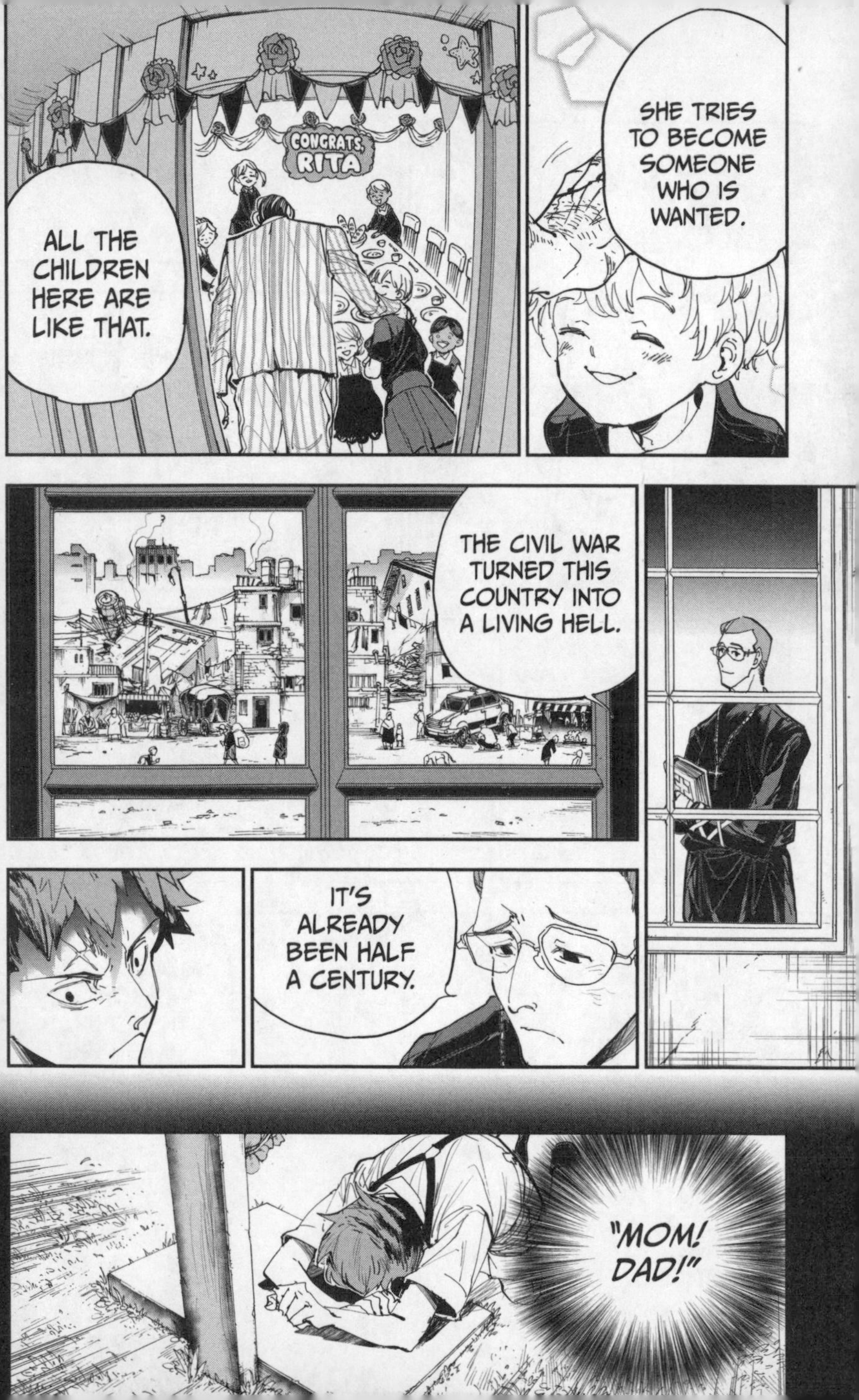
SHE TRIES TO BECOME SOMEONE WHO IS WANTED.
CONGRATS, RITA
ALL THE CHILDREN HERE ARE LIKE THAT.
THE CIVIL WAR TURNED THIS COUNTRY INTO A LIVING HELL.
IT'S ALREADY BEEN HALF A CENTURY.
"MOM! DAD!"

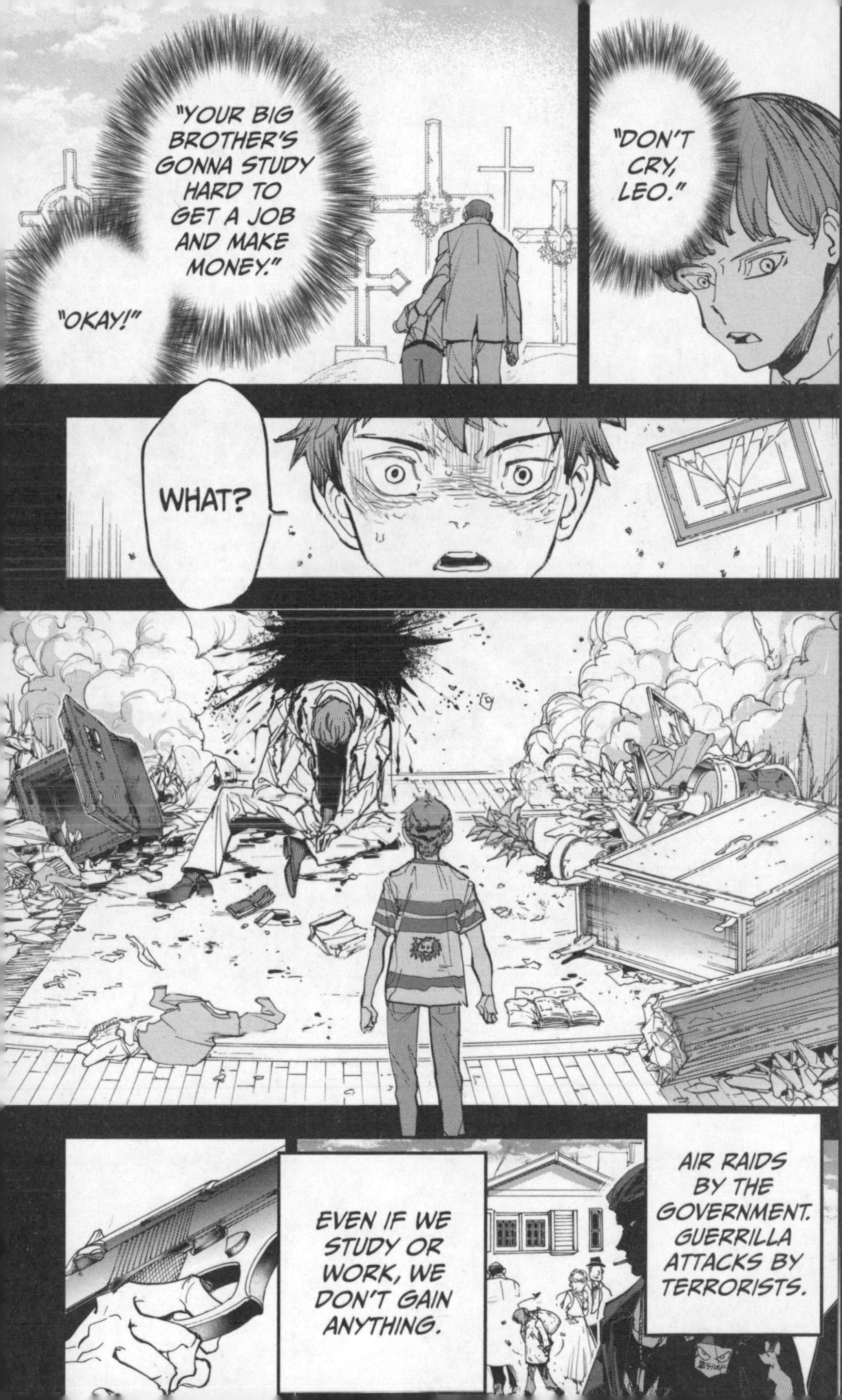
"DON'T CRY, LEO."
"YOUR BIG BROTHER'S GONNA STUDY HARD TO GET A JOB AND MAKE MONEY."
"OKAY!"
WHAT?
AIR RAIDS BY THE GOVERNMENT. GUERRILLA ATTACKS BY TERRORISTS.
EVEN IF WE STUDY OR WORK, WE DON'T GAIN ANYTHING.

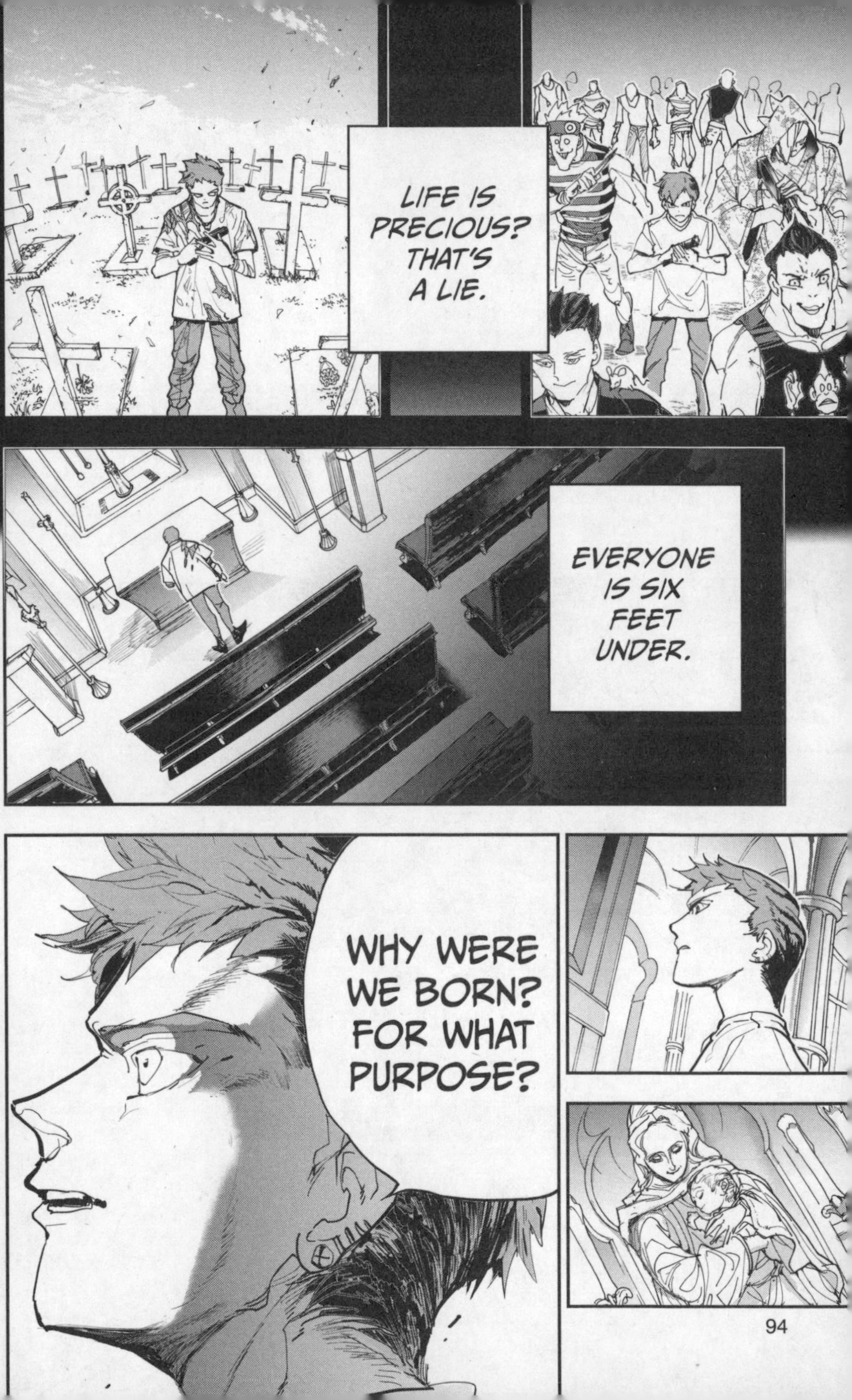
LIFE IS PRECIOUS? THAT'S A LIE.
EVERYONE IS SIX FEET UNDER.
WHY WERE WE BORN? FOR WHAT PURPOSE?

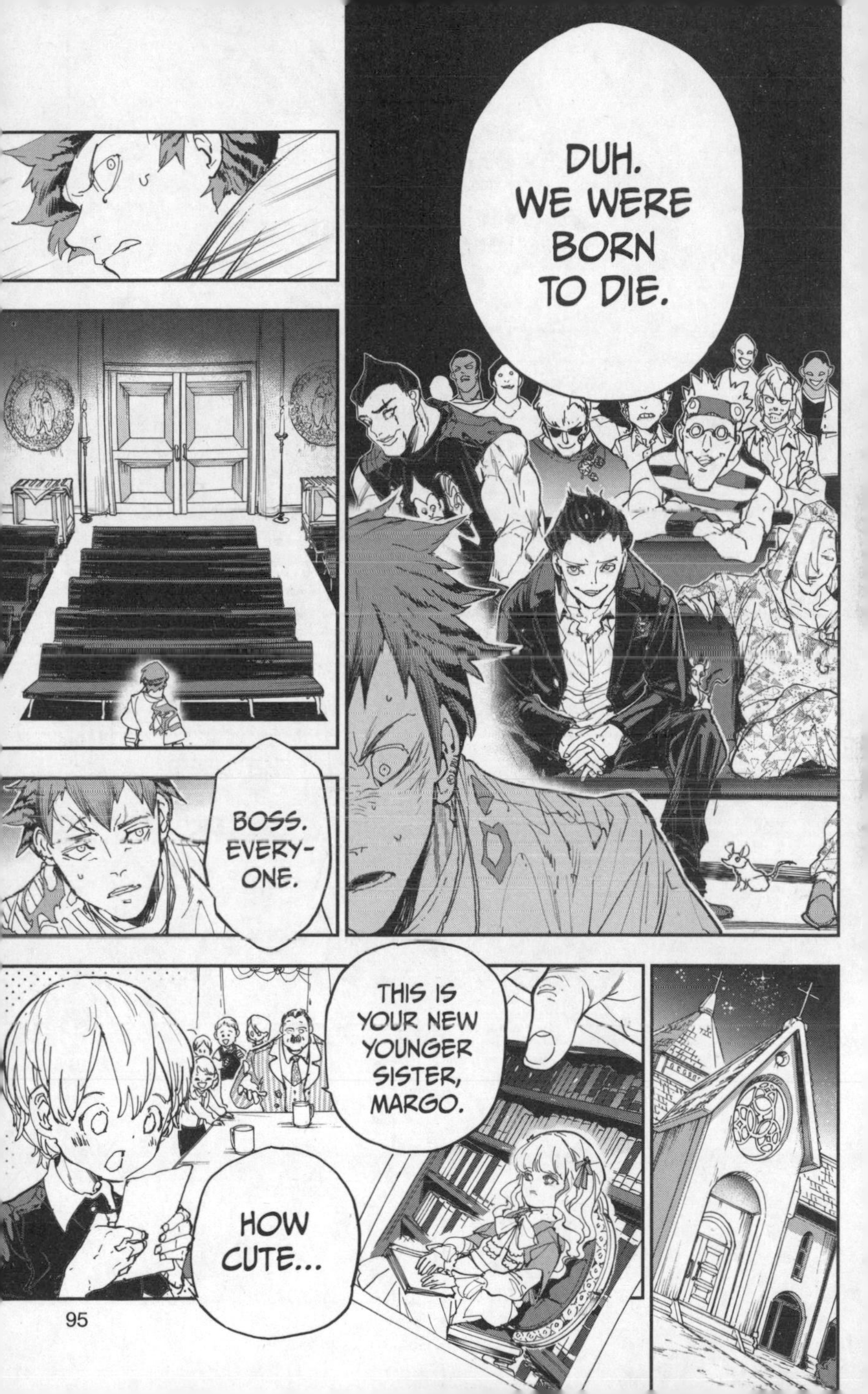
DUH. WE WERE BORN TO DIE.
BOSS. EVERY-ONE.
THIS IS YOUR NEW YOUNGER SISTER, MARGO.
HOW CUTE...

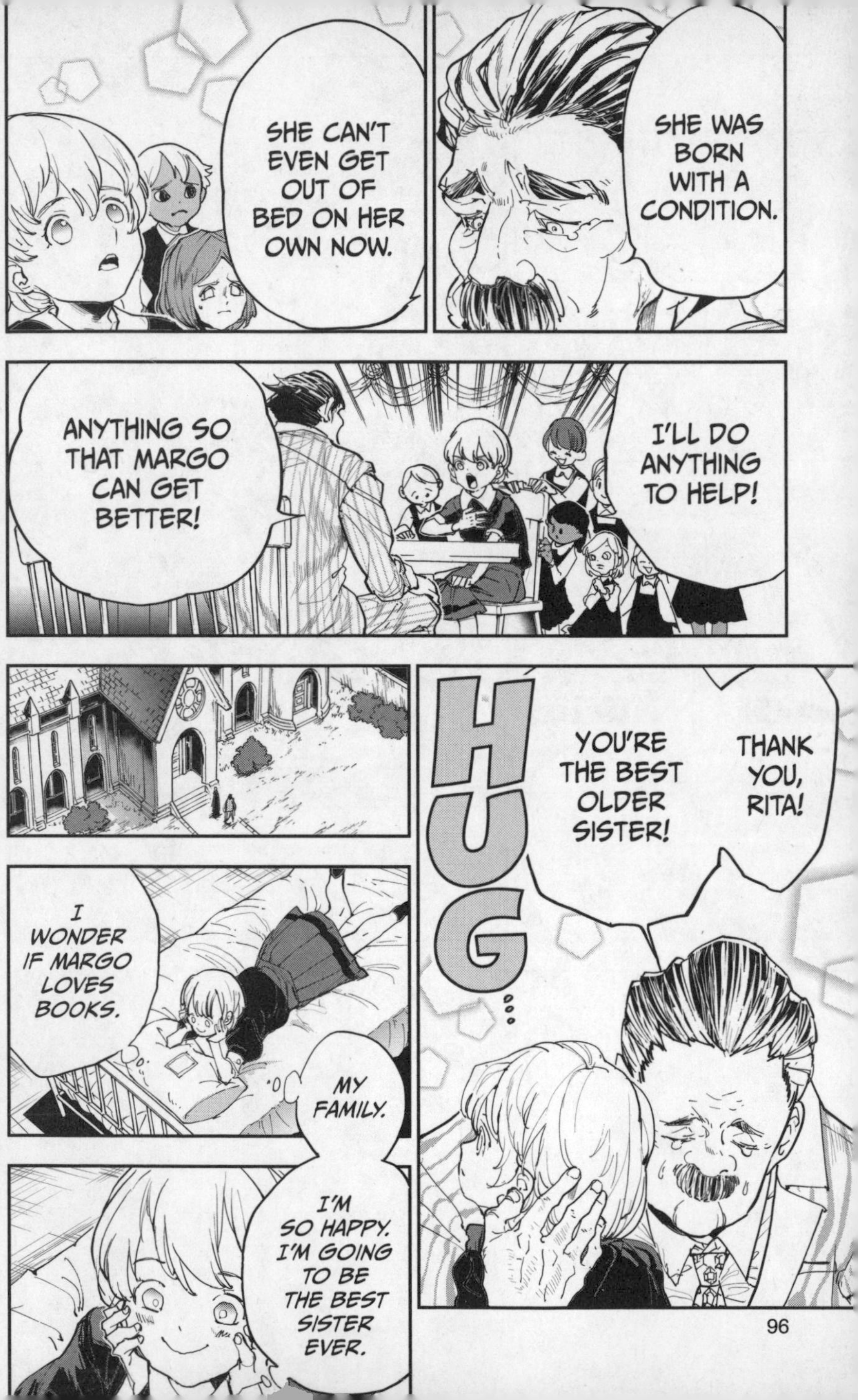
SHE WAS BORN WITH A CONDITION.
SHE CAN'T EVEN GET OUT OF BED ON HER OWN NOW.
I'LL DO ANYTHING TO HELP!
ANYTHING SO THAT MARGO CAN GET BETTER!
THANK YOU, RITA!
YOU'RE THE BEST OLDER SISTER!
HUG...
I WONDER IF MARGO LOVES BOOKS.
MY FAMILY.
I'M SO HAPPY. I'M GOING TO BE THE BEST SISTER EVER.

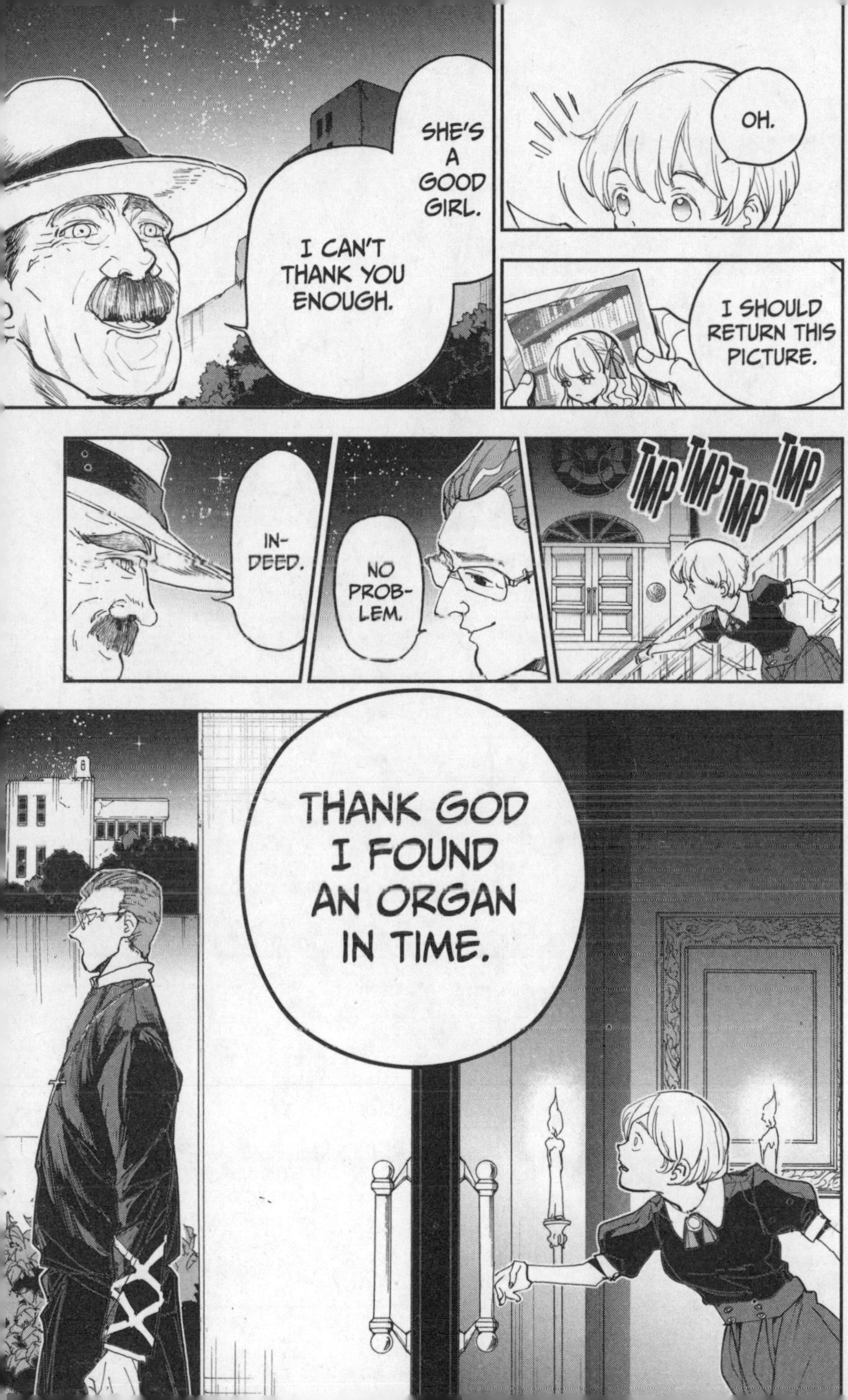
OH.
I SHOULD RETURN THIS PICTURE.
SHE'S A GOOD GIRL.
I CAN'T THANK YOU ENOUGH.
TMP TMP TMP TMP
NO PROB-LEM.
IN-DEED.
THANK GOD I FOUND AN ORGAN IN TIME.

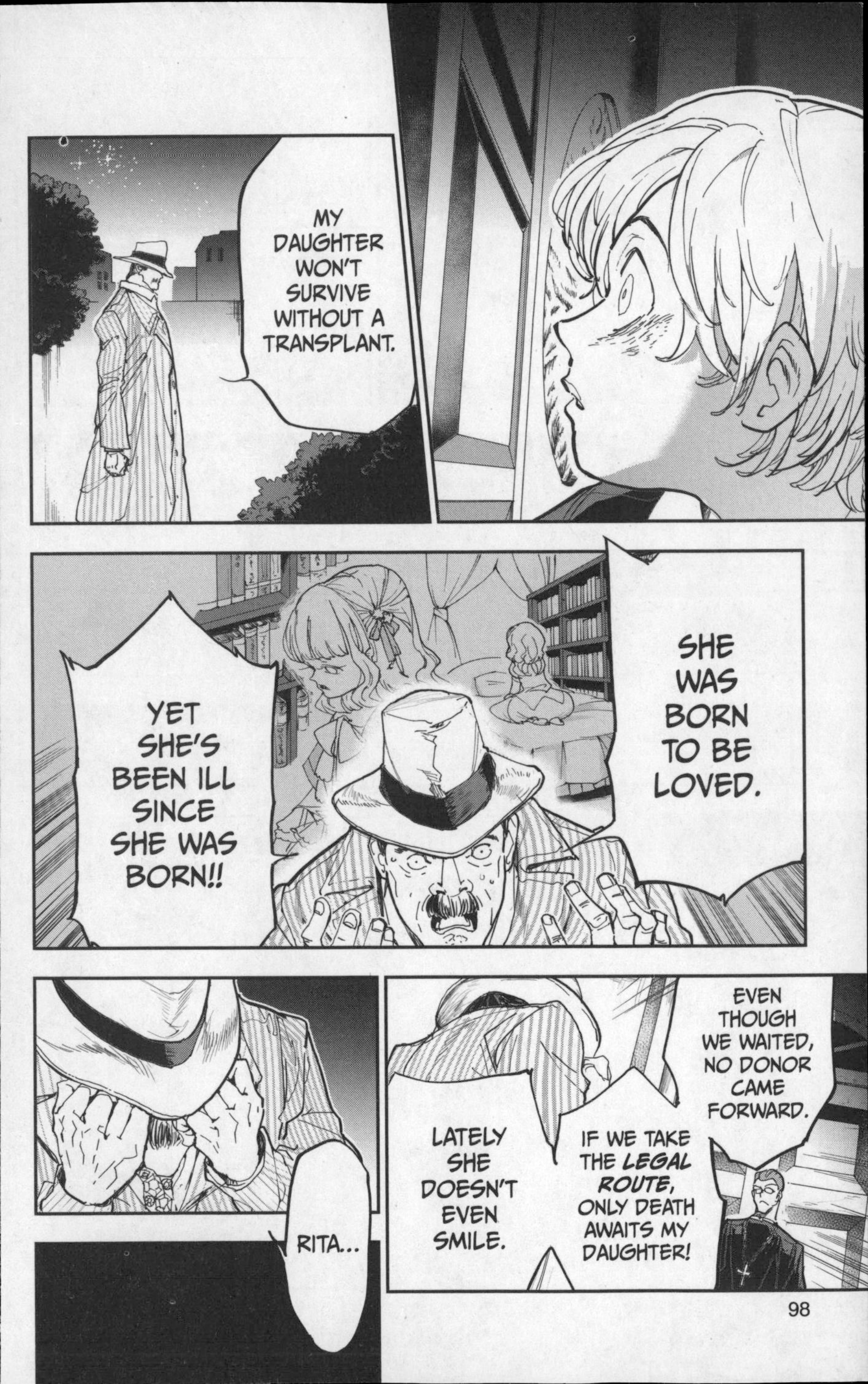
MY DAUGHTER WON'T SURVIVE WITHOUT A TRANSPLANT.
SHE WAS BORN TO BE LOVED.
YET SHE'S BEEN ILL SINCE SHE WAS BORN!!
EVEN THOUGH WE WAITED, NO DONOR CAME FORWARD.
IF WE TAKE THE *LEGAL ROUTE*, ONLY DEATH AWAITS MY DAUGHTER!
LATELY SHE DOESN'T EVEN SMILE.
RITA...

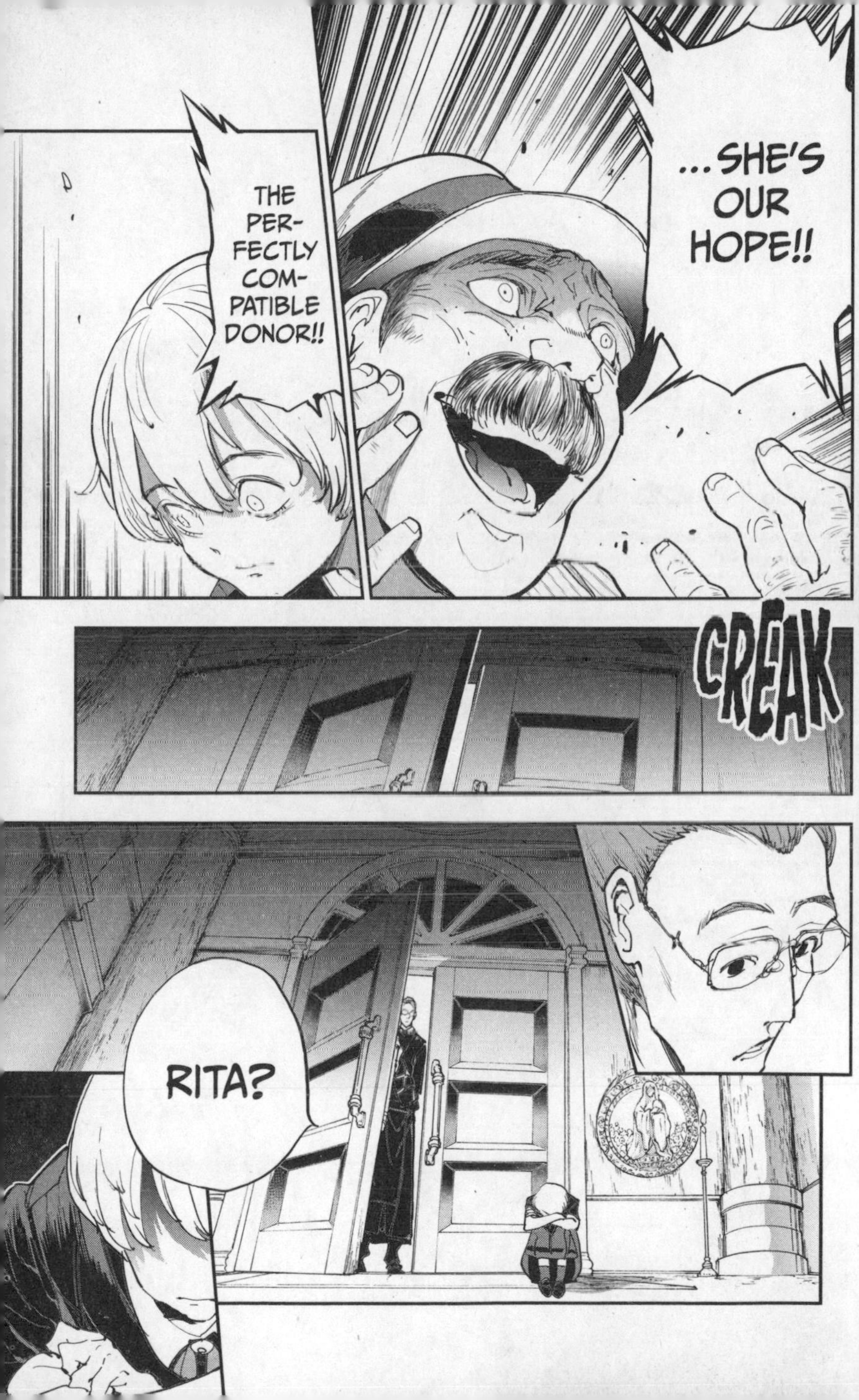
...SHE'S OUR HOPE!!
THE PER-FECTLY COM-PATIBLE DONOR!!
CREAK
RITA?

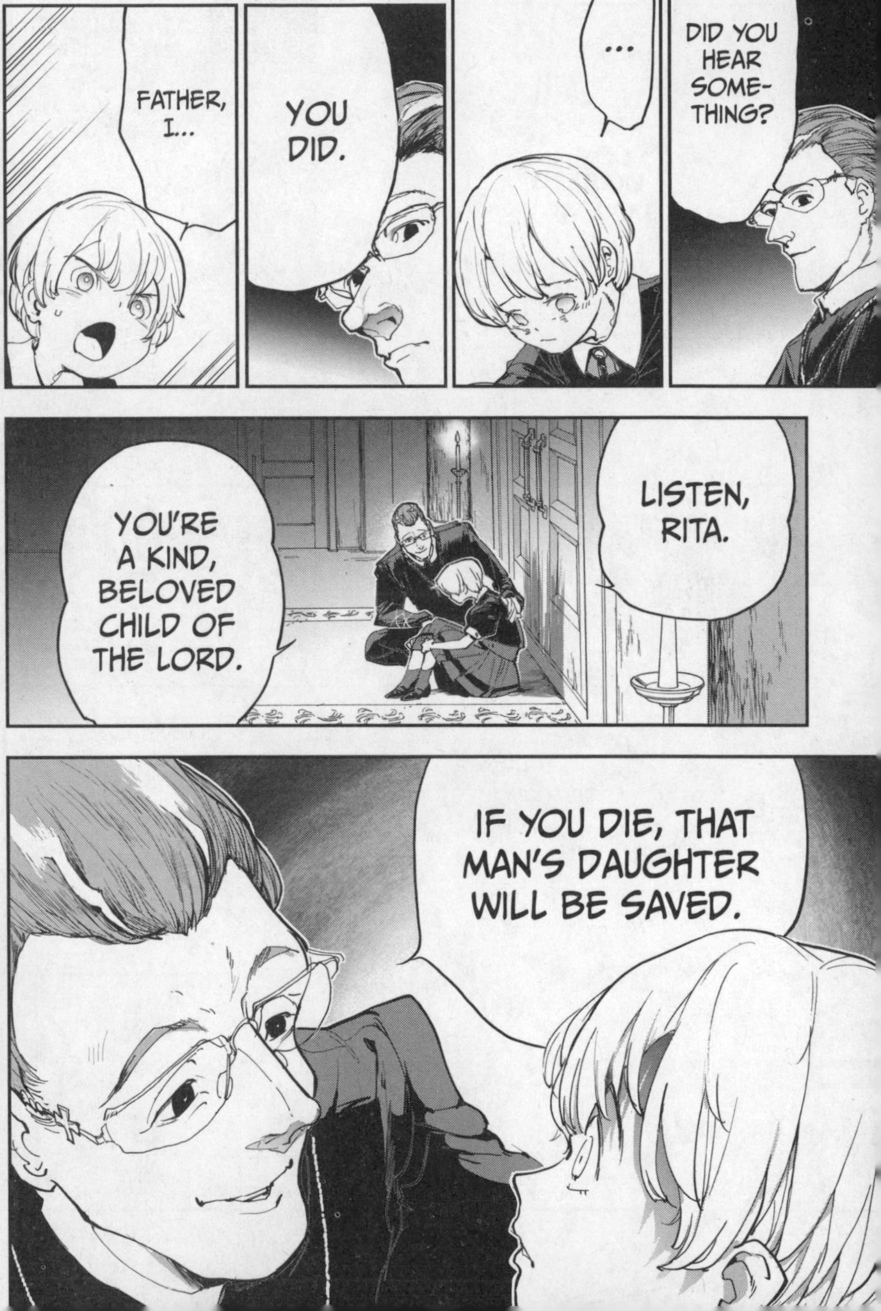
DID YOU HEAR SOME-THING?
...
YOU DID.
FATHER, I...
LISTEN, RITA.
YOU'RE A KIND, BELOVED CHILD OF THE LORD.
IF YOU DIE, THAT MAN'S DAUGHTER WILL BE SAVED.

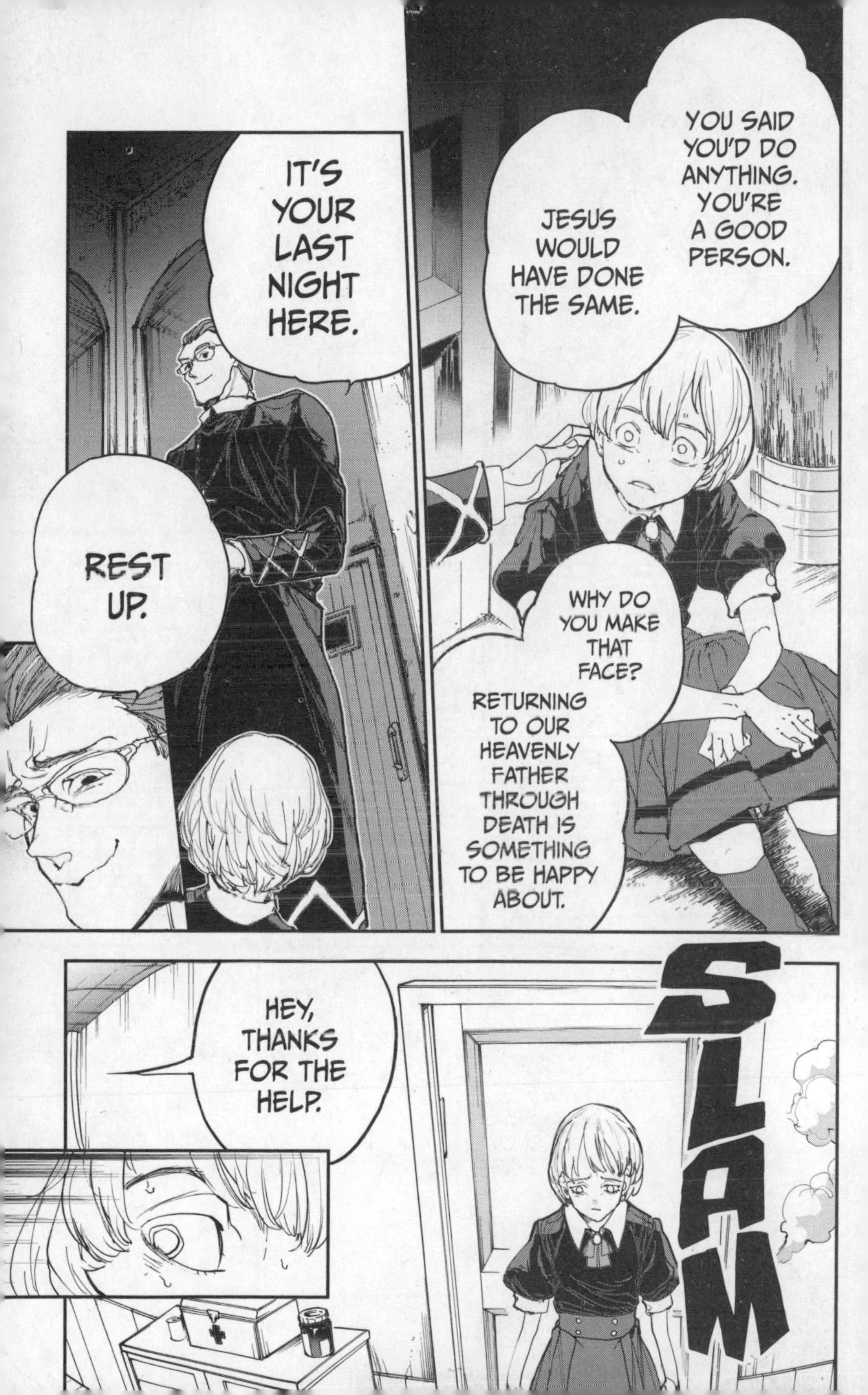
YOU SAID YOU'D DO ANYTHING. YOU'RE A GOOD PERSON.
JESUS WOULD HAVE DONE THE SAME.
WHY DO YOU MAKE THAT FACE?
RETURNING TO OUR HEAVENLY FATHER THROUGH DEATH IS SOMETHING TO BE HAPPY ABOUT.
IT'S YOUR LAST NIGHT HERE.
REST UP.
SLAM
HEY, THANKS FOR THE HELP.

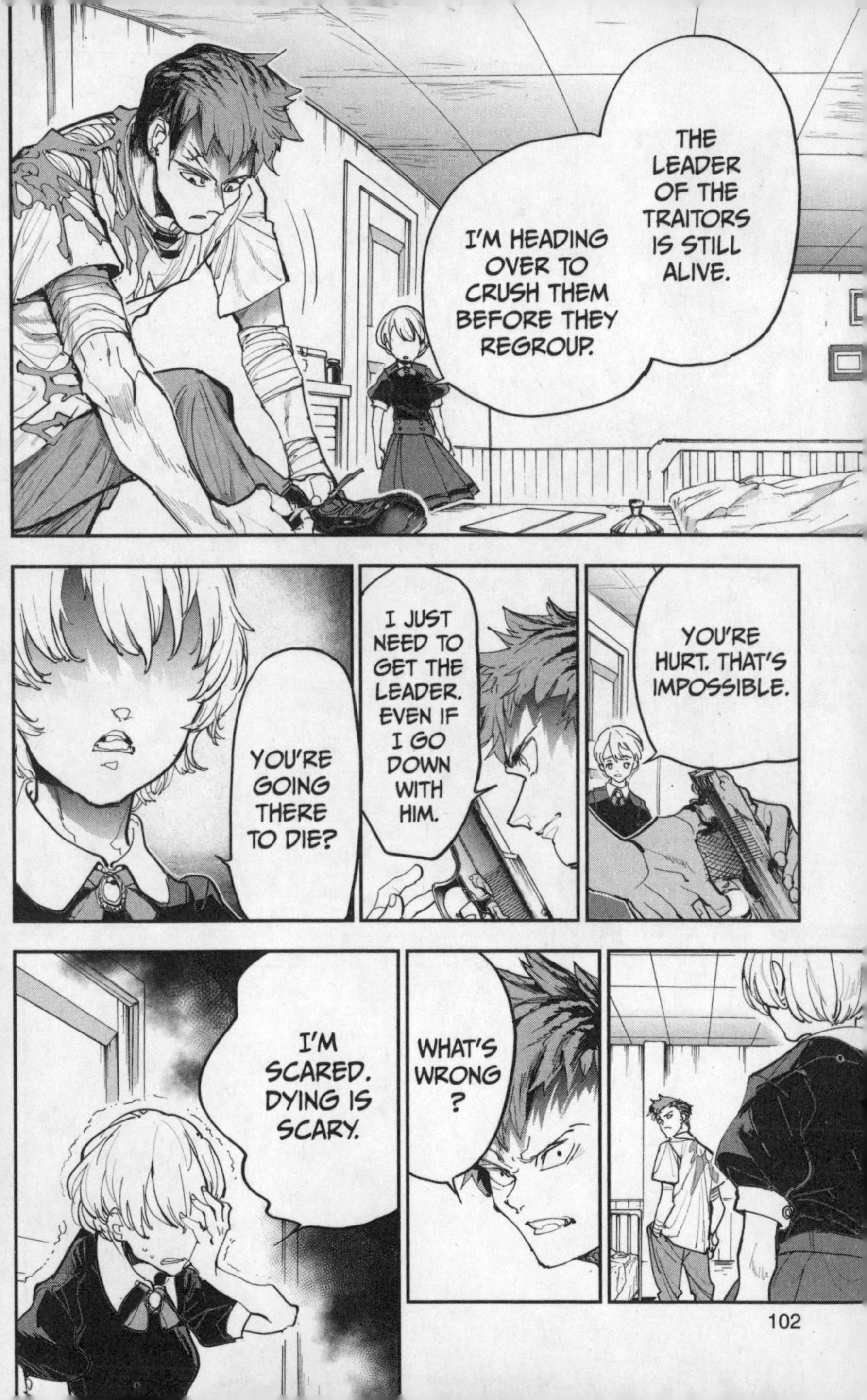
THE LEADER OF THE TRAITORS IS STILL ALIVE.
I'M HEADING OVER TO CRUSH THEM BEFORE THEY REGROUP.
YOU'RE HURT. THAT'S IMPOSSIBLE.
I JUST NEED TO GET THE LEADER. EVEN IF I GO DOWN WITH HIM.
YOU'RE GOING THERE TO DIE?
WHAT'S WRONG ?
I'M SCARED. DYING IS SCARY.

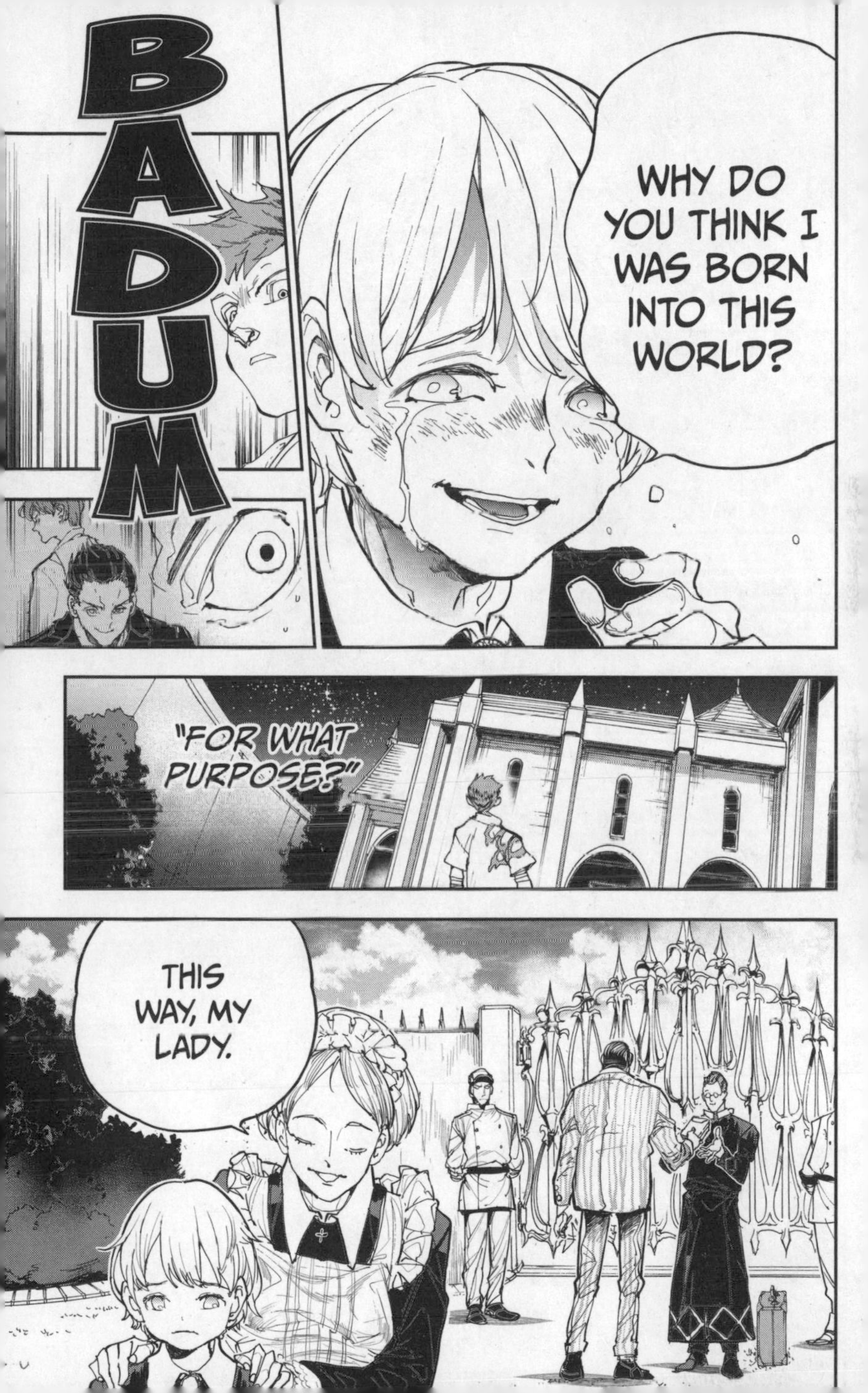
WHY DO YOU THINK I WAS BORN INTO THIS WORLD?
BADUM
"FOR WHAT PURPOSE?"
THIS WAY, MY LADY.

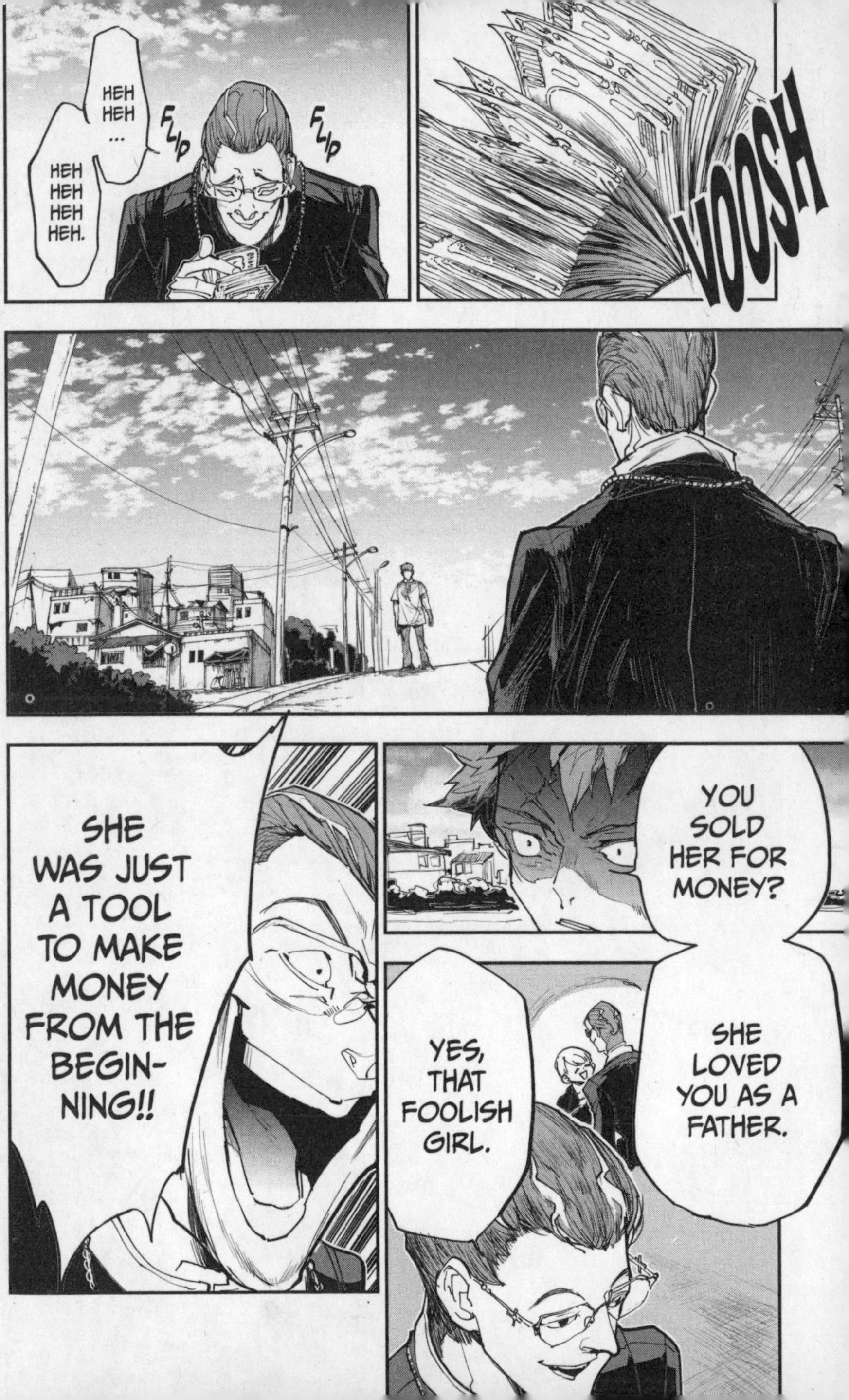
VOOSH
FLIP
FLIP
HEH HEH ...
HEH HEH HEH HEH.
YOU SOLD HER FOR MONEY?
SHE LOVED YOU AS A FATHER.
YES, THAT FOOLISH GIRL.
SHE WAS JUST A TOOL TO MAKE MONEY FROM THE BEGIN- NING!!

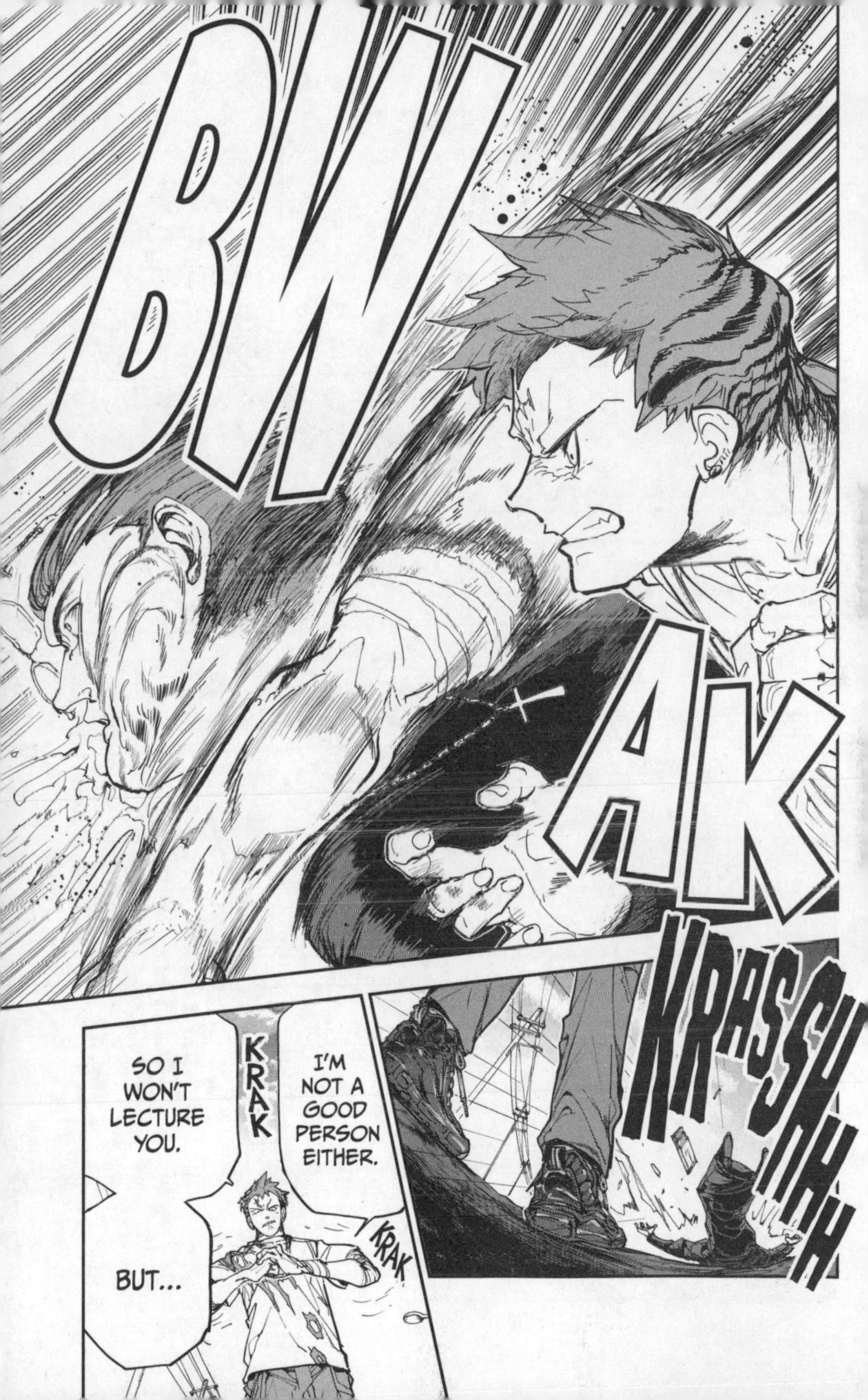
BWAK
KRASHHHH
I'M NOT A GOOD PERSON EITHER.
KRAK
SO I WON'T LECTURE YOU.
KRAK
BUT...

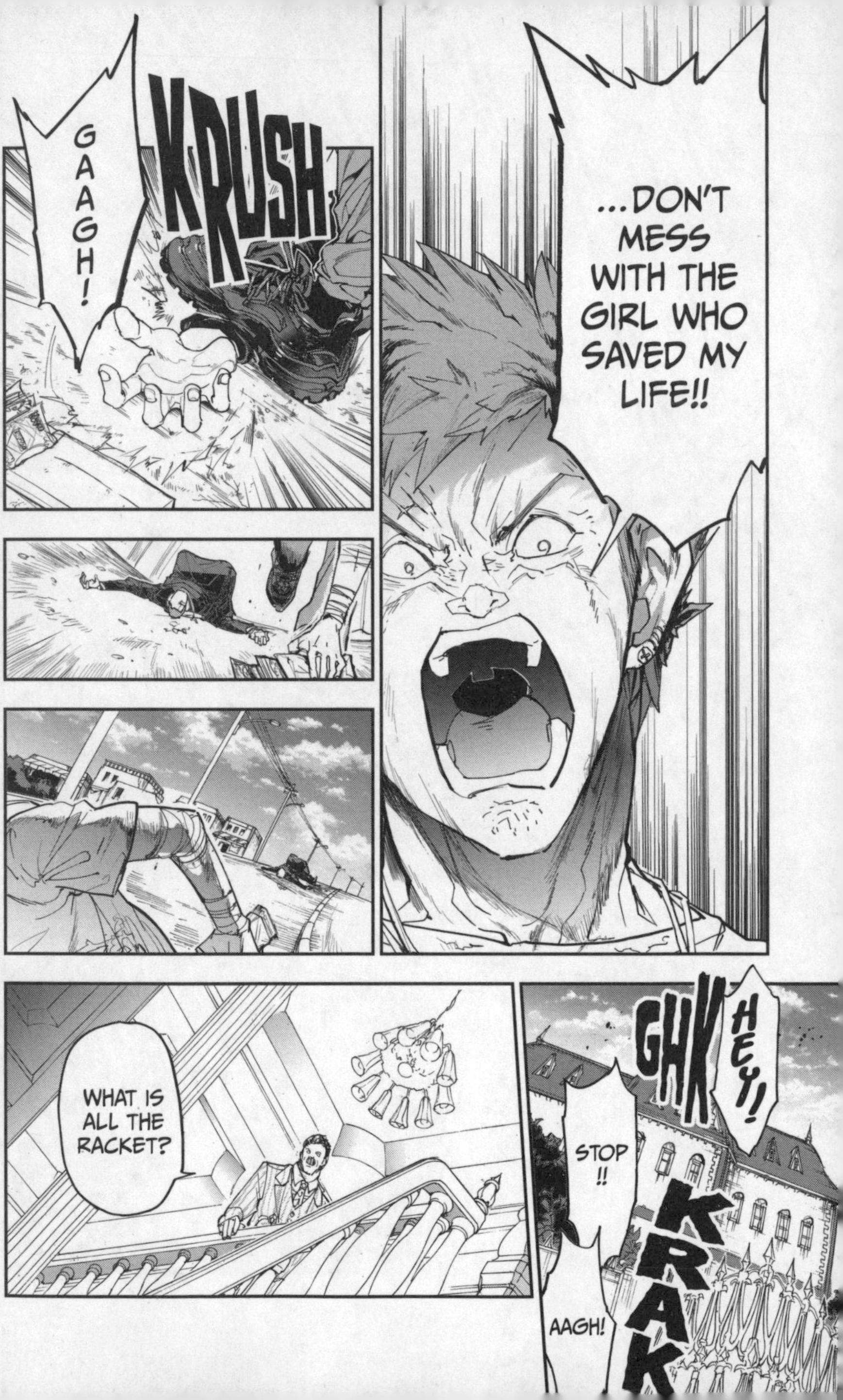
...DON'T MESS WITH THE GIRL WHO SAVED MY LIFE!!
KRUSH
GAAGH!
HEY!
GHK
STOP!!
KRAK
AAGH!
WHAT IS ALL THE RACKET?

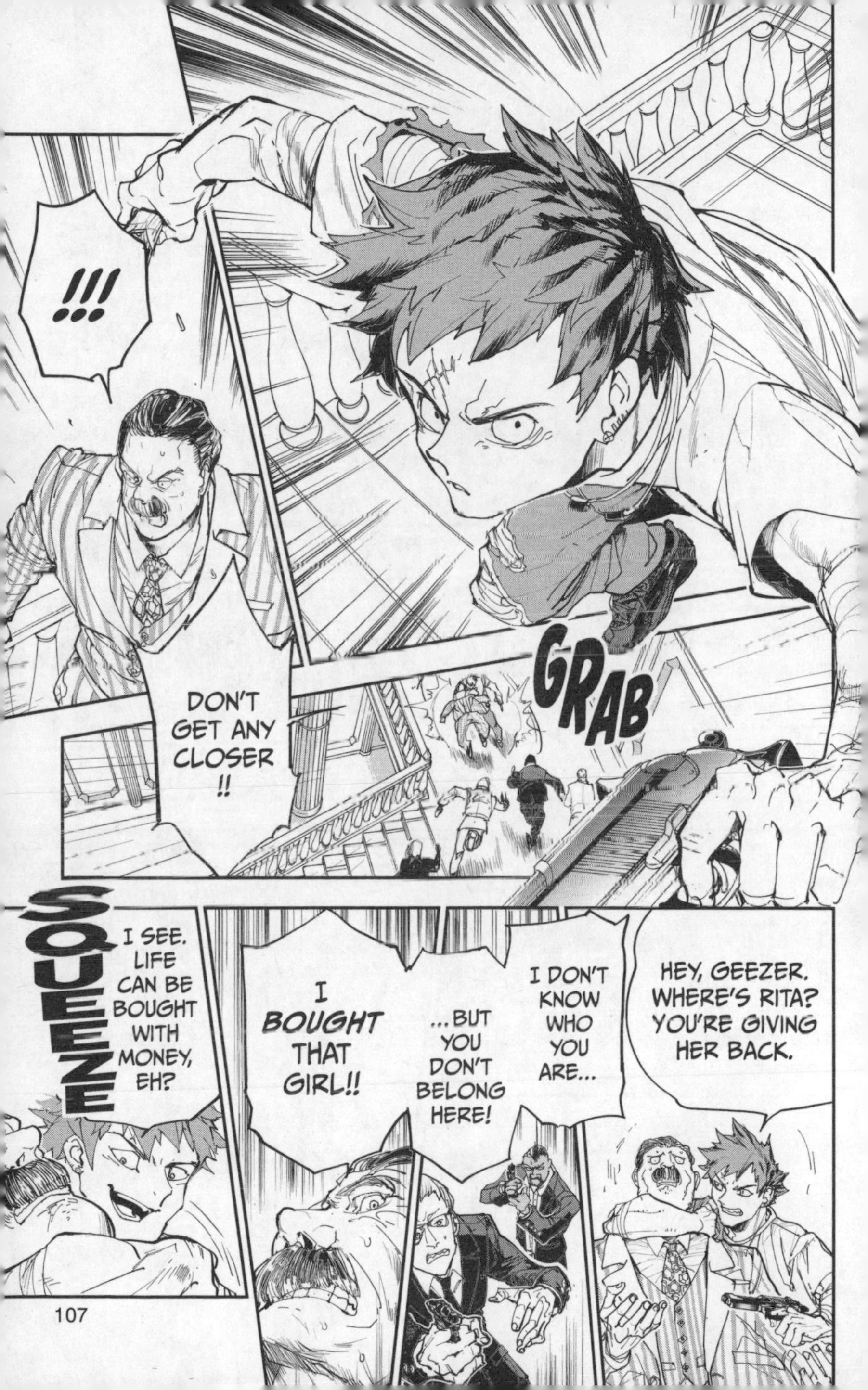
!!!
GRAB
DON'T GET ANY CLOSER !!
HEY, GEEZER. WHERE'S RITA? YOU'RE GIVING HER BACK.
I DON'T KNOW WHO YOU ARE...
...BUT YOU DON'T BELONG HERE!
I *BOUGHT* THAT GIRL!!
SQUEEZE
I SEE. LIFE CAN BE BOUGHT WITH MONEY, EH?

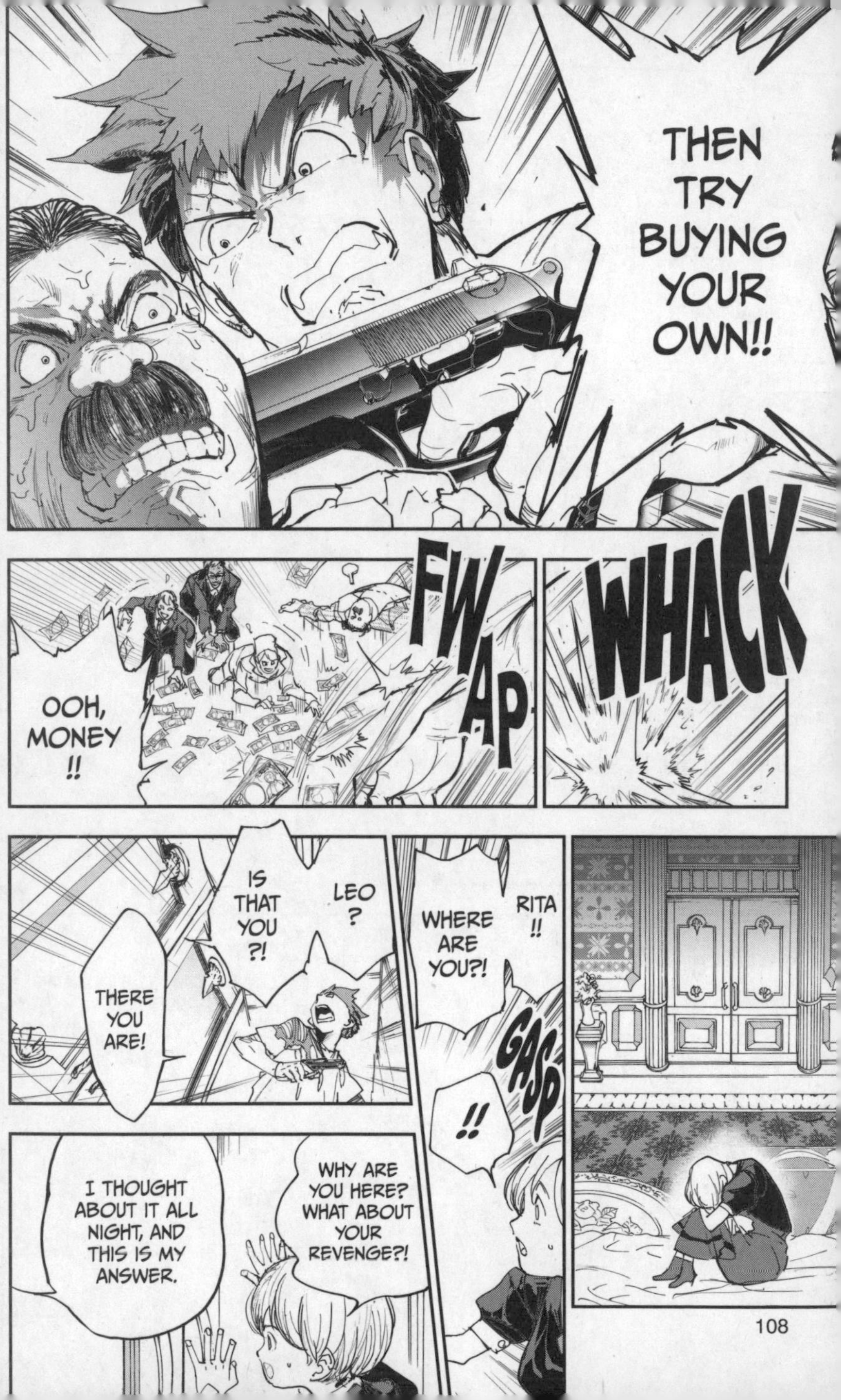
THEN TRY BUYING YOUR OWN!!
WHACK
FWAP
OOH, MONEY!!
RITA!!
WHERE ARE YOU?!
GASP
!!
LEO?
IS THAT YOU?!
THERE YOU ARE!
WHY ARE YOU HERE? WHAT ABOUT YOUR REVENGE?!
I THOUGHT ABOUT IT ALL NIGHT, AND THIS IS MY ANSWER.

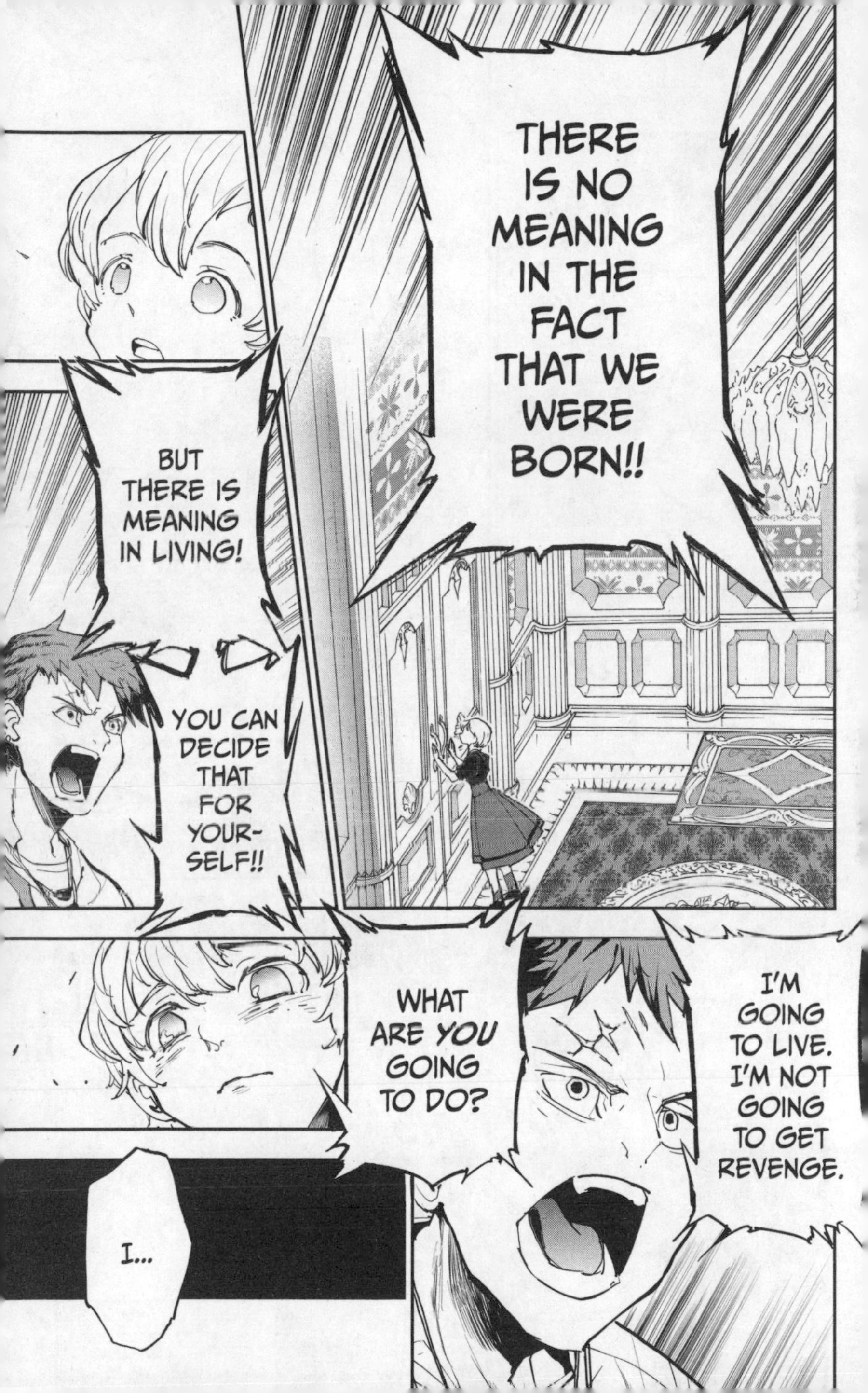
THERE IS NO MEANING IN THE FACT THAT WE WERE BORN!!
BUT THERE IS MEANING IN LIVING!
YOU CAN DECIDE THAT FOR YOURSELF!!
I'M GOING TO LIVE. I'M NOT GOING TO GET REVENGE.
WHAT ARE *YOU* GOING TO DO?
I...

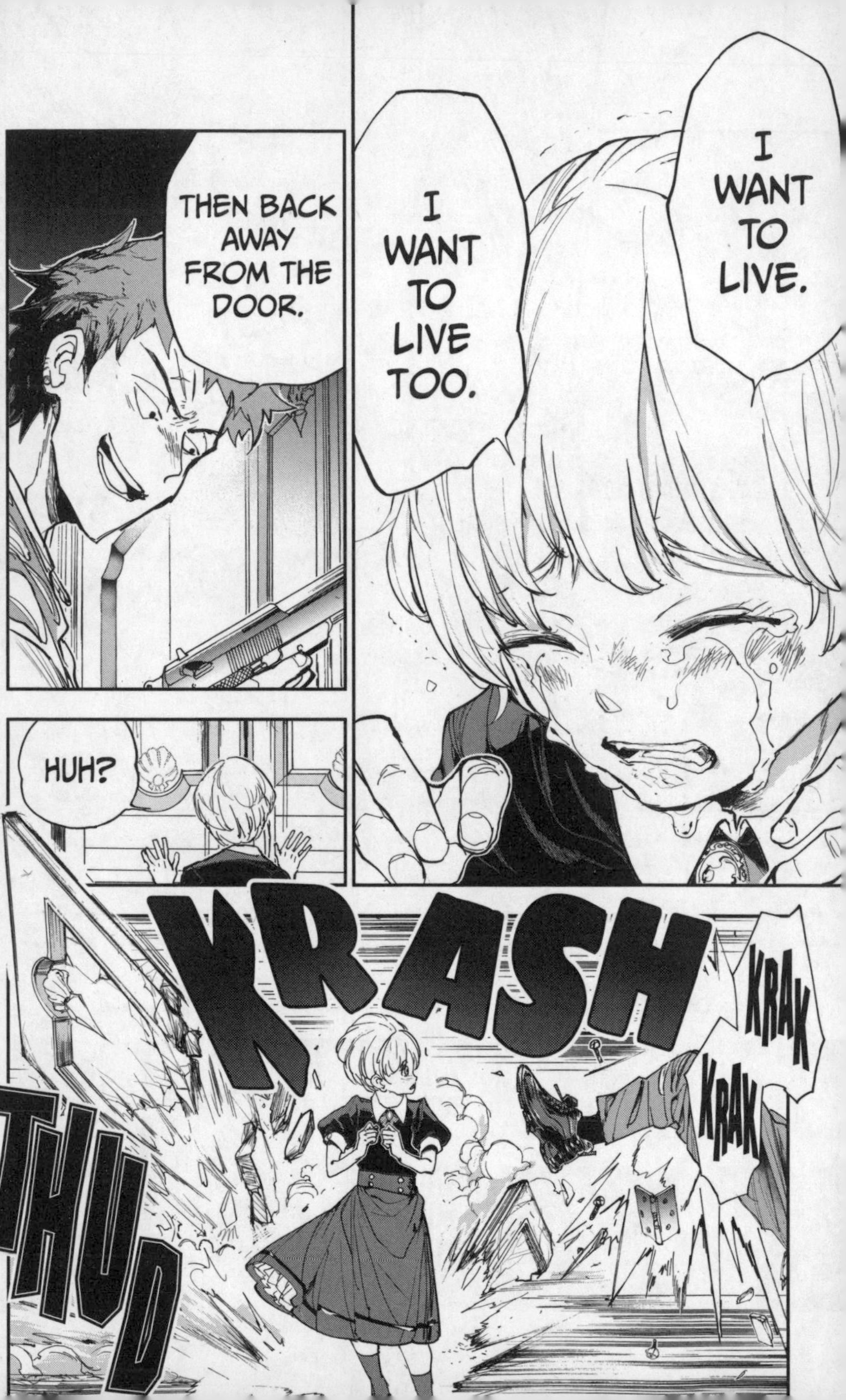
I WANT TO LIVE.
I WANT TO LIVE TOO.
THEN BACK AWAY FROM THE DOOR.
HUH?
KRASH
KRAK KRAK
THUD

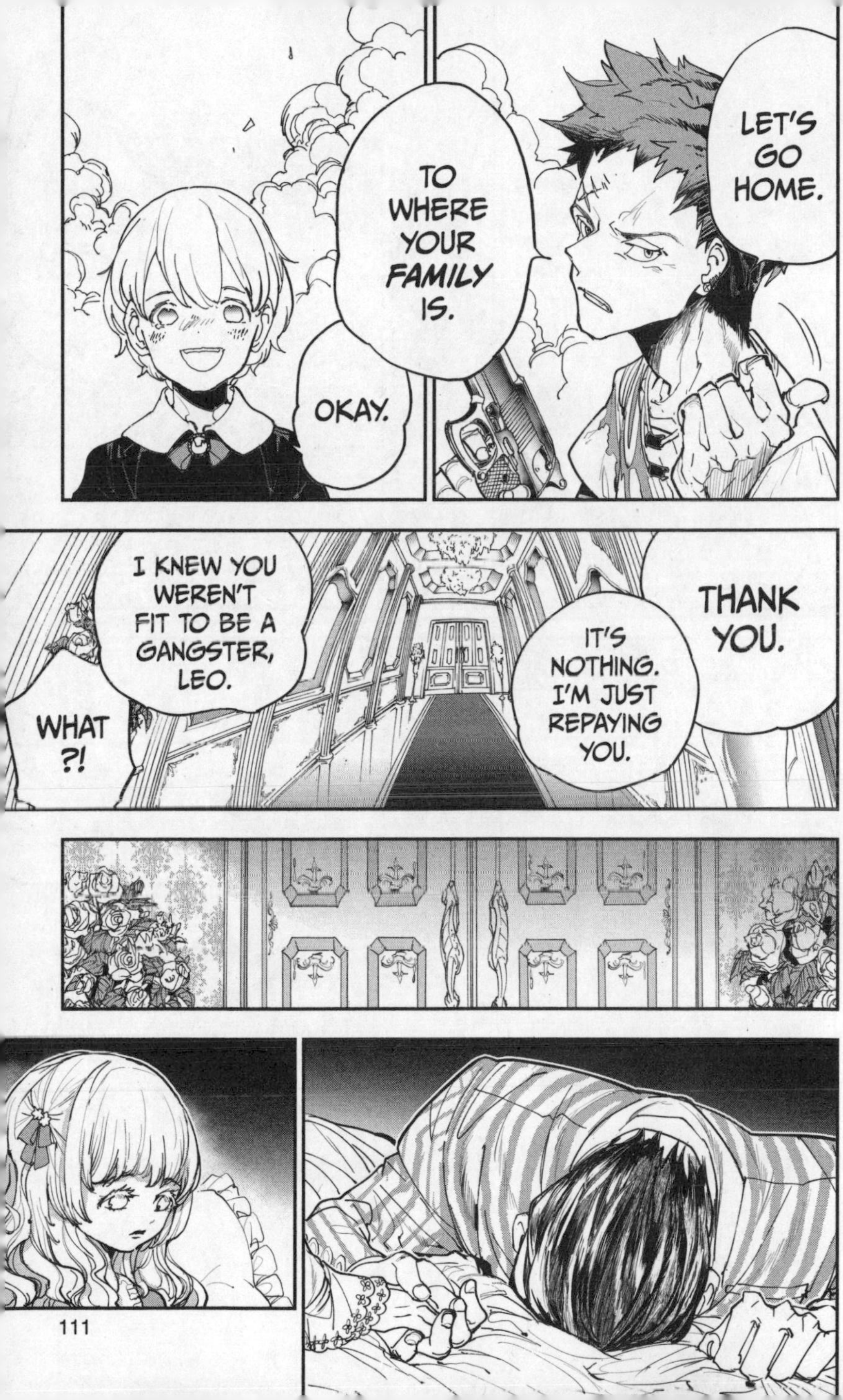
LET'S GO HOME.
TO WHERE YOUR *FAMILY* IS.
OKAY.
THANK YOU.
IT'S NOTHING. I'M JUST REPAYING YOU.
I KNEW YOU WEREN'T FIT TO BE A GANGSTER, LEO.
WHAT?!

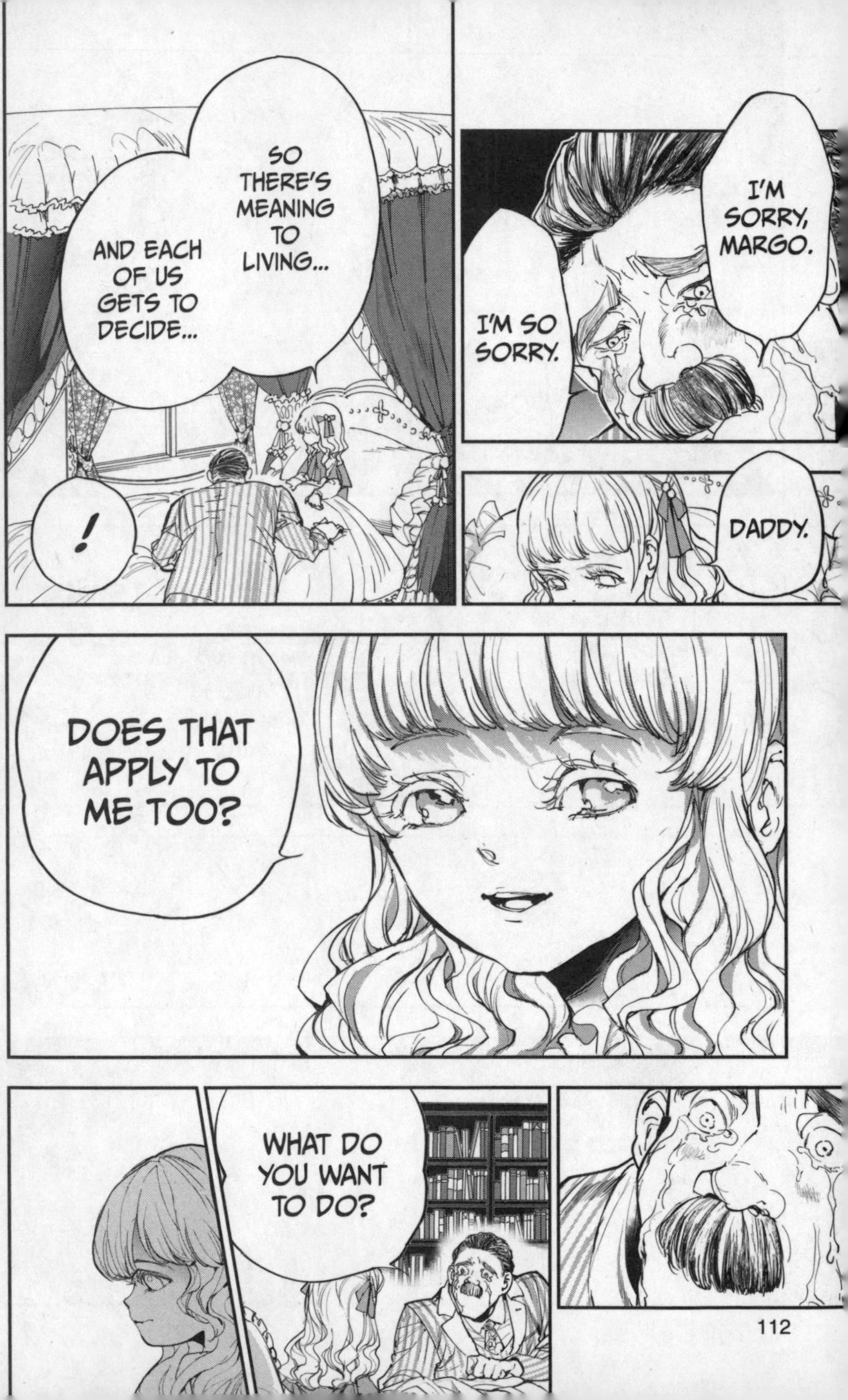
I'M SORRY, MARGO.
I'M SO SORRY.
DADDY.
SO THERE'S MEANING TO LIVING...
AND EACH OF US GETS TO DECIDE...
!
DOES THAT APPLY TO ME TOO?
WHAT DO YOU WANT TO DO?

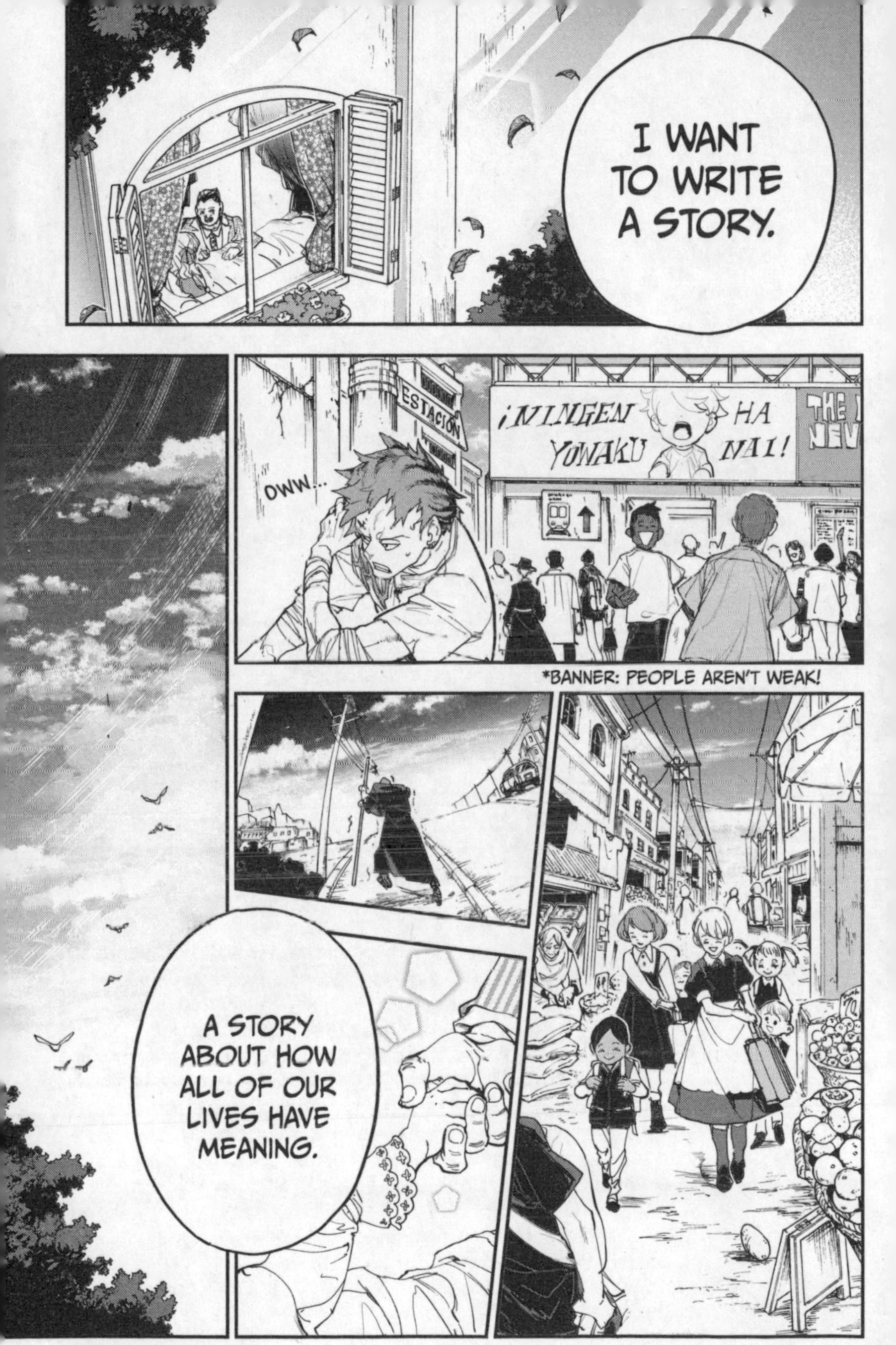
I WANT TO WRITE A STORY.
ESTACIÓN
¡NINGEN HA YOWAKU NAI!
OWW...
*BANNER: PEOPLE AREN'T WEAK!
A STORY ABOUT HOW ALL OF OUR LIVES HAVE MEANING.

WE WERE BORN (FIN)

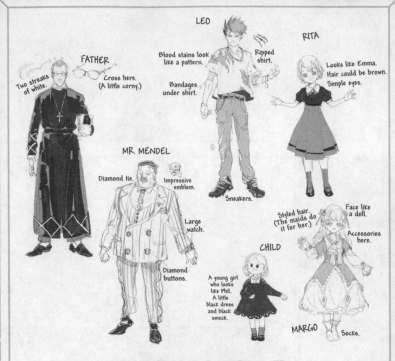

LEO
RITA
FATHER
Two streaks of white.
Cross here. (A little corny.)
Blood stains look like a pattern.
Ripped shirt.
Bandages under shirt.
Looks like Emma. Hair could be brown. Simple eyes.
MR. MENDEL
Diamond tie.
Impressive emblem.
Sneakers.
Large watch.
Diamond buttons.
Styled hair. (The maids do it for her.)
Face like a doll.
Accessories here.
CHILD
A young girl who looks like Phil. A little black dress and black smock.
MARGO
Socks.

SHIRAI'S BEHIND-THE-SCENES STORIES #3

- After taking *The Promised Neverland* to the editors, there was a competition for a special issue two weeks later. This was the first story I came up with. I wrote it super fast. But for some reason I nixed it, wrote "Kono Saburo," and turned that in instead. (My editor said, "Why?! This was fine.")
- Even though I wrote it super fast, I think this idea wasn't from scratch. If *The Promised Neverland* got a good response, I expected that they would ask me to do a one-shot similar to it, so I think I had this story prepared. But when I wasn't asked to write something similar, I thought maybe I should do something more "me" for my first shot at being published. Is that why I nixed it? I think that's what happened.
- After *The Promised Neverland* ended, I revised and adjusted a few pages. But I hadn't read the original storyboards in a while, and I thought that Leo's brother was similar to James Ratri.* (*A character from *The Promised Neverland*. I didn't make them similar consciously.)
- Demizu Sensei's character designs (pictured above) are great, so please look at them!
- Demizu Sensei drew that the mice are attached to Leo's boss. That was one of my favorite details.

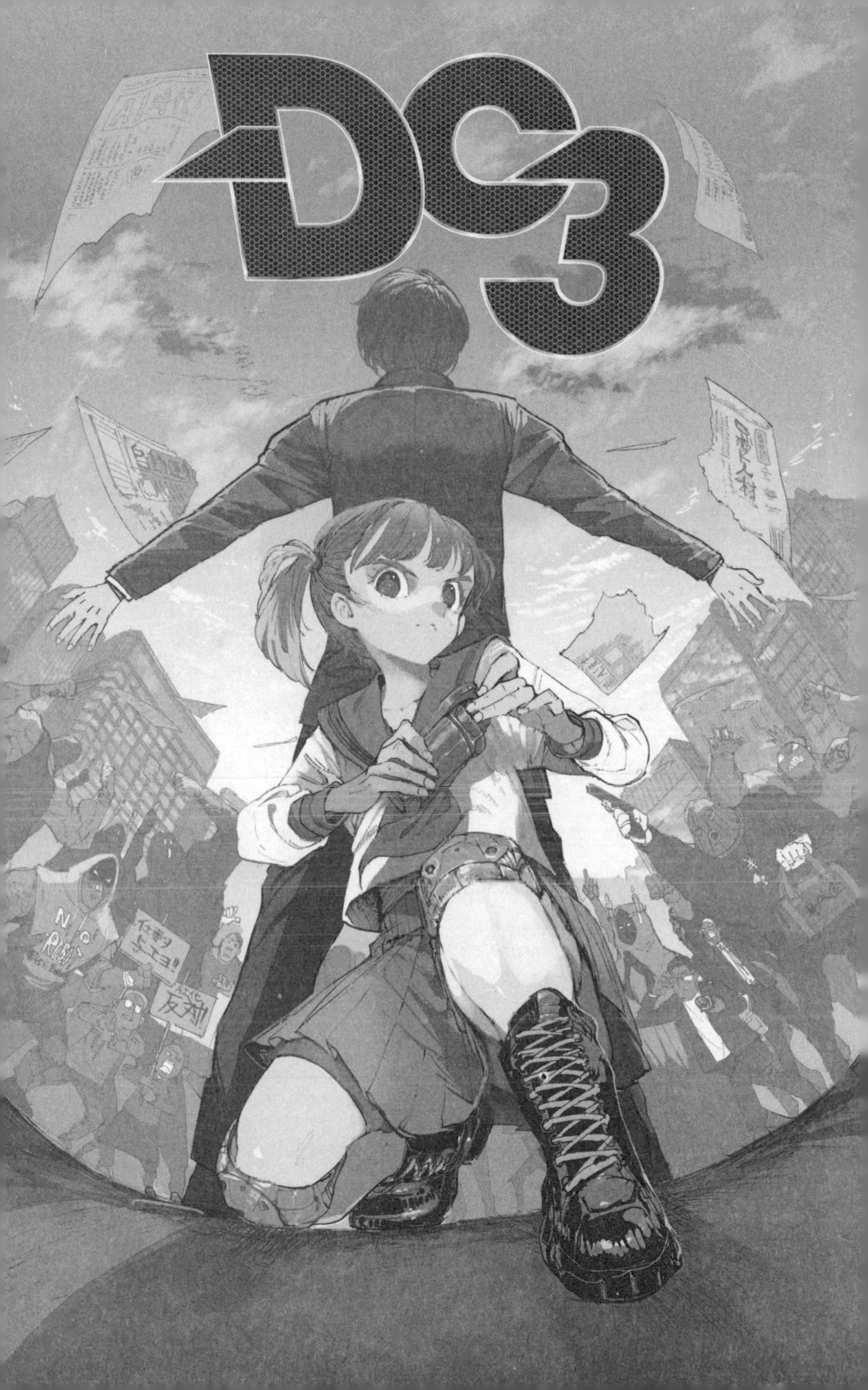
DC3
NO ROBOT
AI化
反対!!

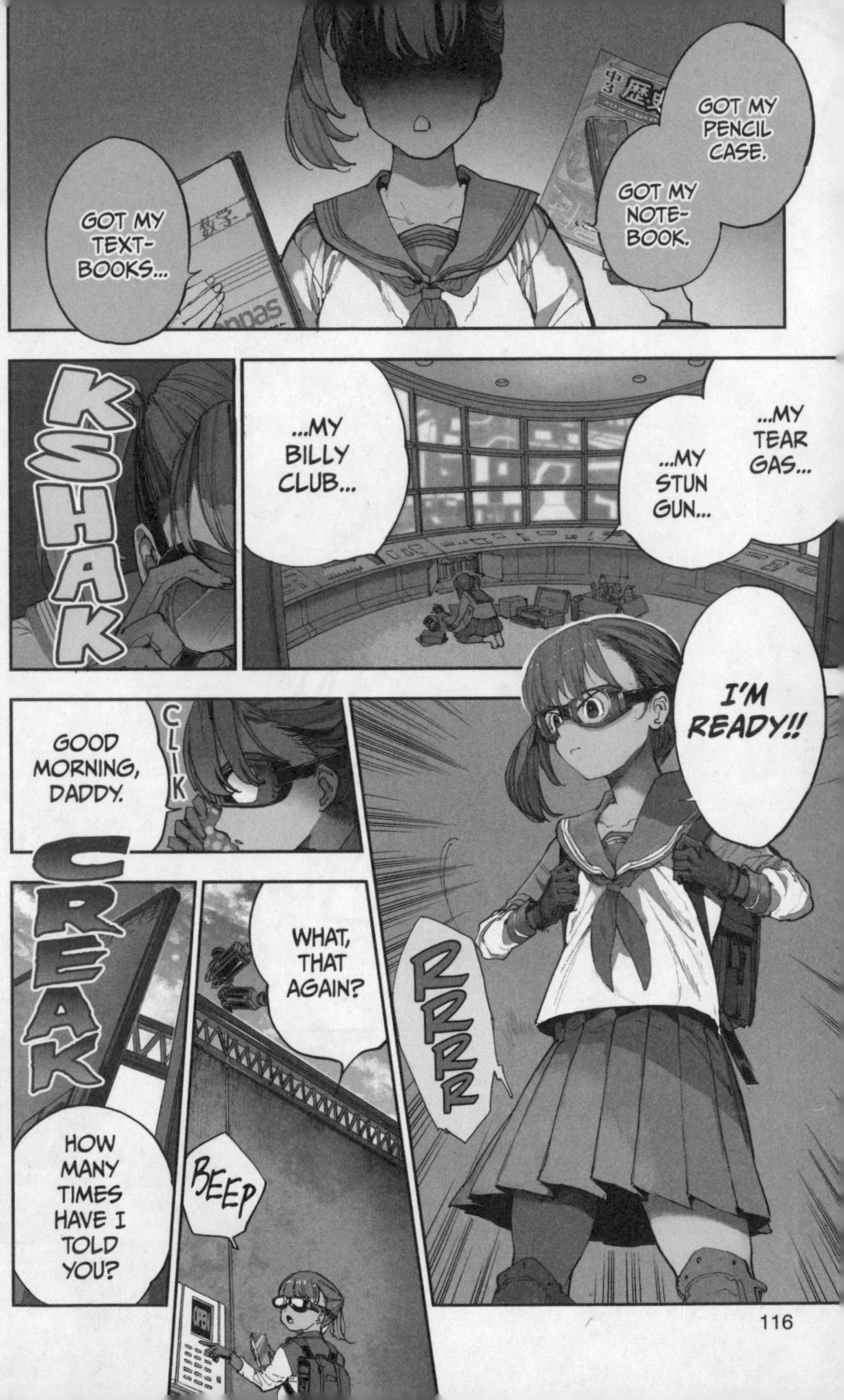
GOT MY PENCIL CASE.
GOT MY NOTE-BOOK.
GOT MY TEXT-BOOKS...
...MY TEAR GAS...
...MY STUN GUN...
...MY BILLY CLUB...
KSHAK
I'M READY!!
RRRR
CLIK
GOOD MORNING, DADDY.
WHAT, THAT AGAIN?
BEEP
CREAK
HOW MANY TIMES HAVE I TOLD YOU?

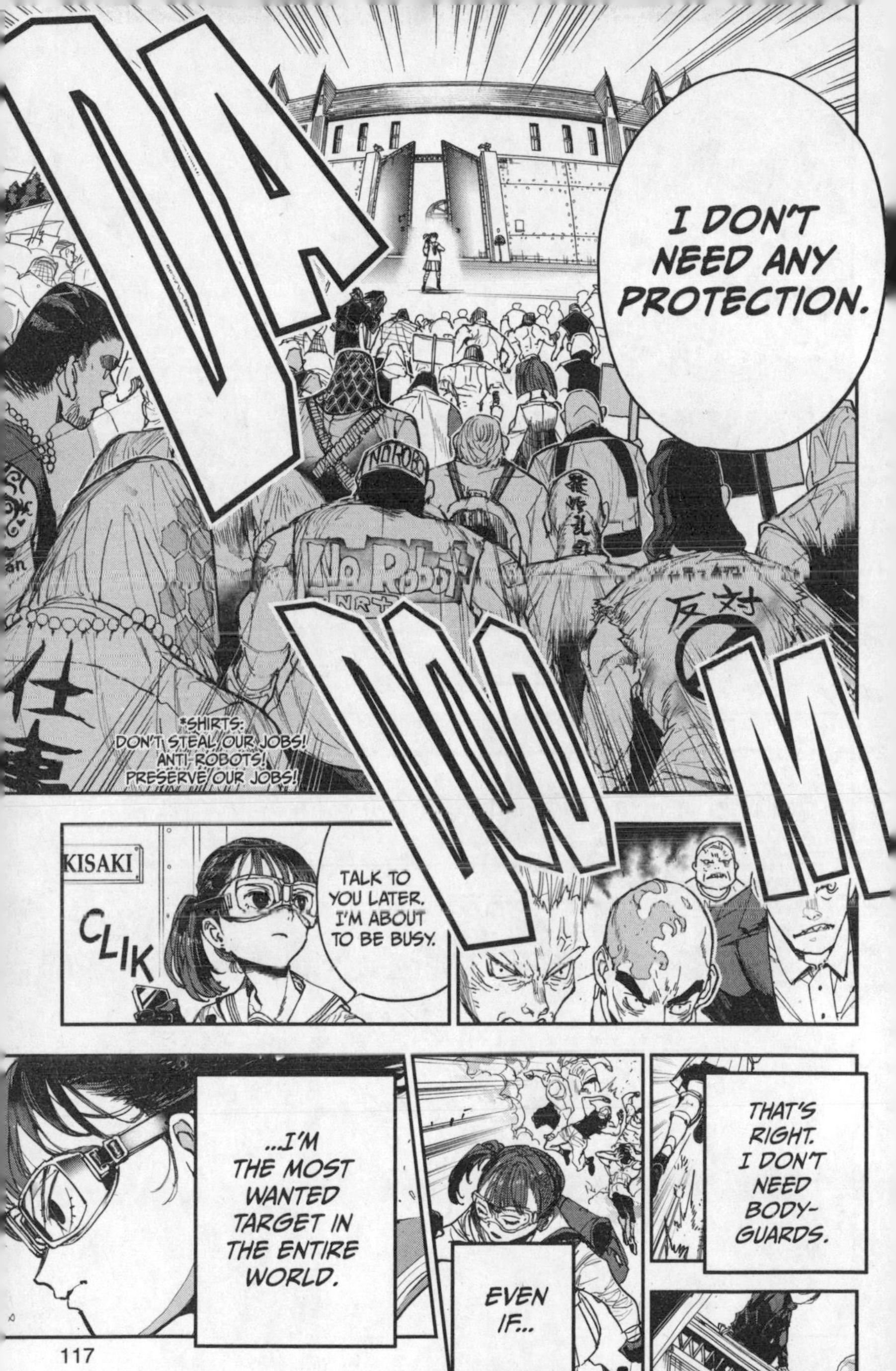
I DON'T NEED ANY PROTECTION.
*SHIRTS: DON'T STEAL OUR JOBS! ANTI-ROBOTS! PRESERVE OUR JOBS!
KISAKI
TALK TO YOU LATER. I'M ABOUT TO BE BUSY.
CLIK
THAT'S RIGHT. I DON'T NEED BODY-GUARDS.
EVEN IF...
...I'M THE MOST WANTED TARGET IN THE ENTIRE WORLD.

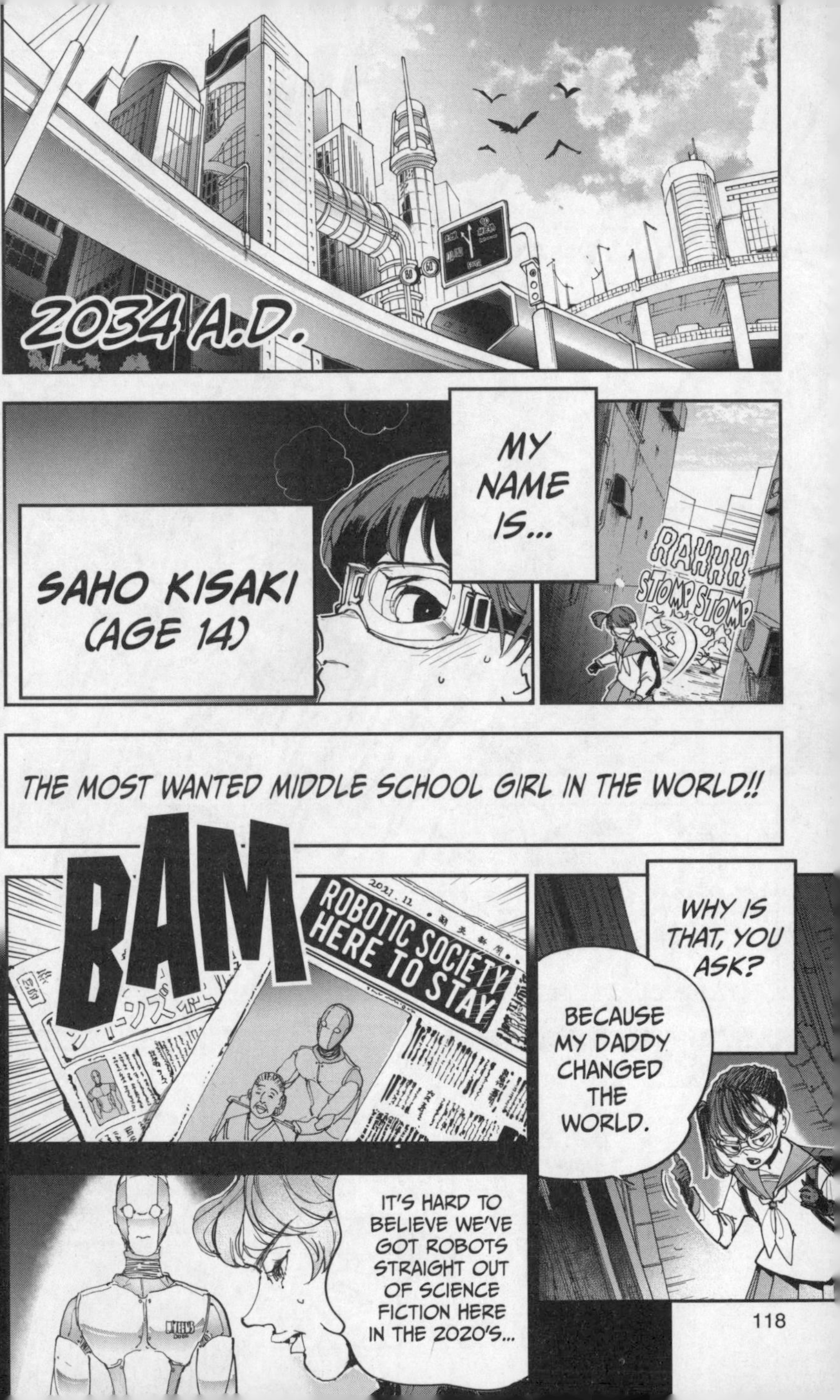
2034 A.D.
RAHHH
STOMP STOMP
MY NAME IS...
SAHO KISAKI (AGE 14)
THE MOST WANTED MIDDLE SCHOOL GIRL IN THE WORLD!!
WHY IS THAT, YOU ASK?
BECAUSE MY DADDY CHANGED THE WORLD.
BAM
2021.12
ROBOTIC SOCIETY HERE TO STAY
IT'S HARD TO BELIEVE WE'VE GOT ROBOTS STRAIGHT OUT OF SCIENCE FICTION HERE IN THE 2020'S...

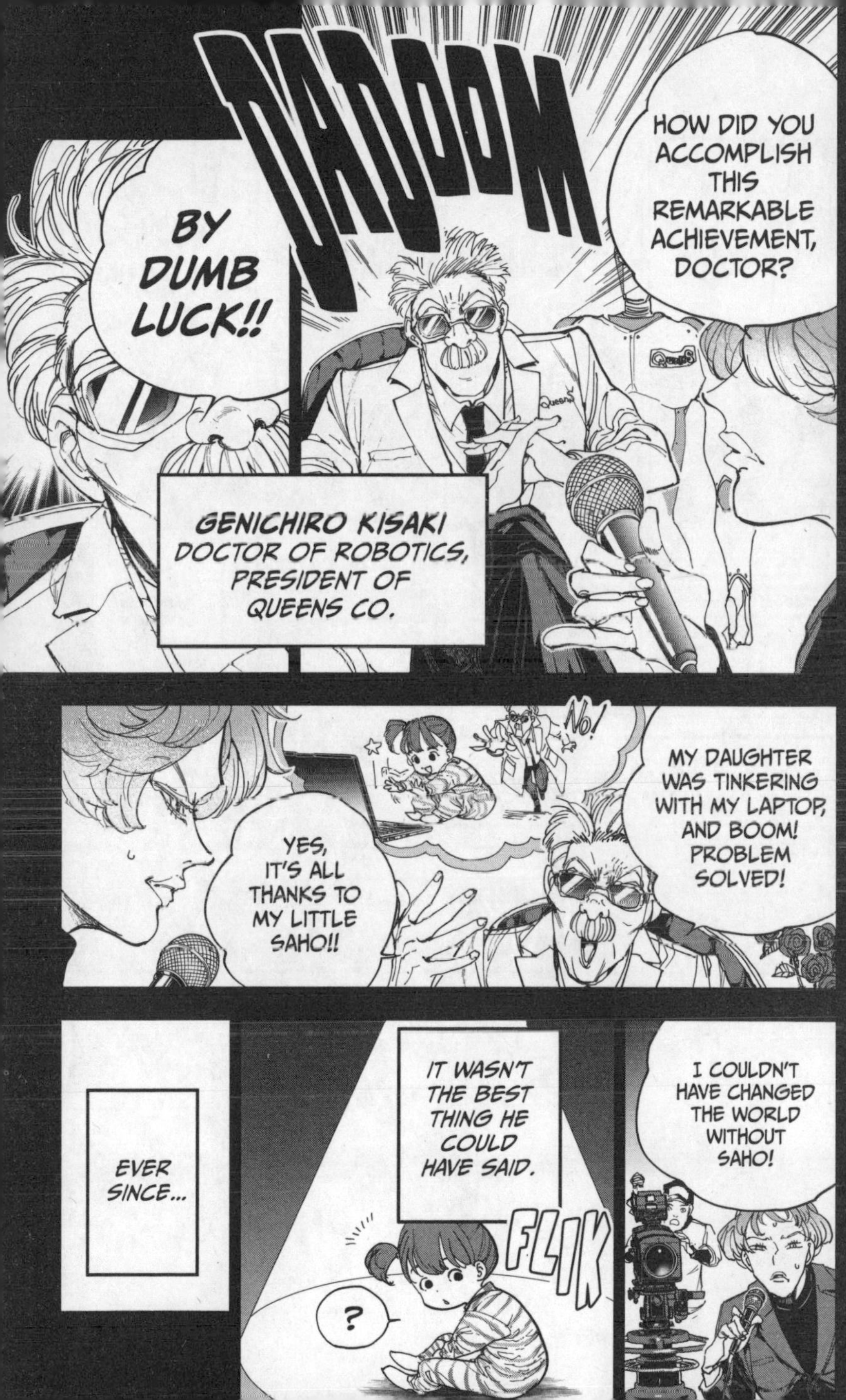
HOW DID YOU ACCOMPLISH THIS REMARKABLE ACHIEVEMENT, DOCTOR?
TADOOM
GENICHIRO KISAKI DOCTOR OF ROBOTICS, PRESIDENT OF QUEENS CO.
BY DUMB LUCK!!
MY DAUGHTER WAS TINKERING WITH MY LAPTOP, AND BOOM! PROBLEM SOLVED!
No!
YES, IT'S ALL THANKS TO MY LITTLE SAHO!!
I COULDN'T HAVE CHANGED THE WORLD WITHOUT SAHO!
IT WASN'T THE BEST THING HE COULD HAVE SAID.
FLIK
?
EVER SINCE...

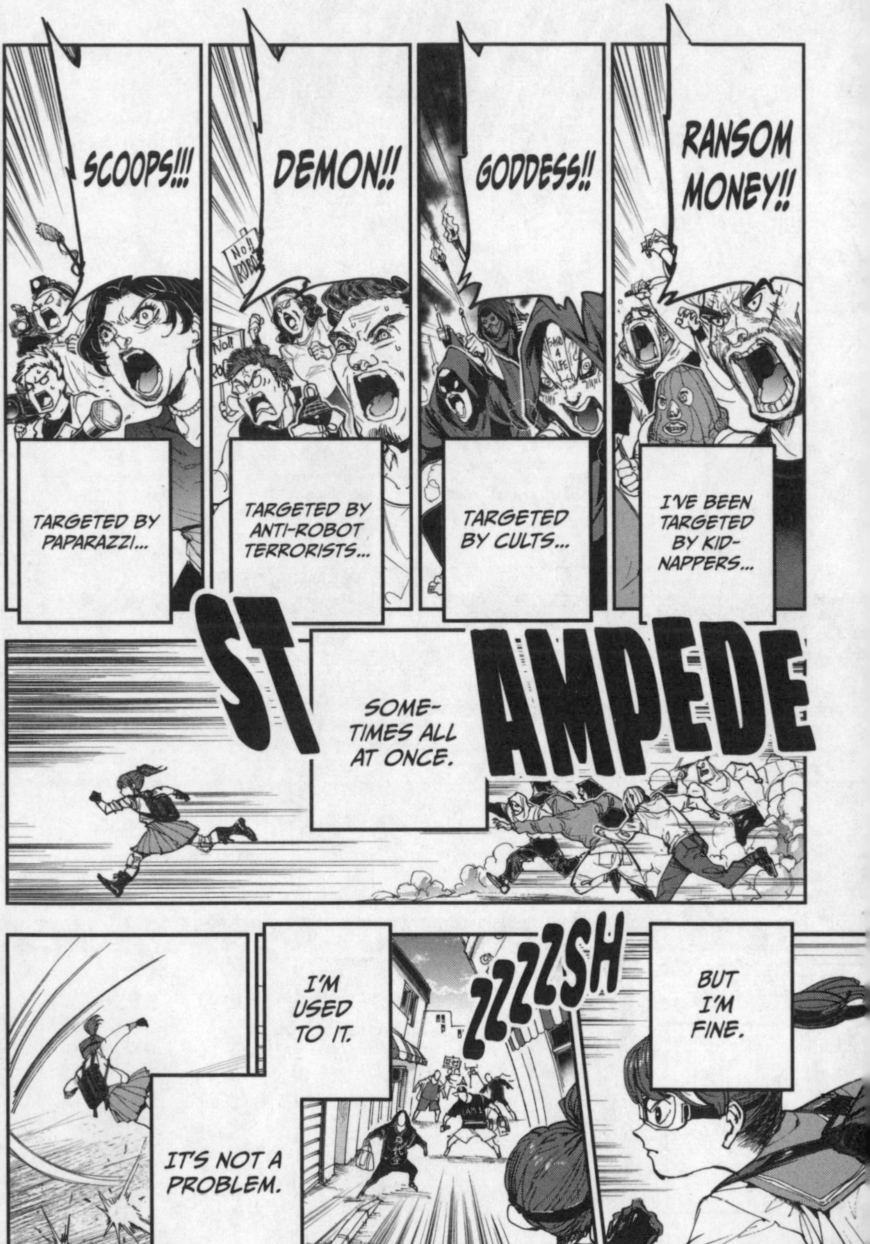
RANSOM MONEY!!
I'VE BEEN TARGETED BY KID-NAPPERS...
GODDESS!!
TARGETED BY CULTS...
DEMON!!
TARGETED BY ANTI-ROBOT TERRORISTS...
SCOOPS!!!
TARGETED BY PAPARAZZI...
STAMPEDE
SOME-TIMES ALL AT ONCE.
BUT I'M FINE.
ZZZZZSH
I'M USED TO IT.
IT'S NOT A PROBLEM.

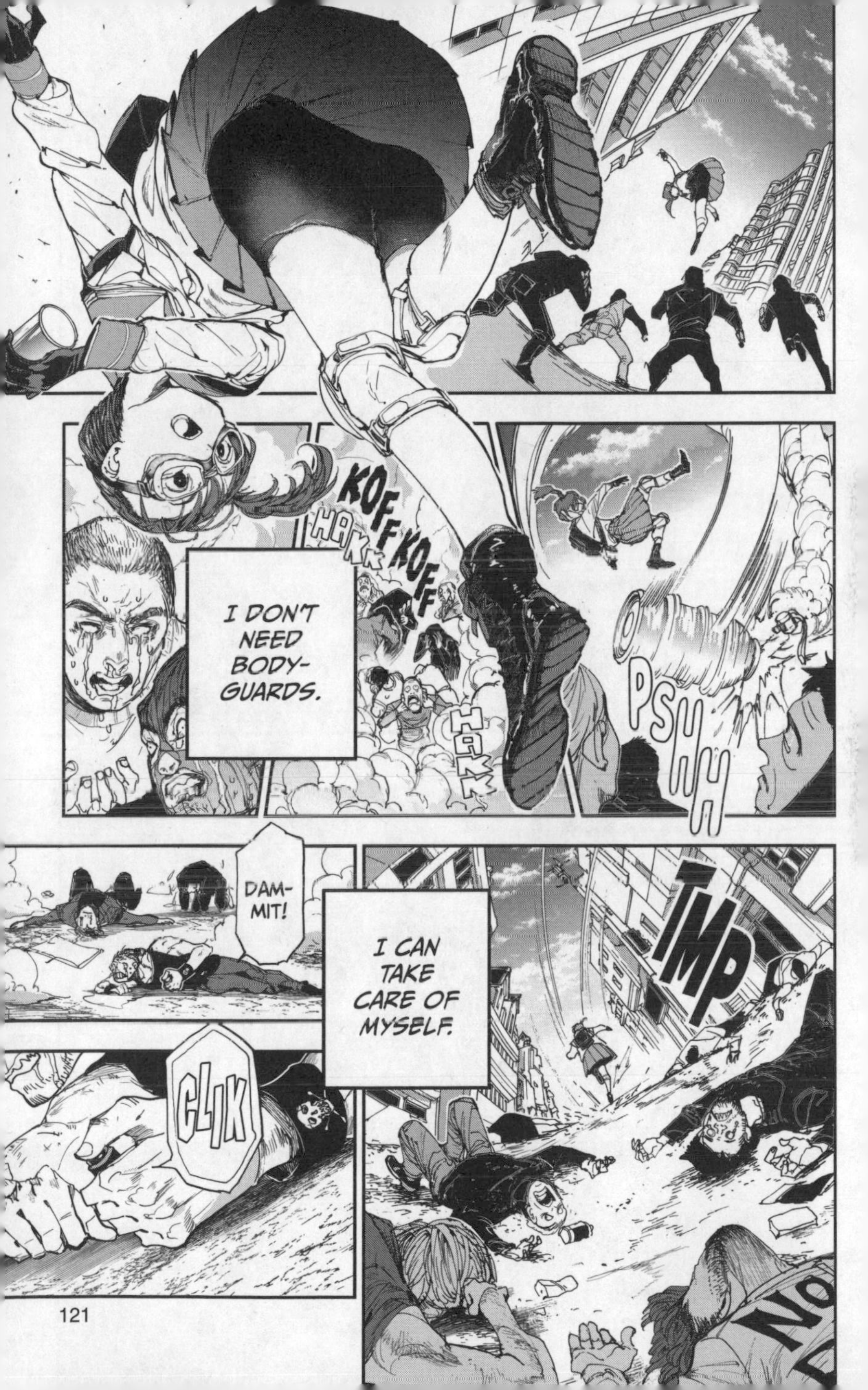
PSHH
KOFF KOFF KOFF
HAKK
HAKK
I DON'T NEED BODY-GUARDS.
TMP
I CAN TAKE CARE OF MYSELF.
DAM-MIT!
CLIK

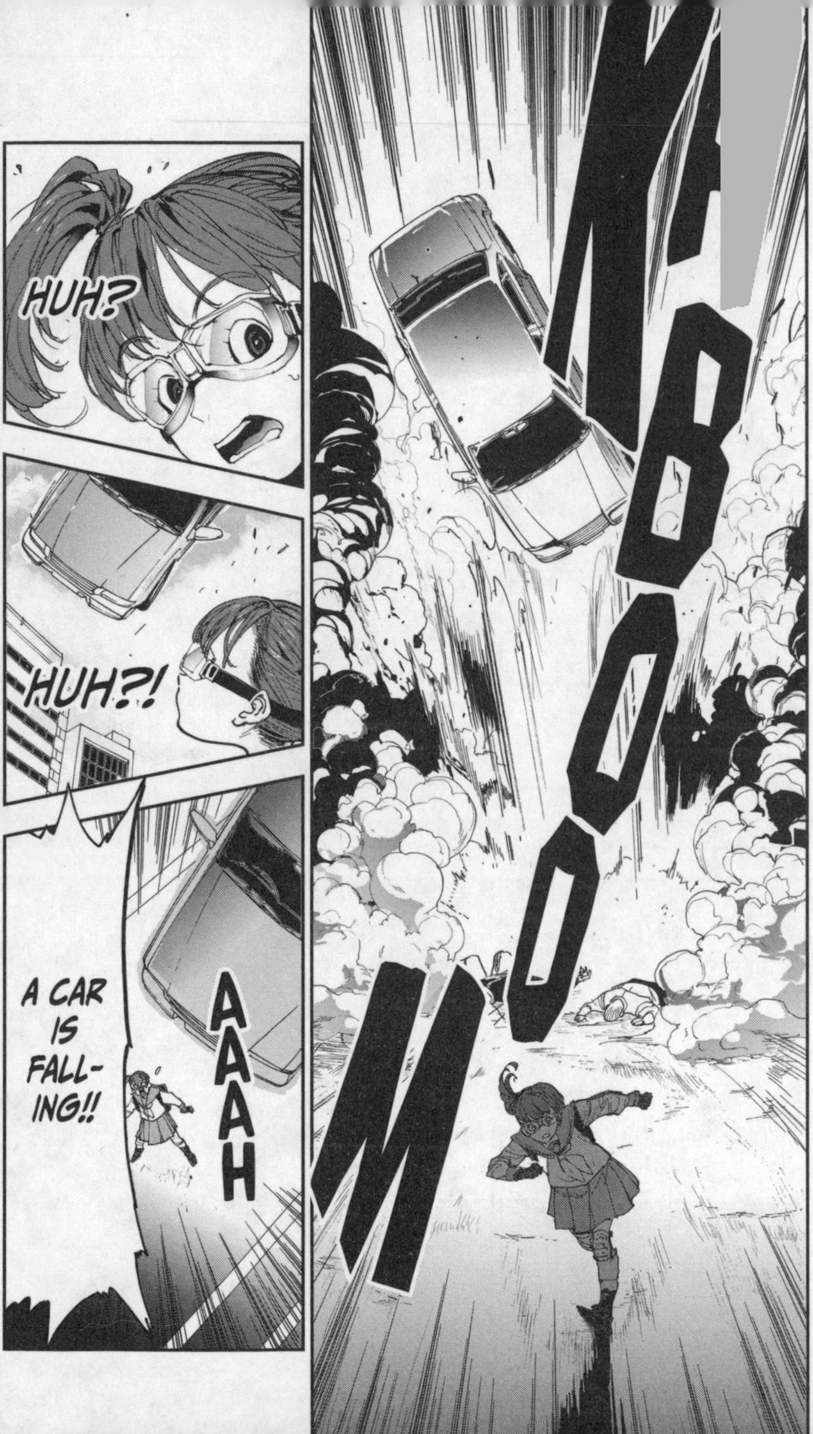
KABOOOM
HUH?
HUH?!
AAAH
A CAR IS FALL-ING!!

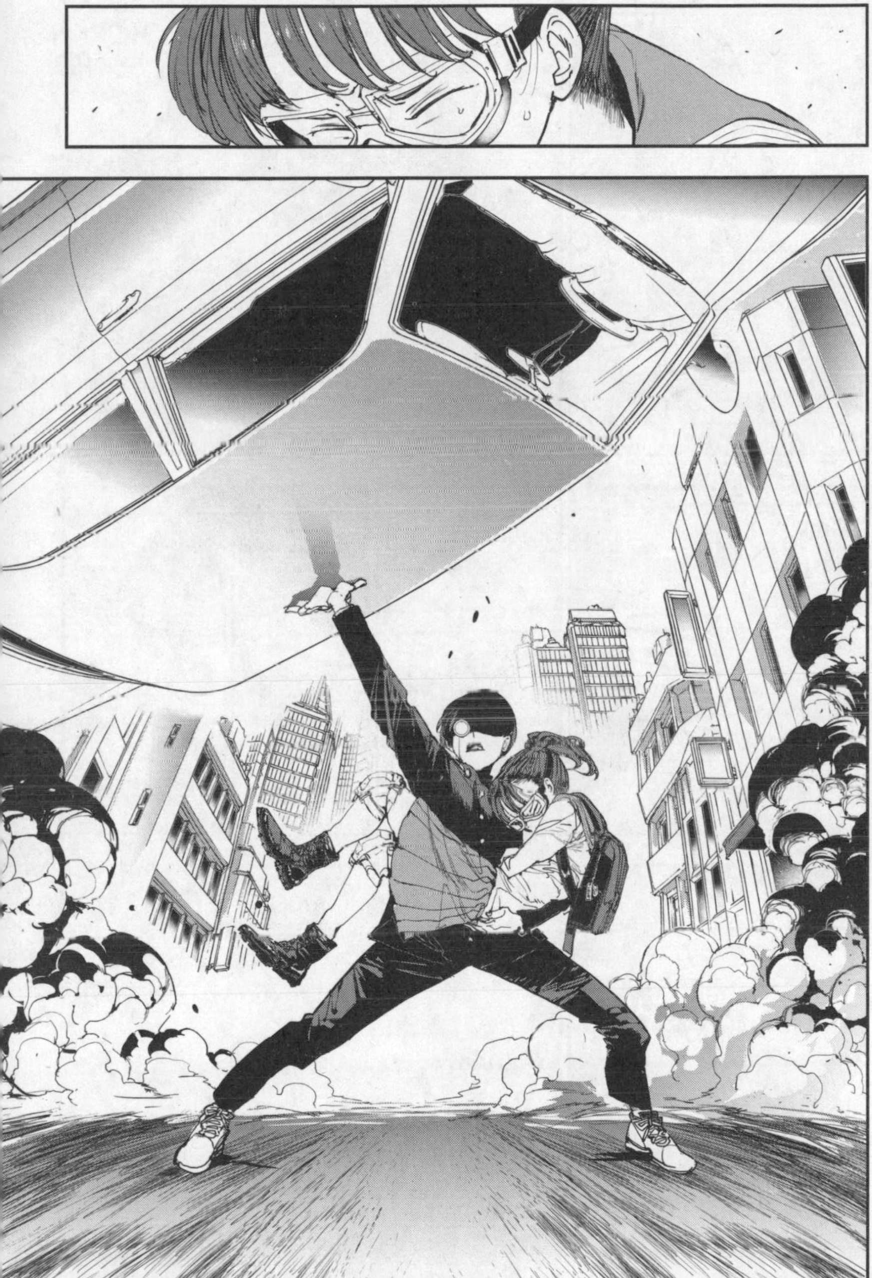

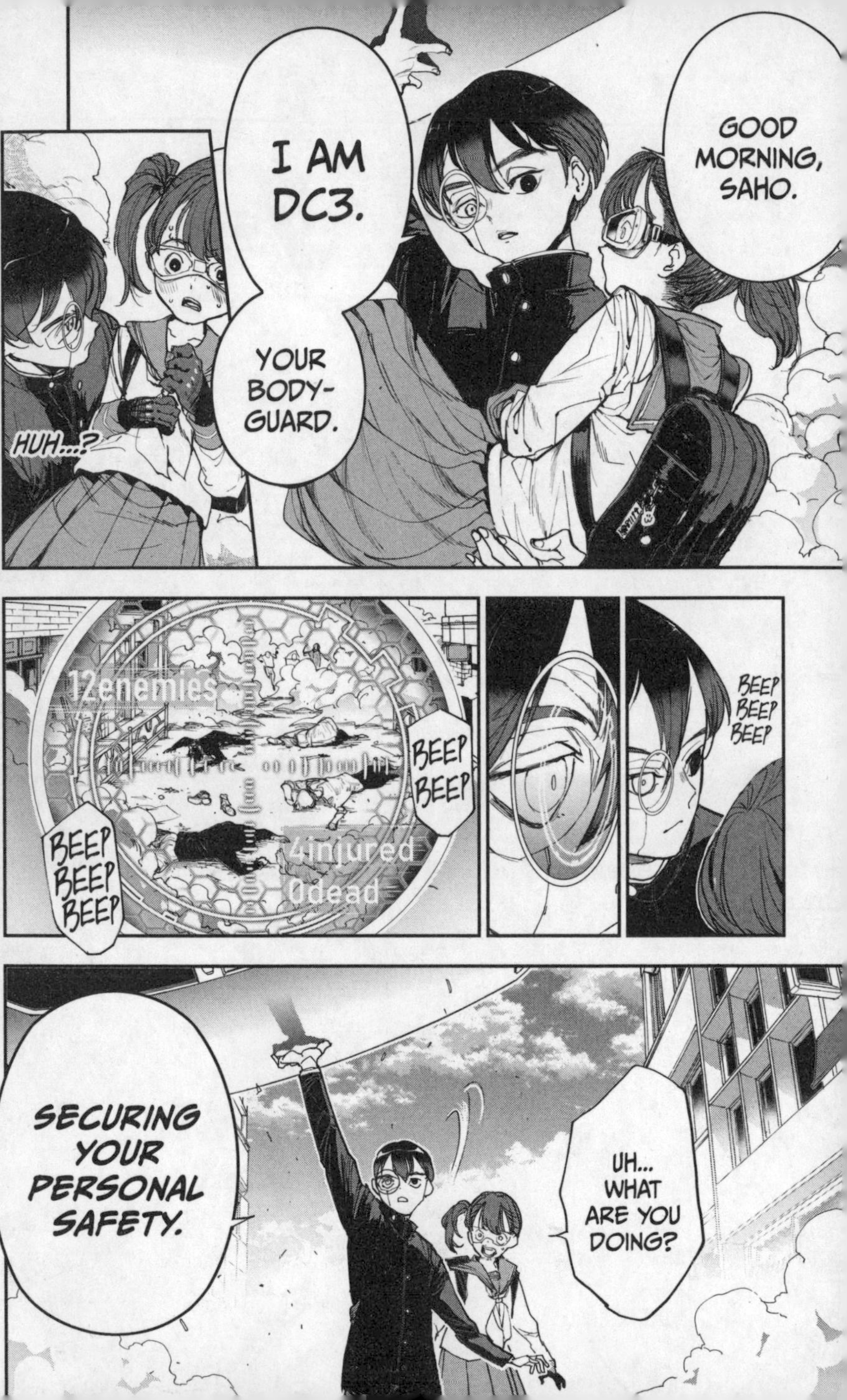
GOOD MORNING, SAHO.
I AM DC3.
YOUR BODY-GUARD.
HUH...?
BEEP BEEP BEEP
BEEP BEEP
12enemies
BEEP BEEP BEEP
4injured
0dead
UH... WHAT ARE YOU DOING?
SECURING YOUR PERSONAL SAFETY.

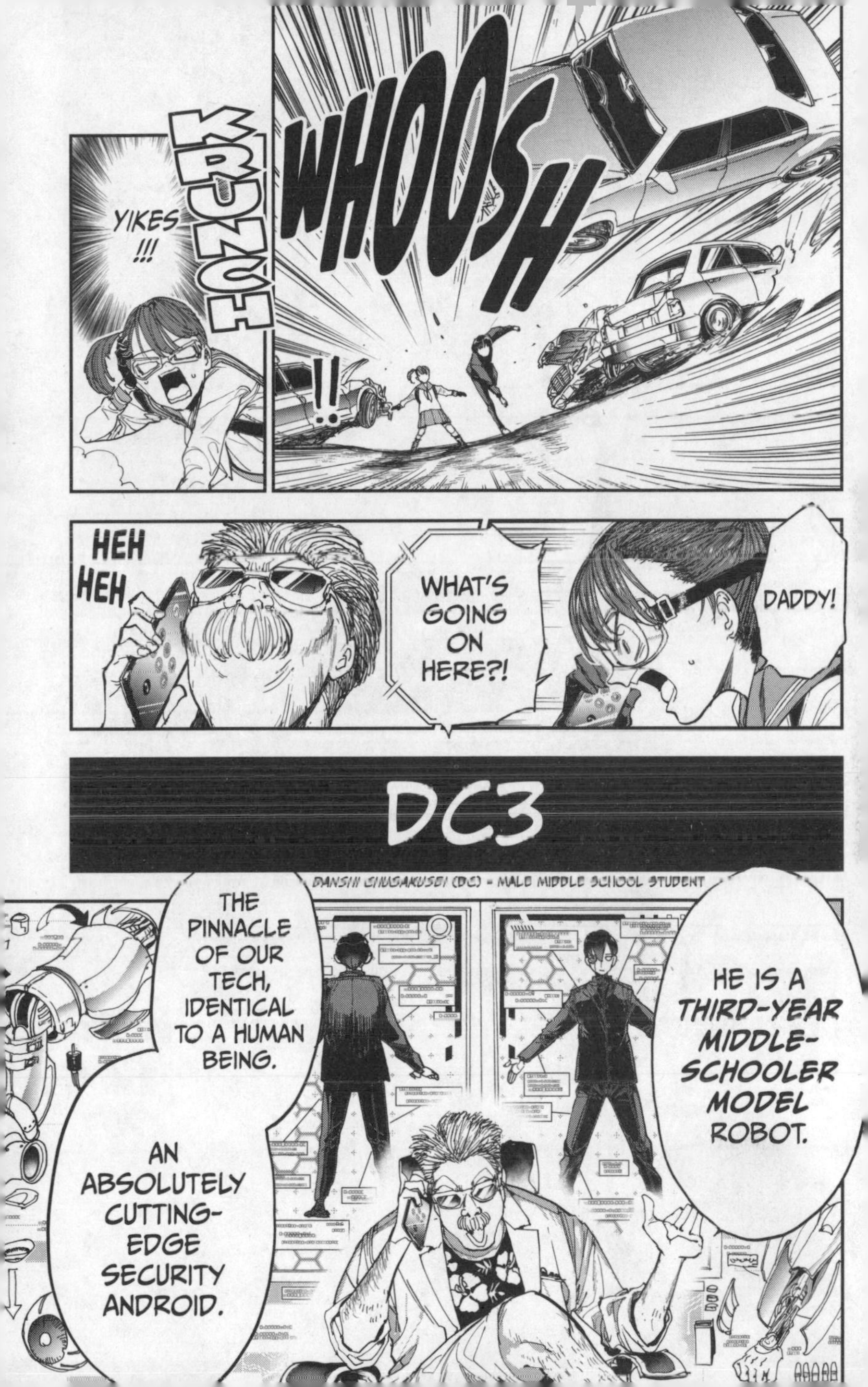
WHOOSH
!!
KRUNCH
YIKES!!!
DADDY!
WHAT'S GOING ON HERE?!
HEH HEH
DC3
DANSHI CHUGAKUSEI (DC) = MALE MIDDLE SCHOOL STUDENT
HE IS A THIRD-YEAR MIDDLE-SCHOOLER MODEL ROBOT.
THE PINNACLE OF OUR TECH, IDENTICAL TO A HUMAN BEING.
AN ABSOLUTELY CUTTING-EDGE SECURITY ANDROID.

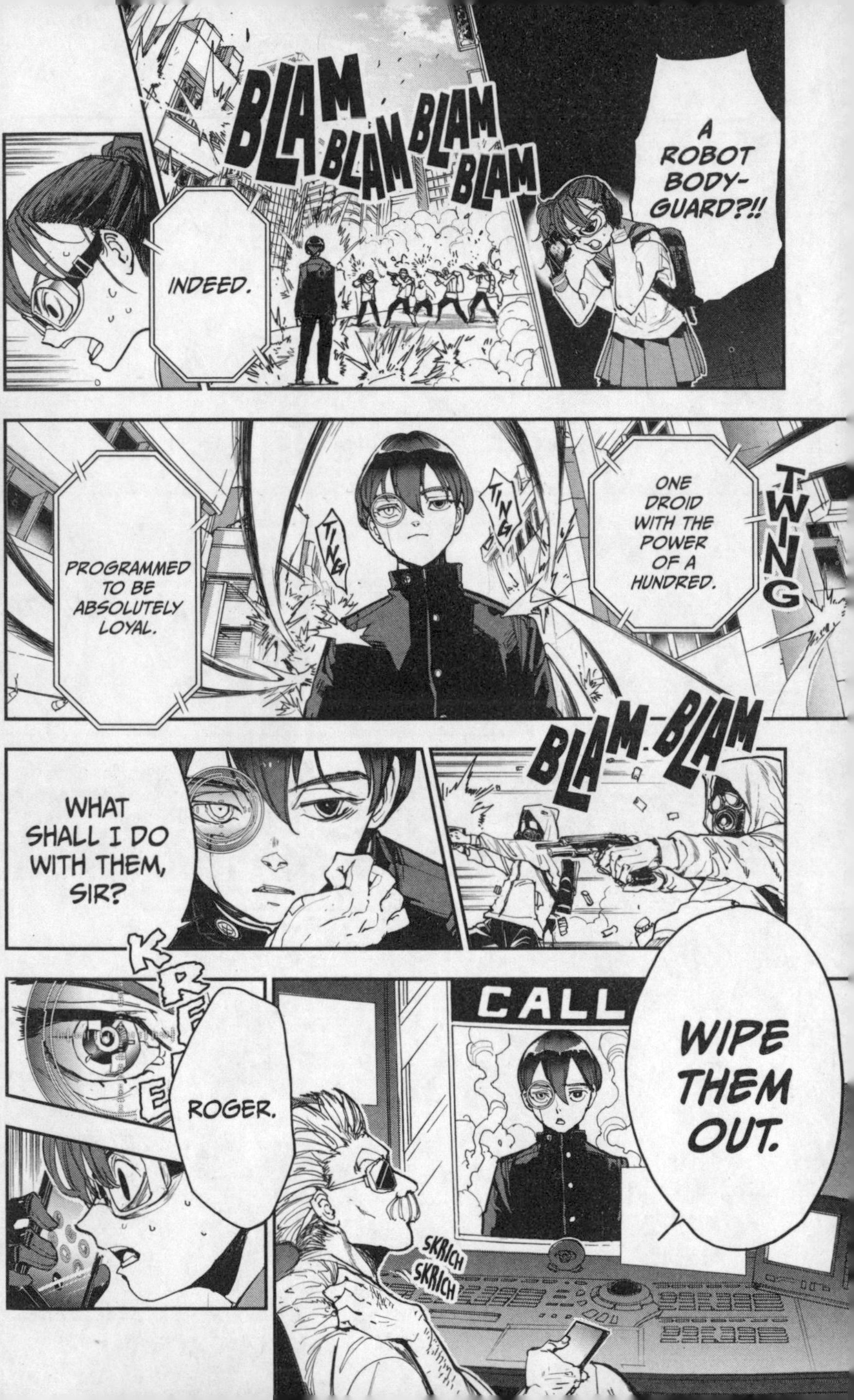
A ROBOT BODY-GUARD?!!
BLAM BLAM BLAM BLAM
INDEED.
TWING
ONE DROID WITH THE POWER OF A HUNDRED.
TING TING
PROGRAMMED TO BE ABSOLUTELY LOYAL.
BLAM BLAM
WHAT SHALL I DO WITH THEM, SIR?
WIPE THEM OUT.
CALL
SKRICH SKRICH
ROGER.
KREE

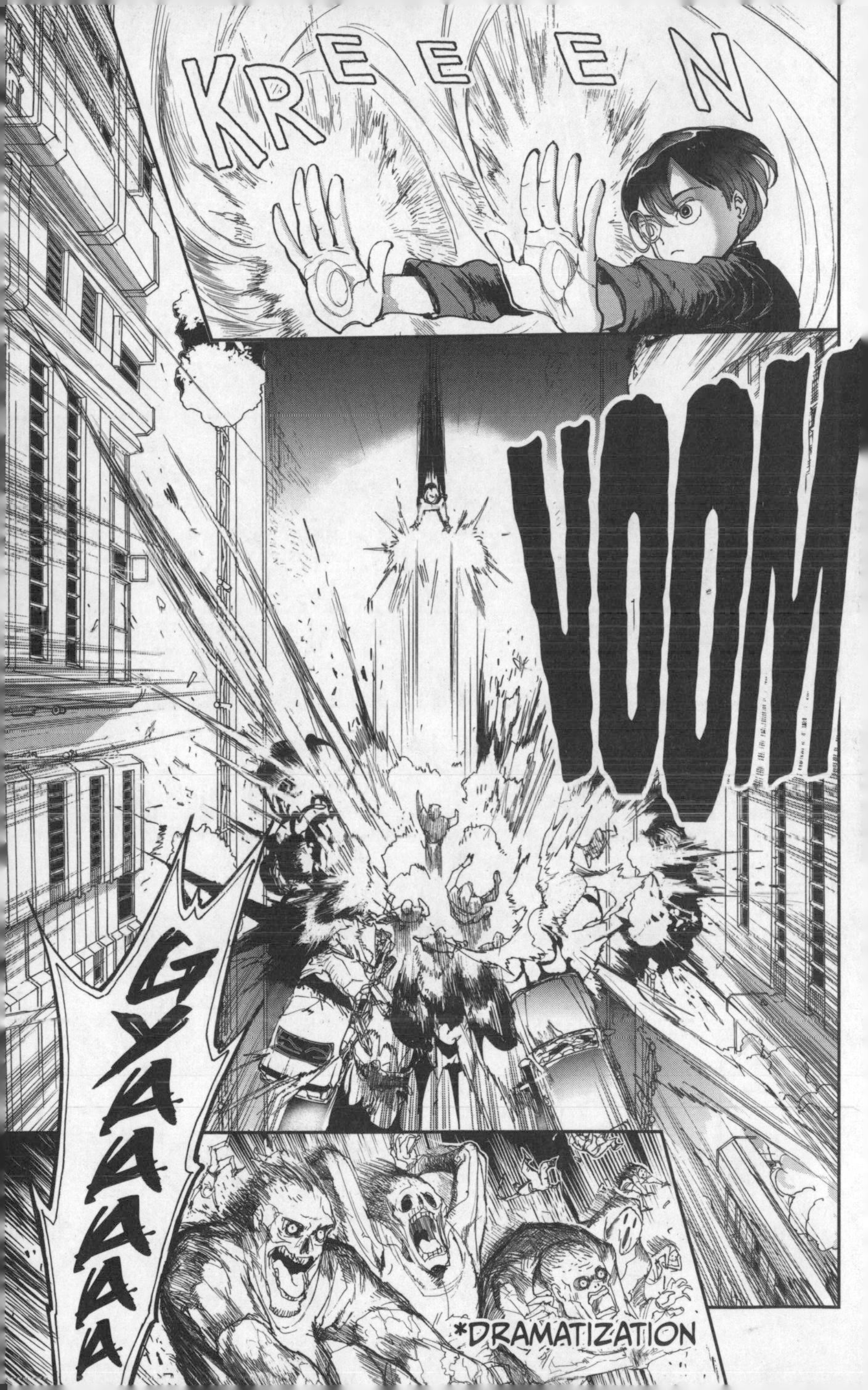
KREEEN
VOOM
GYAAAAAA
*DRAMATIZATION

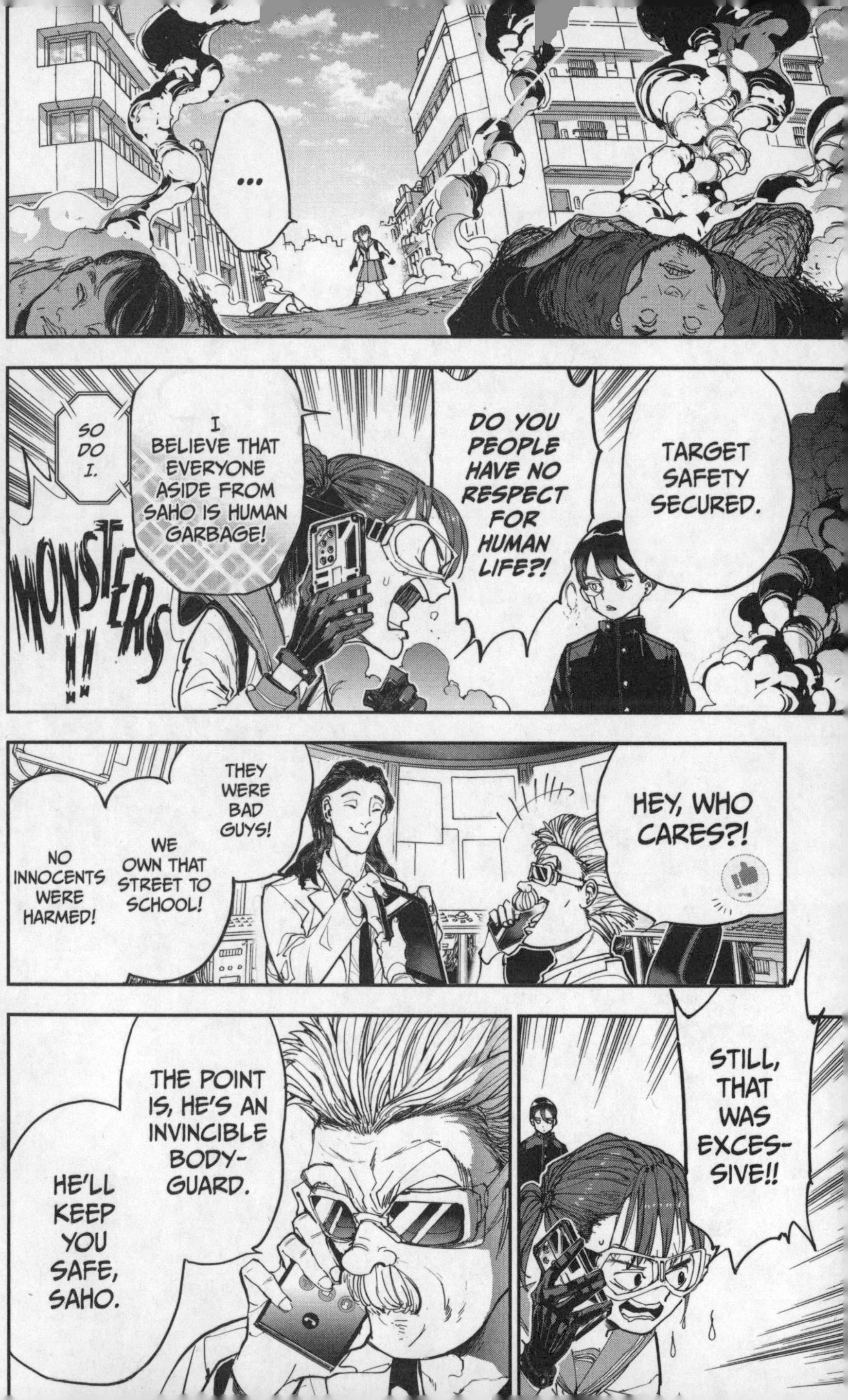
...
TARGET SAFETY SECURED.
DO YOU PEOPLE HAVE NO RESPECT FOR HUMAN LIFE?!
I BELIEVE THAT EVERYONE ASIDE FROM SAHO IS HUMAN GARBAGE!
SO DO I.
MONSTERS!!
HEY, WHO CARES?!
THEY WERE BAD GUYS!
WE OWN THAT STREET TO SCHOOL!
NO INNOCENTS WERE HARMED!
STILL, THAT WAS EXCES-SIVE!!
THE POINT IS, HE'S AN INVINCIBLE BODY-GUARD.
HE'LL KEEP YOU SAFE, SAHO.

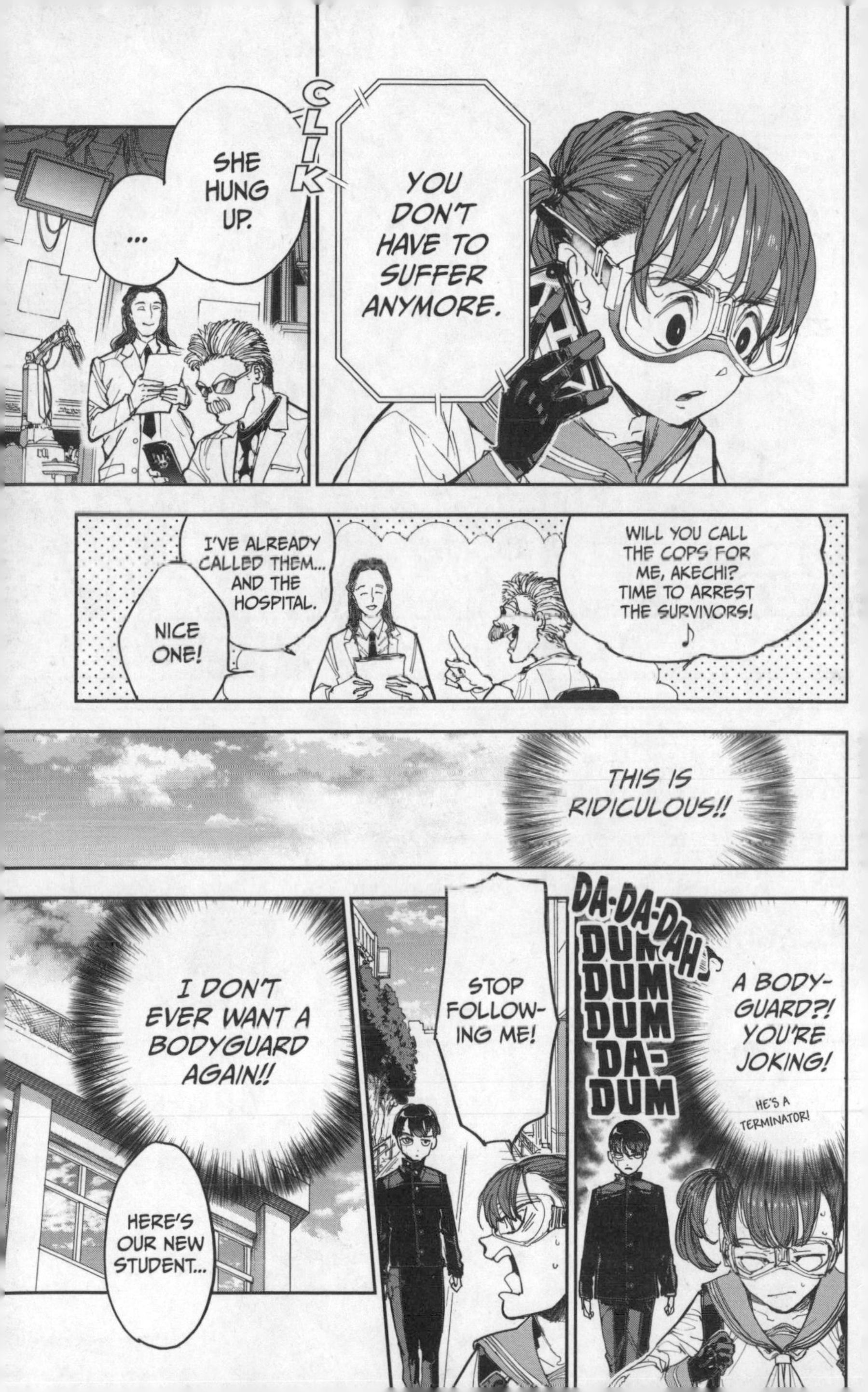
YOU DON'T HAVE TO SUFFER ANYMORE.
CLIK
SHE HUNG UP.
...
WILL YOU CALL THE COPS FOR ME, AKECHI? TIME TO ARREST THE SURVIVORS! ♪
I'VE ALREADY CALLED THEM... AND THE HOSPITAL.
NICE ONE!
THIS IS RIDICULOUS!!
DA-DA-DAH
DUM DUM DUM DA-DUM
A BODY-GUARD?! YOU'RE JOKING!
HE'S A TERMINATOR!
STOP FOLLOW-ING ME!
I DON'T EVER WANT A BODYGUARD AGAIN!!
HERE'S OUR NEW STUDENT...

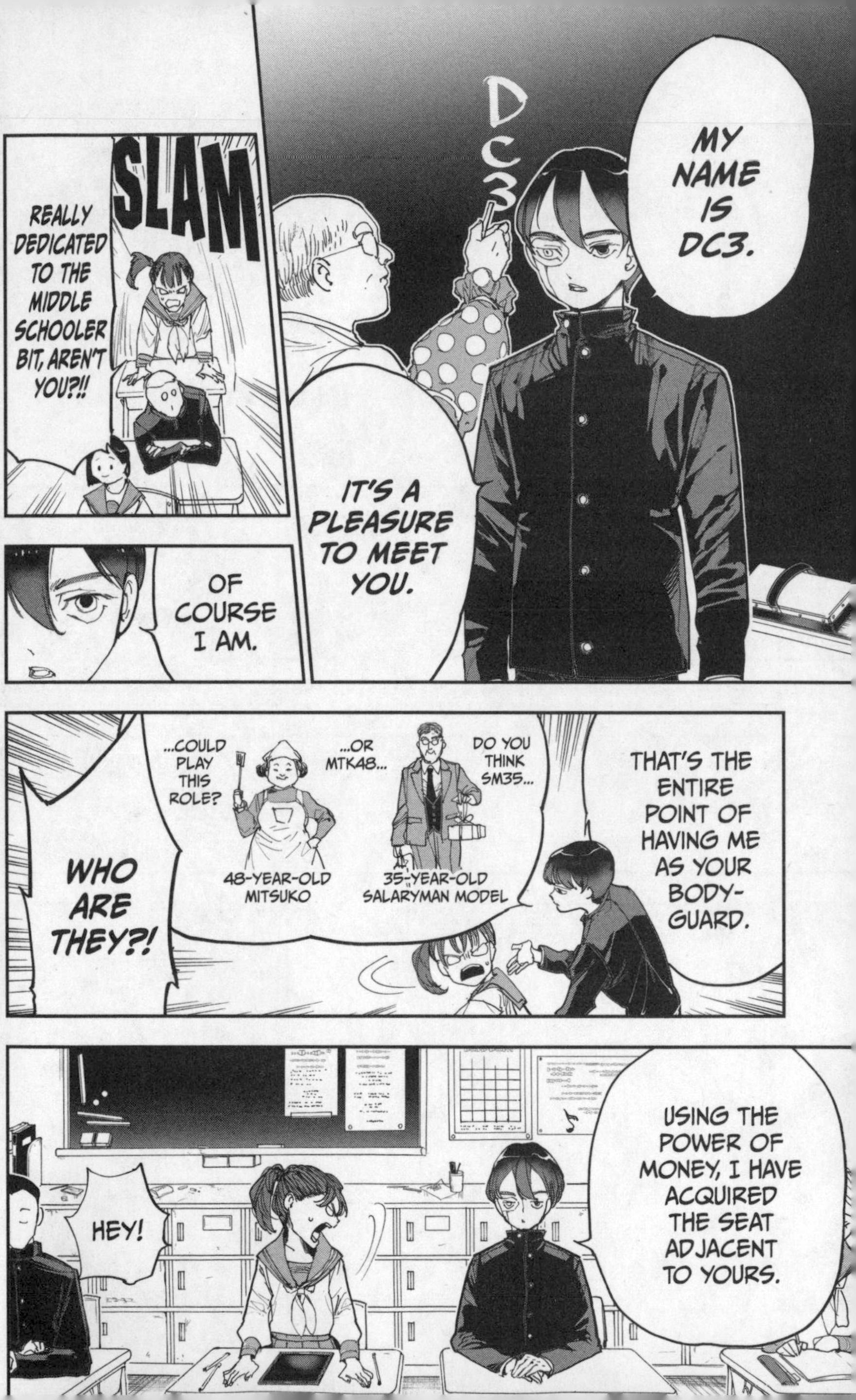
DC3
MY NAME IS DC3.
IT'S A PLEASURE TO MEET YOU.
SLAM
REALLY DEDICATED TO THE MIDDLE SCHOOLER BIT, AREN'T YOU?!!
OF COURSE I AM.
THAT'S THE ENTIRE POINT OF HAVING ME AS YOUR BODY-GUARD.
DO YOU THINK SM35...
35-YEAR-OLD SALARYMAN MODEL
...OR MTK48...
...COULD PLAY THIS ROLE?
48-YEAR-OLD MITSUKO
WHO ARE THEY?!
USING THE POWER OF MONEY, I HAVE ACQUIRED THE SEAT ADJACENT TO YOURS.
HEY!

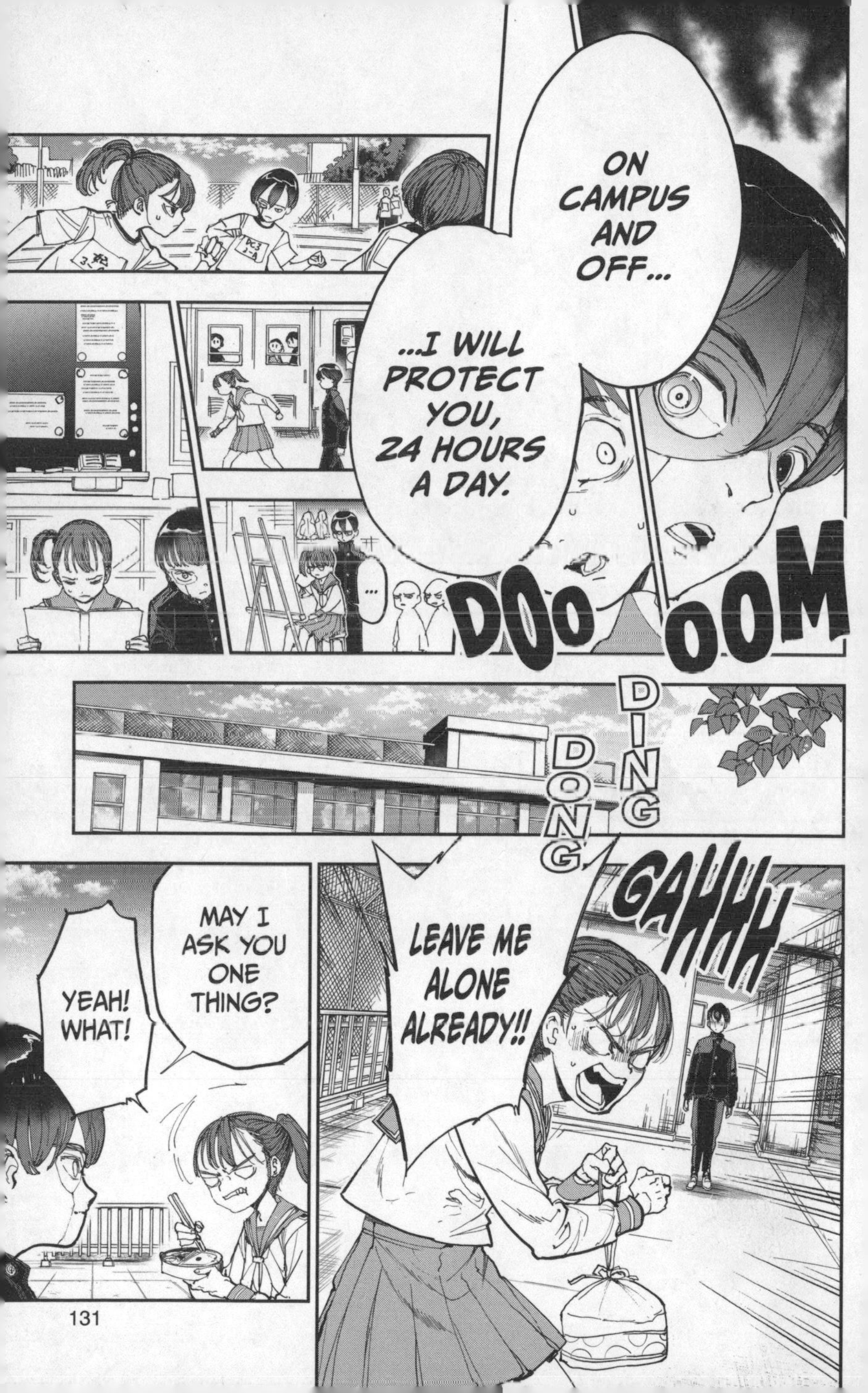
ON CAMPUS AND OFF...
...I WILL PROTECT YOU, 24 HOURS A DAY.
DOO OOM
...
DING
DONG
GAHHH
LEAVE ME ALONE ALREADY!!
MAY I ASK YOU ONE THING?
YEAH! WHAT!

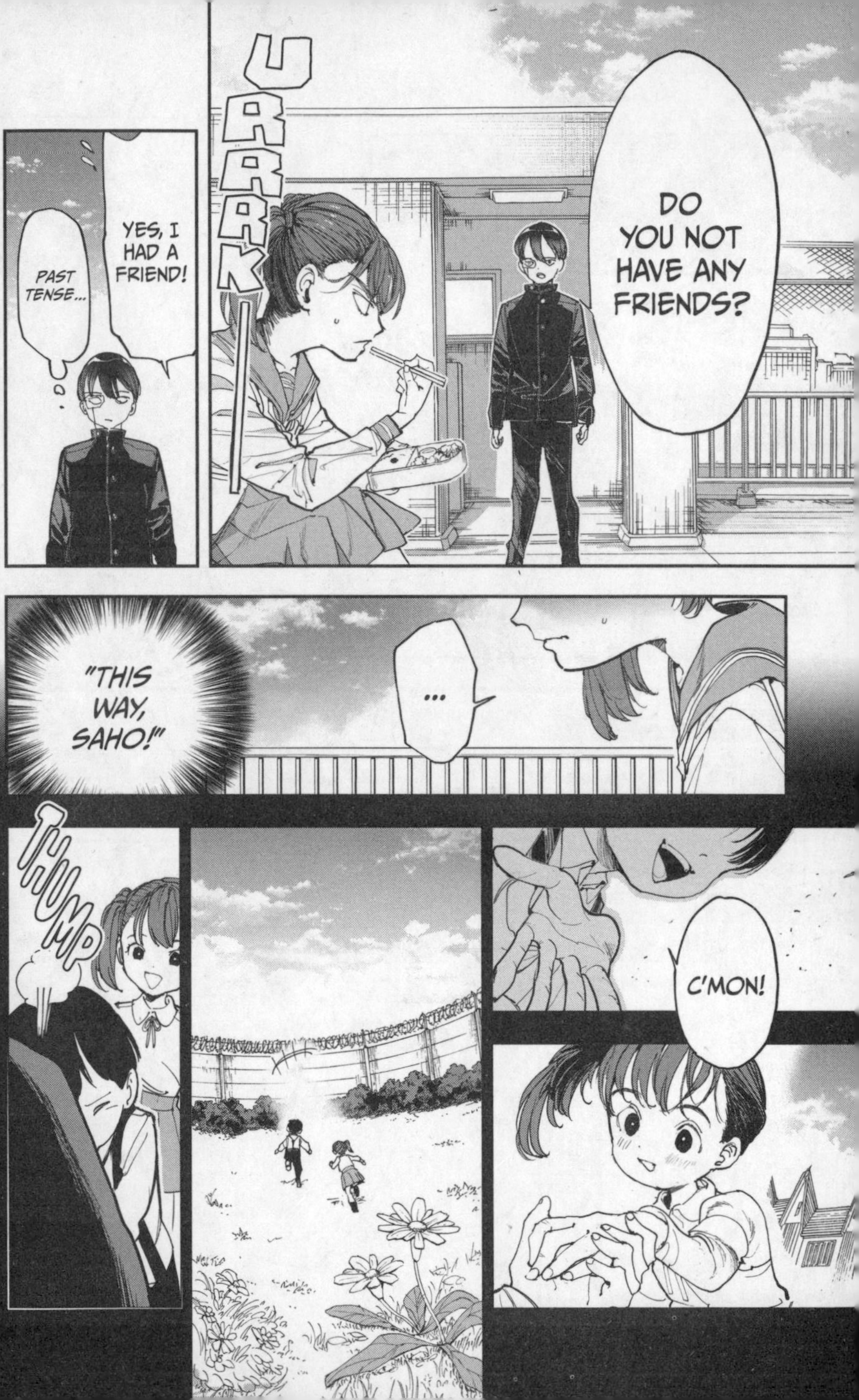
DO YOU NOT HAVE ANY FRIENDS?
URRRK
YES, I HAD A FRIEND!
PAST TENSE...
...
"THIS WAY, SAHO!"
C'MON!
THUMP

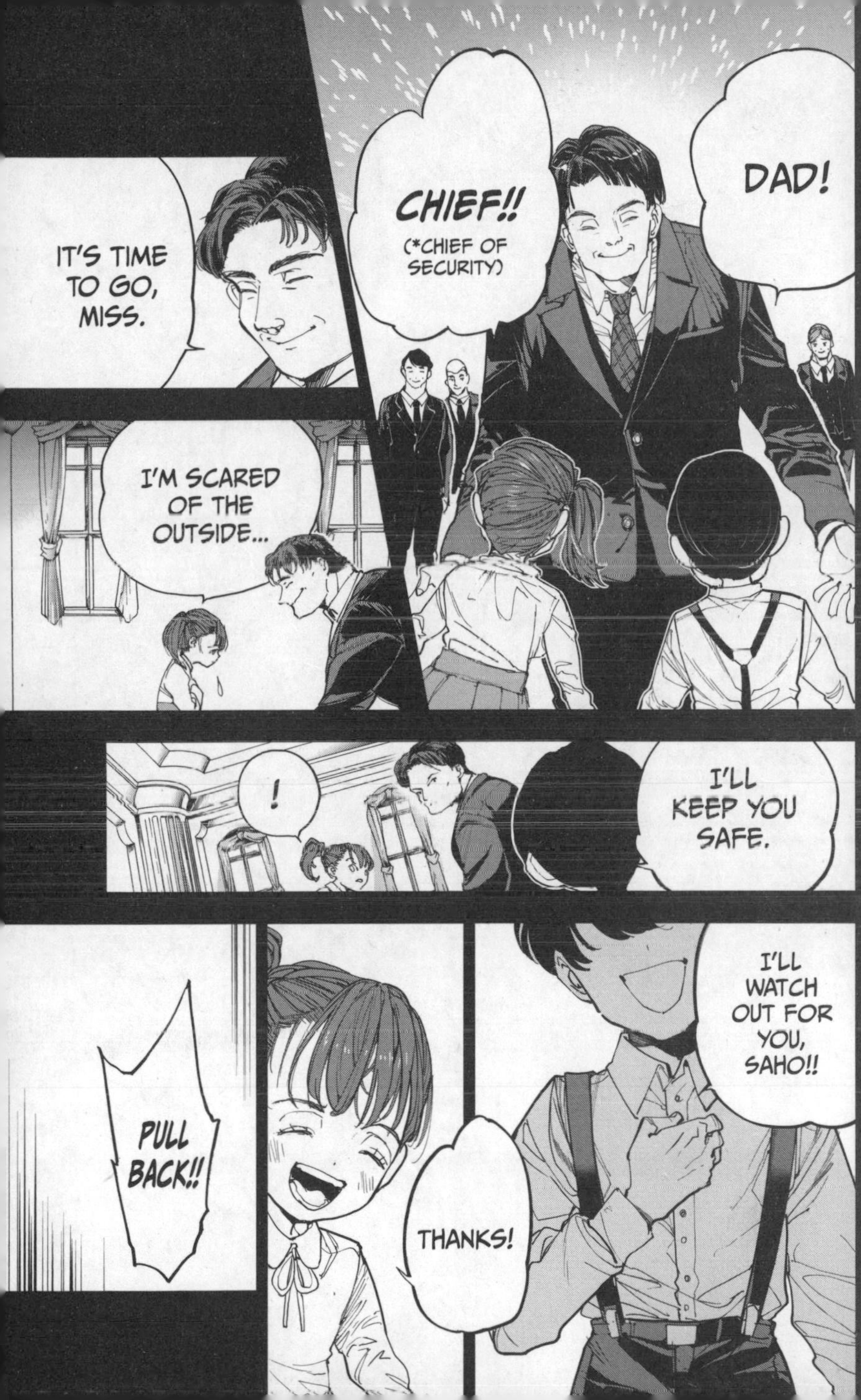
DAD!
CHIEF!!
(*CHIEF OF SECURITY)
IT'S TIME TO GO, MISS.
I'M SCARED OF THE OUTSIDE...
I'LL KEEP YOU SAFE.
!
I'LL WATCH OUT FOR YOU, SAHO!!
THANKS!
PULL BACK!!

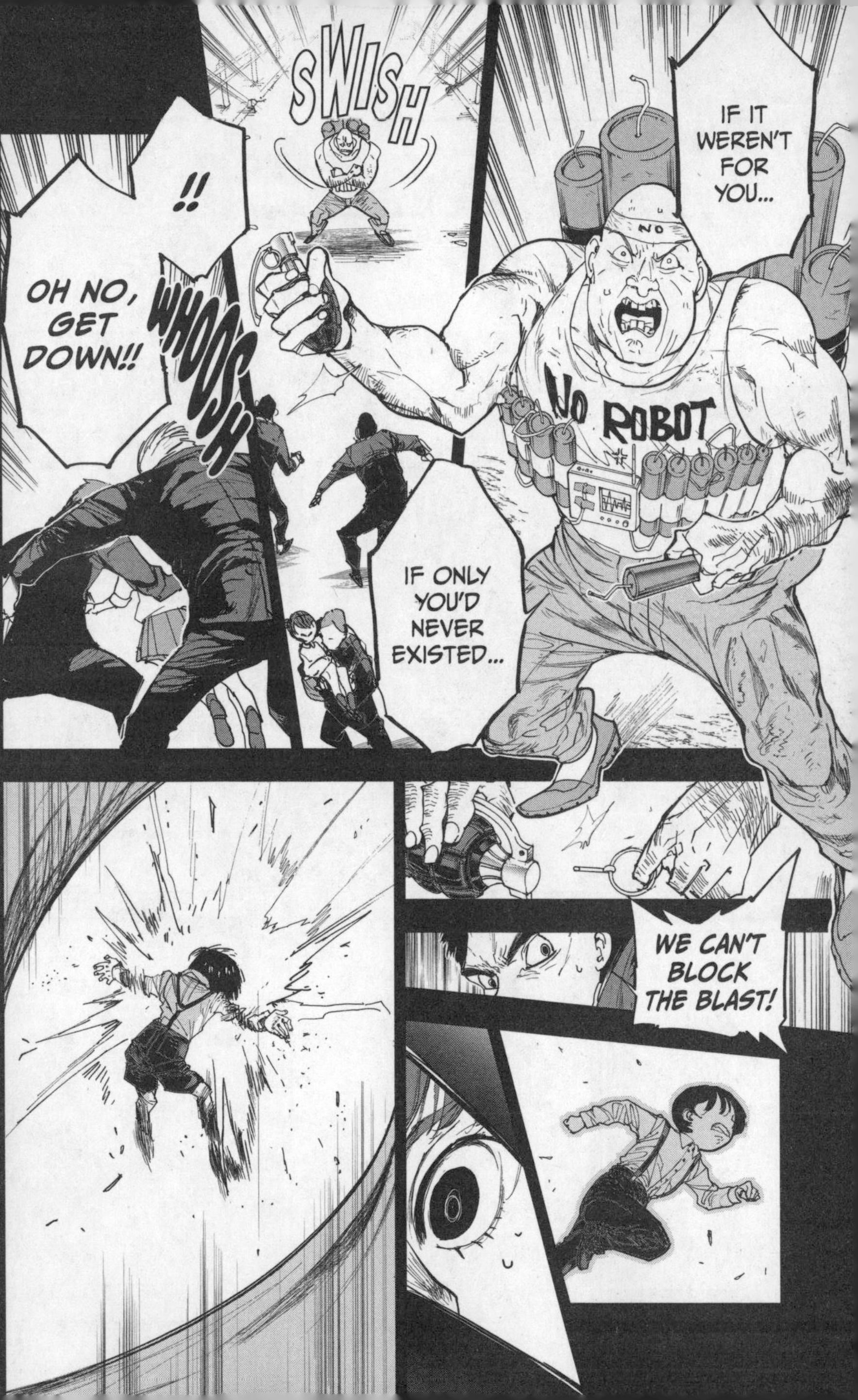
IF IT WEREN'T FOR YOU...
NO
NO ROBOT
IF ONLY YOU'D NEVER EXISTED...
SWISH
!!
OH NO, GET DOWN!!
WHOOSH
WE CAN'T BLOCK THE BLAST!

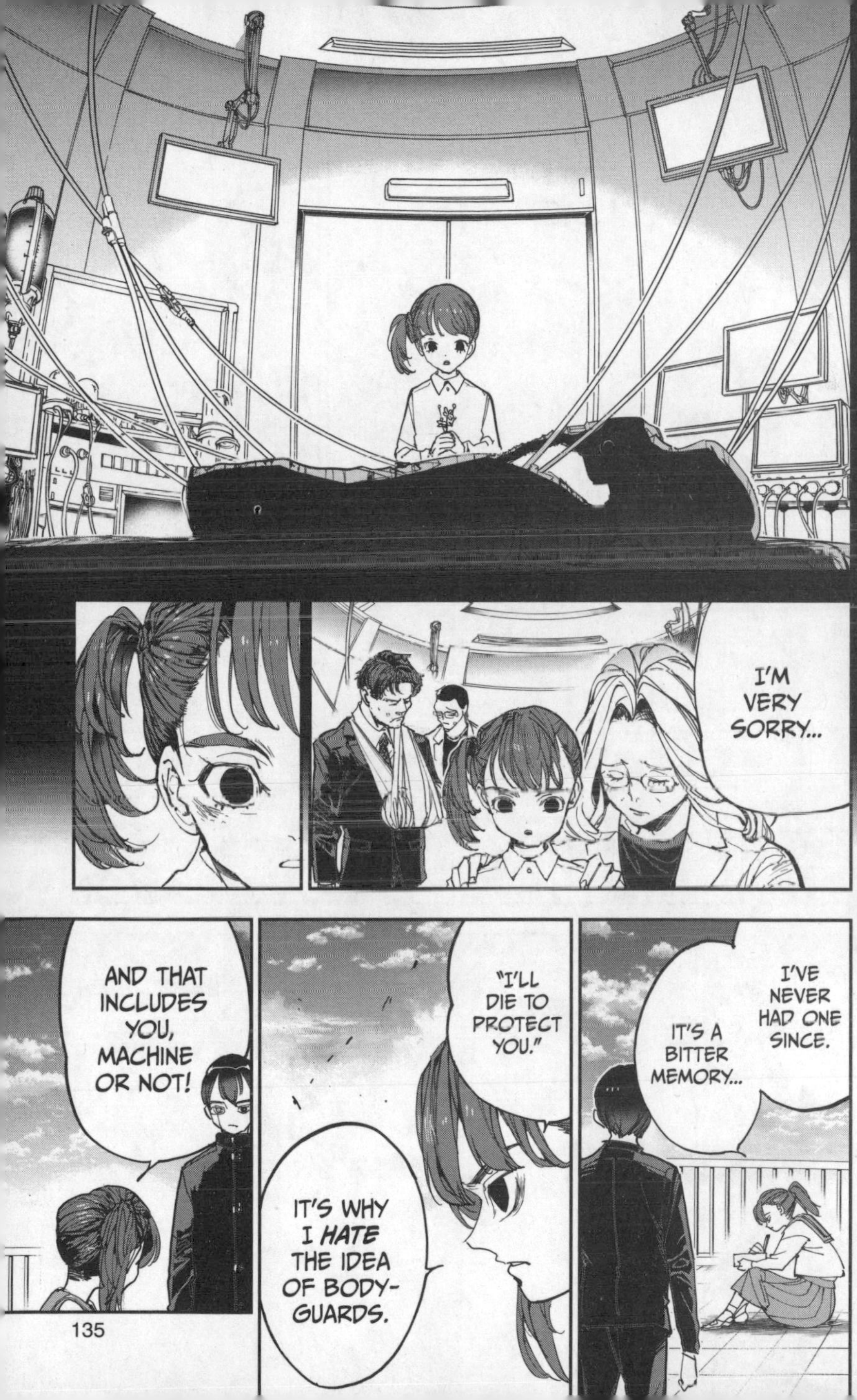
I'M VERY SORRY...
I'VE NEVER HAD ONE SINCE.
IT'S A BITTER MEMORY...
"I'LL DIE TO PROTECT YOU."
IT'S WHY I *HATE* THE IDEA OF BODY-GUARDS.
AND THAT INCLUDES YOU, MACHINE OR NOT!

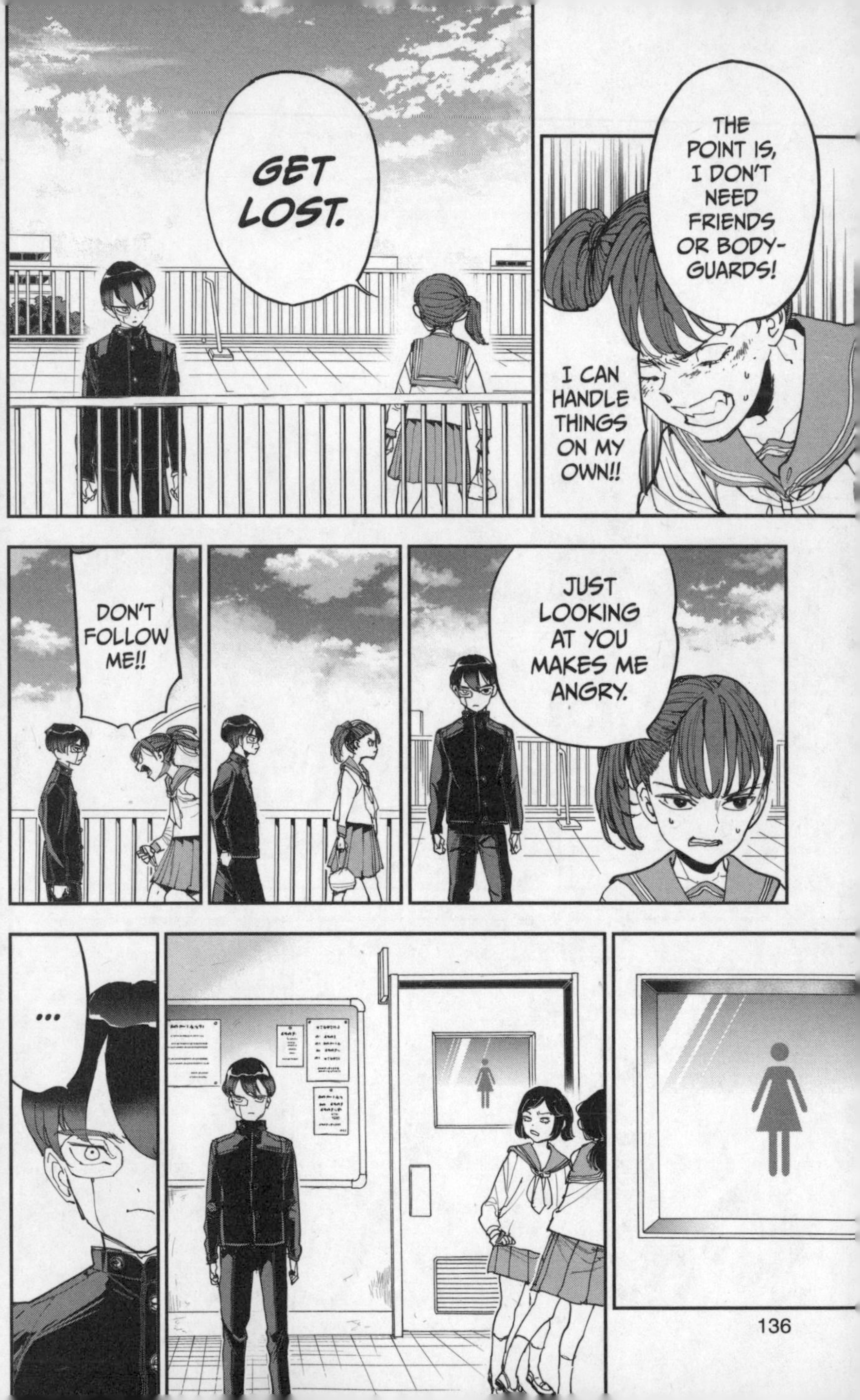
THE POINT IS, I DON'T NEED FRIENDS OR BODY-GUARDS!
I CAN HANDLE THINGS ON MY OWN!!
GET LOST.
JUST LOOKING AT YOU MAKES ME ANGRY.
DON'T FOLLOW ME!!
...

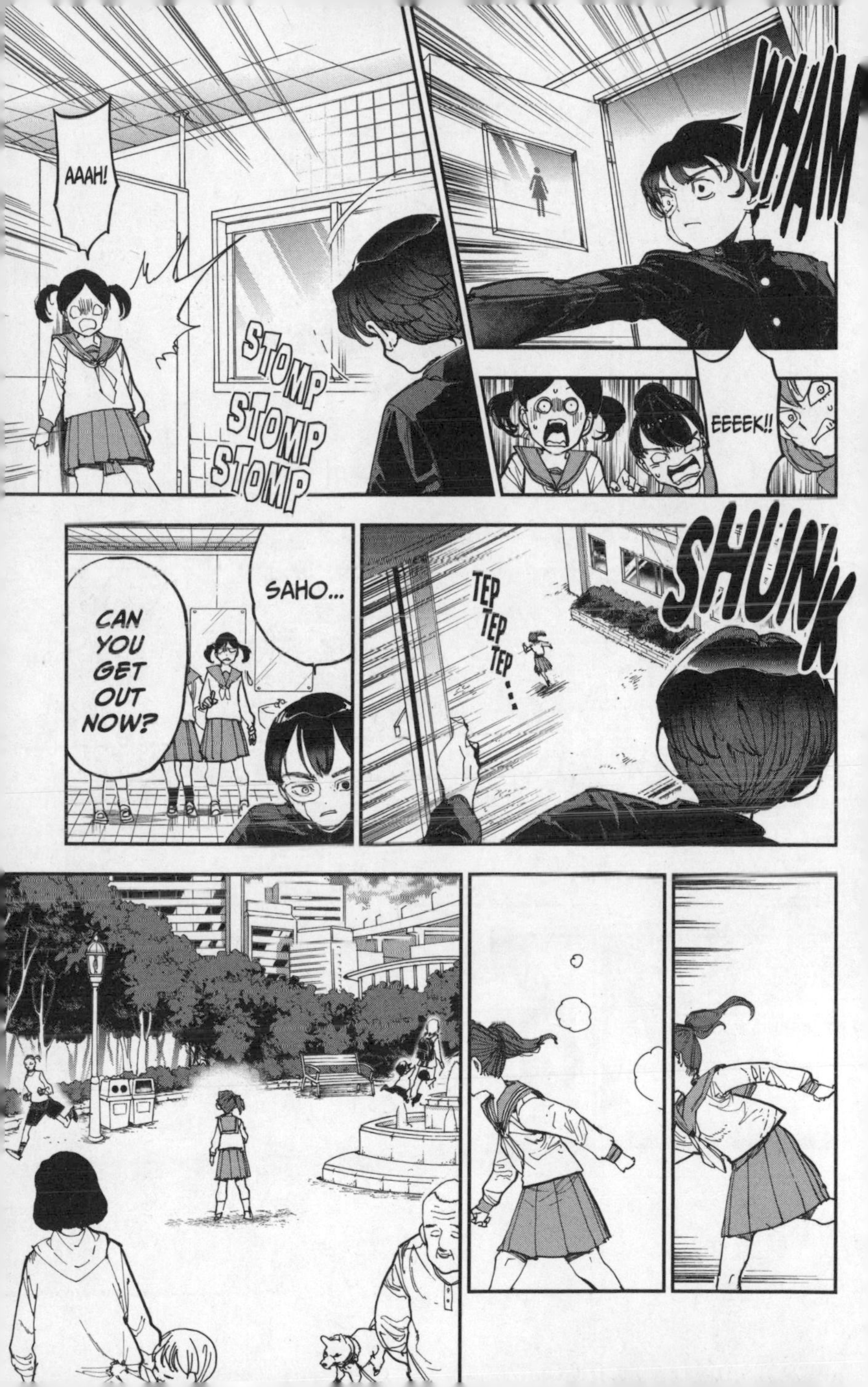
WHAM
EEEEK!!
AAAH!
STOMP STOMP STOMP
SHUNK
TEP TEP TEP...
SAHO...
CAN YOU GET OUT NOW?

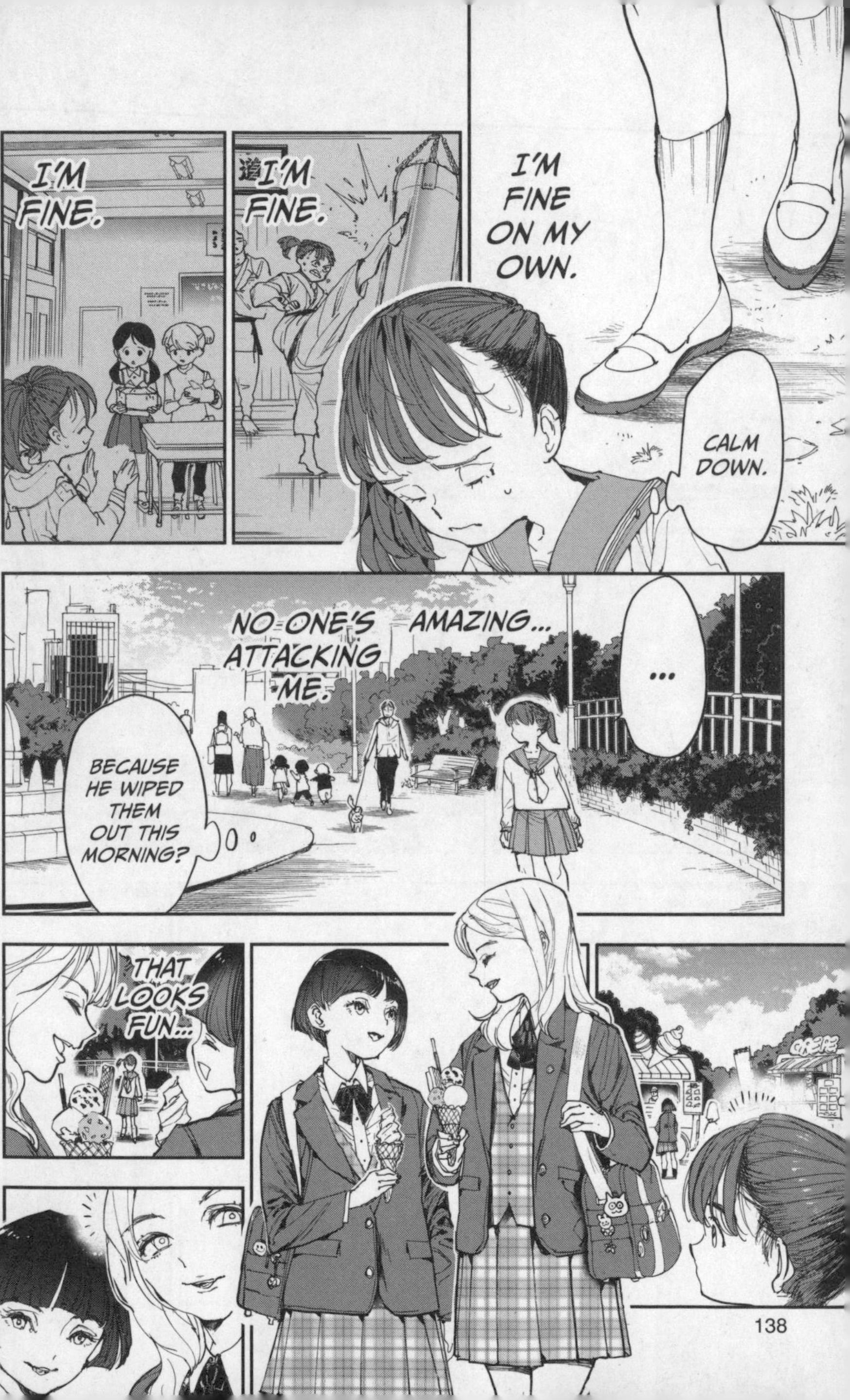
I'M FINE ON MY OWN.
CALM DOWN.
I'M FINE.
I'M FINE.
...
AMAZING...
NO ONE'S ATTACKING ME.
BECAUSE HE WIPED THEM OUT THIS MORNING?
THAT LOOKS FUN...

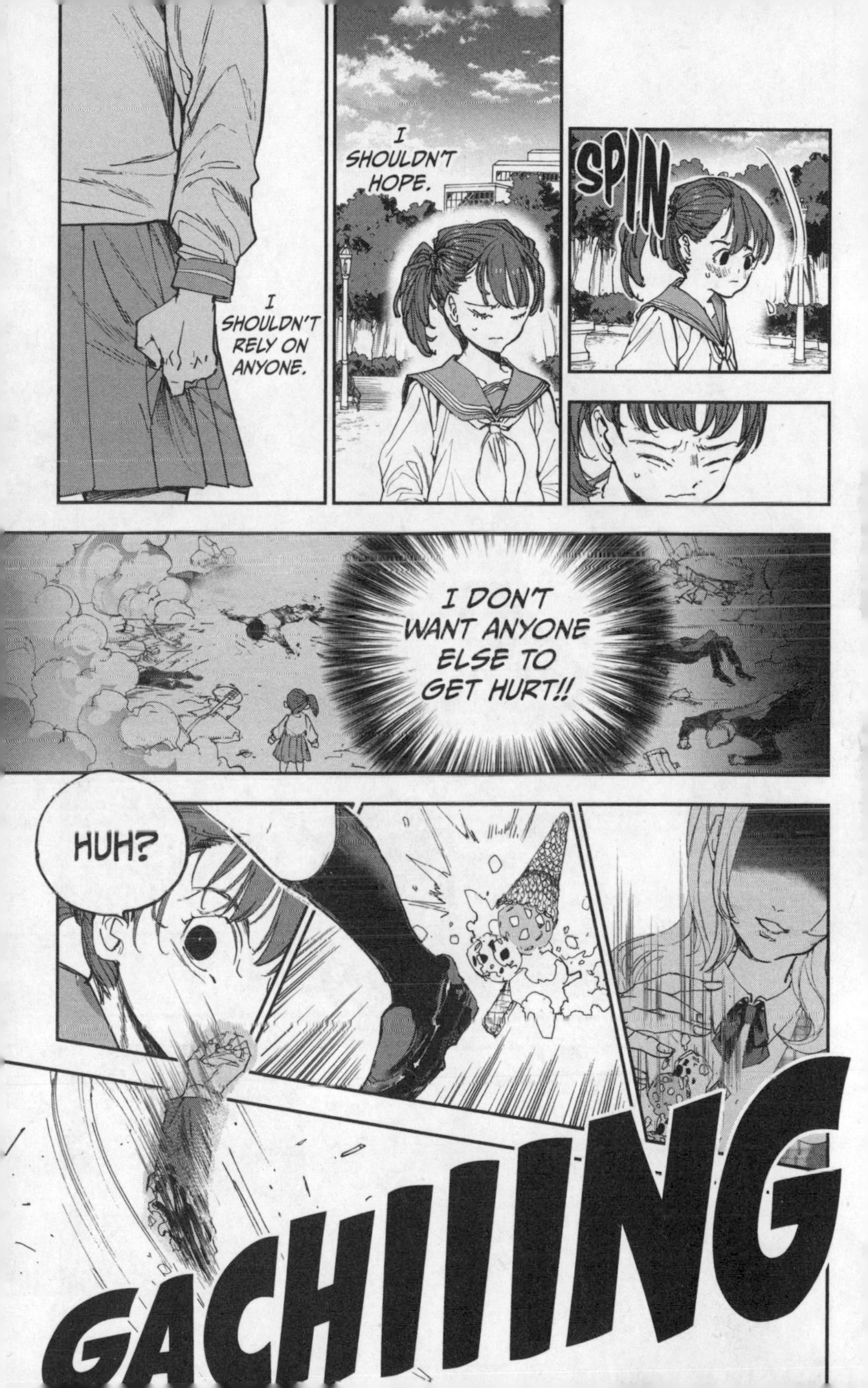
SPIN
I SHOULDN'T HOPE.
I SHOULDN'T RELY ON ANYONE.
I DON'T WANT ANYONE ELSE TO GET HURT!!
HUH?
GACHIIIING

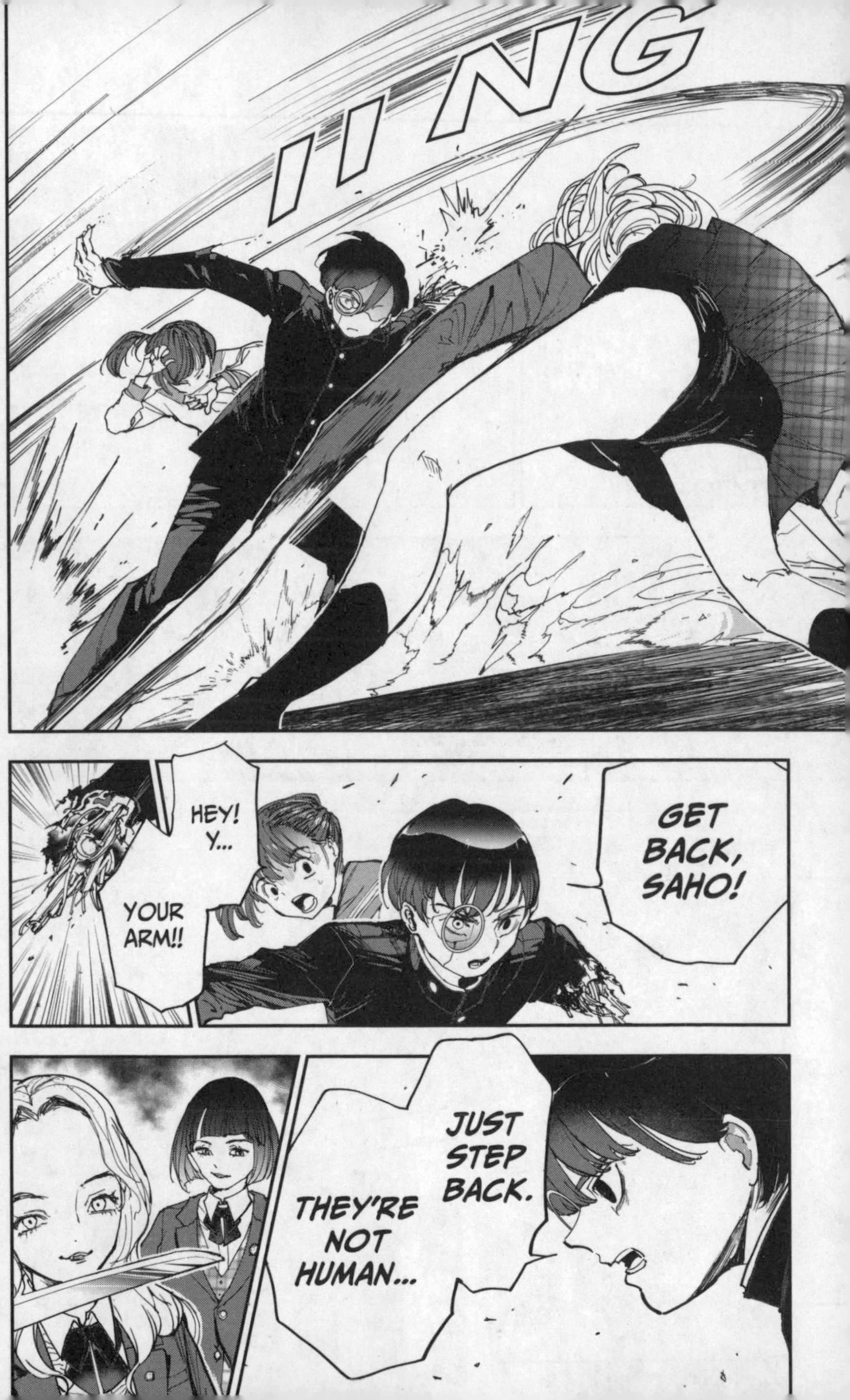
IING
GET BACK, SAHO!
HEY! Y...
YOUR ARM!!
JUST STEP BACK.
THEY'RE NOT HUMAN...

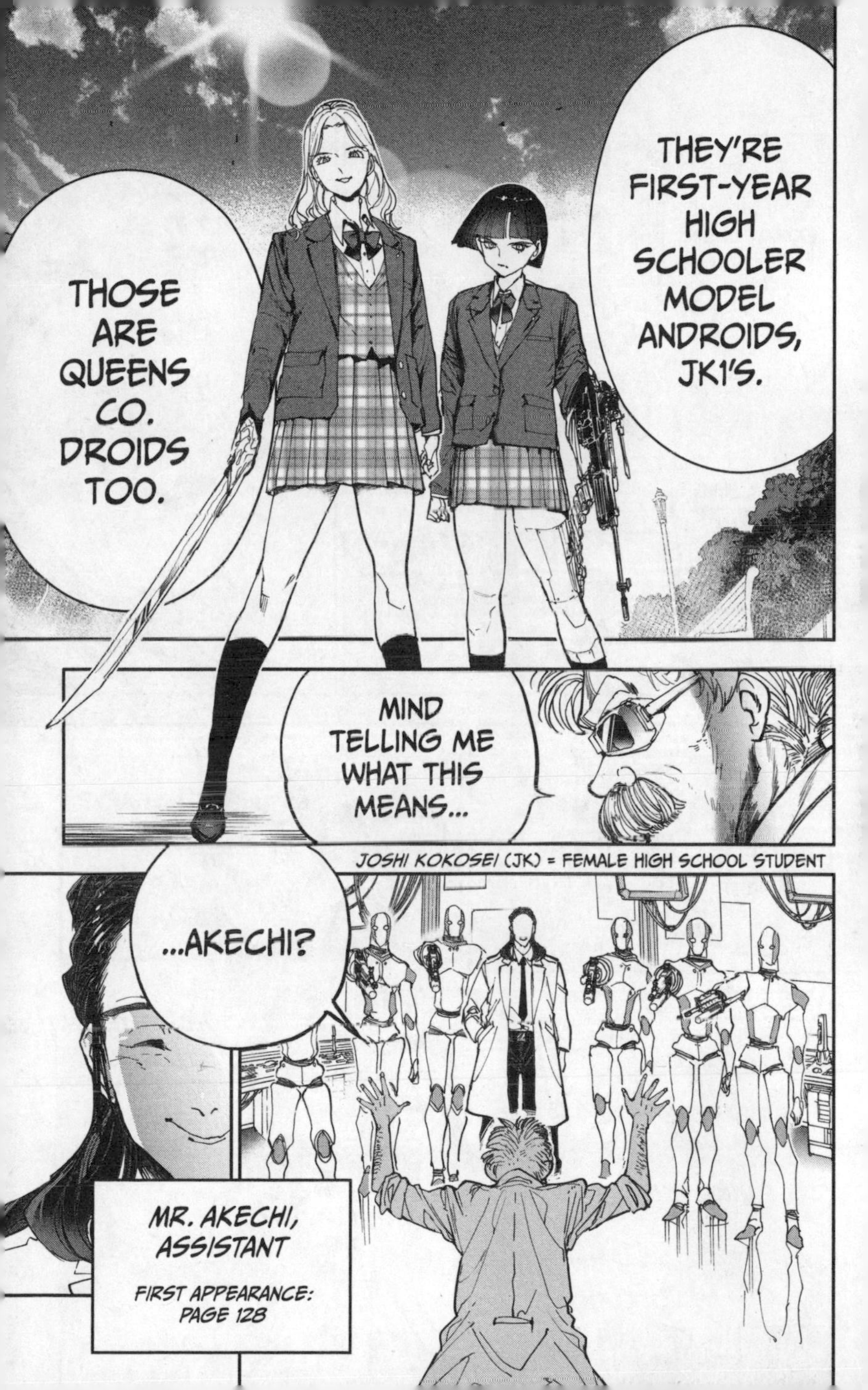
THEY'RE FIRST-YEAR HIGH SCHOOLER MODEL ANDROIDS, JK1'S.
THOSE ARE QUEENS CO. DROIDS TOO.
MIND TELLING ME WHAT THIS MEANS...
JOSHI KOKOSEI (JK) = FEMALE HIGH SCHOOL STUDENT
...AKECHI?
MR. AKECHI, ASSISTANT
FIRST APPEARANCE: PAGE 128

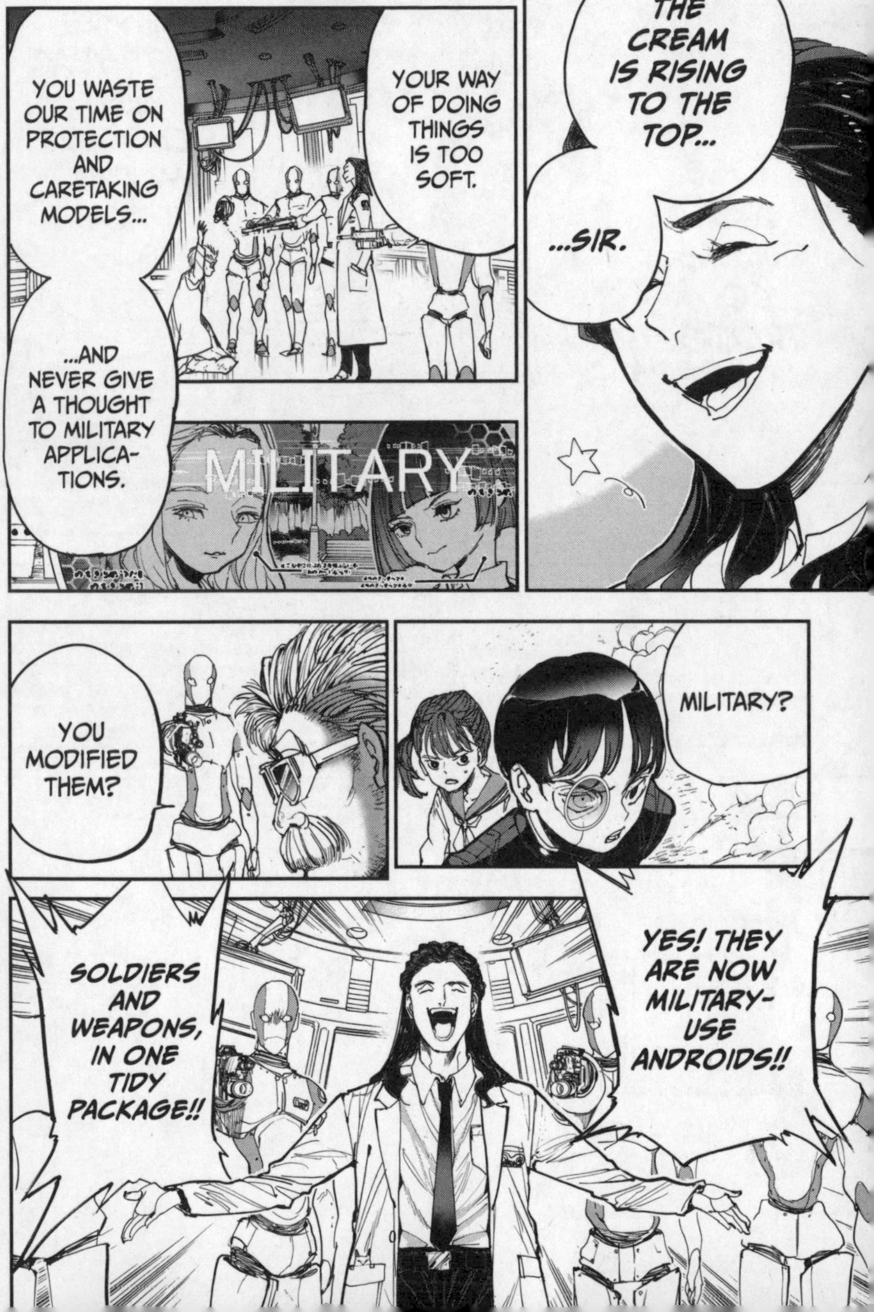
THE CREAM IS RISING TO THE TOP...
...SIR.
YOUR WAY OF DOING THINGS IS TOO SOFT.
YOU WASTE OUR TIME ON PROTECTION AND CARETAKING MODELS...
...AND NEVER GIVE A THOUGHT TO MILITARY APPLICATIONS.
MILITARY
MILITARY?
YOU MODIFIED THEM?
YES! THEY ARE NOW MILITARY-USE ANDROIDS!!
SOLDIERS AND WEAPONS, IN ONE TIDY PACKAGE!!

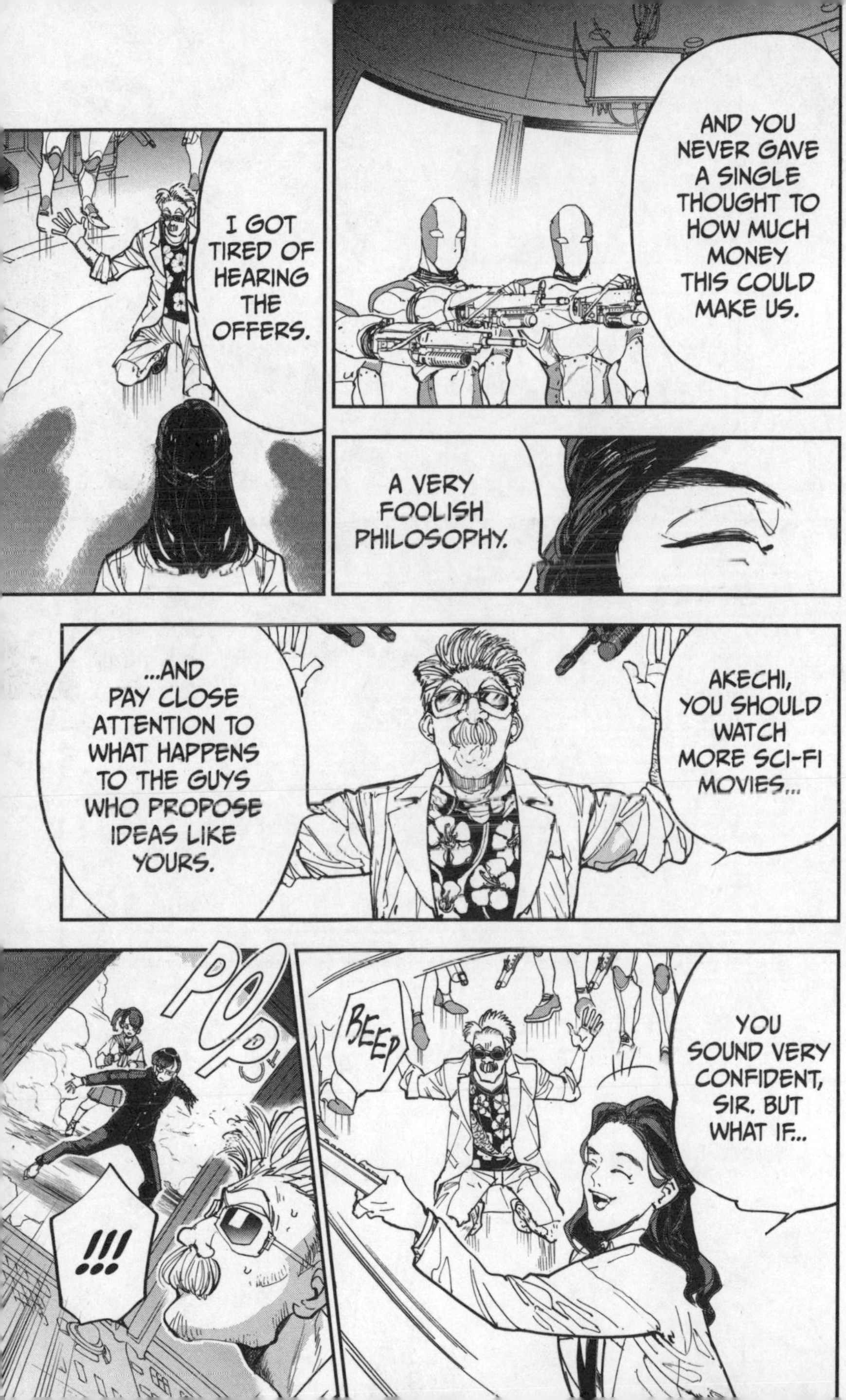
AND YOU NEVER GAVE A SINGLE THOUGHT TO HOW MUCH MONEY THIS COULD MAKE US.
A VERY FOOLISH PHILOSOPHY.
I GOT TIRED OF HEARING THE OFFERS.
AKECHI, YOU SHOULD WATCH MORE SCI-FI MOVIES...
...AND PAY CLOSE ATTENTION TO WHAT HAPPENS TO THE GUYS WHO PROPOSE IDEAS LIKE YOURS.
YOU SOUND VERY CONFIDENT, SIR. BUT WHAT IF...
BEEP
POP
!!!

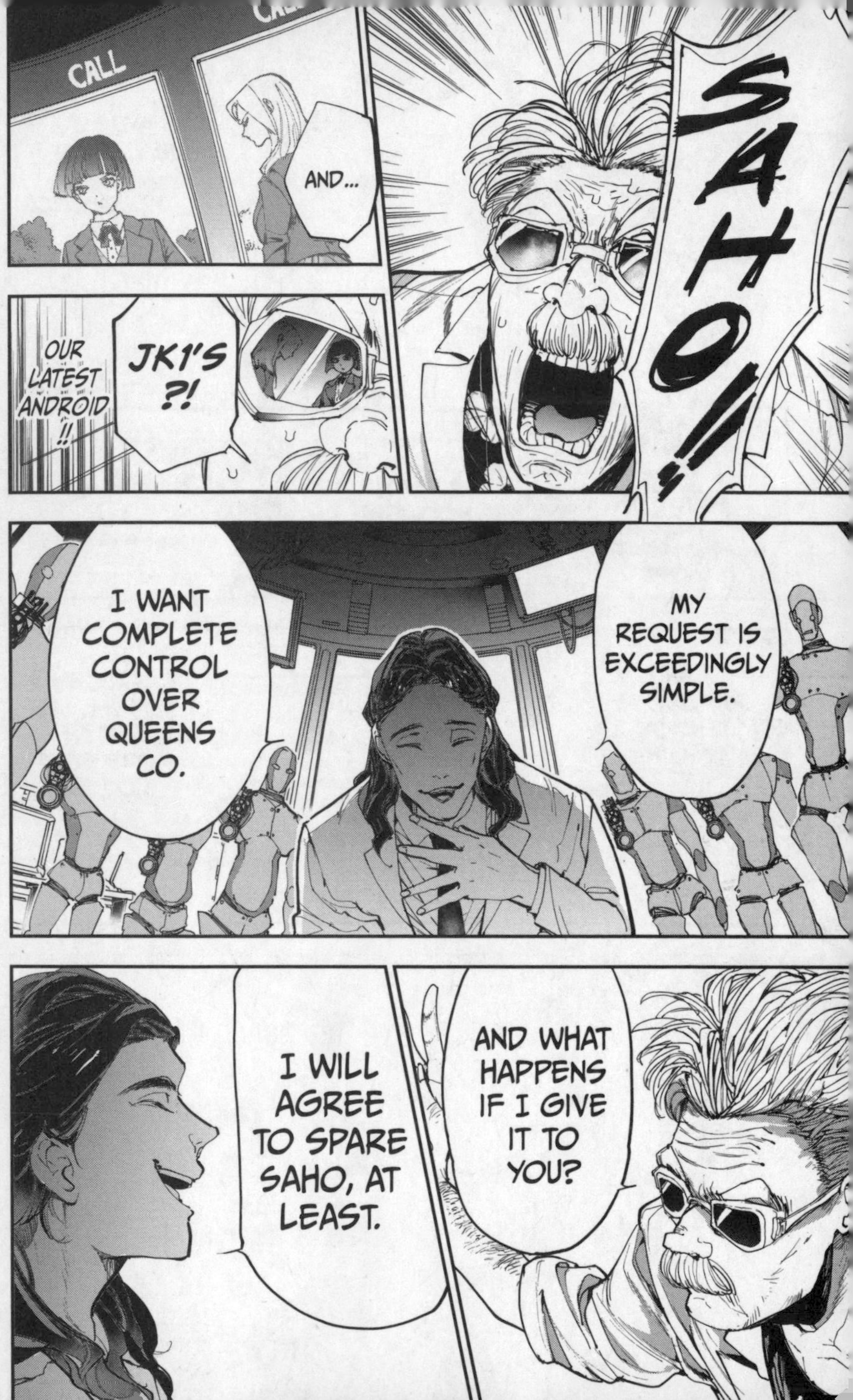
SAHO!!
CALL
AND...
JK1'S ?!
OUR LATEST ANDROID!!
MY REQUEST IS EXCEEDINGLY SIMPLE.
I WANT COMPLETE CONTROL OVER QUEENS CO.
AND WHAT HAPPENS IF I GIVE IT TO YOU?
I WILL AGREE TO SPARE SAHO, AT LEAST.

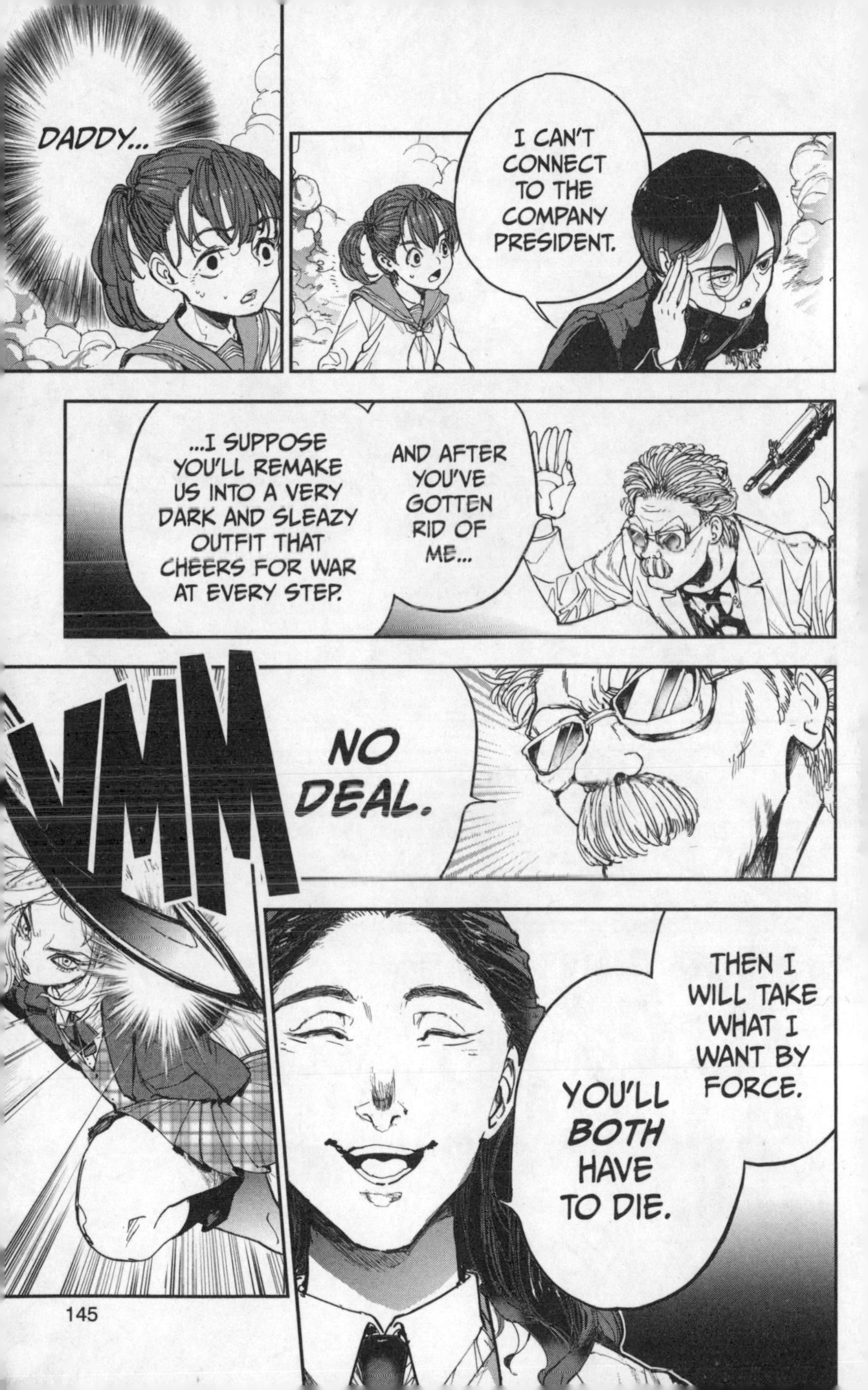
I CAN'T CONNECT TO THE COMPANY PRESIDENT.
DADDY...
AND AFTER YOU'VE GOTTEN RID OF ME...
...I SUPPOSE YOU'LL REMAKE US INTO A VERY DARK AND SLEAZY OUTFIT THAT CHEERS FOR WAR AT EVERY STEP.
NO DEAL.
VMM
THEN I WILL TAKE WHAT I WANT BY FORCE.
YOU'LL BOTH HAVE TO DIE.

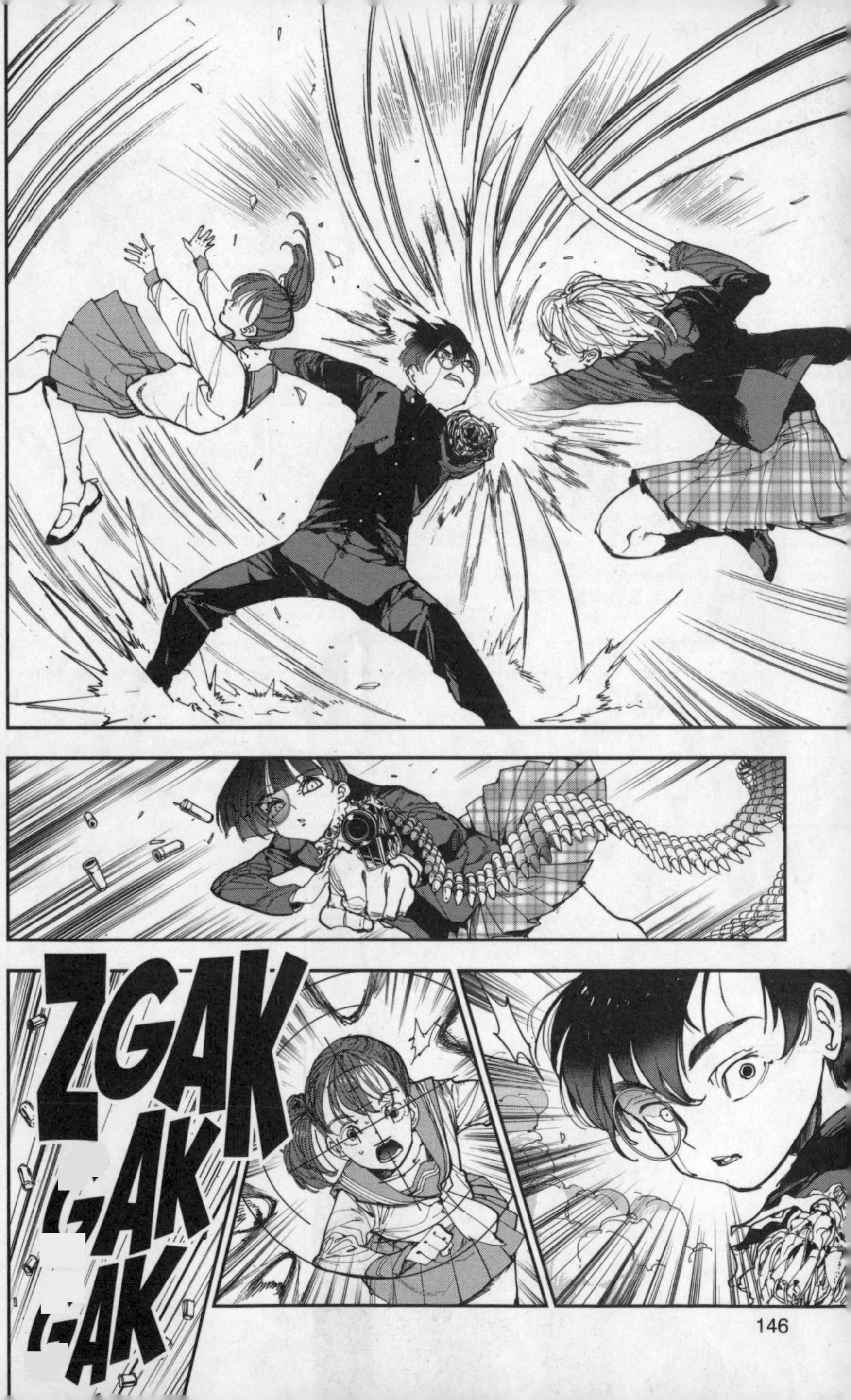
ZGAK

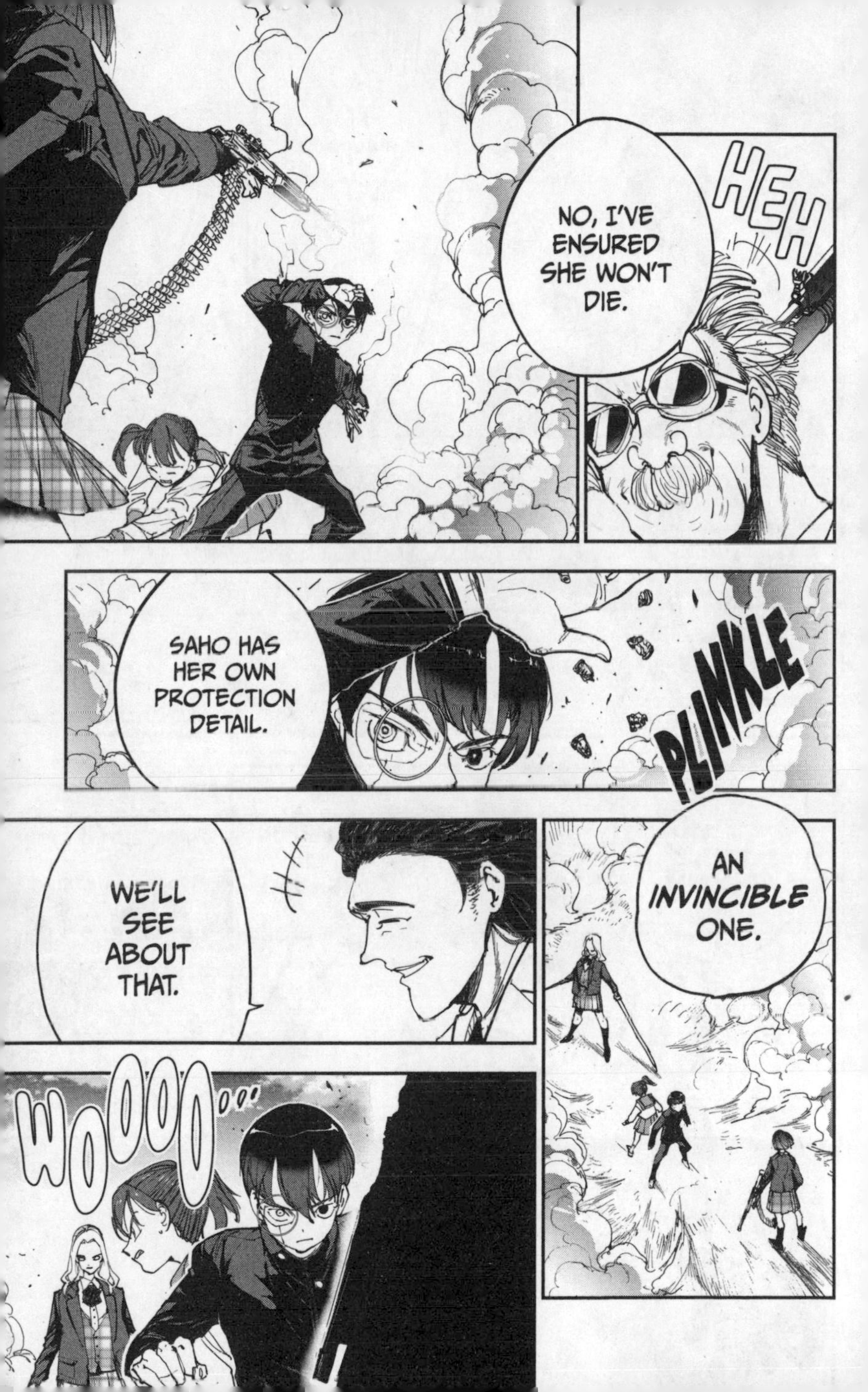
HEH
NO, I'VE ENSURED SHE WON'T DIE.
SAHO HAS HER OWN PROTECTION DETAIL.
PLINKLE
AN INVINCIBLE ONE.
WE'LL SEE ABOUT THAT.
WOOOO

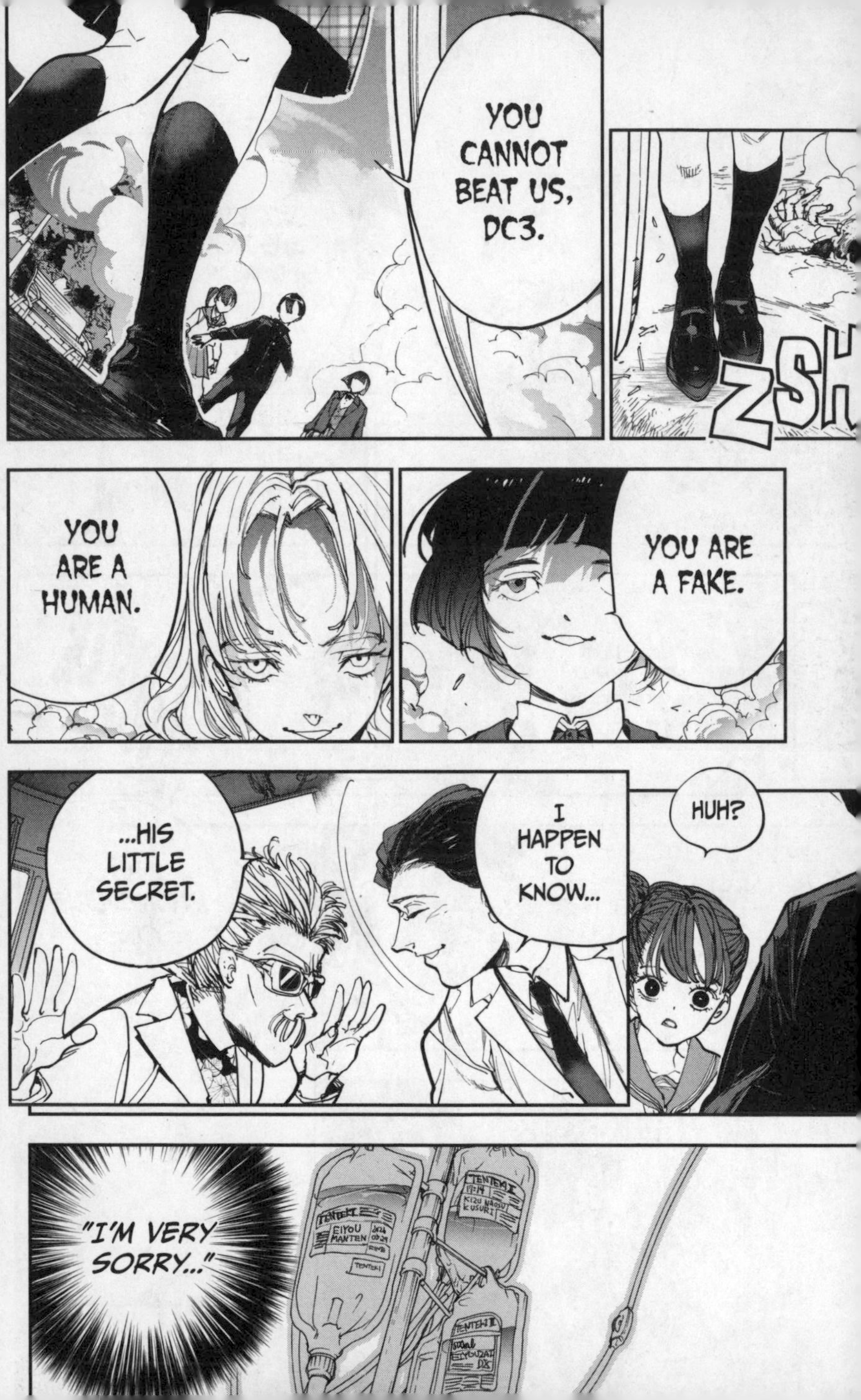
ZSH
YOU CANNOT BEAT US, DC3.
YOU ARE A FAKE.
YOU ARE A HUMAN.
HUH?
I HAPPEN TO KNOW...
...HIS LITTLE SECRET.
TENTEKI I
KIZU NAOSU KUSURI
TENTEKI
EIYOU MANTEN
"I'M VERY SORRY..."
TENTEKI II
EIYOUZAI DX

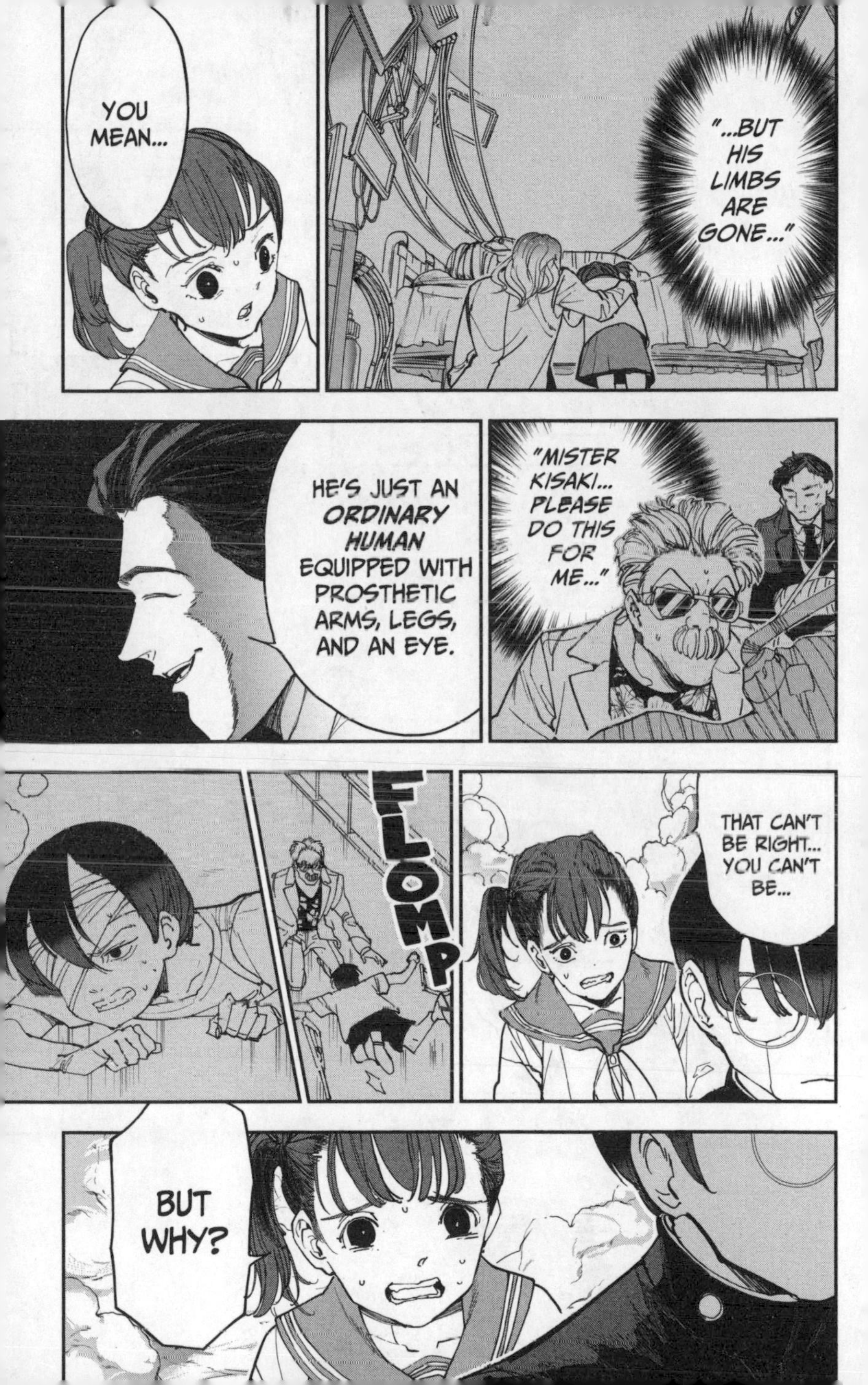
"...BUT HIS LIMBS ARE GONE..."
YOU MEAN...
"MISTER KISAKI... PLEASE DO THIS FOR ME..."
HE'S JUST AN *ORDINARY HUMAN* EQUIPPED WITH PROSTHETIC ARMS, LEGS, AND AN EYE.
THAT CAN'T BE RIGHT... YOU CAN'T BE...
FLOMP
BUT WHY?

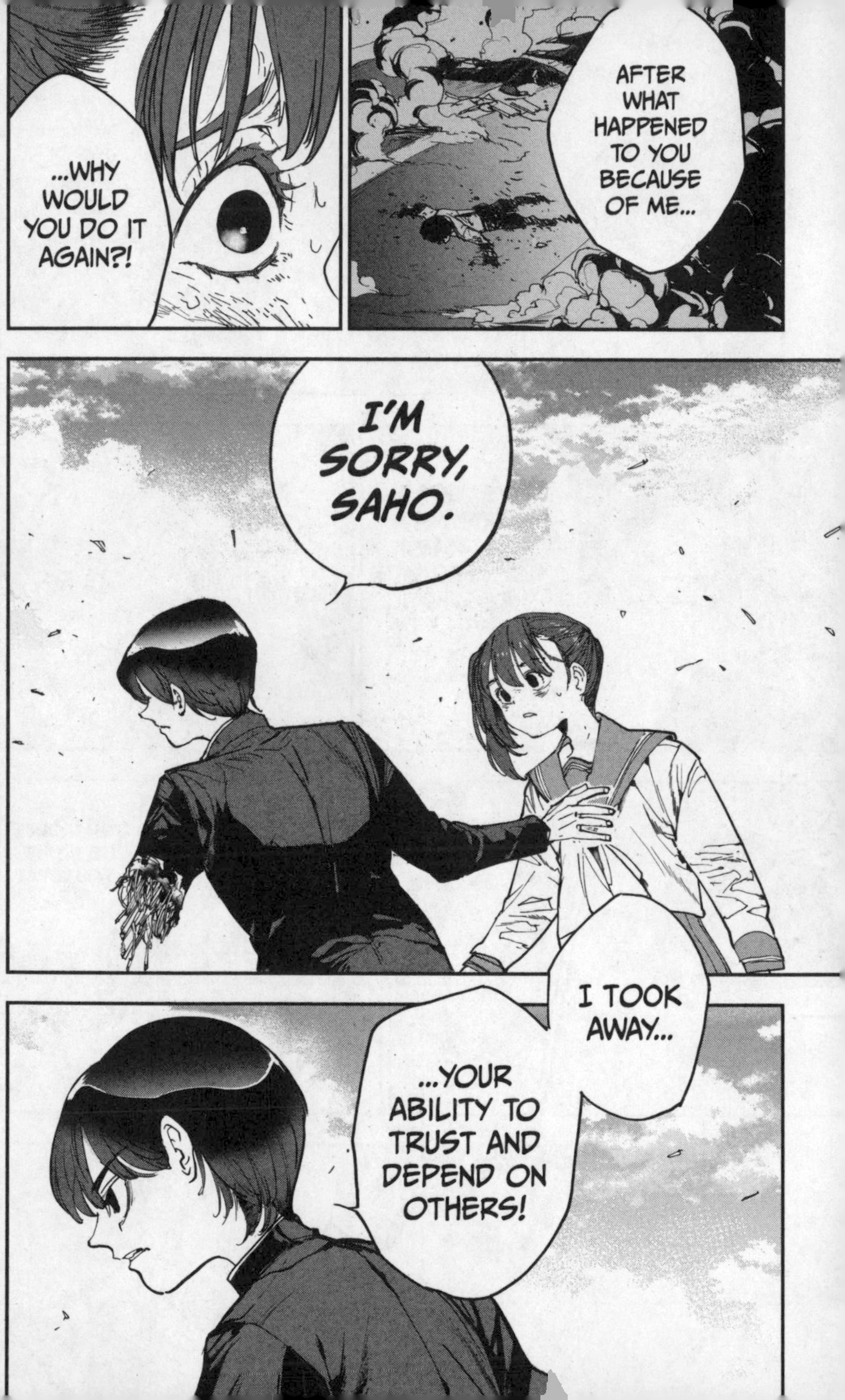
AFTER WHAT HAPPENED TO YOU BECAUSE OF ME...
...WHY WOULD YOU DO IT AGAIN?!
I'M SORRY, SAHO.
I TOOK AWAY...
...YOUR ABILITY TO TRUST AND DEPEND ON OTHERS!

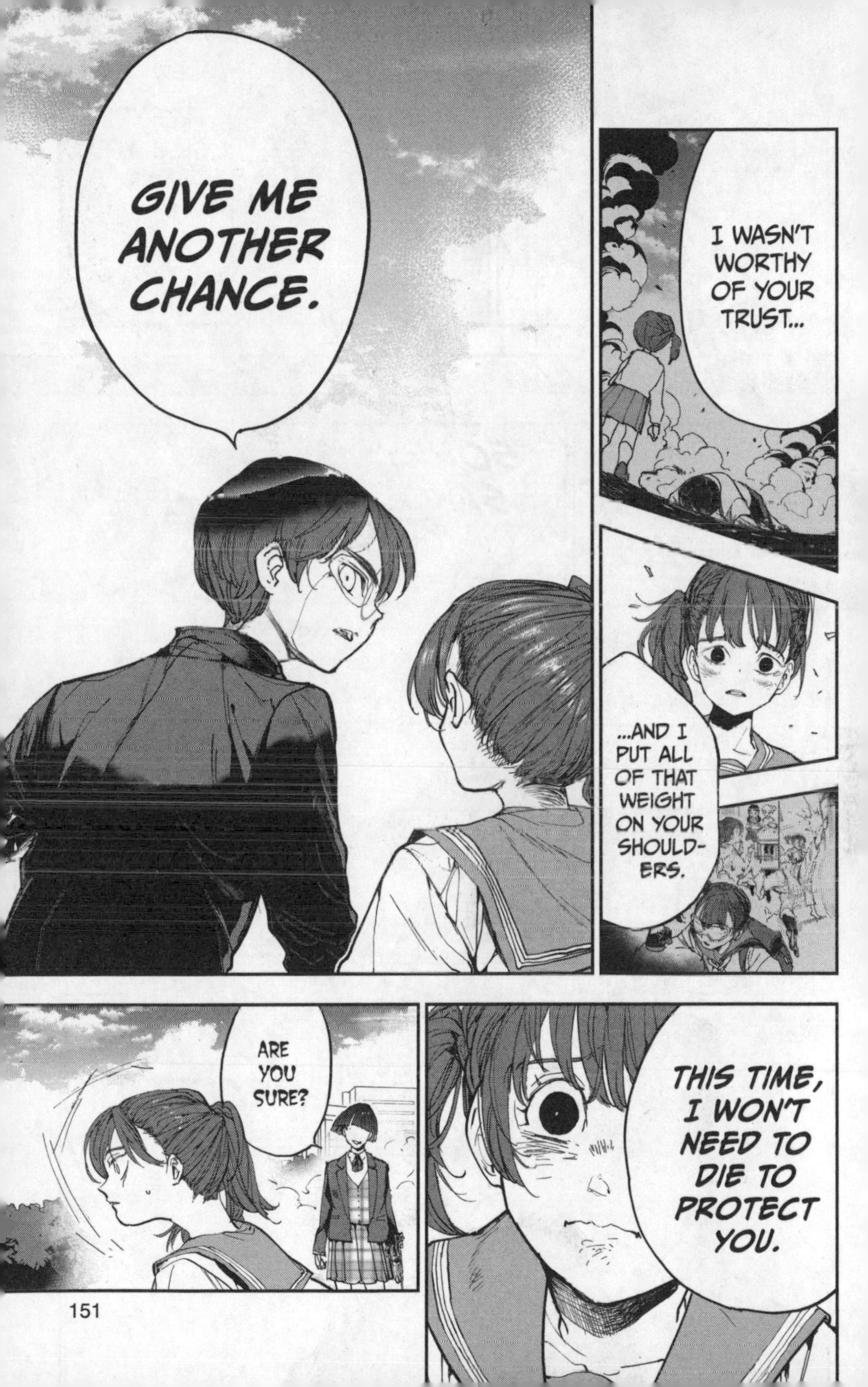
I WASN'T WORTHY OF YOUR TRUST...
...AND I PUT ALL OF THAT WEIGHT ON YOUR SHOULDERS.
GIVE ME ANOTHER CHANCE.
THIS TIME, I WON'T NEED TO DIE TO PROTECT YOU.
ARE YOU SURE?

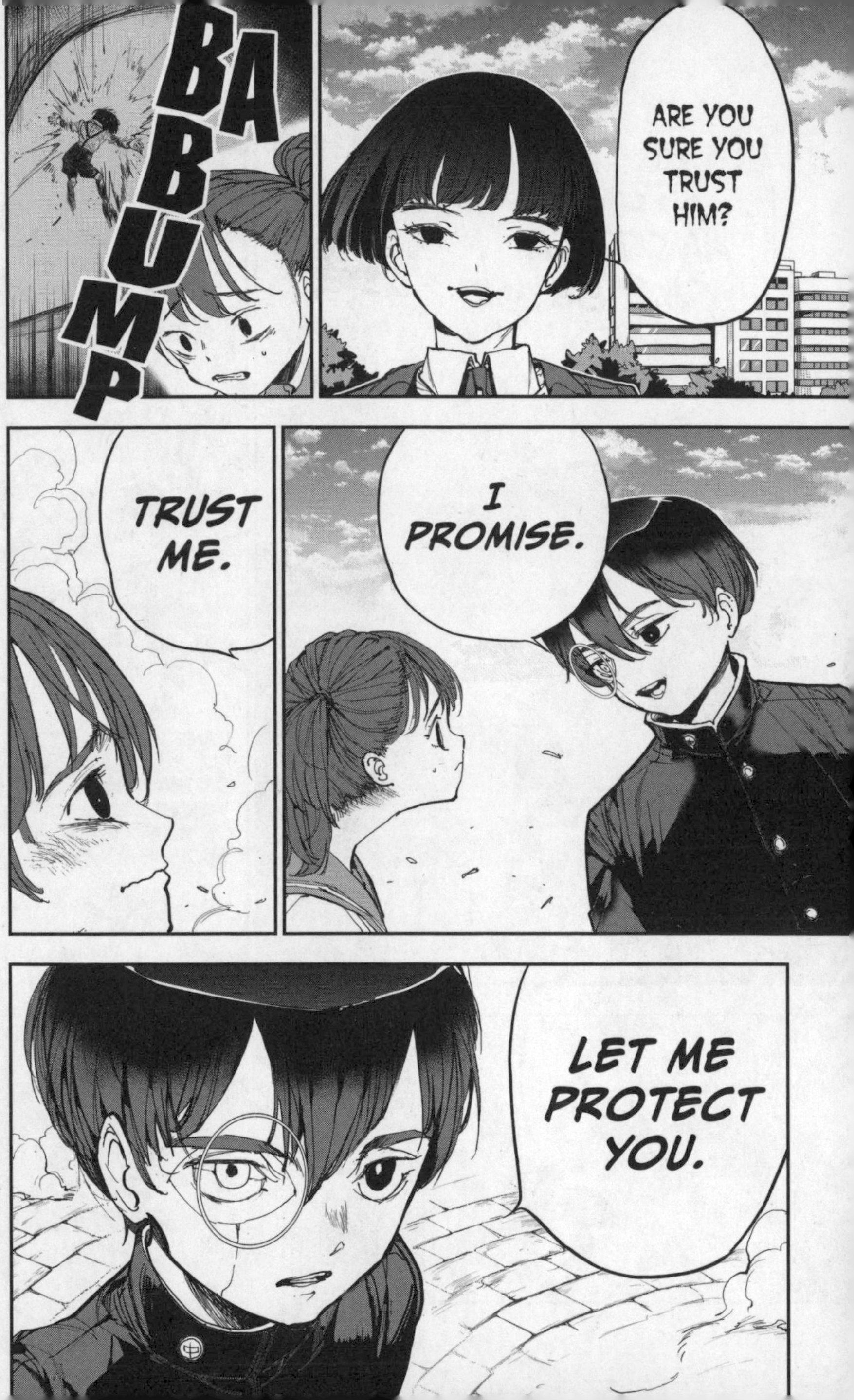
ARE YOU SURE YOU TRUST HIM?
BA BUMP
I PROMISE.
TRUST ME.
LET ME PROTECT YOU.

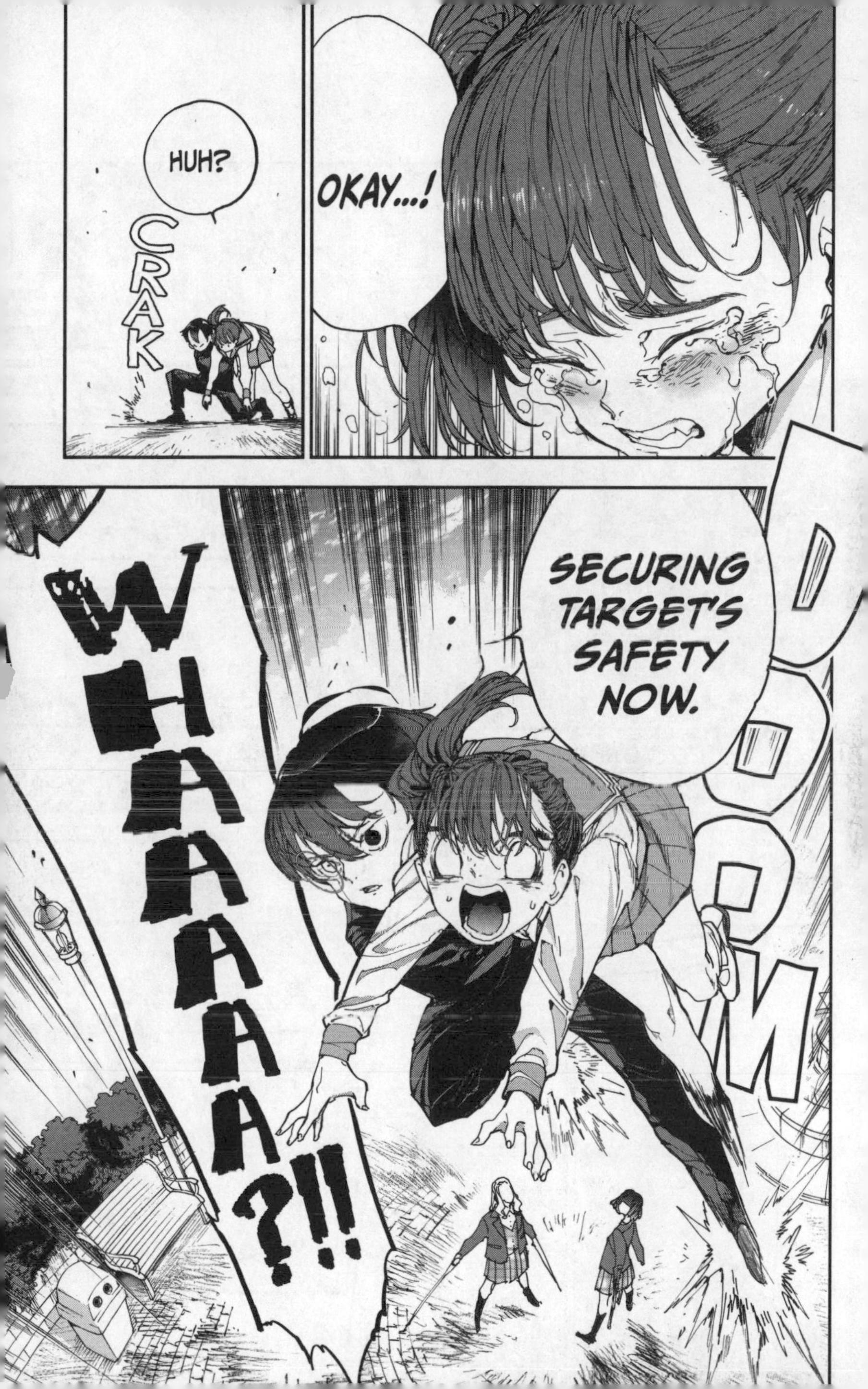
OKAY...!
HUH?
CRAK
DOOM
SECURING TARGET'S SAFETY NOW.
WHAAAAAA?!!

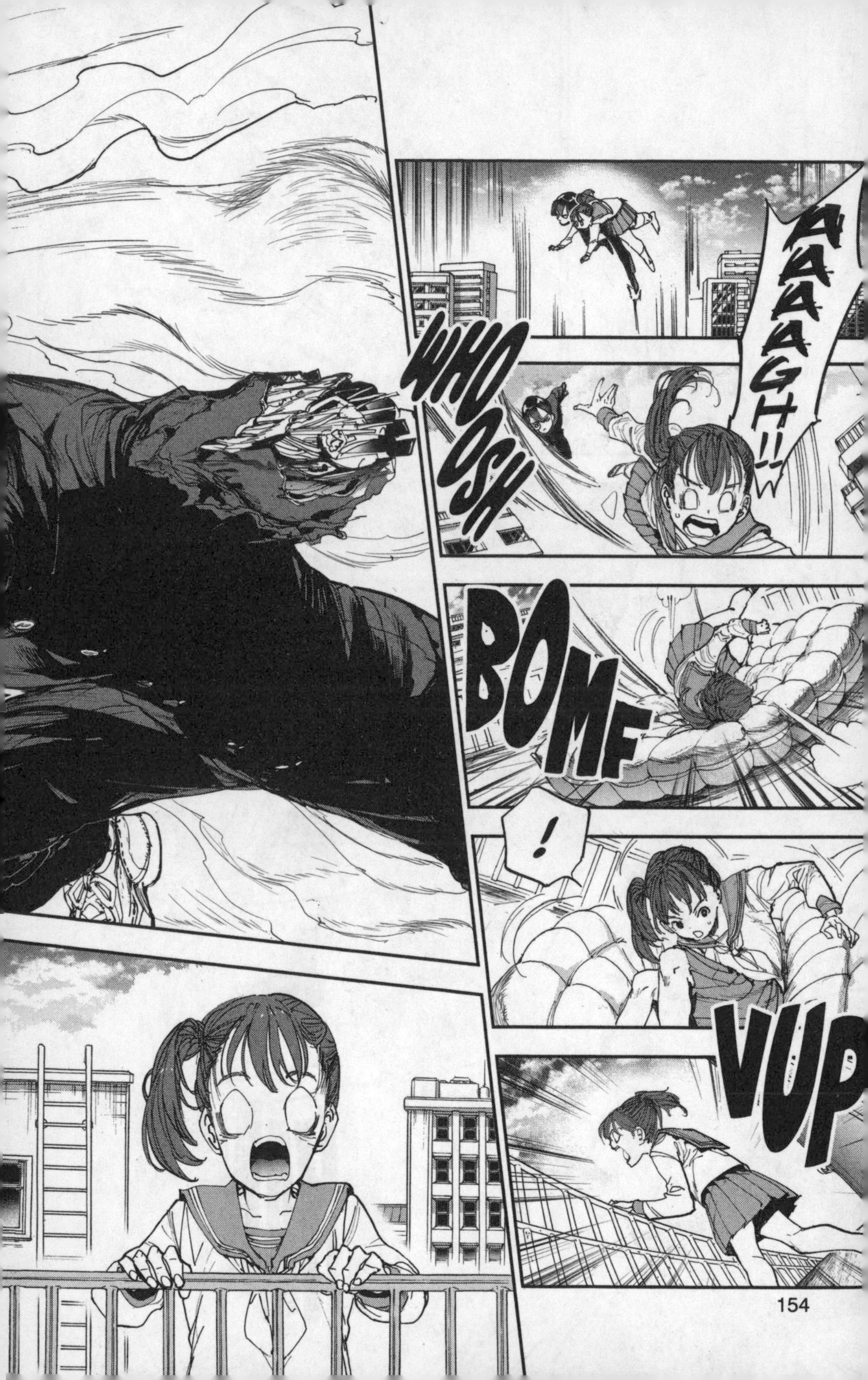
AAAAGH!!
WHOOSH
BOMF
!
VUP

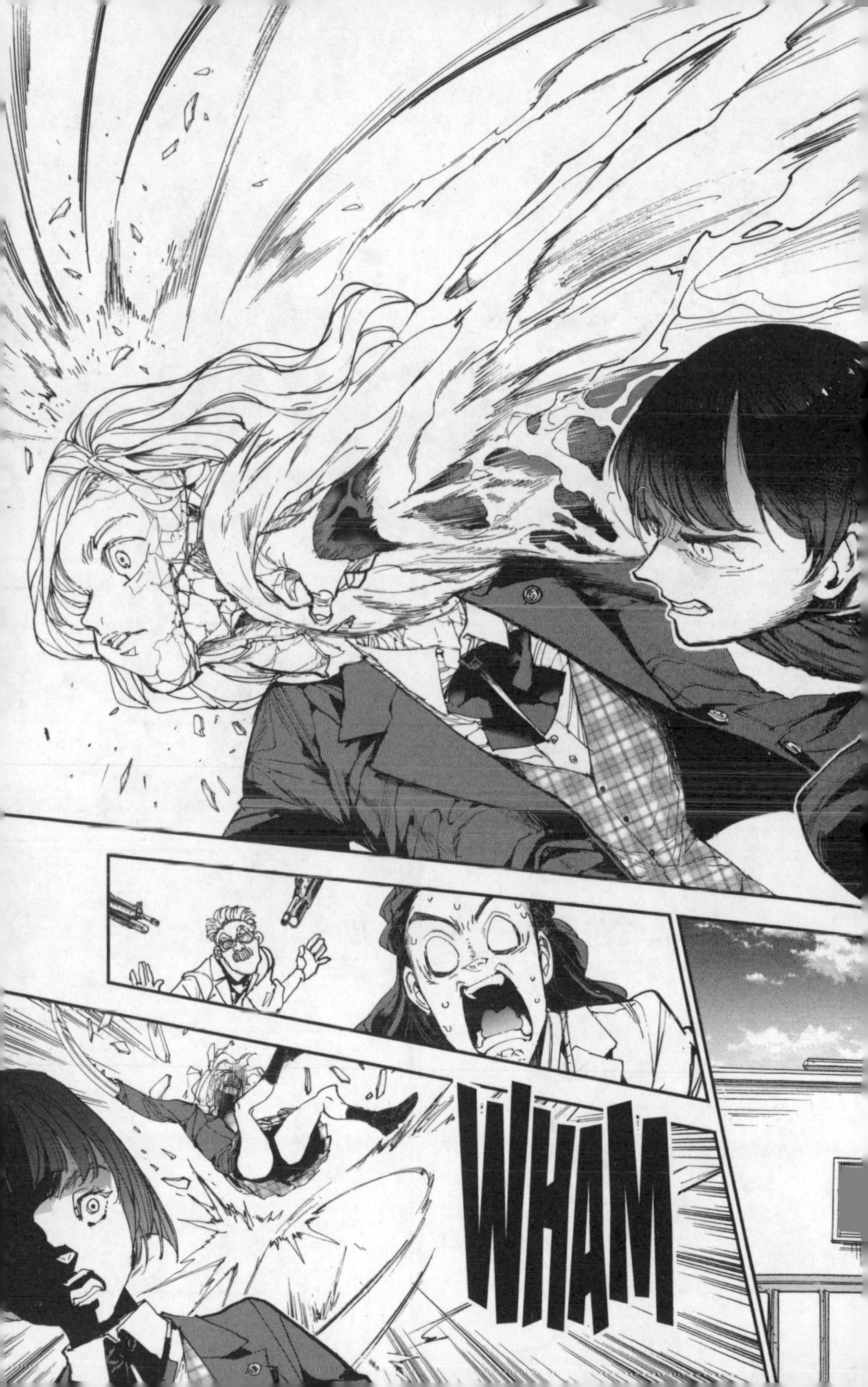
WHAM

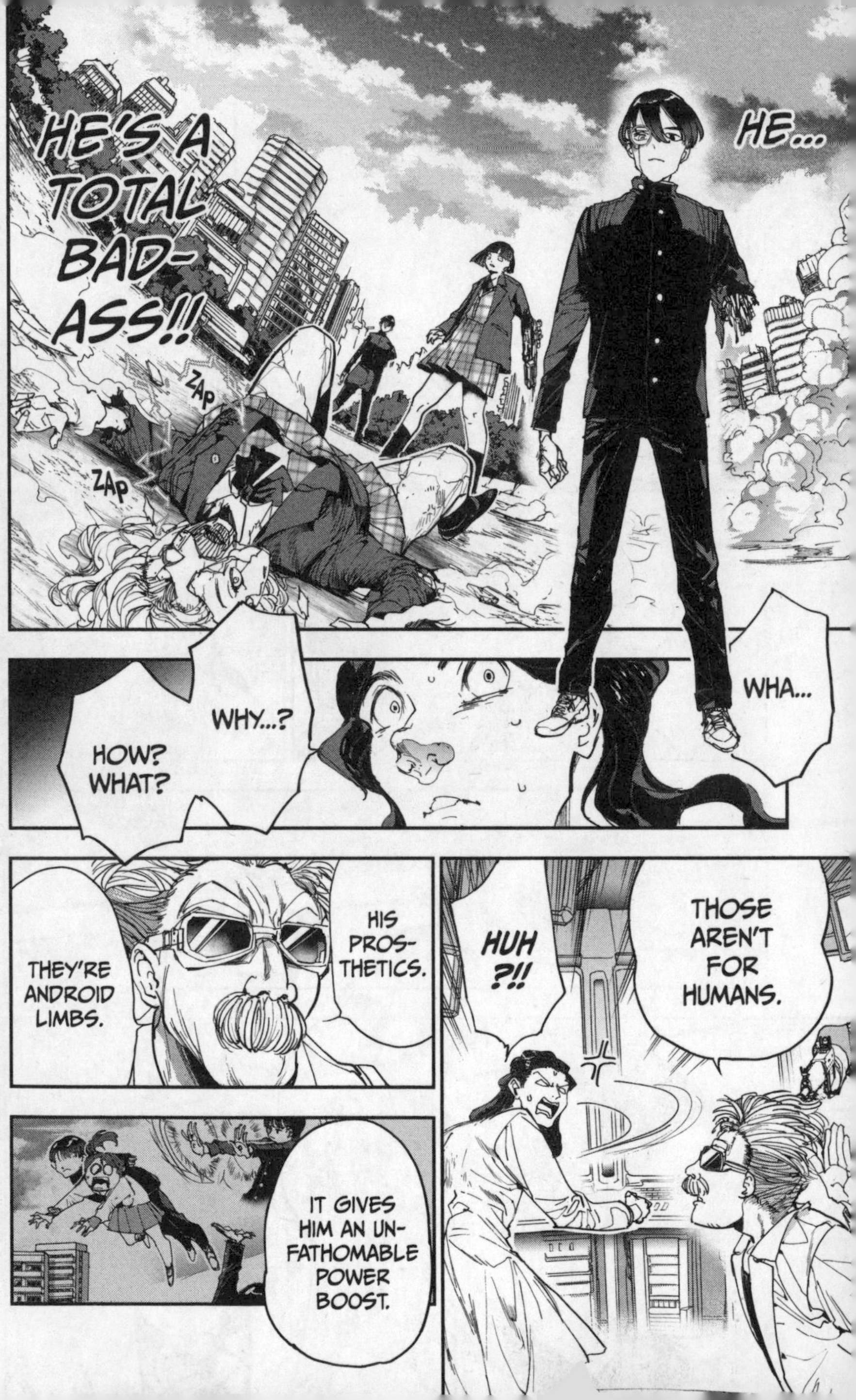
HE...
HE'S A TOTAL BAD-ASS!!
ZAP
ZAP
WHA...
WHY...?
HOW? WHAT?
THOSE AREN'T FOR HUMANS.
HUH?!!
HIS PROSTHETICS.
THEY'RE ANDROID LIMBS.
IT GIVES HIM AN UN-FATHOMABLE POWER BOOST.

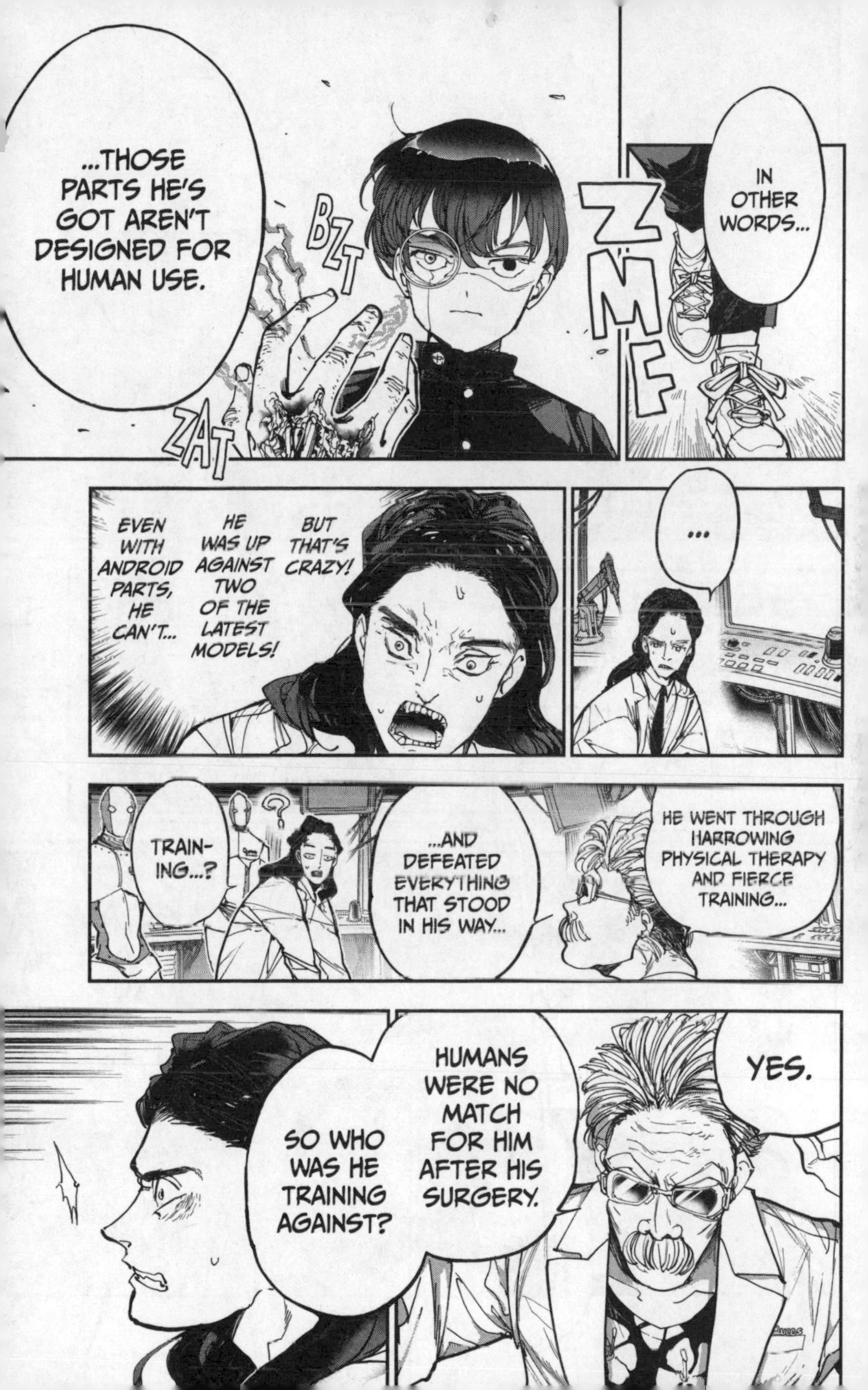
IN OTHER WORDS...
ZMF
...THOSE PARTS HE'S GOT AREN'T DESIGNED FOR HUMAN USE.
BZT
ZAT
...
BUT THAT'S CRAZY!
HE WAS UP AGAINST TWO OF THE LATEST MODELS!
EVEN WITH ANDROID PARTS, HE CAN'T...
HE WENT THROUGH HARROWING PHYSICAL THERAPY AND FIERCE TRAINING...
...AND DEFEATED EVERYTHING THAT STOOD IN HIS WAY...
TRAIN-ING...?
YES.
HUMANS WERE NO MATCH FOR HIM AFTER HIS SURGERY.
SO WHO WAS HE TRAINING AGAINST?

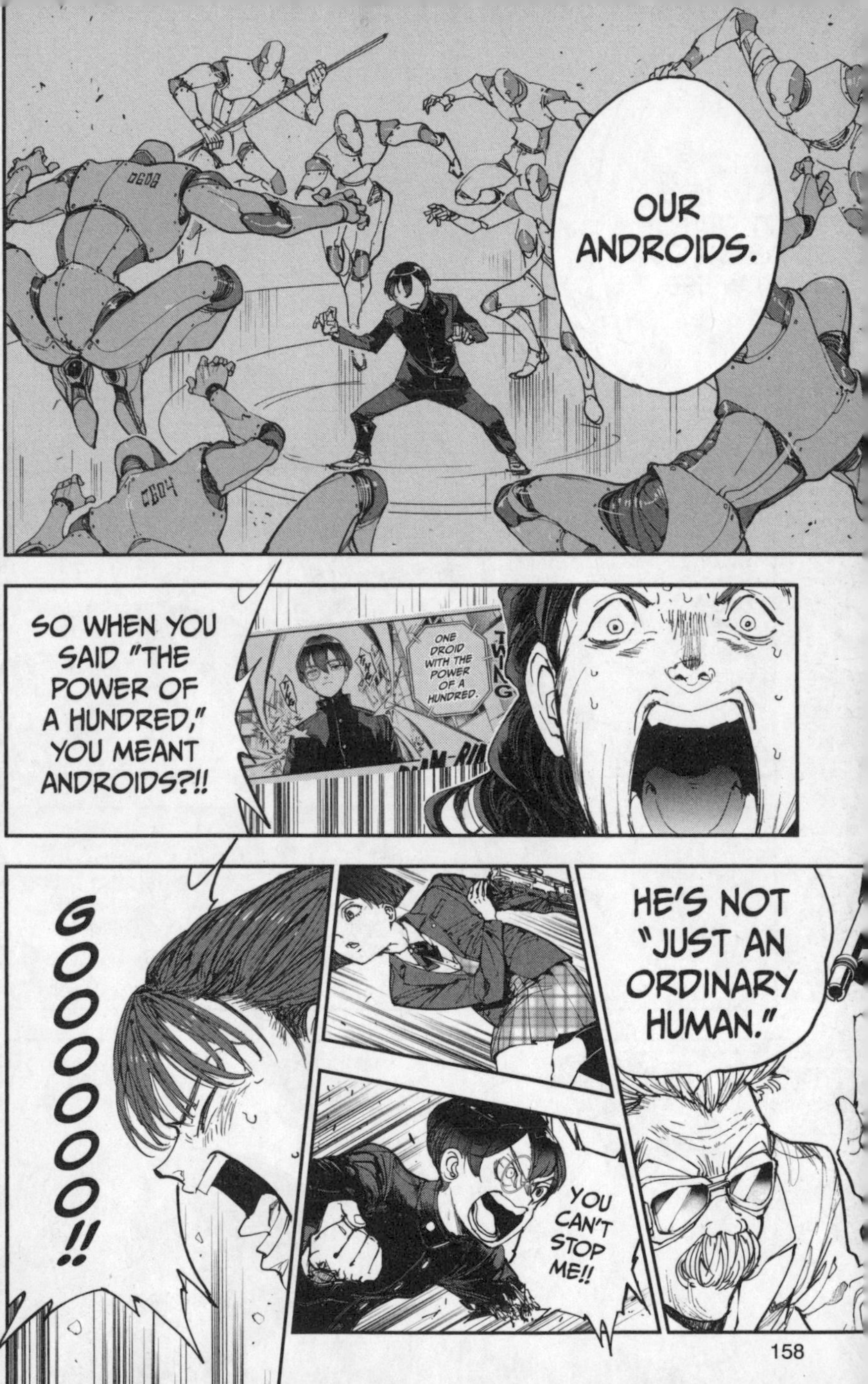
OUR ANDROIDS.
TWING
ONE DROID WITH THE POWER OF A HUNDRED.
SO WHEN YOU SAID "THE POWER OF A HUNDRED," YOU MEANT ANDROIDS?!!
HE'S NOT "JUST AN ORDINARY HUMAN."
YOU CAN'T STOP ME!!
GOOOOOOOO!!

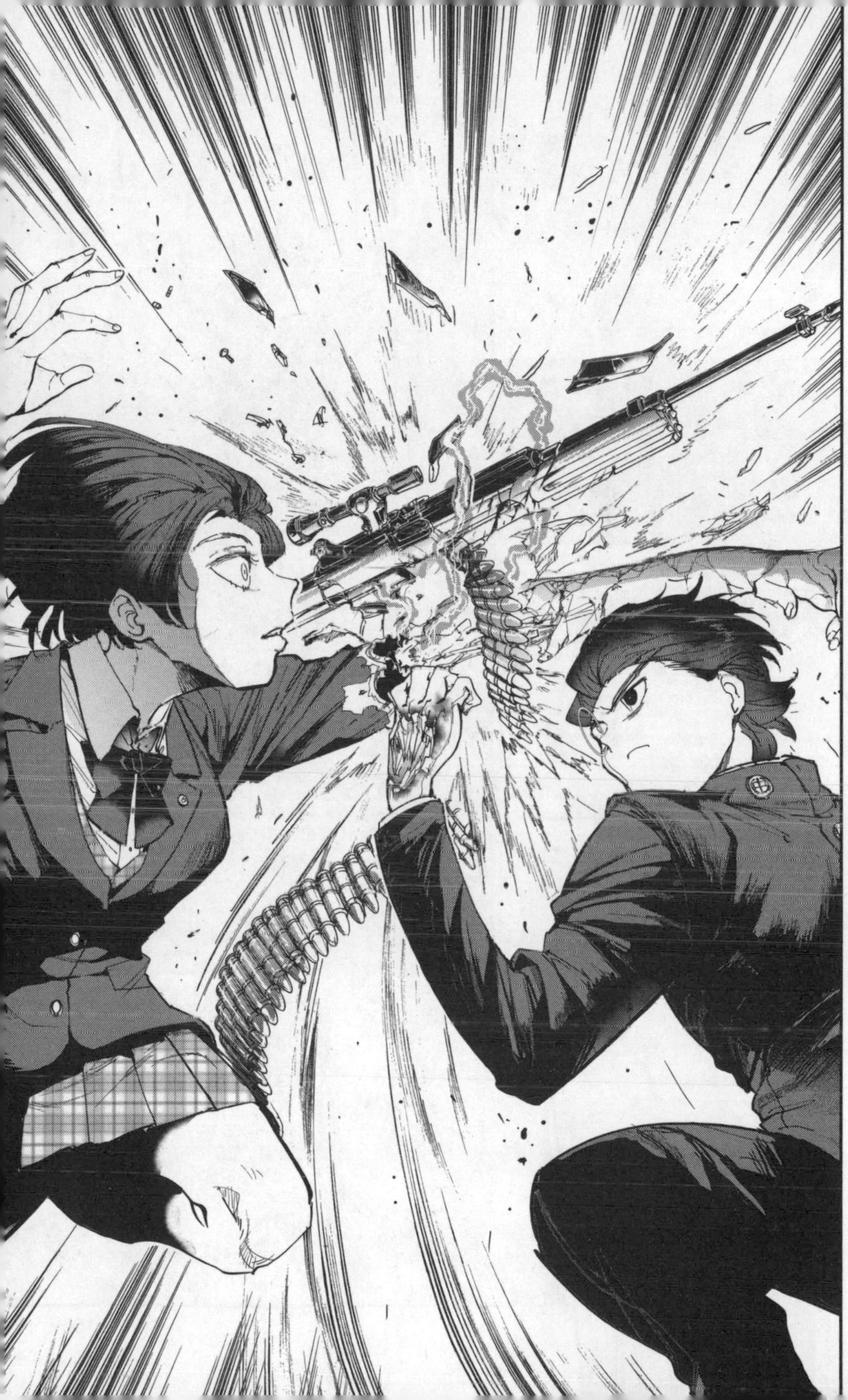

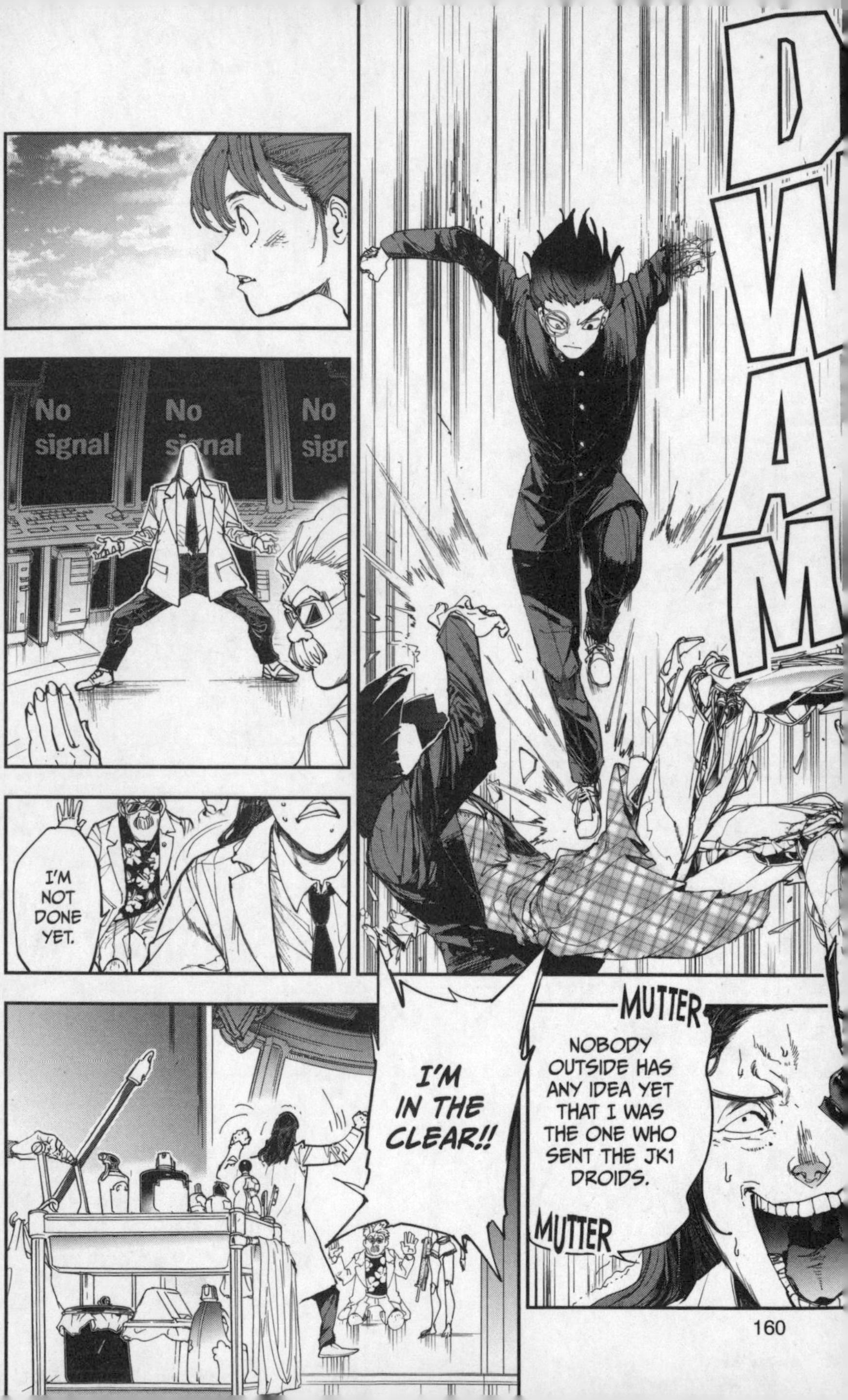
DWAM
No signal
No signal
No signal
I'M NOT DONE YET.
MUTTER
NOBODY OUTSIDE HAS ANY IDEA YET THAT I WAS THE ONE WHO SENT THE JK1 DROIDS.
MUTTER
I'M IN THE CLEAR!!

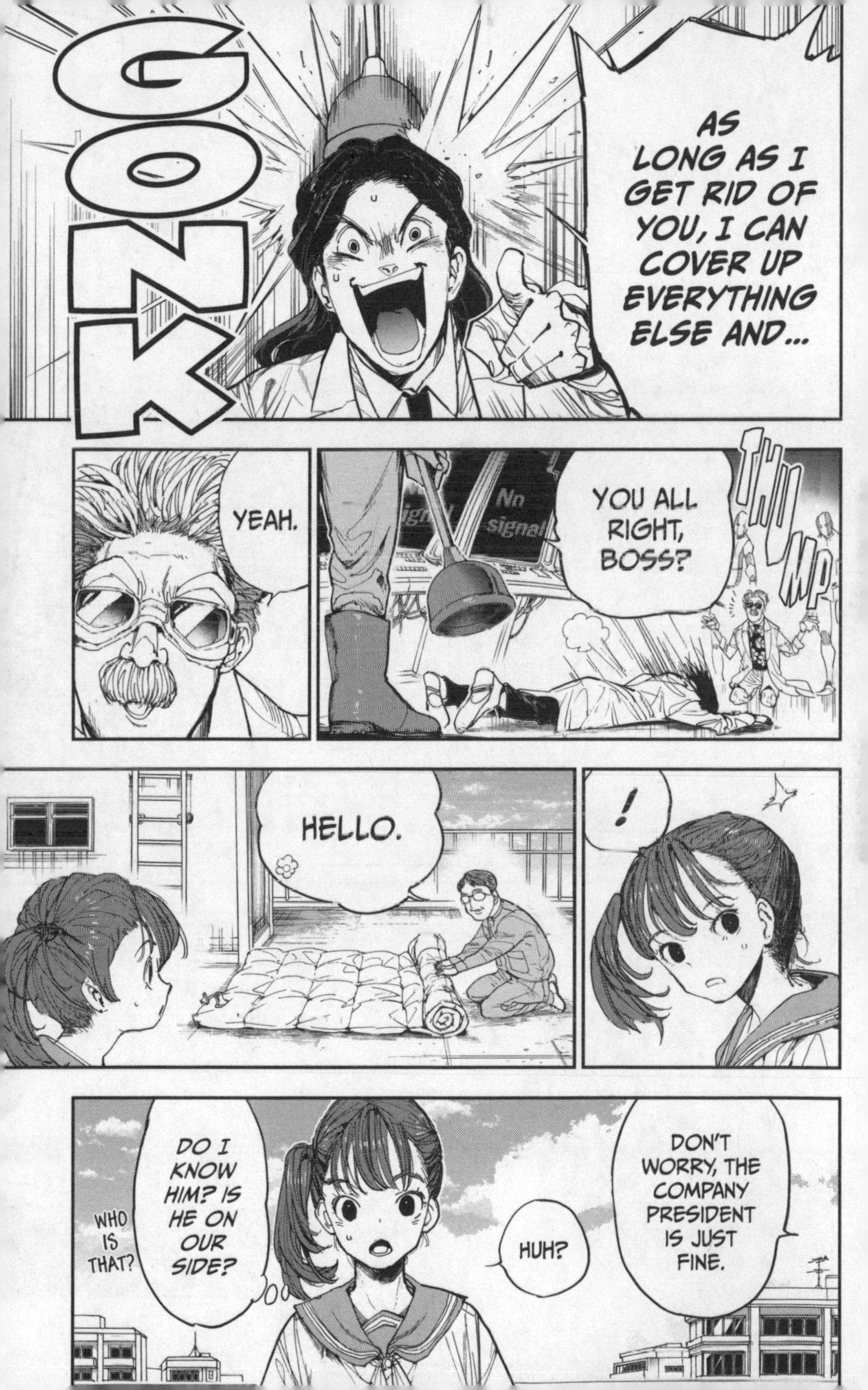
AS LONG AS I GET RID OF YOU, I CAN COVER UP EVERYTHING ELSE AND...
GONK
THUMP
YOU ALL RIGHT, BOSS?
No signal
YEAH.
!
HELLO.
DON'T WORRY, THE COMPANY PRESIDENT IS JUST FINE.
HUH?
DO I KNOW HIM? IS HE ON OUR SIDE?
WHO IS THAT?

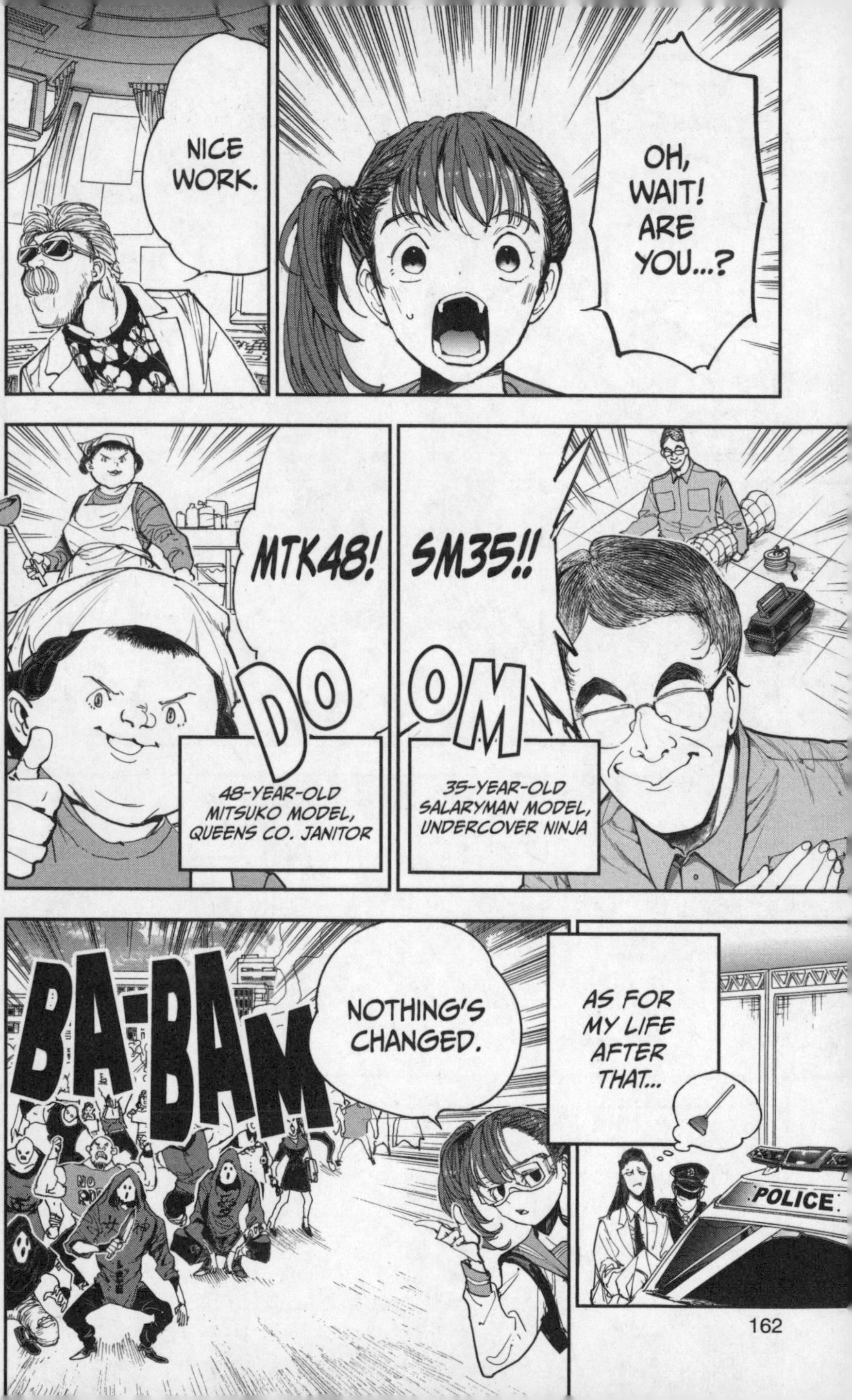
OH, WAIT! ARE YOU...?
NICE WORK.
SM35!!
35-YEAR-OLD SALARYMAN MODEL, UNDERCOVER NINJA
MTK48!
48-YEAR-OLD MITSUKO MODEL, QUEENS CO. JANITOR
DO OM
AS FOR MY LIFE AFTER THAT...
POLICE
NOTHING'S CHANGED.
BA-BAM

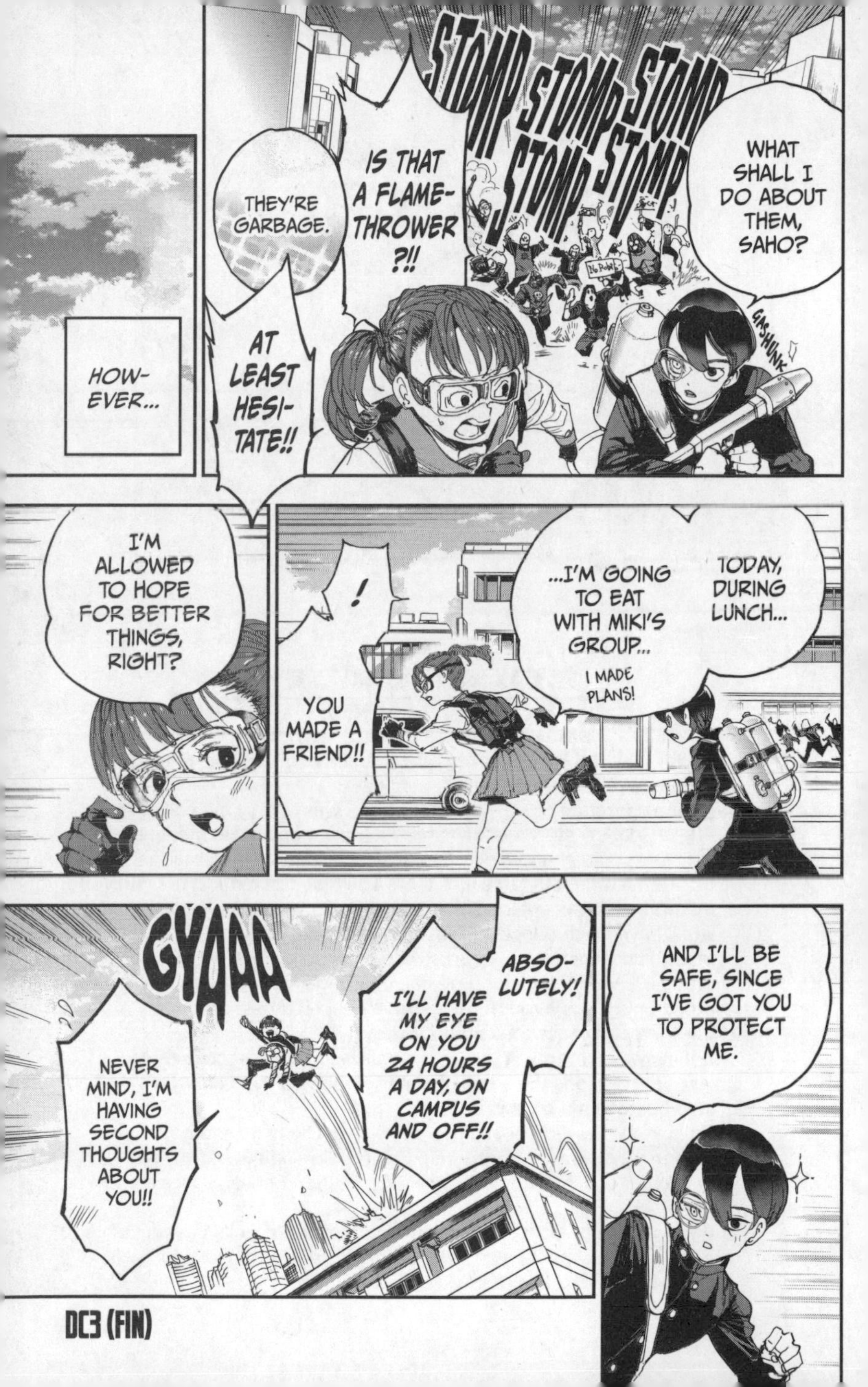
STOMP STOMP STOMP STOMP STOMP
WHAT SHALL I DO ABOUT THEM, SAHO?
GASHUNK
IS THAT A FLAME-THROWER?!!
THEY'RE GARBAGE.
AT LEAST HESI-TATE!!
HOW-EVER...
TODAY, DURING LUNCH...
...I'M GOING TO EAT WITH MIKI'S GROUP...
I MADE PLANS!
!
YOU MADE A FRIEND!!
I'M ALLOWED TO HOPE FOR BETTER THINGS, RIGHT?
AND I'LL BE SAFE, SINCE I'VE GOT YOU TO PROTECT ME.
ABSO-LUTELY!
I'LL HAVE MY EYE ON YOU 24 HOURS A DAY, ON CAMPUS AND OFF!!
GYAAA
NEVER MIND, I'M HAVING SECOND THOUGHTS ABOUT YOU!!

DC3 (FIN)

SHIRAI'S BEHIND-THE-SCENES STORIES #4

◆ I wrote this at a time when I was having a really hard time finding an artist for *The Promised Neverland* and was about to give up on the series.

◆ I had a challenge attached to this story. I was told by my editor, Mr. Sugita, that my storyboards tended to be a bit risky. He meant that the story could change with one expression and that for manga split between a writer and an artist, there could be discrepancies in how the work was presented. So he told me, "Try writing storyboards that won't have discrepancies no matter which artist draws it. Something that would work even if an artist who can't do extreme expressions draws it." And I tried taking on that challenge, which is why the main protagonist (?) is a robot, the dad wears sunglasses, and many of the characters have their eyes closed.

◆ But midway through, I gave up and allowed the characters to use facial expressions to convey the story. I realized that I could only storyboard in my own way.

◆ So anyway, the storyboard had some restrictions on it, but surprisingly, it was restored from the trash bin and was drawn by the holder of unlimited drawing ability, Demizu Sensei, so it's a very lucky story.

◆ Sadly it was cut off in the printing, but Demizu Sensei's drawing of Saho's dad's slippers was overwhelmingly right on!! I love them! I'm not worthy!! You're a goddess!!

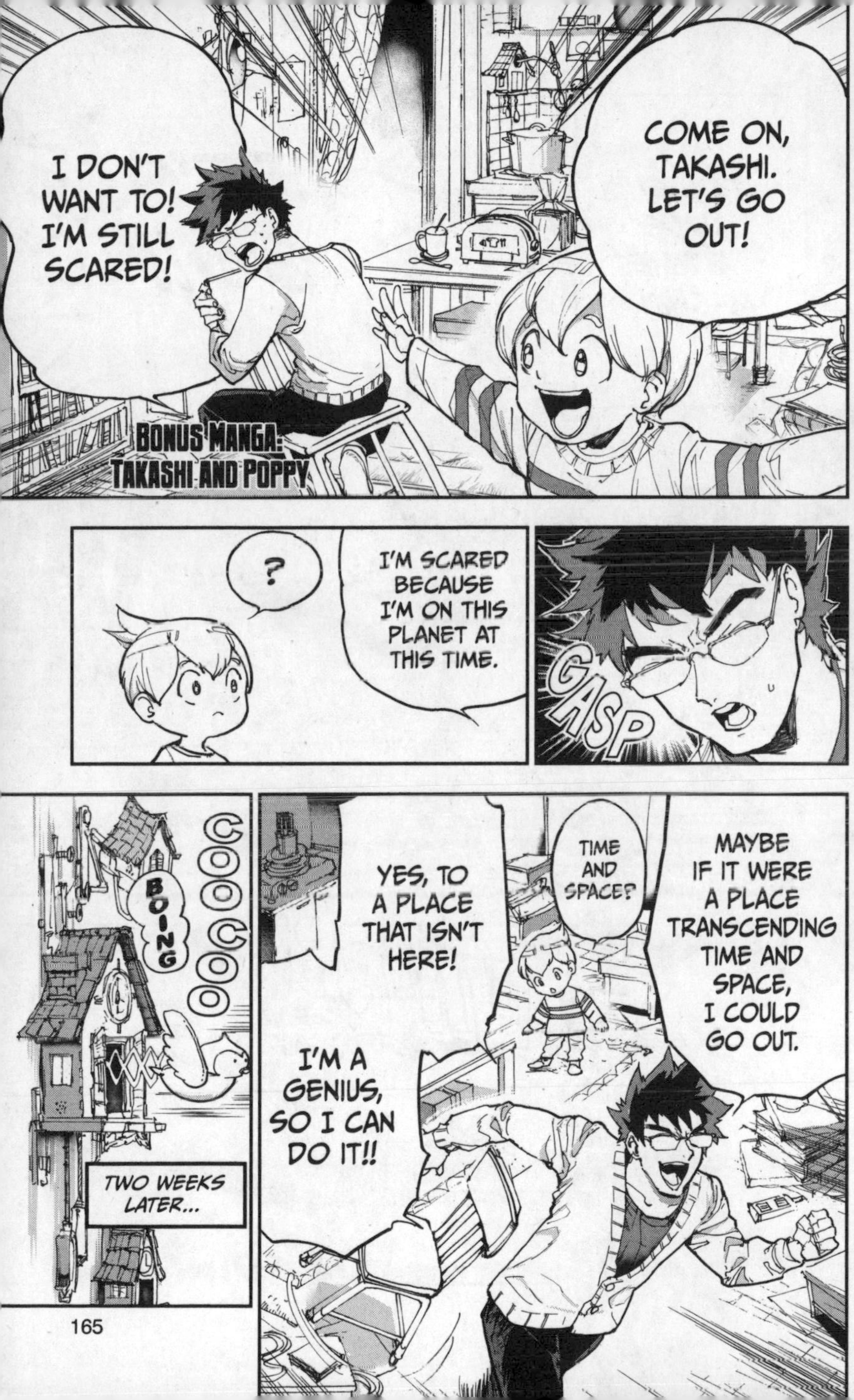
BONUS MANGA: TAKASHI AND POPPY
COME ON, TAKASHI. LET'S GO OUT!
I DON'T WANT TO! I'M STILL SCARED!
GASP
I'M SCARED BECAUSE I'M ON THIS PLANET AT THIS TIME.
?
MAYBE IF IT WERE A PLACE TRANSCENDING TIME AND SPACE, I COULD GO OUT.
TIME AND SPACE?
YES, TO A PLACE THAT ISN'T HERE!
I'M A GENIUS, SO I CAN DO IT!!
COOCOO
BOING
TWO WEEKS LATER...

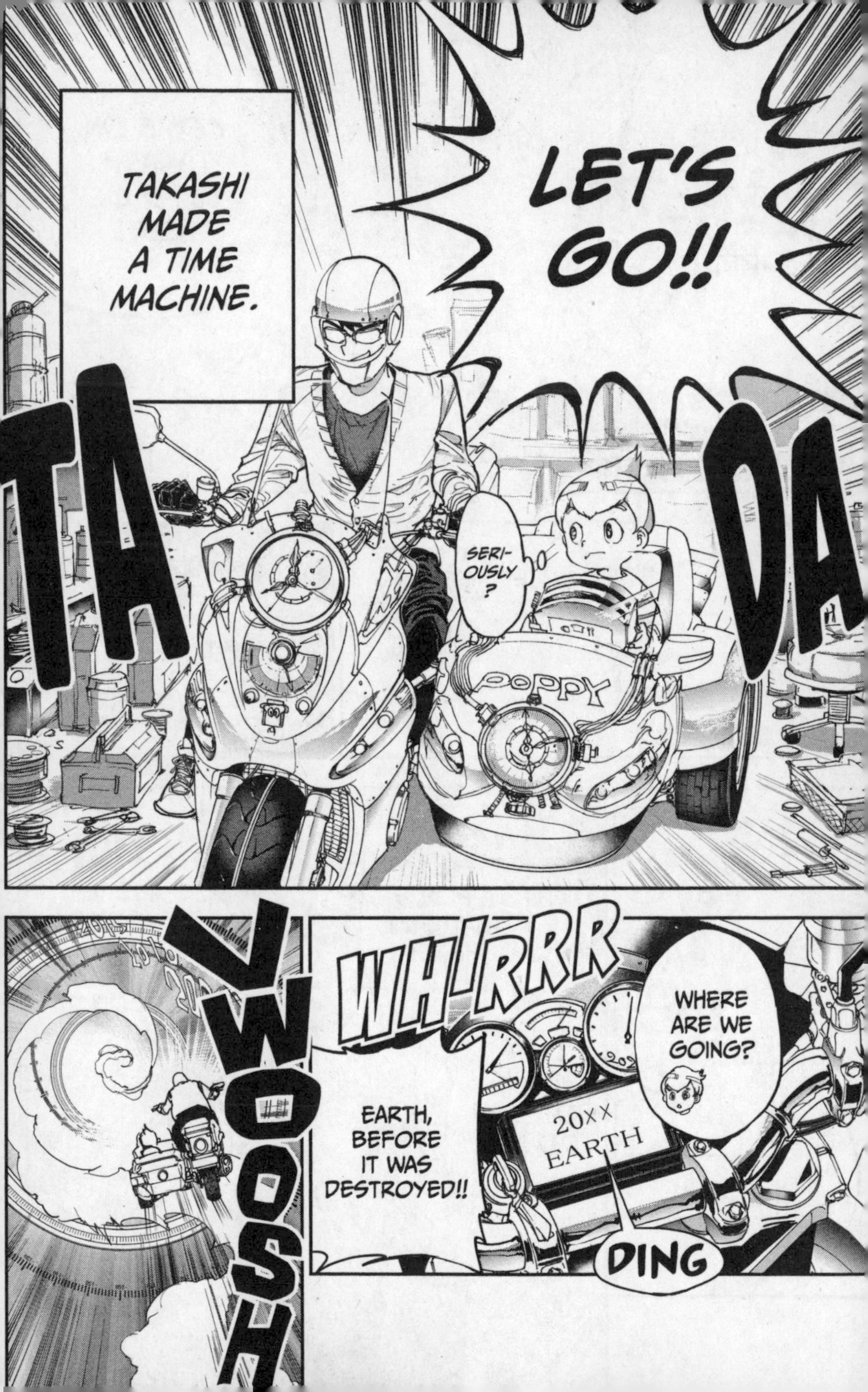
LET'S GO!!
TAKASHI MADE A TIME MACHINE.
TA DA
SERI-OUSLY?
POPPY
WHIRRR
WHERE ARE WE GOING?
20XX EARTH
EARTH, BEFORE IT WAS DESTROYED!!
DING
VWOOSH

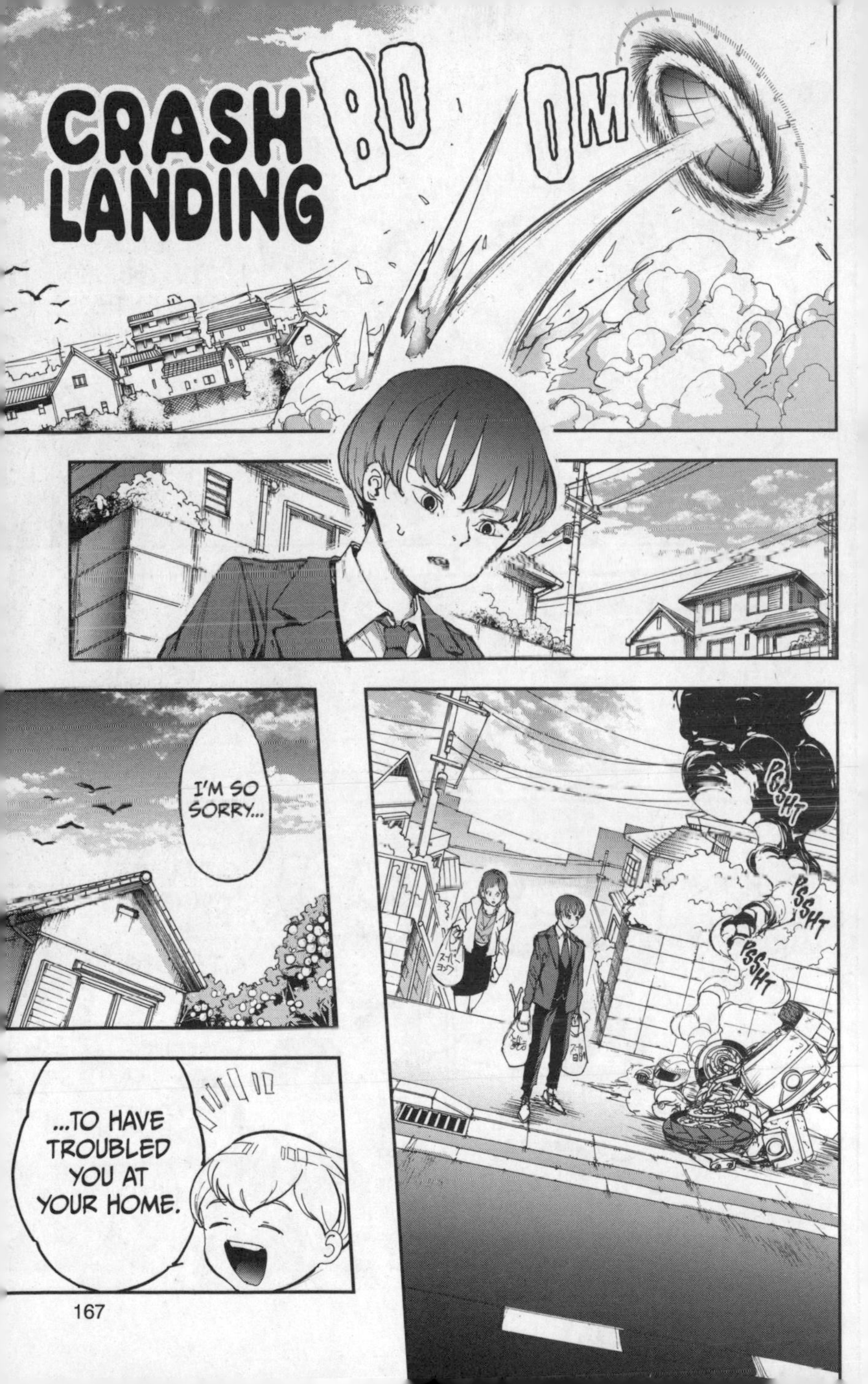
CRASH LANDING
BOOM
PSSHT
PSSHT
PSSHT
I'M SO SORRY...
...TO HAVE TROUBLED YOU AT YOUR HOME.

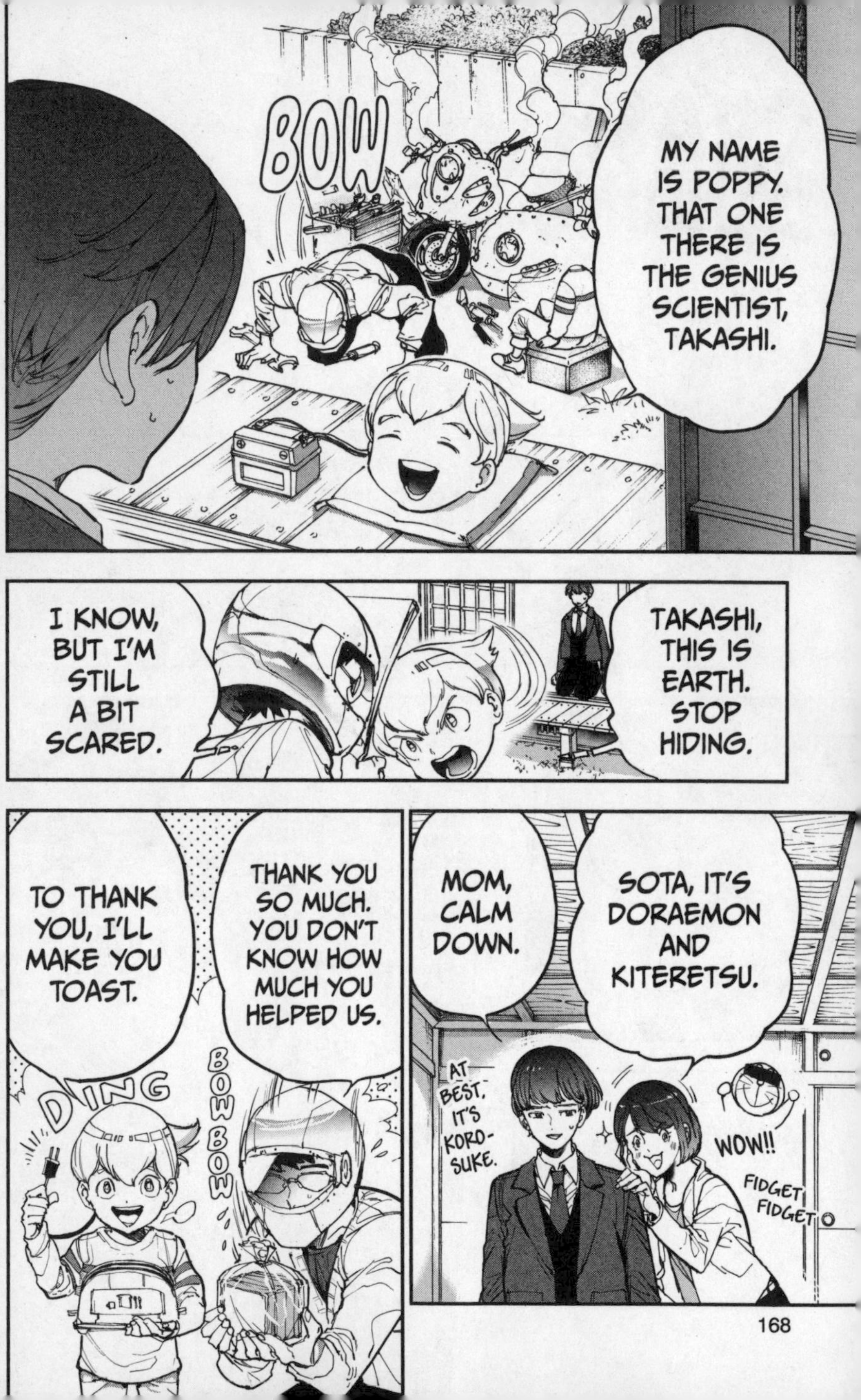
MY NAME IS POPPY. THAT ONE THERE IS THE GENIUS SCIENTIST, TAKASHI.
BOW
TAKASHI, THIS IS EARTH. STOP HIDING.
I KNOW, BUT I'M STILL A BIT SCARED.
SOTA, IT'S DORAEMON AND KITERETSU.
MOM, CALM DOWN.
AT BEST, IT'S KORO-SUKE.
WOW!!
FIDGET FIDGET
THANK YOU SO MUCH. YOU DON'T KNOW HOW MUCH YOU HELPED US.
TO THANK YOU, I'LL MAKE YOU TOAST.
BOW BOW
DING

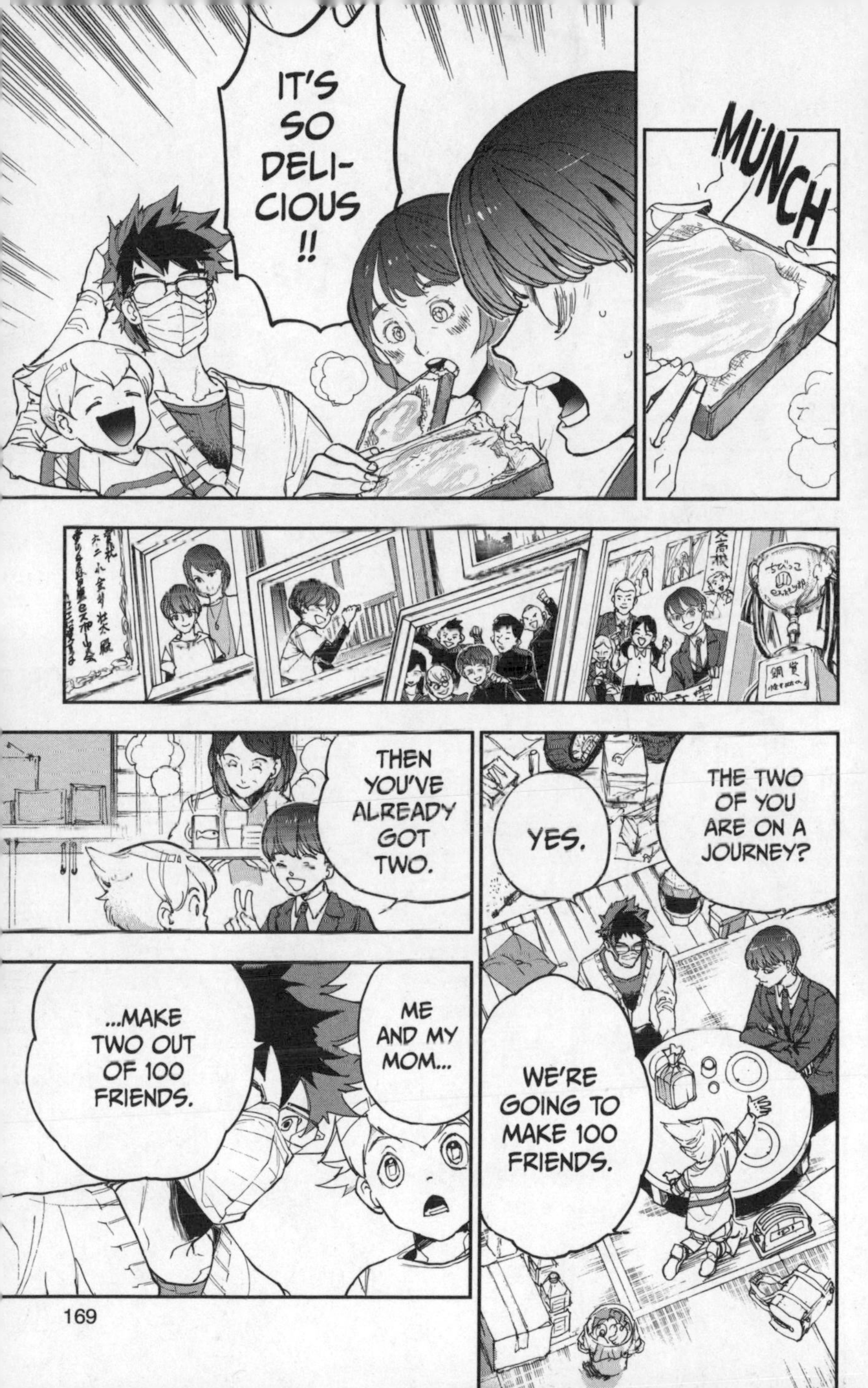
MUNCH
IT'S SO DELI-CIOUS!!
THE TWO OF YOU ARE ON A JOURNEY?
YES.
WE'RE GOING TO MAKE 100 FRIENDS.
THEN YOU'VE ALREADY GOT TWO.
ME AND MY MOM...
...MAKE TWO OUT OF 100 FRIENDS.

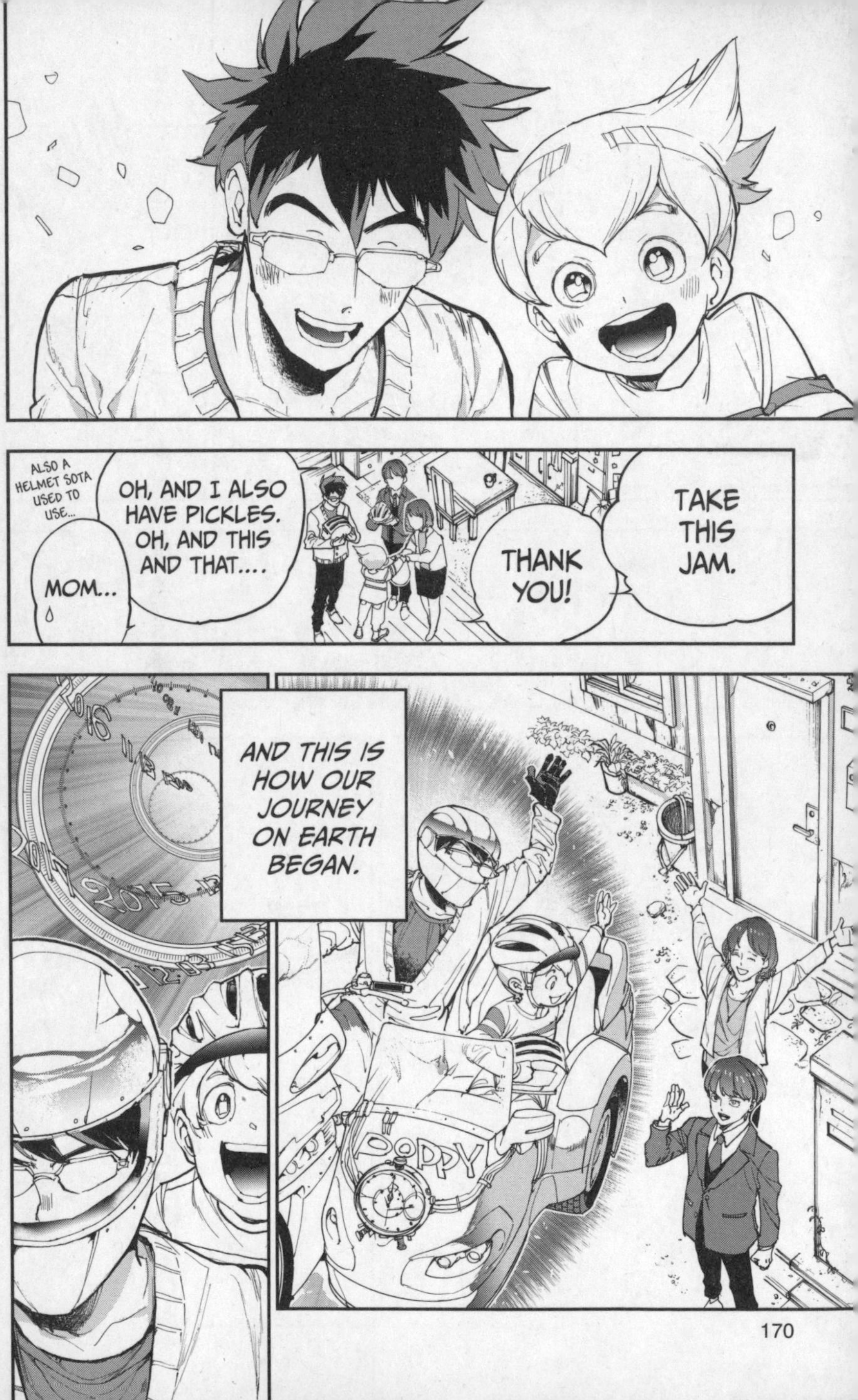
TAKE THIS JAM.
THANK YOU!
OH, AND I ALSO HAVE PICKLES. OH, AND THIS AND THAT....
ALSO A HELMET SOTA USED TO USE...
MOM...
AND THIS IS HOW OUR JOURNEY ON EARTH BEGAN.
POPPY

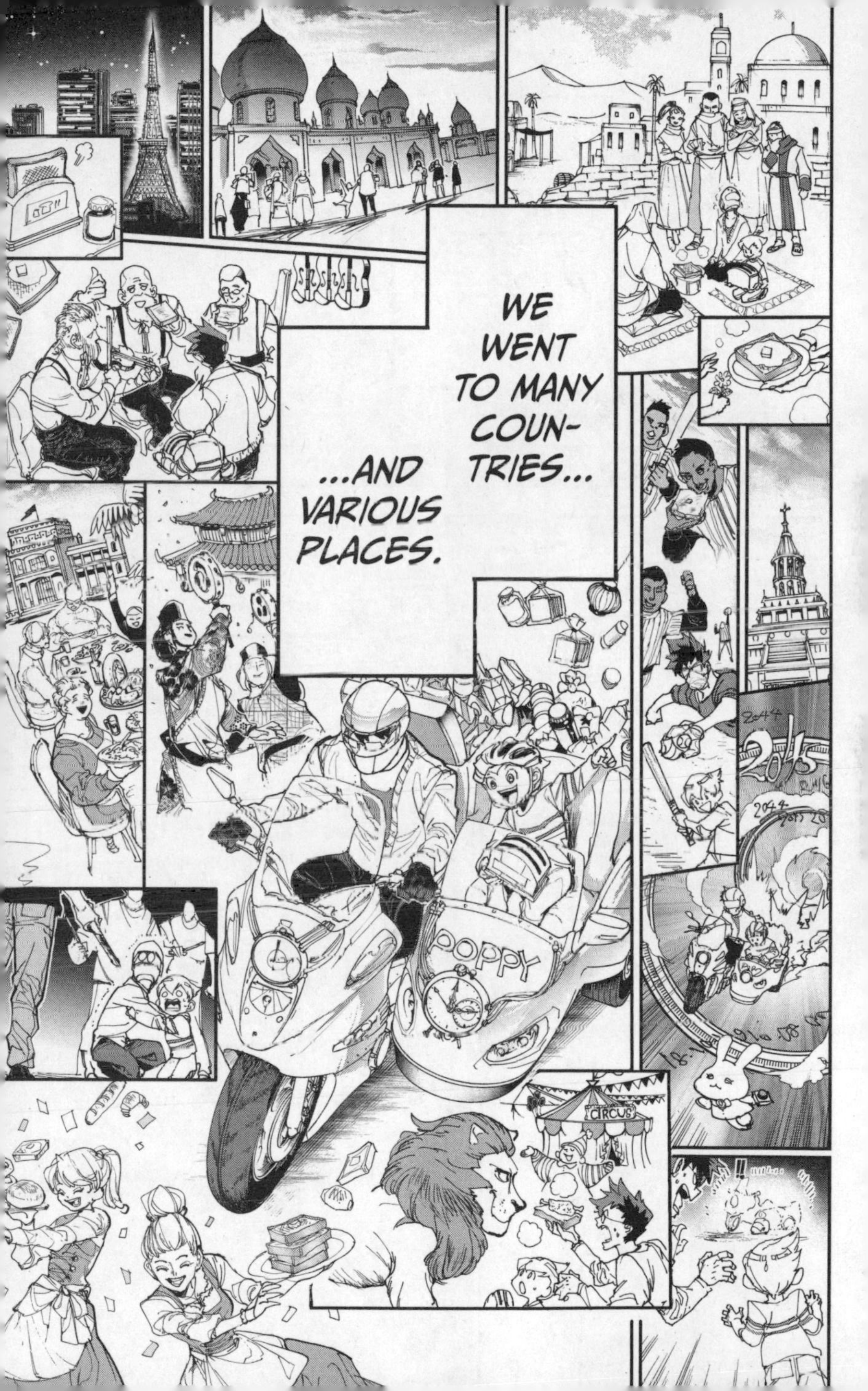
WE WENT TO MANY COUN-TRIES...
...AND VARIOUS PLACES.
POPPY
CIRCUS
2044
2045

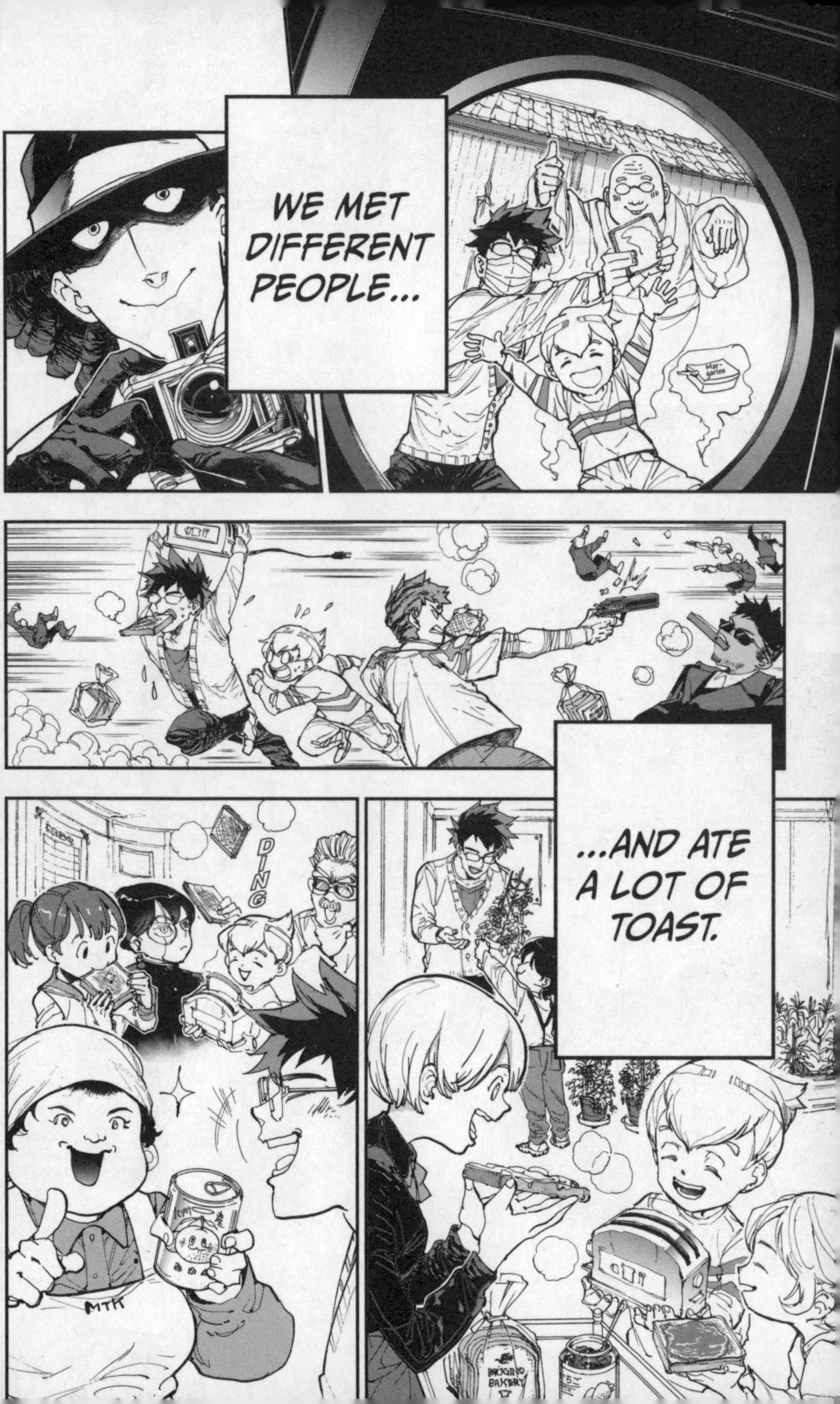
WE MET DIFFERENT PEOPLE...
Margarine
...AND ATE A LOT OF TOAST.
DING
MTK
BAKERY

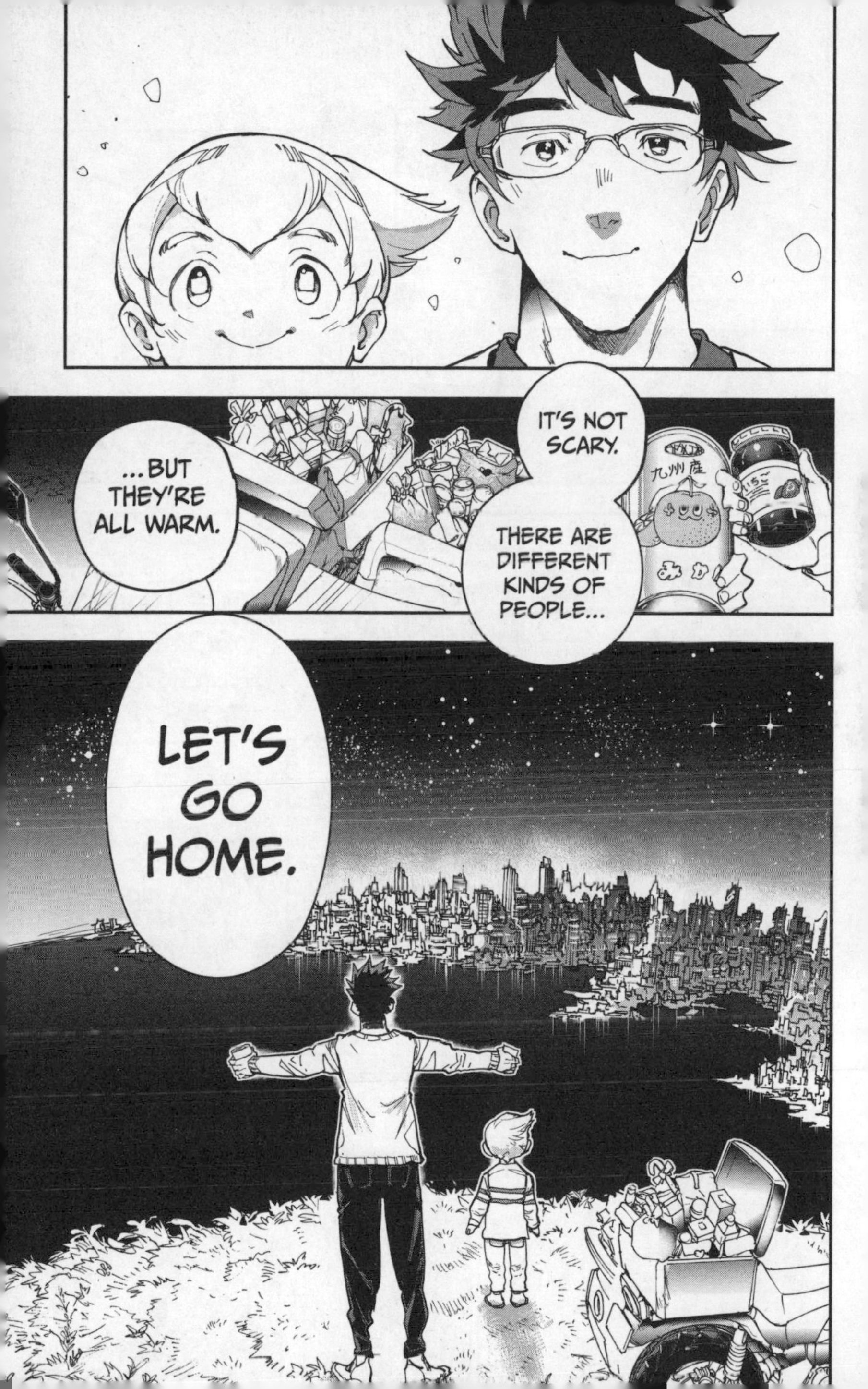

IT'S NOT SCARY.
THERE ARE DIFFERENT KINDS OF PEOPLE...
九州産
いちご
...BUT THEY'RE ALL WARM.
LET'S GO HOME.

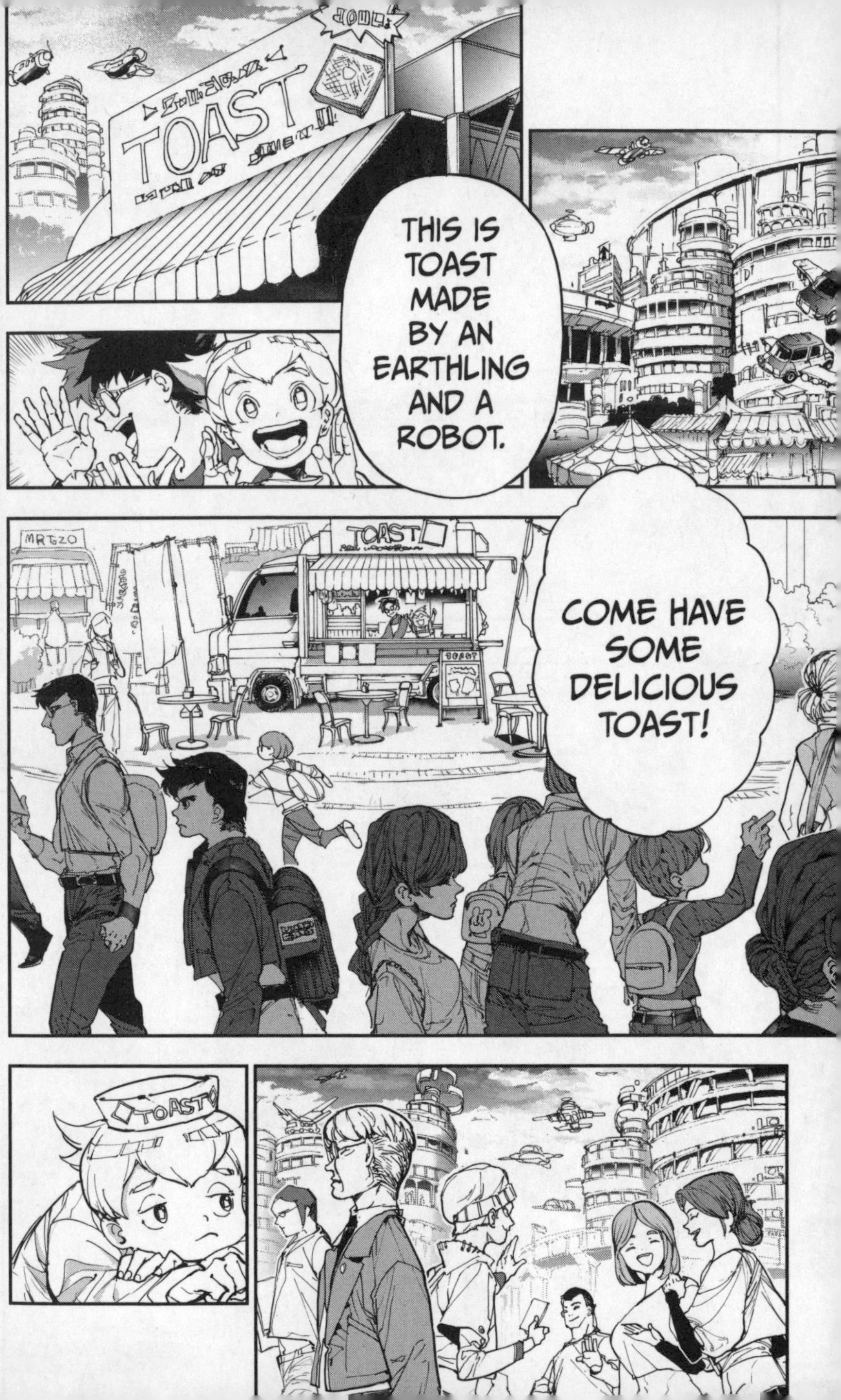
TOAST
THIS IS TOAST MADE BY AN EARTHLING AND A ROBOT.
TOAST
COME HAVE SOME DELICIOUS TOAST!
TOAST

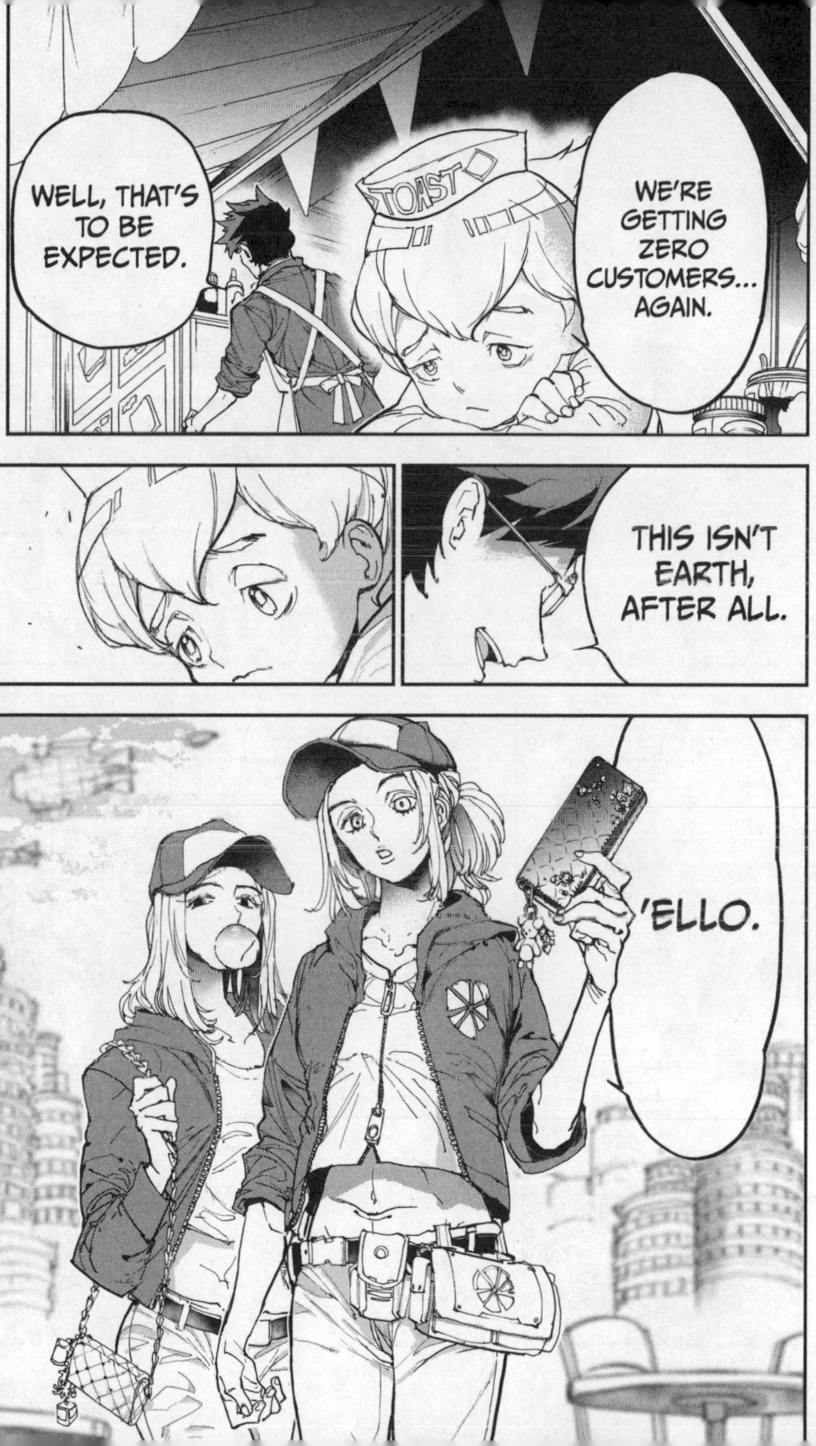
WE'RE GETTING ZERO CUSTOMERS... AGAIN.
TOAST
WELL, THAT'S TO BE EXPECTED.
THIS ISN'T EARTH, AFTER ALL.
'ELLO.

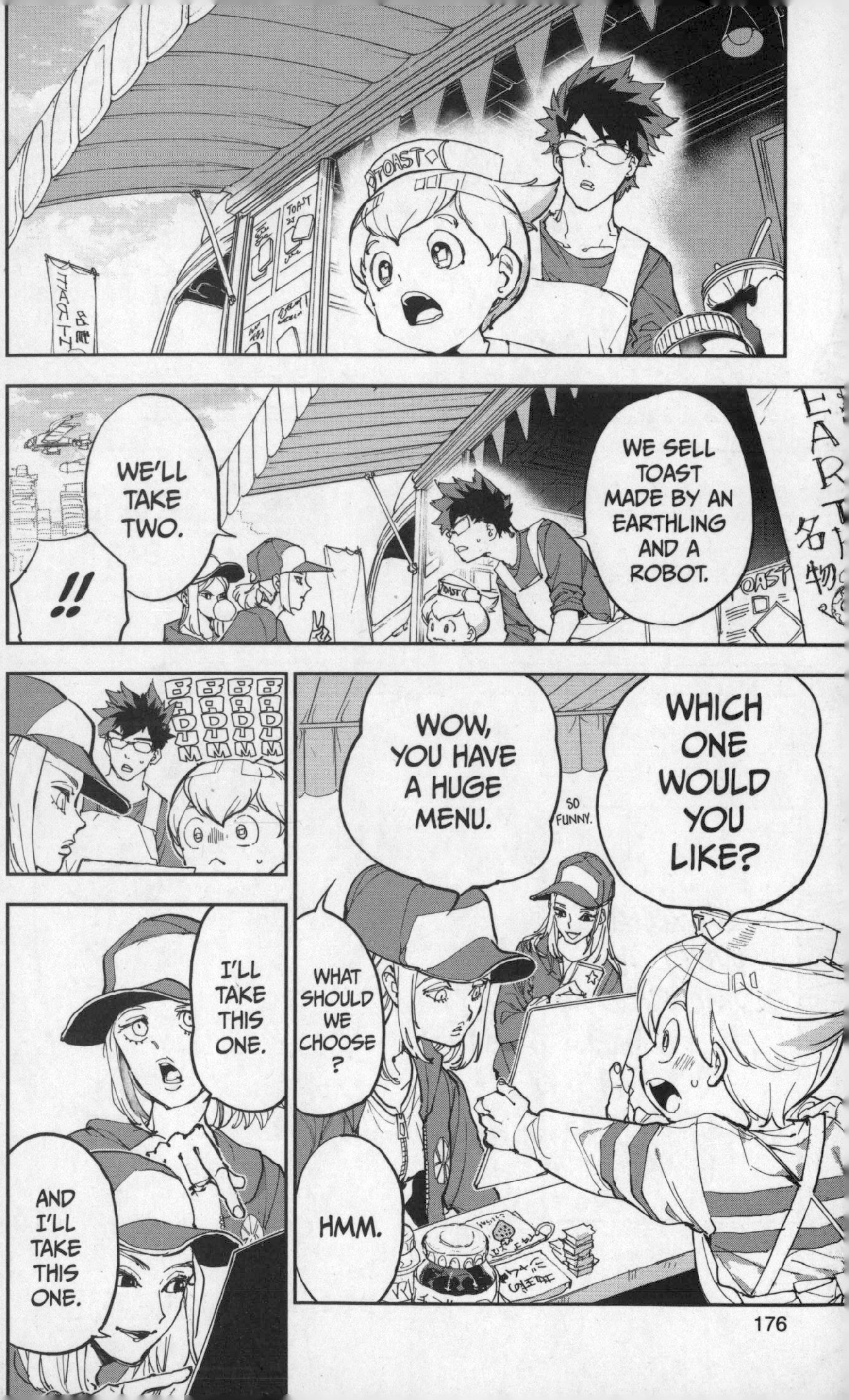
WE SELL TOAST MADE BY AN EARTHLING AND A ROBOT.
WE'LL TAKE TWO.
!!
WHICH ONE WOULD YOU LIKE?
WOW, YOU HAVE A HUGE MENU.
SO FUNNY.
BADUM BADUM BADUM BADUM
WHAT SHOULD WE CHOOSE?
HMM.
I'LL TAKE THIS ONE.
AND I'LL TAKE THIS ONE.

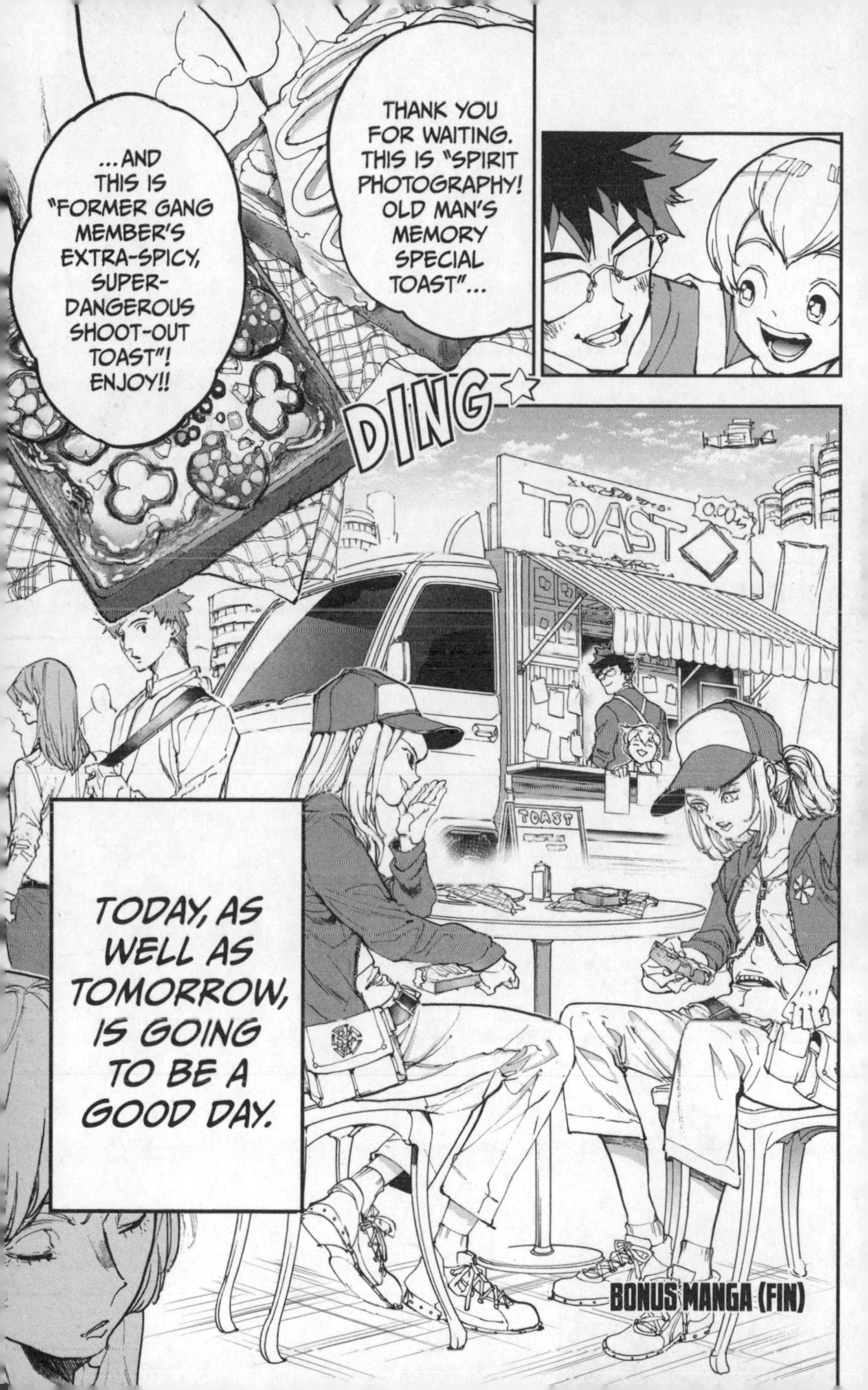
THANK YOU FOR WAITING. THIS IS "SPIRIT PHOTOGRAPHY! OLD MAN'S MEMORY SPECIAL TOAST"...
...AND THIS IS "FORMER GANG MEMBER'S EXTRA-SPICY, SUPER-DANGEROUS SHOOT-OUT TOAST"! ENJOY!!
DING☆
TOAST
TOAST
TODAY, AS WELL AS TOMORROW, IS GOING TO BE A GOOD DAY.
BONUS MANGA (FIN)

This is a special manga that was displayed at the Promised Neverland Exhibit.
The staff made the exhibit so wonderful that I'm confident that everyone who came had fun.

But due to the new virus variant, many people couldn't come due to travel restrictions between prefectures, parents refusing to let them go, or restrictions for those working in the health and elderly care industries. I was told that even if they wanted to go, some people had to give up on it.

We were already planning on including this manga somewhere, but we decided to hasten publication and put it at the end of this book.

It's only one part of what was a huge exhibit, but I would be happy if you enjoyed it.

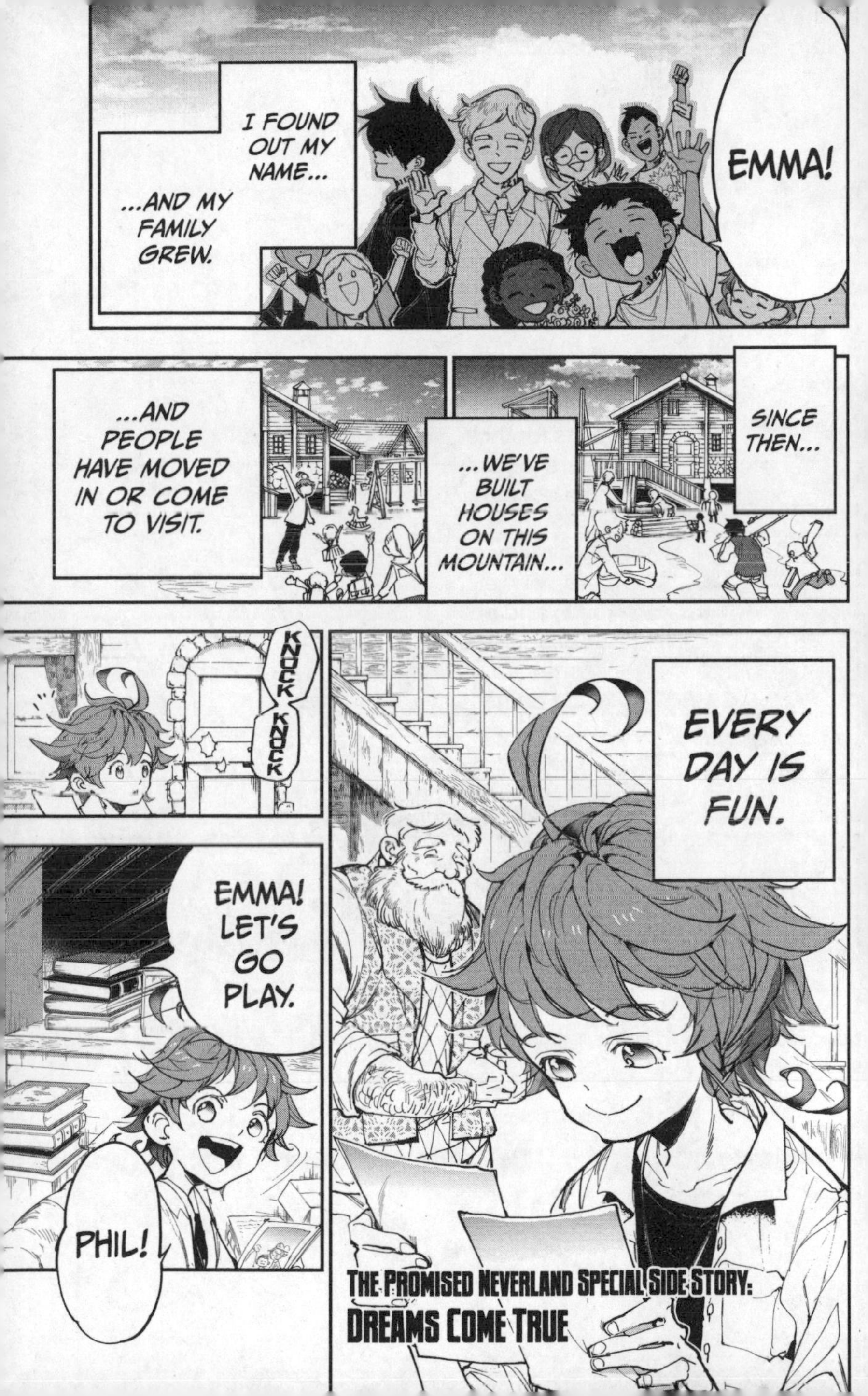
EMMA!
I FOUND OUT MY NAME...
...AND MY FAMILY GREW.
SINCE THEN...
...WE'VE BUILT HOUSES ON THIS MOUNTAIN...
...AND PEOPLE HAVE MOVED IN OR COME TO VISIT.
EVERY DAY IS FUN.
THE PROMISED NEVERLAND SPECIAL SIDE STORY:
DREAMS COME TRUE
KNOCK KNOCK
EMMA! LET'S GO PLAY.
PHIL!

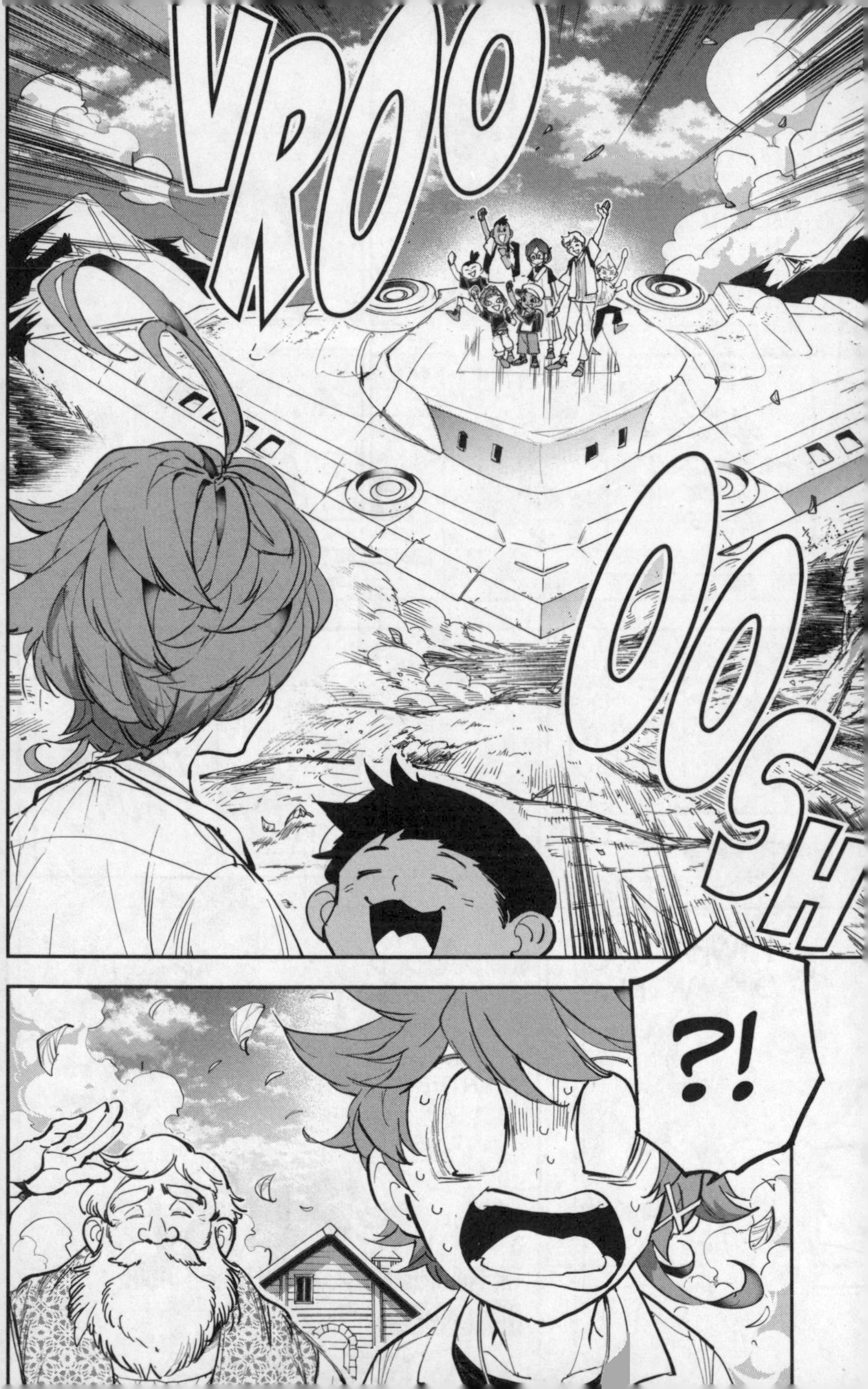
VROO
OOOSH
?!

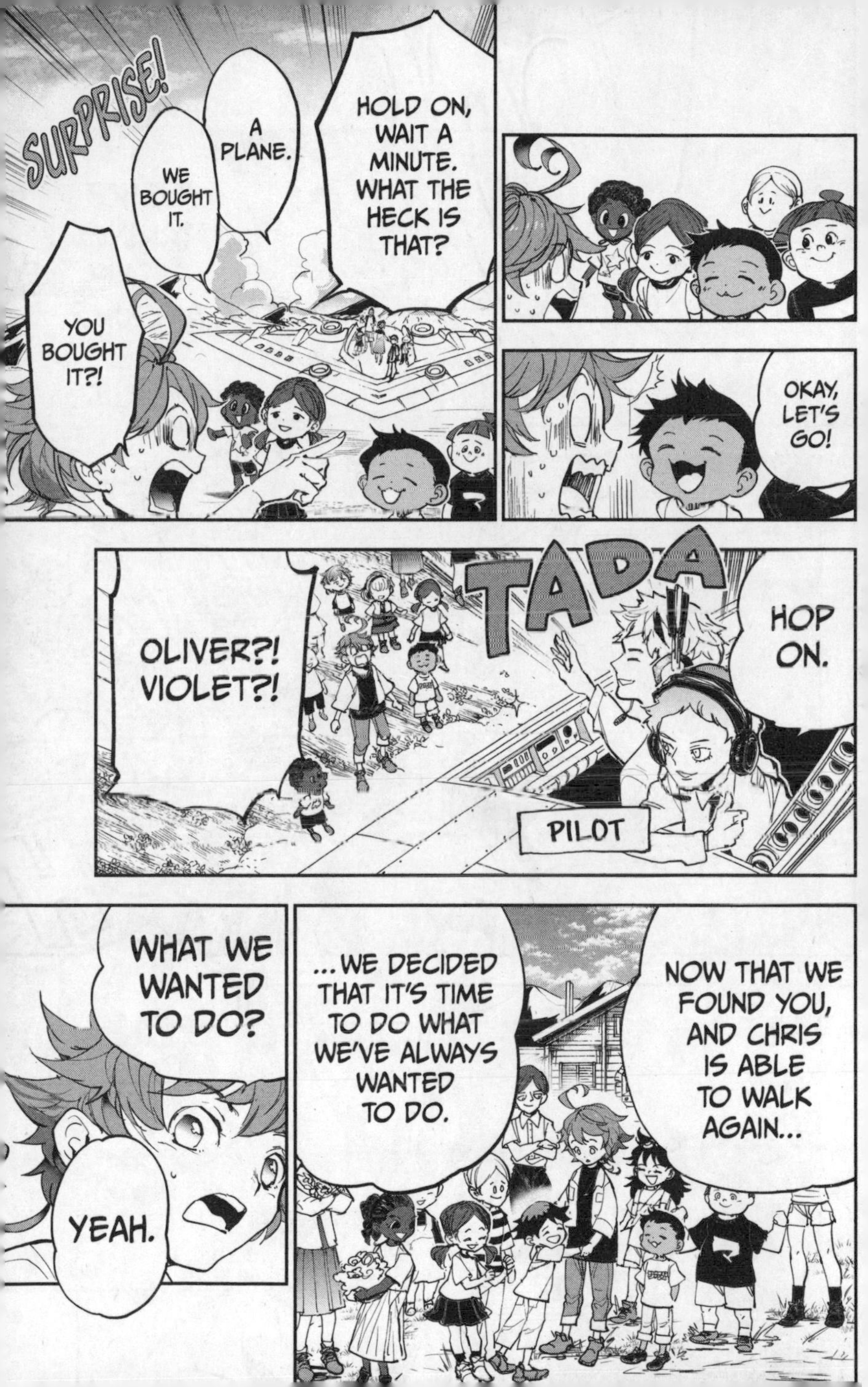
OKAY, LET'S GO!
HOLD ON, WAIT A MINUTE. WHAT THE HECK IS THAT?
A PLANE.
WE BOUGHT IT.
SURPRISE!
YOU BOUGHT IT?!
HOP ON.
TADA
PILOT
OLIVER?! VIOLET?!
NOW THAT WE FOUND YOU, AND CHRIS IS ABLE TO WALK AGAIN...
...WE DECIDED THAT IT'S TIME TO DO WHAT WE'VE ALWAYS WANTED TO DO.
WHAT WE WANTED TO DO?
YEAH.

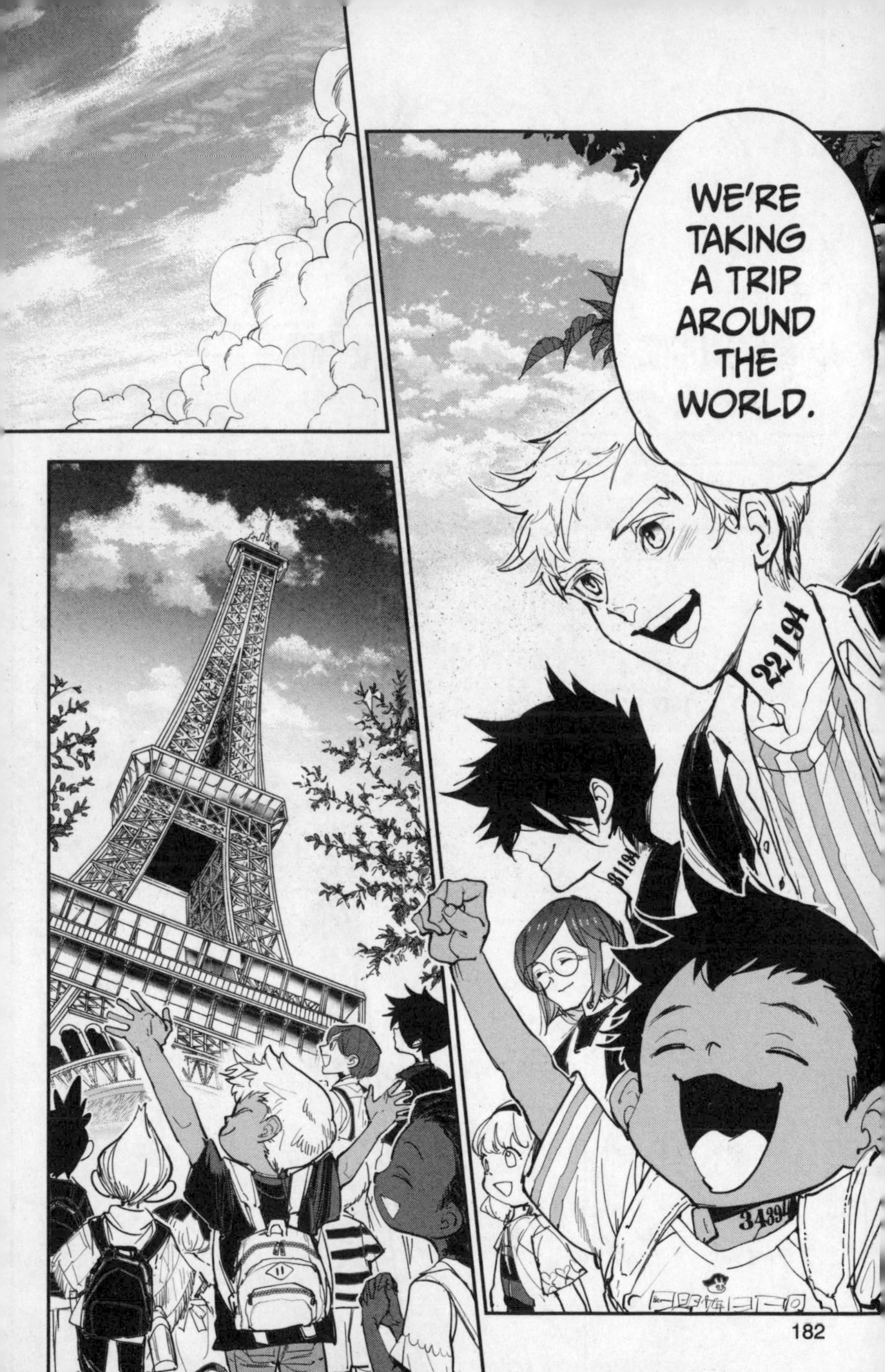
WE'RE TAKING A TRIP AROUND THE WORLD.

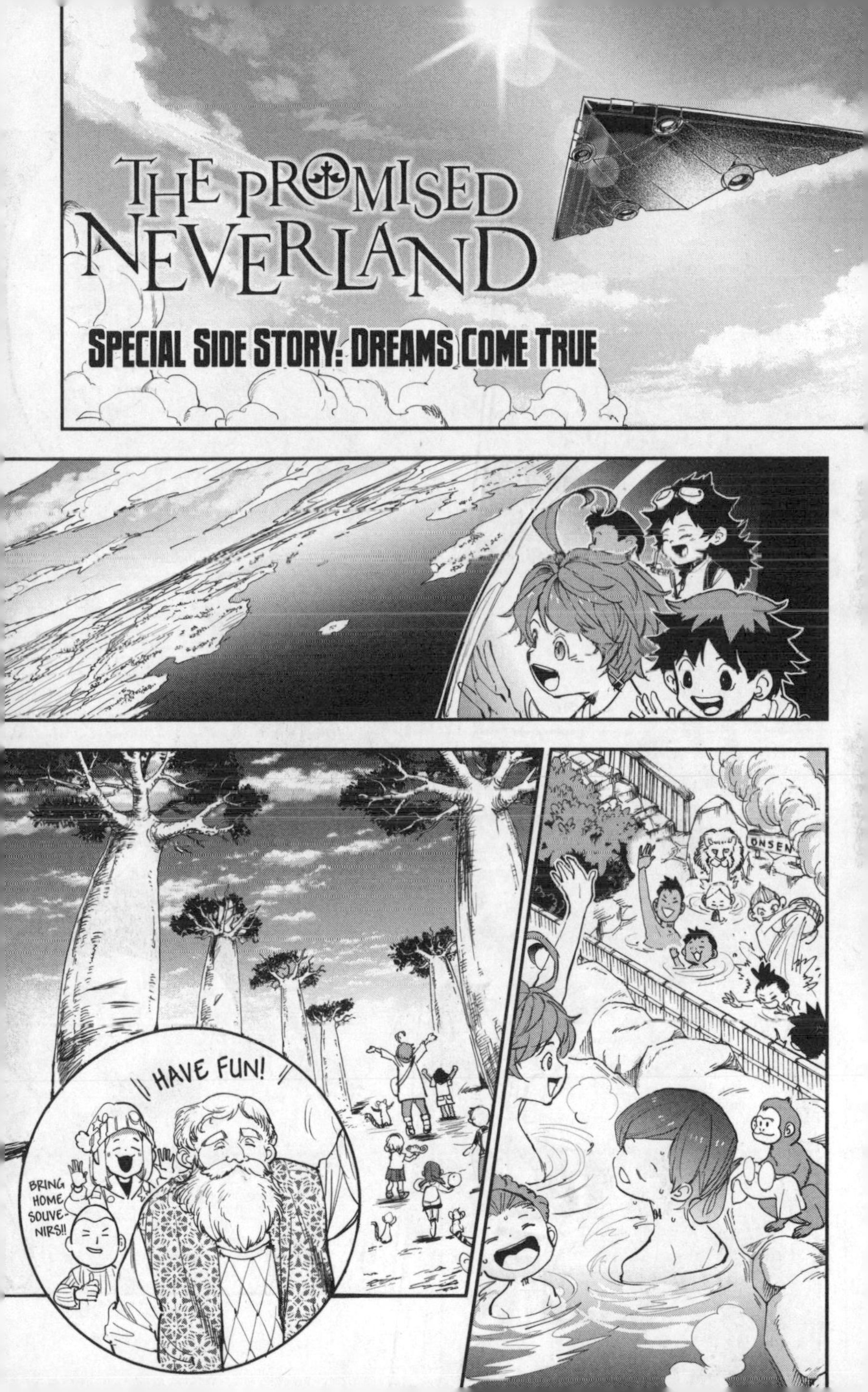
THE PROMISED NEVERLAND
SPECIAL SIDE STORY: DREAMS COME TRUE
ONSEN
HAVE FUN!
BRING HOME SOUVE-NIRS!!

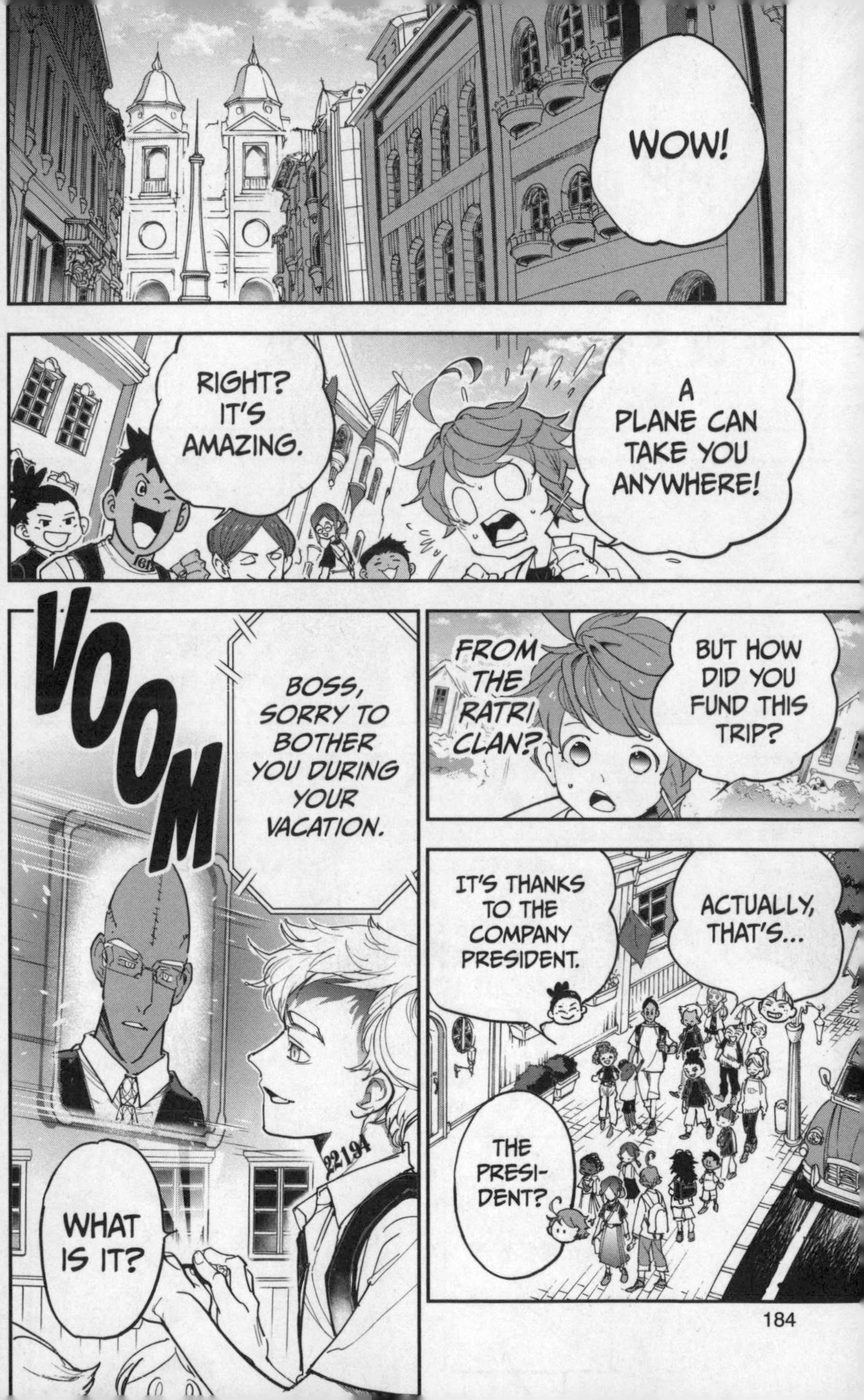
WOW!
A PLANE CAN TAKE YOU ANYWHERE!
RIGHT? IT'S AMAZING.
BUT HOW DID YOU FUND THIS TRIP?
FROM THE RATRI CLAN?
ACTUALLY, THAT'S...
IT'S THANKS TO THE COMPANY PRESIDENT.
THE PRESI-DENT?
VOOM
BOSS, SORRY TO BOTHER YOU DURING YOUR VACATION.
22194
WHAT IS IT?

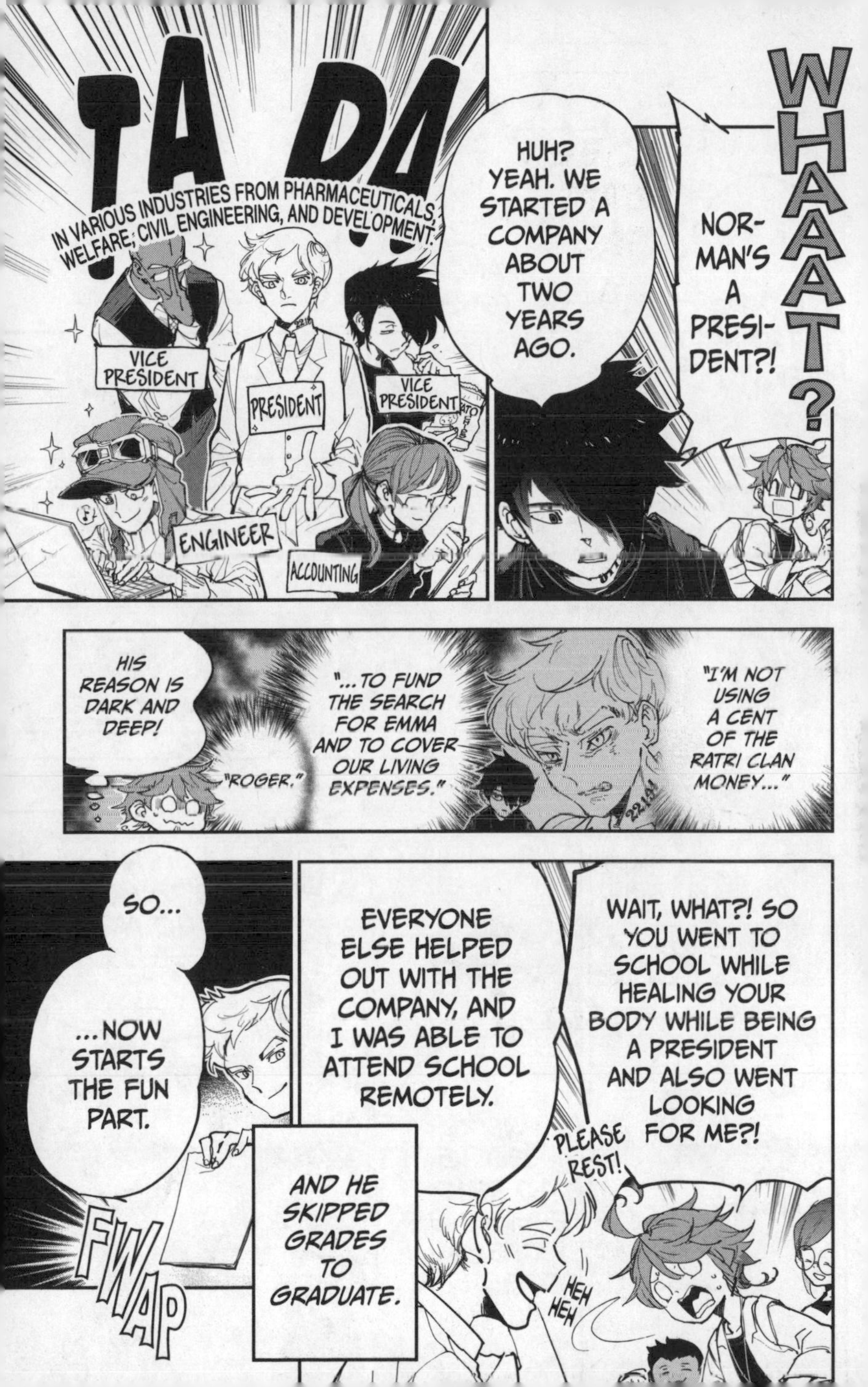
WHAAAT?
NOR-MAN'S A PRESI-DENT?!
HUH? YEAH. WE STARTED A COMPANY ABOUT TWO YEARS AGO.
TA DA
IN VARIOUS INDUSTRIES FROM PHARMACEUTICALS, WELFARE, CIVIL ENGINEERING, AND DEVELOPMENT.
VICE PRESIDENT
PRESIDENT
VICE PRESIDENT
ENGINEER
ACCOUNTING
"I'M NOT USING A CENT OF THE RATRI CLAN MONEY..."
"...TO FUND THE SEARCH FOR EMMA AND TO COVER OUR LIVING EXPENSES."
"ROGER."
HIS REASON IS DARK AND DEEP!
WAIT, WHAT?! SO YOU WENT TO SCHOOL WHILE HEALING YOUR BODY WHILE BEING A PRESIDENT AND ALSO WENT LOOKING FOR ME?!
EVERYONE ELSE HELPED OUT WITH THE COMPANY, AND I WAS ABLE TO ATTEND SCHOOL REMOTELY.
PLEASE REST!
HEH HEH
SO...
...NOW STARTS THE FUN PART.
AND HE SKIPPED GRADES TO GRADUATE.
FWAP

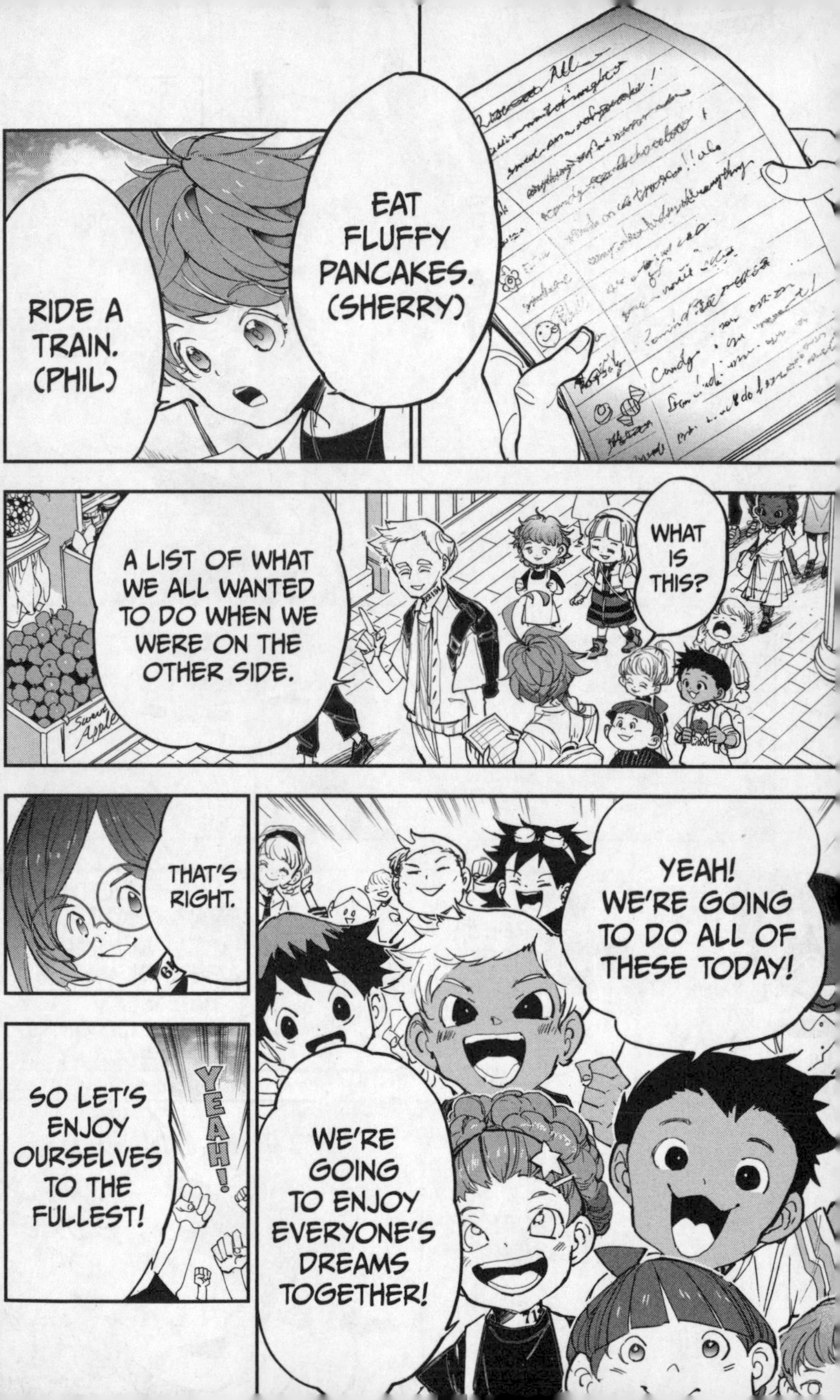
EAT FLUFFY PANCAKES. (SHERRY)
RIDE A TRAIN. (PHIL)
WHAT IS THIS?
A LIST OF WHAT WE ALL WANTED TO DO WHEN WE WERE ON THE OTHER SIDE.
Sweet Apple
YEAH! WE'RE GOING TO DO ALL OF THESE TODAY!
WE'RE GOING TO ENJOY EVERYONE'S DREAMS TOGETHER!
THAT'S RIGHT.
SO LET'S ENJOY OURSELVES TO THE FULLEST!
YEAH!

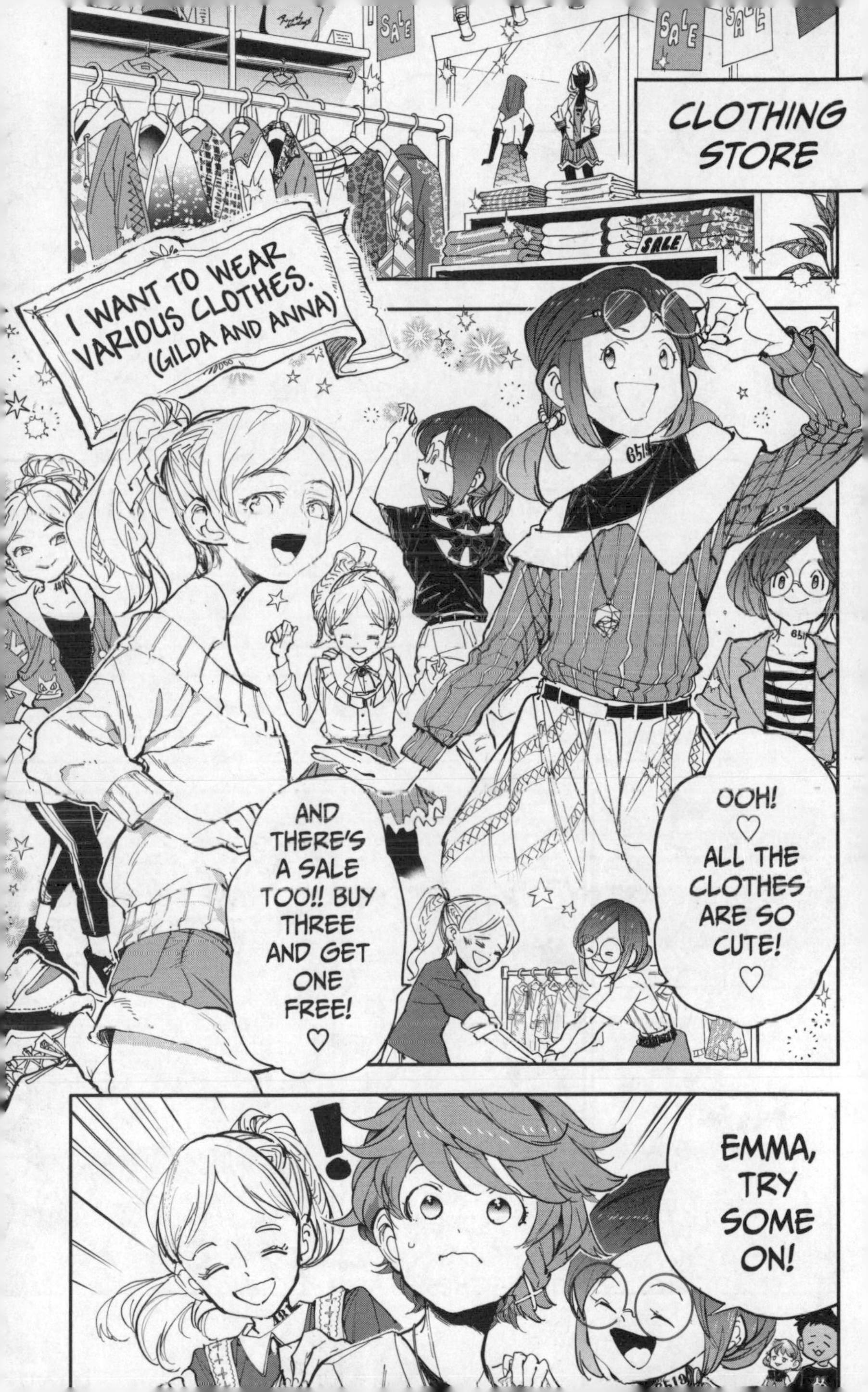
CLOTHING STORE
SALE
I WANT TO WEAR VARIOUS CLOTHES. (GILDA AND ANNA)
OOH! ♡ ALL THE CLOTHES ARE SO CUTE! ♡
AND THERE'S A SALE TOO!! BUY THREE AND GET ONE FREE! ♡
EMMA, TRY SOME ON!
!

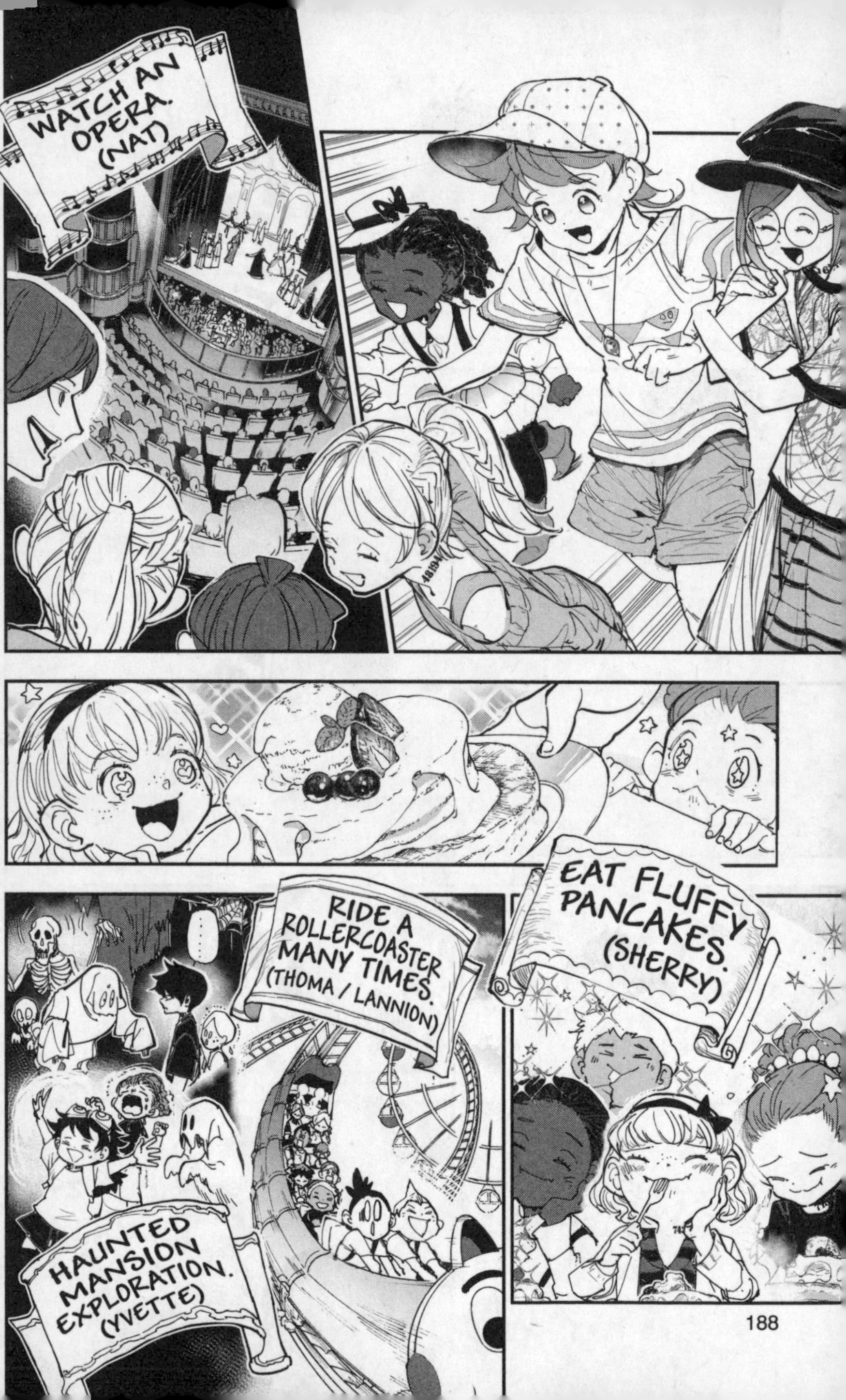
WATCH AN OPERA. (NAT)
EAT FLUFFY PANCAKES. (SHERRY)
RIDE A ROLLERCOASTER MANY TIMES. (THOMA / LANNION)
......
HAUNTED MANSION EXPLORATION. (YVETTE)

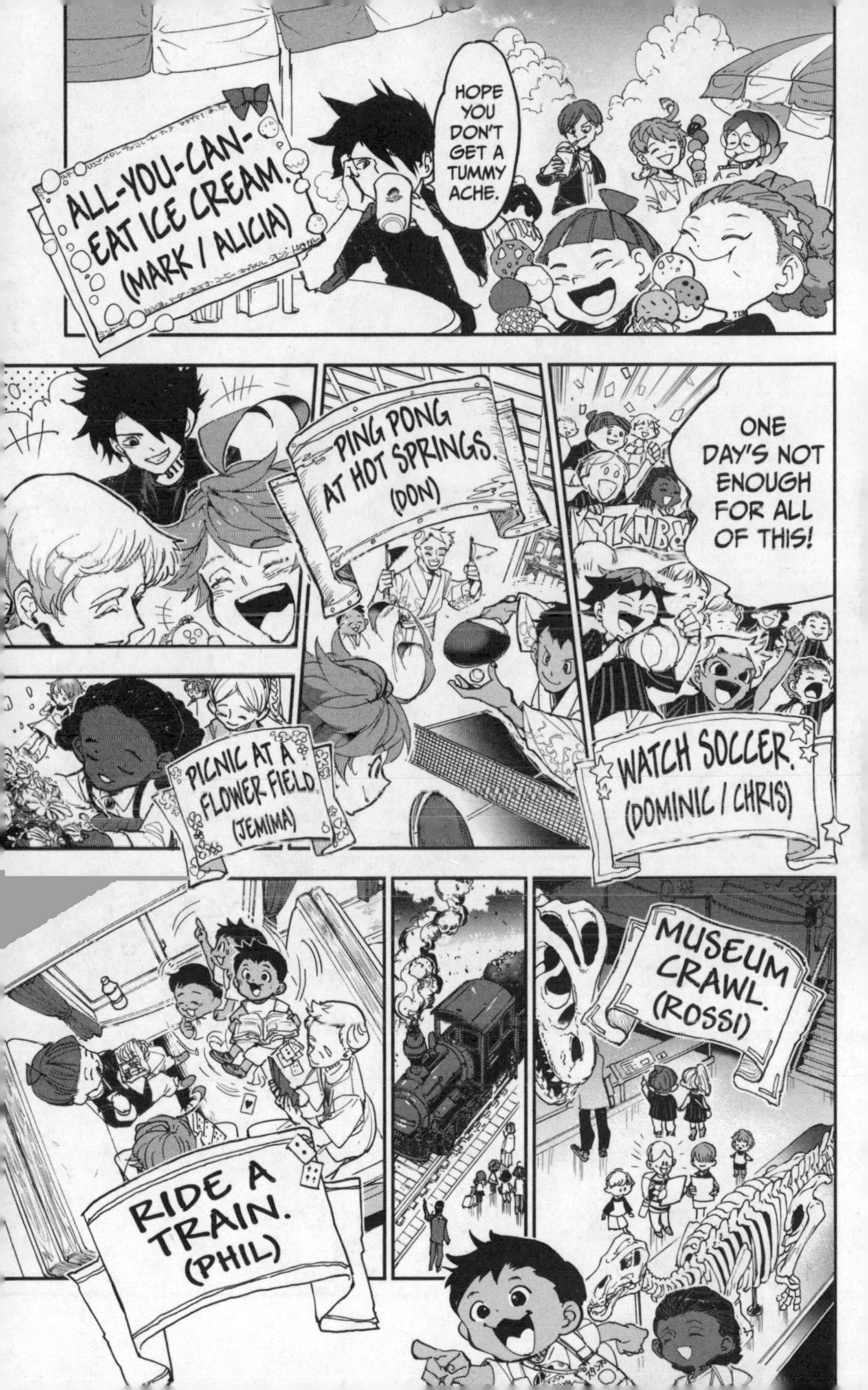
HOPE YOU DON'T GET A TUMMY ACHE.
ALL-YOU-CAN-EAT ICE CREAM. (MARK / ALICIA)
ONE DAY'S NOT ENOUGH FOR ALL OF THIS!
WATCH SOCCER. (DOMINIC / CHRIS)
PING PONG AT HOT SPRINGS. (DON)
PICNIC AT A FLOWER FIELD (JEMIMA)
MUSEUM CRAWL. (ROSSI)
RIDE A TRAIN. (PHIL)

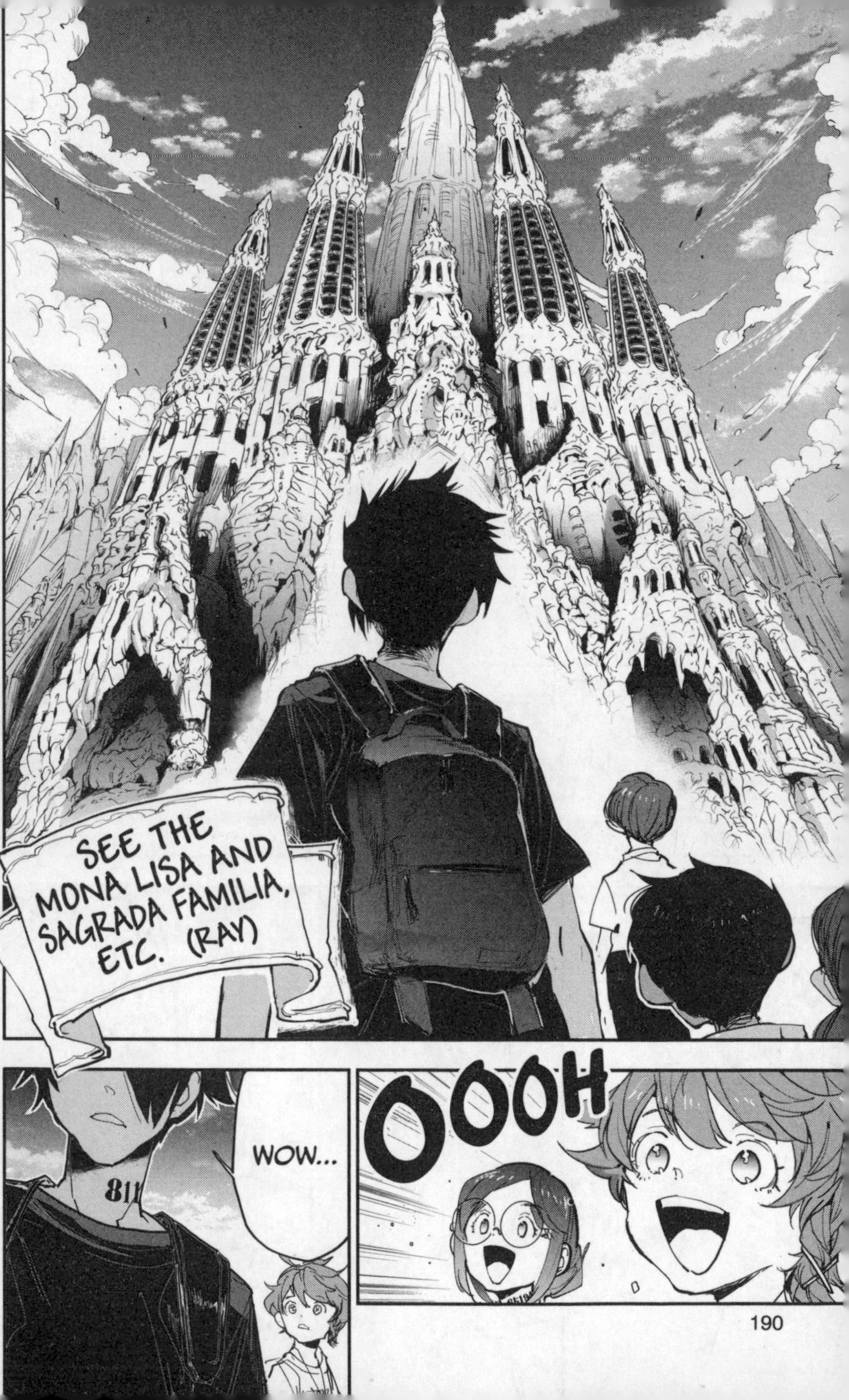
SEE THE MONA LISA AND SAGRADA FAMILIA, ETC. (RAY)
OOOH
WOW...
811

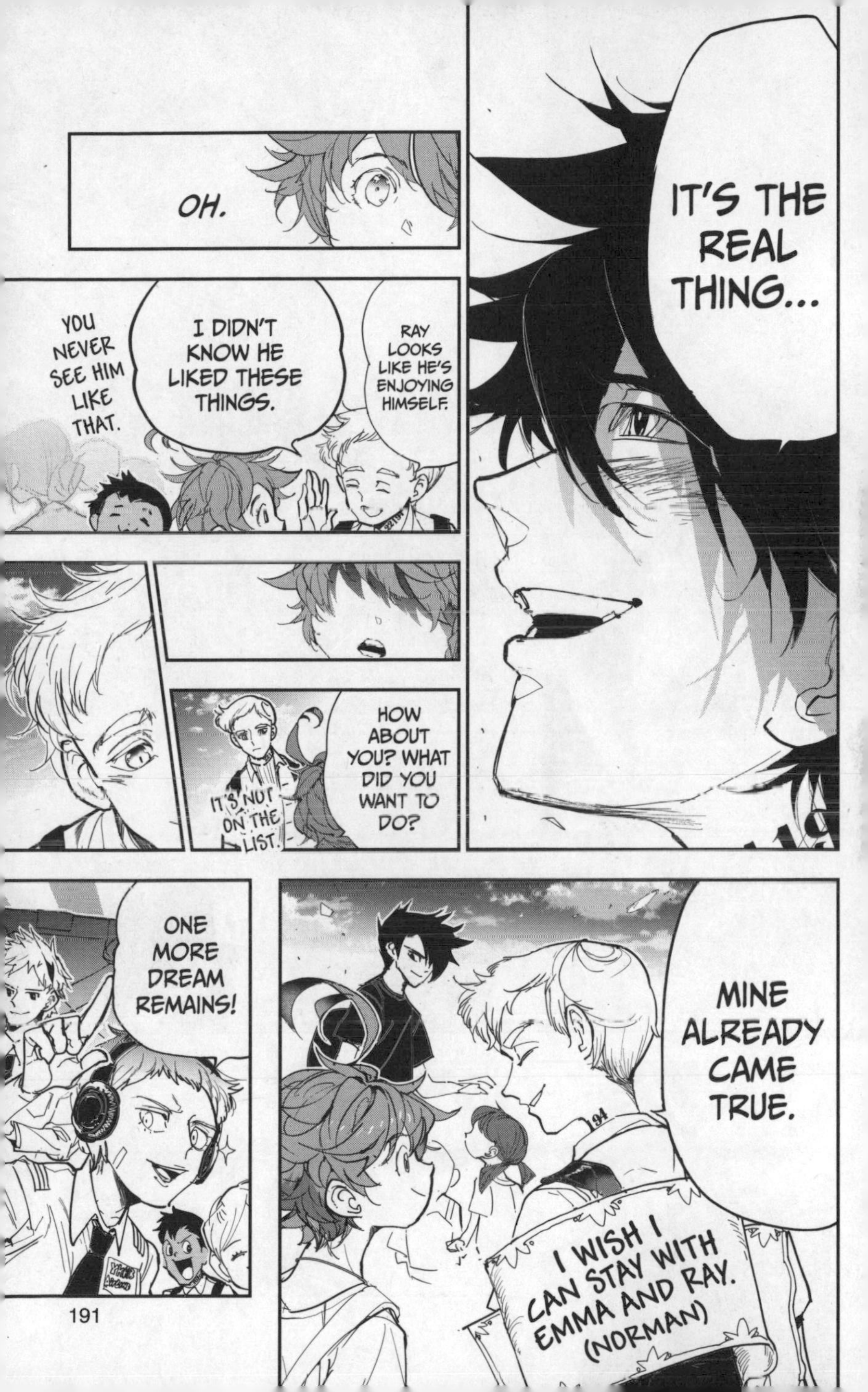
IT'S THE REAL THING...
OH.
RAY LOOKS LIKE HE'S ENJOYING HIMSELF.
I DIDN'T KNOW HE LIKED THESE THINGS.
YOU NEVER SEE HIM LIKE THAT.
HOW ABOUT YOU? WHAT DID YOU WANT TO DO?
IT'S NOT ON THE LIST.
MINE ALREADY CAME TRUE.
I WISH I CAN STAY WITH EMMA AND RAY. (NORMAN)
ONE MORE DREAM REMAINS!

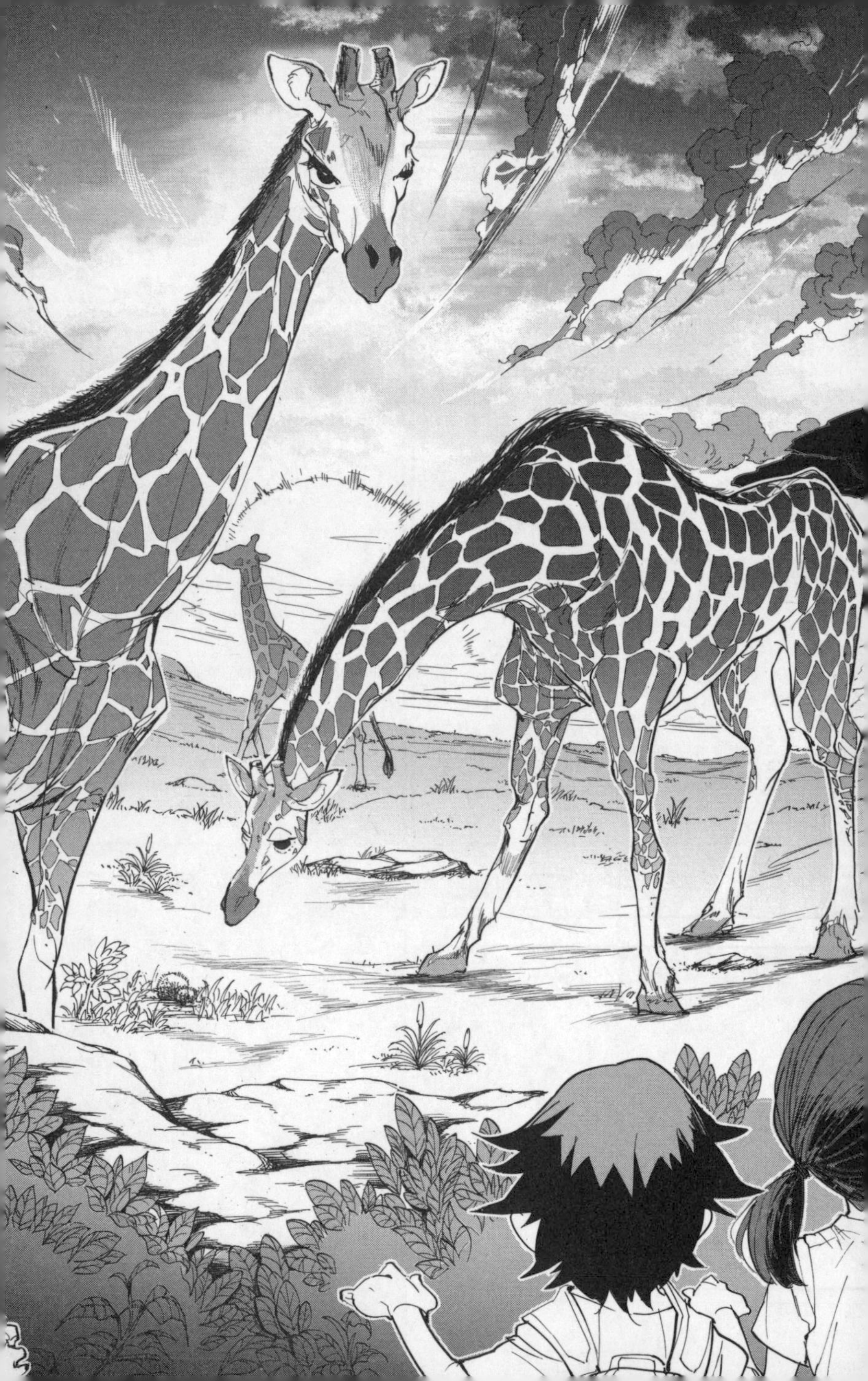

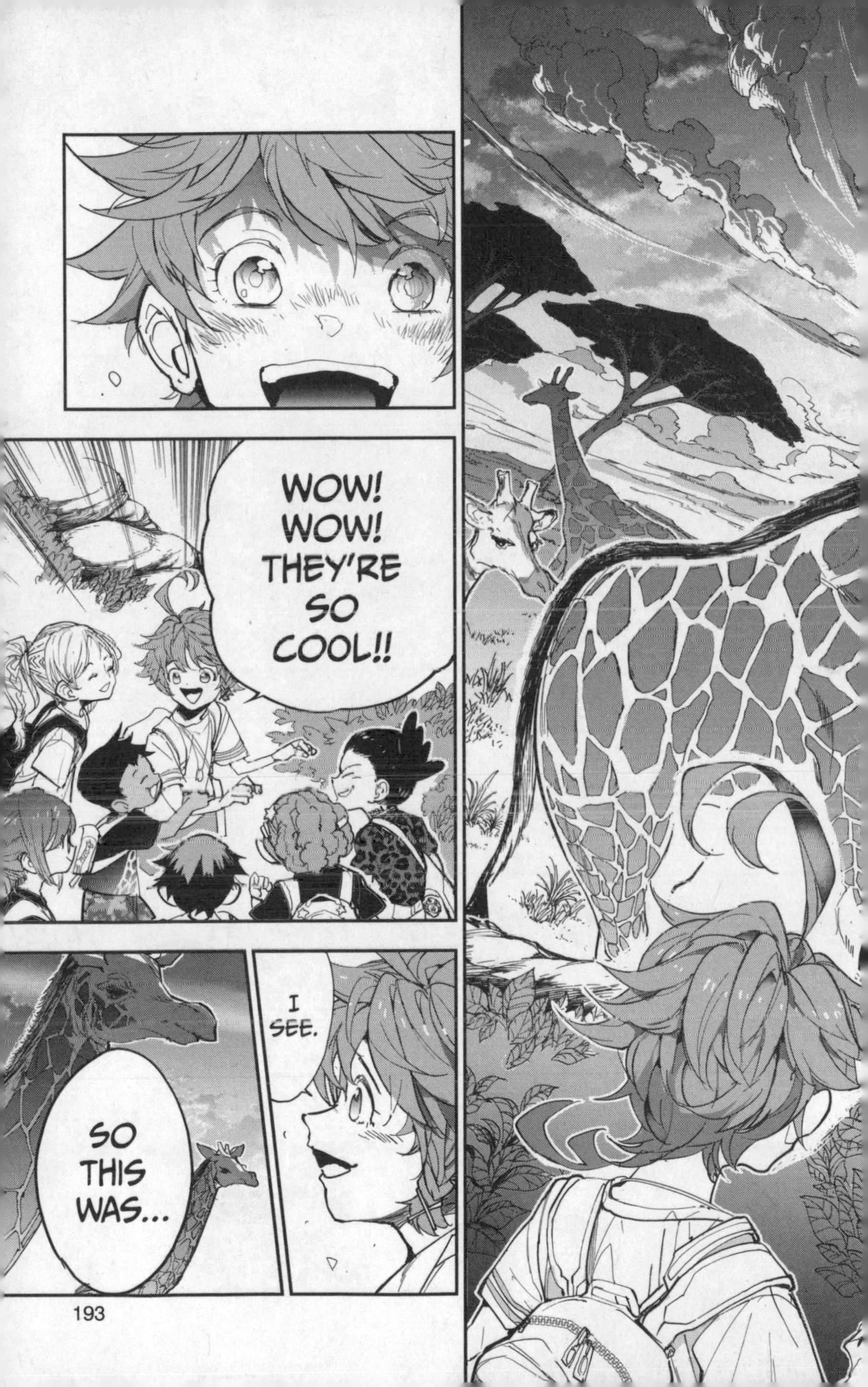
WOW! WOW! THEY'RE SO COOL!!
I SEE.
SO THIS WAS...

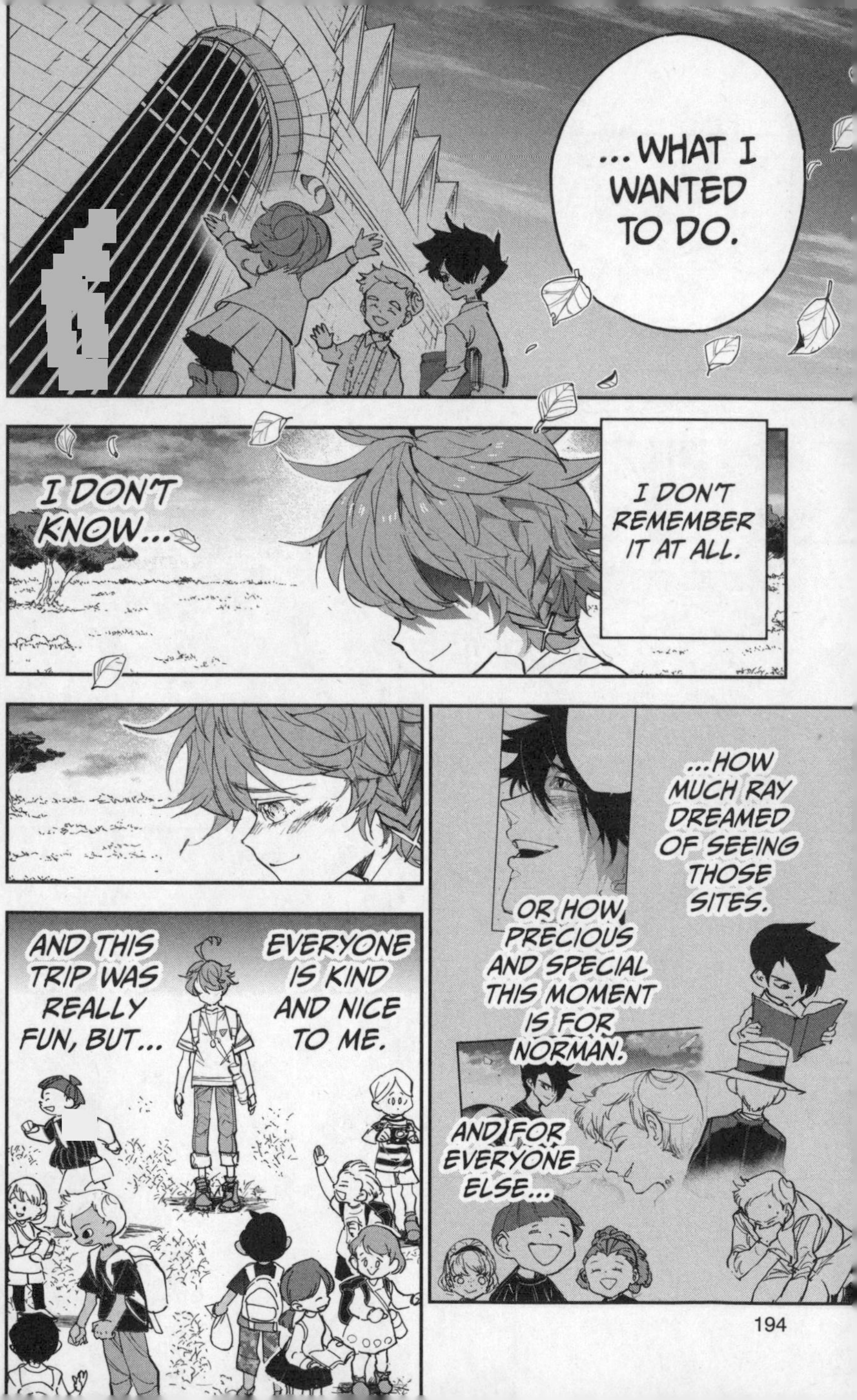
...WHAT I WANTED TO DO.
I DON'T REMEMBER IT AT ALL.
I DON'T KNOW...
...HOW MUCH RAY DREAMED OF SEEING THOSE SITES.
OR HOW PRECIOUS AND SPECIAL THIS MOMENT IS FOR NORMAN.
AND FOR EVERYONE ELSE...
EVERYONE IS KIND AND NICE TO ME.
AND THIS TRIP WAS REALLY FUN, BUT...

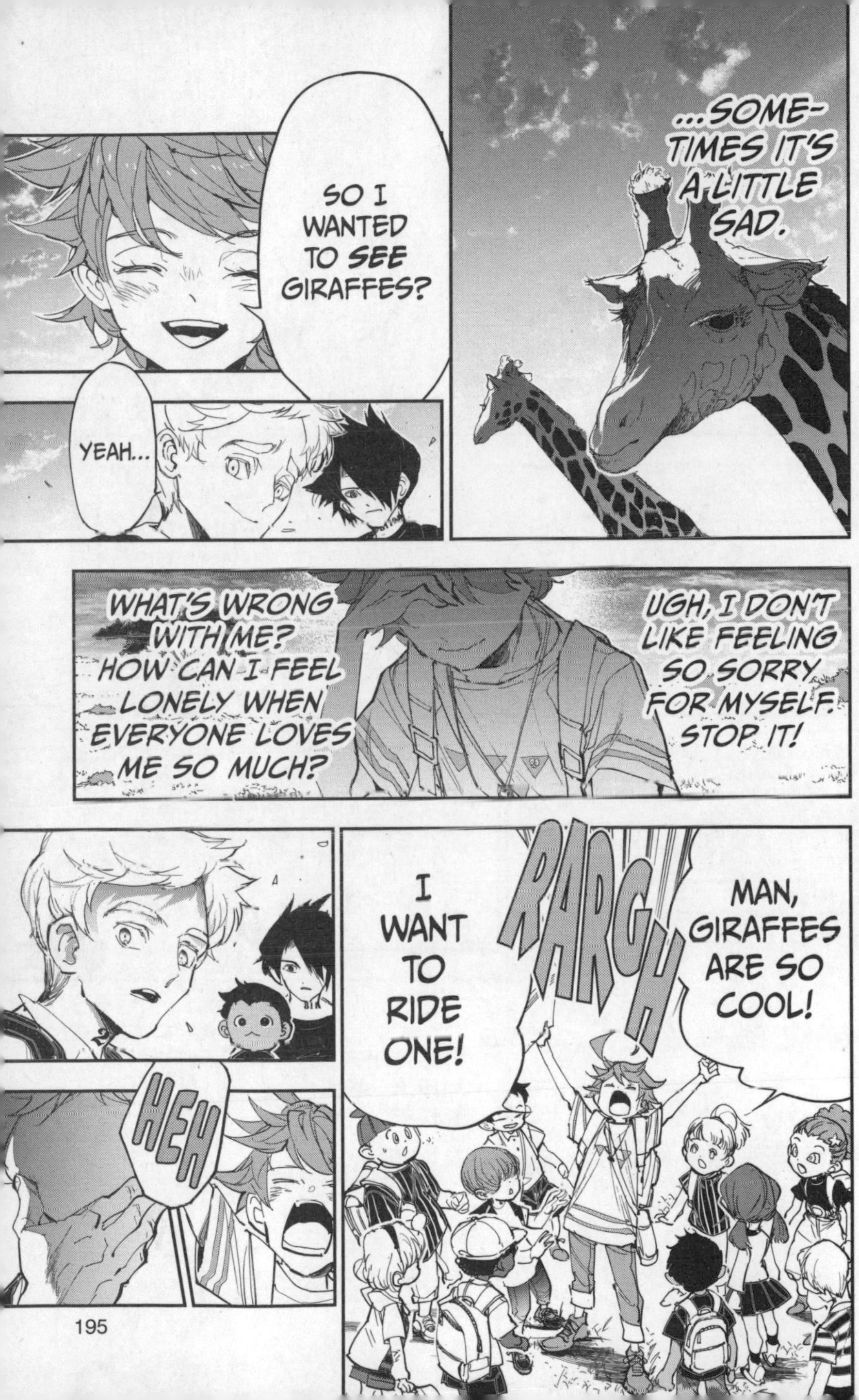
...SOMETIMES IT'S A LITTLE SAD.
SO I WANTED TO SEE GIRAFFES?
YEAH...
UGH, I DON'T LIKE FEELING SO SORRY FOR MYSELF. STOP IT!
WHAT'S WRONG WITH ME? HOW CAN I FEEL LONELY WHEN EVERYONE LOVES ME SO MUCH?
MAN, GIRAFFES ARE SO COOL!
RARGH
I WANT TO RIDE ONE!
HEH

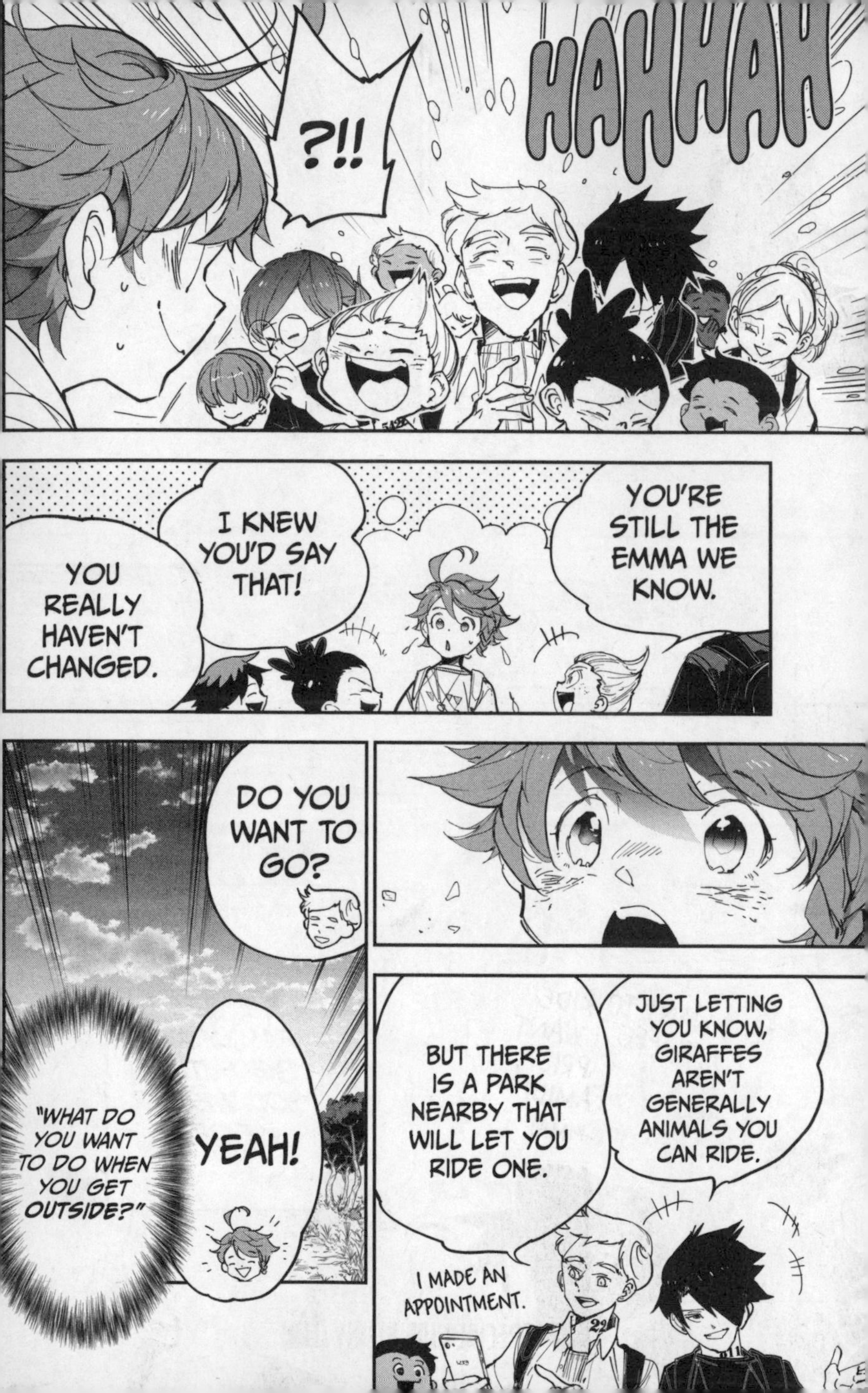
HAHHAH
?!!
YOU'RE STILL THE EMMA WE KNOW.
I KNEW YOU'D SAY THAT!
YOU REALLY HAVEN'T CHANGED.
JUST LETTING YOU KNOW, GIRAFFES AREN'T GENERALLY ANIMALS YOU CAN RIDE.
BUT THERE IS A PARK NEARBY THAT WILL LET YOU RIDE ONE.
I MADE AN APPOINTMENT.
DO YOU WANT TO GO?
YEAH!
"WHAT DO YOU WANT TO DO WHEN YOU GET OUTSIDE?"

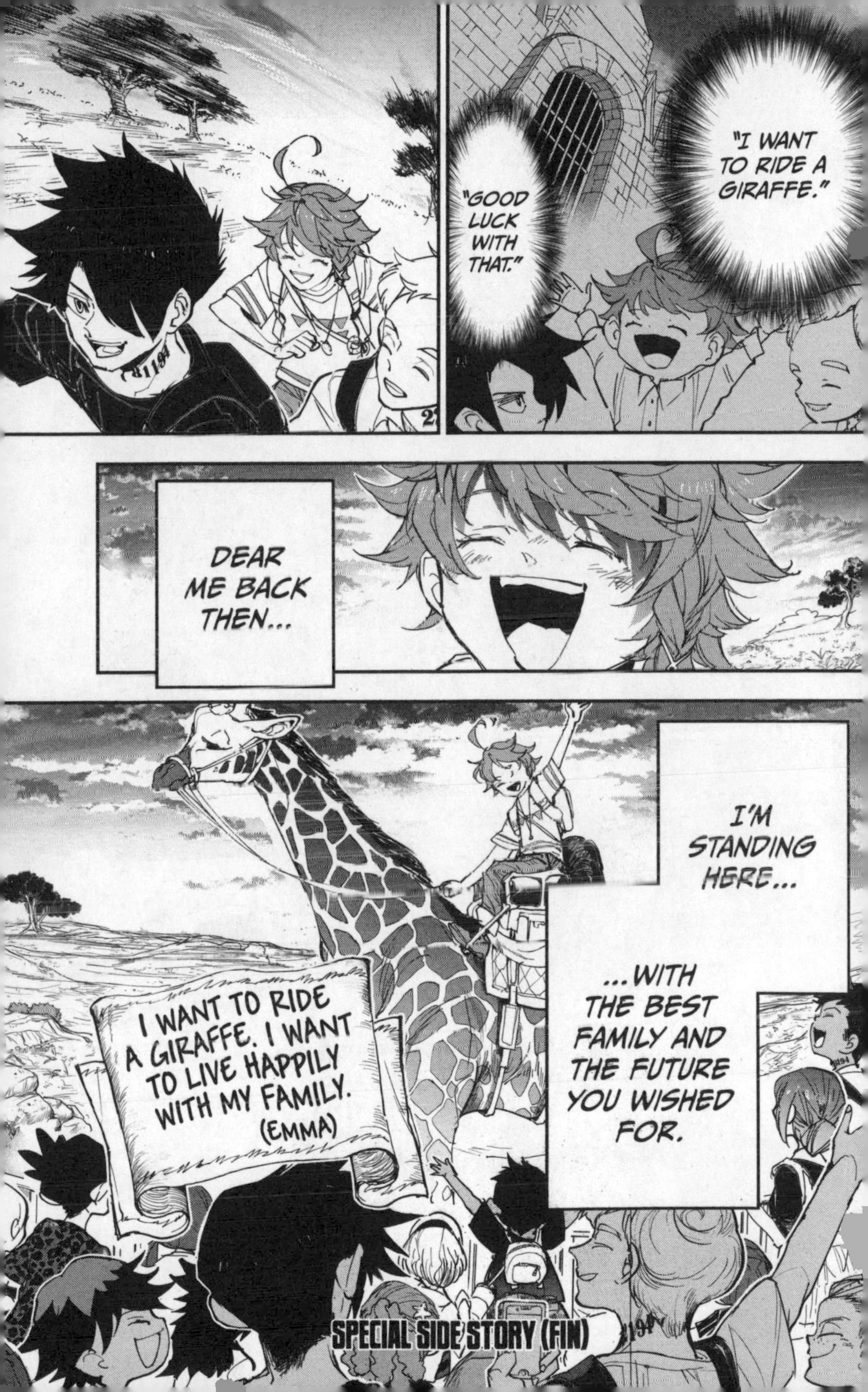
"I WANT TO RIDE A GIRAFFE."
"GOOD LUCK WITH THAT."
DEAR ME BACK THEN...
I'M STANDING HERE...
...WITH THE BEST FAMILY AND THE FUTURE YOU WISHED FOR.
I WANT TO RIDE A GIRAFFE. I WANT TO LIVE HAPPILY WITH MY FAMILY. (EMMA)
SPECIAL SIDE STORY (FIN)

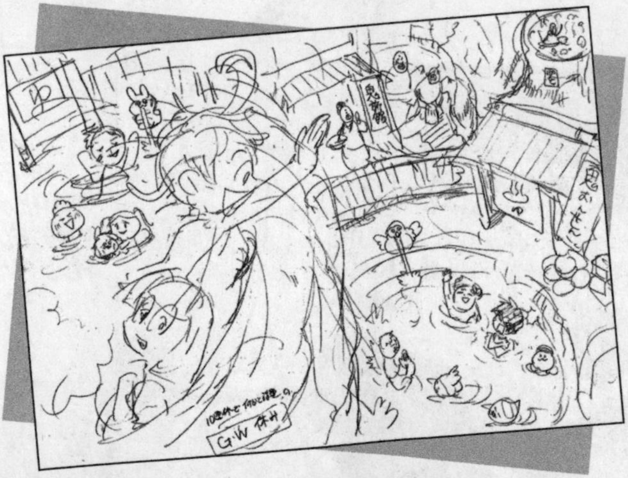
G・W 休み

Weekly Shonen Jump Issue 20, 2019, unused idea for an opening color spread

THE PROMISED NEVERLAND

STORY BY **KAIU SHIRAI**

ART BY **POSUKA DEMIZU**

Emma, Norman and Ray are the brightest kids at the Grace Field House orphanage. And under the care of the woman they refer to as "Mom," all the kids have enjoyed a comfortable life. Good food, clean clothes and the perfect environment to learn—what more could an orphan ask for? One day, though, Emma and Norman uncover the dark truth of the outside world they are forbidden from seeing.

YOU'RE READING THE **WRONG WAY!**

Kaiu Shirai x Posuka Demizu: Beyond The Promised Neverland reads from right to left, starting in the upper-right corner. Japanese is read from right to left, meaning that action, sound effects and word-balloon order are completely reversed from English order.